Mapping Norwood

Mapping Norwood

An Irish American Memoir

CHARLES FANNING

University of Massachusetts Press
AMHERST AND BOSTON

Printed in the United States of America

LC 2010014694
ISBN 978-1-55849-810-5 (paper); 809-9 (library cloth)

Designed by Sally Nichols
Set in Aldus
Printed and bound by Thomson-Shore, Inc.

Library of Congress Cataloging-in-Publication Data

Fanning, Charles.
Mapping Norwood : an Irish American memoir / Charles Fanning.
p. cm.
ISBN 978-1-55849-810-5 (pbk. : alk. paper) — ISBN 978-1-55849-809-9 (library cloth : alk. paper)
1. Fanning, Charles—Childhood and youth. 2. Fanning, Charles—Family. 3. Irish Americans—Massachusetts—Norwood (Town)—Biography. 4. Norwood (Mass. : Town)—Biography. 5. Irish Americans—Massachusetts—Boston Metropolitan Area—History. I. Title.
F74.N99F36 2010
929′.20973—dc22

2010014694

British Library Cataloguing in Publication data are available.

To Fran, Stephen, and Ellen

Each one of us, then, should speak of his roads, his crossroads,
his roadside benches; each one of us should make a
surveyor's map of his lost fields and meadows.

—Gaston Bachelard, *The Poetics of Space*

Contents

Illustrations

Preface

As the title indicates, this book is an act of mapmaking, of plotting out overlapping territories, both topographical and temporal. These include the Boston area from colonial times to the recent past, the American Civil War, Ireland and Germany in the nineteenth century, encounters with Boston's Museum of Fine Arts and with Harvard College, and aspects of family life in a Massachusetts town from the 1930s to the 1960s. In her essay "Place in Fiction," Eudora Welty was right, of course. "Location" is "the heart's field," in life as in writing. "Place," she says, "absorbs our earliest notice and attention, it bestows on us our original awareness; and our critical powers spring up from the study of it and the growth of experience inside it. It perseveres in bringing us back to earth when we fly too high. It never really stops informing us, for it is forever astir, alive, changing, reflecting, like the mind of man itself." As for applicability further down the road, Welty asserts that "one place comprehended can make us understand other places better. Sense of place gives equilibrium; extended, it is sense of direction too."

For me, that place was Norwood, Massachusetts. This book begins there, with the effort of remembering my own "original awareness." Mapping that territory as I experienced it in the late 1940s and the 1950s has made me realize just how full of advantage this town of 16,000 was for me. I had only to be born there to receive the gift of a secure base from which to grow. In "Endpoint," his valedictory poetic sequence, John Updike acknowledges his hometown of Shillington, Pennsylvania, in reverential terms with which I completely agree:

> Perhaps
> we meet our heaven at the start and not
> the end of life. Even then were tears
> and fear and struggle, but the town itself
> draped in plain glory the passing days.

This book contains a chapter for each of my parents and their families, a tangle of tales that counters the "Irish American" subtitle. (As we all know, nobody's story is that simple.) I am half Irish, to be sure, but also a quarter German and a quarter New England Yankee, and all parts of that mix have contributed to my own sense of self. Both of my parents had been born and raised in Norwood as well. They shared the steadying power of the place, which was also the site of painful losses. Born in 1909 to hybrid Irish Yankee parents, my father, Charles Frederick "Chick" Fanning, was the second of five children. His mother died when he was eight, two years later the family was burned out of an apartment in the middle of the night, and he left school to go to work after sixth grade. His father failed at a number of business ventures even before the Depression, which hit the Fannings hard. The fourth of five, all girls, my mother, Frances Patricia Balduf, was born in 1913 to German and Irish parents. When "Pat" Balduf was sixteen, her mother died and she took over the household, thus ending her dream of college and a teaching career. Before that, her family's small ethnic community had been rocked by anti-German sentiment during World War I. In addition, her father endured his last illness during the rise of Hitler's Third Reich. None of this kept my parents from providing their three children with a stable and salutary place in which to grow up.

Though I've thought a lot about the Fannings and Baldufs, there is much about them that I'll never understand, and that is one of the lessons of this project. I remain encouraged by William Maxwell, who says in *Time Will Darken It* that "the history of one's parents has to be pieced together from fragments, their motives and character guessed at, and the truth about them remains deeply buried, like a boulder that projects one small surface above the level of smooth lawn, and when you come to dig around it, proves to be too large ever to move, though each year's frost forces it up a little higher."

I knew only one of my grandparents, my father's father, Charles Winslow Fanning. I didn't come close to meeting the other three. Mary Ann Shedd Fanning died at age forty in 1918, Johanna Frances McAuliffe Balduf at fifty in 1930, and Edward Everett Balduf at sixty-two in 1941—a year before I was born. Back beyond these four, I've found archetypal stories and retold them in my parents' chapters. My mother's German ancestors include two generations of fugitives from endemic militarism. I've been to the hometowns of these Kulds and Baldufs in the province of Baden. My father's grandfather, John, the first Fanning born on American soil, abandoned his own family and disappeared into the West. It was I who discovered his hidden life and his grave in Illinois.

There are two chapters here for ancestors further back: great-great-grandfathers on my father's side, an Irish immigrant and a New Hampshire Yankee. Each was profoundly affected by his tribe's great mid-nineteenth-century catastrophe. Born in 1828 in County Monaghan, Phillip Fanning left Ireland in March 1851 in the wake of the Great Famine. In Boston he met and married another Irish immigrant, Margaret Bohan. Atypically for their generation, they left the city to start a farm, in Needham, Massachusetts. Born in the Granite State in 1823, Winslow Radcliff came down to Massachusetts as a young man. There he met and married Sophia Ann Draper, a member of a formidably old-line Dedham family. In August 1862, Winslow joined the Thirty-fifth Massachusetts Volunteer Infantry Regiment and went off to the Civil War. A survivor of the battles of Antietam and Fredericksburg, he never recovered from the horrors of the experience. In the end, he took his own life.

These two men provide detailed examples of the links we all have to larger historical happenings. I am guided here by the Irish writer Michael Coady, who looks back over his own engagement with family history, from which emerged the book *All Souls*, to declare that "all of this has to do with the process of memory and the flux of time, with human destinies and the written word, with what is hidden, and what is revealed. The purpose of genealogy should not be the neat assembly of pedigree culminating smugly in self, but its exact opposite: the extension of the personal beyond the self to encounter the intimate unknown of others in our blood."

The three last chapters bring the story back home. One describes the expansive adventure of my childhood—taking Saturday painting classes at the Boston Museum of Fine Arts in seventh grade. One is my "Prelude," a reckoning of the four key elements in my entirely ordinary upbringing in Norwood: listening to the radio, reading, playing baseball, and going to school. In the final chapter, I recall my four years as a first-generation college student at Harvard, class of 1964. A couple of themes take clear definition here. The first is how insistent in my life, career, and historical sense has been the conundrum of Yankee and Irish confrontation and coexistence in the Boston area. The second is the corroboration of a truism. I grew up on the calm upslope of a great divide in American life, in which the watershed event was the assassination of President John Kennedy on November 22, 1963. After that, nothing was the same.

Putting these chapters together has been the most positive writing experience I've had. The pages that follow allow me to answer in the resounding affirmative Marilynne Robinson's question in *Housekeeping*: "For why do our thoughts turn to some gesture of a hand, the fall of a sleeve, some corner of a room on a particular anonymous afternoon, even when we are asleep, and even when we are so old that our thoughts have abandoned other business? What are all these fragments for, if not to be knit up finally?"

Mapping Norwood

1

Place Lore of Norwood

> I am a town boy. I am of the old confederacy of towns. I came of age in midcontinent at midcentury, during the final throes of a true town ethos in America—a dissolution foreordained half a century earlier, when cement highways began to pave over the frontier. I grew up at the end of an era, a fact of which I was clam-happily unaware. The Town, for me as a boy, was what I believed eternity must look like.
>
> —Ron Powers, *Far from Home*

My brother and I walked the downtown streets of Norwood, Massachusetts, with our mother on Friday evenings all the year round in the early 1950s. We had moved from Winslow Avenue up to Walpole Street in the summer of 1951 when I was eight and Geoffrey was six. Our sister Patti had been born into the new house in September of that same year. As part of the old Post Road between Boston and Providence, Walpole Street had been a major artery since colonial times. It was less than a mile to the intersection of Walpole with Washington Street, "the main drag," as my father called it, of our town. He never made this Friday trip, because somebody had to stay home with Patti. Also, he hated shopping. In the earliest years of this weekly ritual, when our legs were still too short for the longer haul on foot, Geoffrey and I would wait with Mum across the street from our house for the bus. This was the week's height of adventure, and now I'm thinking of one such night that can stand for all of them.

Here is a late fall evening, near enough to my November birthday and Thanksgiving and Christmas to make even the most ordinary trip exciting. It's cold and windy with spatters of rain, and fallen leaves skidding and then sticking on the wet, black asphalt of Walpole Street. The three of us are huddled on the corner, waiting. It's full dark at 6:15, and suddenly the bus is here, ablaze with light and the promise of warmth that hits us with the hiss of the opening door, though the metal rail is cold on which my brother and I pull ourselves up and inside. The sign proclaims the route: "Walpole / Norwood Center." Less than a mile back, this bus has stopped at the corner of the street on which my mother was born and raised, so she greets several of the dozen or so people who look up as we skitter down the aisle, off balance as the gears engage and we head for downtown. Some nights, depending on whether or not the driver knows Mum, we kids don't have to pay the nickel fare. Tonight we ride for free, which makes us feel important. The ride down Walpole Street takes us past several buildings that figure in my mother's town geography. Some are the large houses of old-line Yankee inheritors—Tucker, Chickering, Shattuck, Briggs. We also pass the First Congregational Church, the origins of which go all the way back to the founding of the Massachusetts Bay Colony in the seventeenth century. At the crest of the next hill I wave at my home away from home, the town's public library, then I sit back as the bus rumbles down onto Washington Street.

We climb out at the first stop on the main drag—in front of the Guild Theater. The fun begins right here. It's much the smaller of downtown Norwood's two movie houses, a nonthreatening place that shows one film at a time and costs twelve cents. On each side of the double doors is a poster for *The Desert Fox: The Story of Rommel,* starring James Mason as Hitler's brilliant military tactician. Immediately, I start pestering Mum to let me see this show tomorrow afternoon. She remains noncommittal, employing the standard phrase that drives my brother and me crazy: "We'll see." Still a bright memory, my first movie had been *Treasure Island,* the previous year. Exploring our new backyard, large and overgrown, I am often Jim Hawkins, innocent yet clever, expecting to find crazy old Ben Gunn or the essential pirate, Long John Silver himself, definitive in his mixture of sinister threat and oily allure, around every turn of the path we have beaten down. In these years before television, the Guild and the imposing Norwood Theater several blocks ahead on the Town Square are my one connection to the wider world of American visual entertainment. (I am already an enthusiastic radio listener.)

Next door to the theater is the Guild Taxi, an intriguing hole-in-the-wall place, hardly wider than its door. The cigar-smoking dispatcher sits behind his desk back in the gloom, like a spider at the center of a web. A cab idles at the curb. We've been known to take a taxi back or forth between home and here, but only in lashing rain or bitter cold. Also along this stretch is a step-up stone portico that leads into the foyer of the Talbot Block, in which, above the street-level stores, are two floors of apartments whose windows overlook Washington Street and seem to me a fine and mysterious place to hang one's hat. I imagine myself at one of those windows looking down.

The one on the third floor with the table lamp and potted plant. One tenant—I know this because my father told me—is the principal of my elementary school, the austere and solemn Miss Agnes Hedberg. There's something incongruous, though I can't quite articulate it, about where she lives and what she does. The portico is framed by standing columns that I swing slowly around as we pass. I'm hoping to get a glimpse of Miss Hedburg coming or going, but there's no such luck tonight.

Next we stop in front of the one store to which I have a personal connection. Callahan's Norwood Furniture Company is owned and run by the father and uncle of Dan Callahan, one of the two friends that I made in the first week after we moved to Walpole Street. (We've been friends from that day to this—well over fifty years.) In business "since 1895," Callahan's is a Norwood institution, "four floors of fine furniture," well known for many towns around as a first-class operation. I don't think we've ever bought anything there, but the two big front windows provide me with a weekly dose of "gracious living," as the Sunday papers put it. Tonight there's a living room set up, my favorite kind of scene. Two striped and silky wing chairs, a shiny, dark wood coffee table, and a deep patterned oriental rug—all resting in a warm and cozy pool of light pouring from under the off-white shade of a glittering brass standing lamp. I see myself up there as well, nestled in one of the chairs with my nose in a book.

Now we pass "Bert's Thom McAn, Men's and Boys' Shoes," a store I know as the local outlet for Buster Brown: "I got shoes, you got shoes, everybody's gotta have shoes! But there's only one kind of shoes for me—GOOD OLD BUSTER BROWN SHOES!" This jingle is permanently soldered into my mind, because I get the hard sell every Saturday morning from "Smilin' Ed" McConnell on his radio show for kids. The shoes are much too expensive, though, and we never go in here, not even when prompted by the "free" Buster Brown comic books that Smilin' Ed says would be mine just for crossing the threshold. My mother knows better than to fall for this ploy.

The first store that the three of us enter is Kordette's, "Norwood's Leading Shop for Women and Children—Charge and Budget Accounts Invited." My mother does in fact have such an account here, and a few dollars change hands every week or so. Sometimes she buys a sweater or a blouse, and there's always conversation with the friendly proprietors, Mr. and Mrs. Fine. It's the weather, what's new in town, and how are Geoffrey and I doing in school. (I like it, he makes a face, and everyone laughs.) Tonight is special, because Mum finds a hat—she loves hats—and asks Mrs. Fine to put it away till the end of the month. After a cursory glance into the window of the Alice Shop—novelty clocks, greeting cards, ashtrays, vases—knicks and knacks, as we call them, and of no interest to us kids—we enter the thrilling vortex of Friday night life for my brother and me. Norwood in the Fifties has three "Five-and-Tens," all virtually in a row in the middle of town: W. T. Grant's, F. W. Woolworth's, and McClellan's.

Somewhere in this cornucopia of low-budget marvels is our best chance of a "treat," a nickel or dime item that Geoffrey and I may possibly persuade Mum to buy for us. All three stores have well-worn, thin-plank wooden floors and shoulder high (to me) counters stretching away toward the darker reaches of drapery and fabric bolts on the far back walls. Big fans spin lazily from the ceilings. Woolworth's has a lunch counter, and the store smells like coffee, popcorn, and hot dogs, invariably causing a pang of hunger. Grant's has an unambitious pet department consisting of doleful goldfish, scruffy parakeets, and a few smelly hamsters tiredly spinning their wheels. The stuff we covet is right up front, though: packs of baseball cards with gum, individual military figures, yo-yos, kite kits, small cars, trucks, and airplanes. Most of these toys are still made of cheap postwar plastic from "Occupied Japan." Tonight, maybe because Mum found a hat, I come away with a small but piercing red plastic whistle on a loop of string that fits around my neck. She will regret this indulgence before the evening is over. Geoffrey gets a one-piece dump truck, two inches long with no moving parts, so it neither dumps nor spins on its wheels, which bothers him not at all.

The big show for me is our department store, Parke-Snow's, an architectural wonder because it has a wide, sweeping staircase with shiny chrome railings to a second floor, and, most exciting, a basement, also full of merchandise, with its own back exit to a parking lot on a lower level. Here I am delighted to find a smaller version of the Washington Street storefront—a glass double door with narrow (but lighted) display windows on either side. We have no reason to go out this way, but, to my mother's annoyance, I love stepping into the unlighted lot and looking back in at the bustling aisles and color-filled counters. ("Both in and out of the game, and watching and wondering at it," as Walt Whitman says.) This underground, miniature entrance is a magical place. It's where I test my tolerance for fear, standing out there in the dark for as long as I can, threatened by Long John Silver or the Desert Fox, then walking back inside just in time.

Reaching the corner of the Town Square, we cross Washington Street and head back up the other side in the direction of home. First comes Orent Brothers Dry Goods, at which we barely glance. Neither Geoffrey nor I find any interest in clothes. The designation "dry goods" does interest me, though. Why does this refer to clothes, I wonder? And what would constitute "wet goods"? Also, the site and the label are bound up with my first inkling of conflict in Norwood between the Irish and the Yankees—us and them. I had come home from elementary school one afternoon to report that our Memorial Day assembly speaker had been "Commander" Rice, a tiny, doddering old man who had been introduced as a Civil War veteran. I was thrilled at this brush with history—the Civil War! My mother snorted, and pointed out to me that the math on this was as shaky as the Commander. Well, I said, Miss Hedberg had explained that he was a drummer boy, which meant he was still a kid while serving. If this were so, Mum responded, he'd be over a hundred years old by now, and that wasn't likely, was it? She also recalled that in her youth the window of his family's clothing store, Rice's Dry Goods (where Orent's now stands), had featured a sign announcing that "No Irish Need Apply" for jobs therein.

After Orent's, we linger in front of Norwood's two high-end specialty food shops, Dreyfus & White and Humphrey's Market, side by side and set back on a wide step up from the general line of store fronts. By now, supper is a distant memory, and so the window shopping starts to have a bite to it. Tonight the fresh fruits and vegetables at Dreyfus & White sit regally in tilted wooden cases just inside the white-trimmed, sparkling, small-paned glass doors that stretch across the front of the store. My brother and I play the game of asking Mum to identify the exotic produce:

"What are those bumpy green ones?"

"What are those little orange things?"

"Is that a cantaloupe?"

Next door at Humphrey's, "Live Lobsters a Specialty," we can see these strangest of edible creatures poking and bumping around in their big, murky, water-filled cases in the left-hand window:

"That one looks like you!"

"Does not!

"Does too. Look at his nose!"

And in the other window, laid out on their beds of crushed ice, whole fish, wetly iridescent and two feet long, peer out at us accusingly through glittering black eyes. Who knows how far they've traveled to end up here in our own downtown?

Also on the way back is a narrow storefront complex toward which my feelings are decidedly mixed. It is, first off, a miracle of compression, and because I love small, organized spaces, it's pleasant just to step into the open, tiled entryway. On the right side is Jack's Taxi and Travel Bureau, "Agency for Greyhound Bus Line, Cars for Funerals, Weddings and Private Parties." This is the smallest place with the broadest mandate that I can imagine. Inside, there's a dispatcher (is it Jack?) sitting at the desk wedged against the front window. Two or three faded posters of palm trees and Irish castles hang on the wall, and I can't quite believe that anyone can get to Miami or Galway from here. But passing this storefront also makes me uncomfortable for an entirely different, a familial reason. On the left side of the entry, tall windows that start at my belt line reveal a narrow corridor of leather-bottomed chairs with magazines flopped on them. There's barely room for the knees and no stretching out. I know this because I've sat in these chairs many times. This is the waiting area of Eddie Armour's Barber Shop, where my father and I get our haircuts. Straight ahead, through the glass door, are three oversized barber chairs, eerily shrouded in sheets and doubled in the huge mirror that extends the length of the shop. I turn away with a shiver, and not just because it's November, for this is the place where a few years ago I made my father really mad for the first time.

After this disturbing encounter, the way back up Washington Street holds just a few more places of distracting interest. There are more shoe and clothing stores, a drugstore, a restaurant—not much excitement here—but we do stop and look twice more. At Gertrude's Pastry Shop the three of us check the window for wedding cakes, those wonderfully concentric, pure white platforms festooned with sugary garlands and swags, the harbingers of tomorrow's big local events, the Saturday "nuptials"—a vaguely menacing word that I've picked up from the newspapers. There are two cakes tonight, but only one has the miniature couple perched on top, holding hands and looking steadily out through the window into their future.

The last store we sometimes enter is Regina's, a gift shop specializing in "Religious Articles," which in our town means heavy-duty *Catholic* stuff. Tonight we walk in, gingerly as always, because the narrow aisles are full of breakable glassware and china. Here are row upon row of statues, colored and plain: Holy Families, Blessed Mothers, Pietàs, Infants of Prague (the baby Jesus wearing a crown and holding a globe of the world). Here are bins of rosaries, their decades divided by all manner of markers, from sparkling jewels to austere bits of plain wood. Here are crucifixes, holy-water fonts, Guardian Angel night lights, bas-reliefs of the suffering savior with his Sacred Heart burning red. Here are Mass cards and holy cards, prayer books and missals ("Daily and Sunday"), pictures framed and unframed of all imaginable religious events and possibilities. The effect of this barrage is confusing but undeniably impressive, and I am reminded now that it was at Regina's that Catholicism in the 1950s was most real to me. Sunday Mass at St. Catherine's in those days before Vatican II was less than engaging. The experience consisted mostly of listening to Latin while looking at the priest's back. On the other hand, the honky-tonk splendor of the Church Entrepreneurial really got my attention.

The rest of our excursion is a gauntlet of emporia which we run on much depleted energy, with crankiness building steadily. Also, a cold rain has begun to fall. Hurrying past the last few storefronts of downtown, we end up at the bus stop across the street from the Guild Theater where Washington meets Walpole Street. We are in front of Cullen's Corset Shop, which is always good for a laugh. Tonight we act out the joke of "perusing" (a favorite word in our family) with mock solemnity the array of girdles modeled by trunk-only manikins in the window. Now it's back on the bus. We scramble wearily aboard, and Geoffrey and I tumble into our favorite seat—the right front, just behind the metal divider and the doors, with a full picture-window view out the windshield. The bus picks up speed. The wipers glide with ponderous ease. All's right with the world. And then, as we start up the hill for home, to my mother's consternation and my brother's great glee, I blow my new whistle.

Aaron Guild and the Irish Heaven

Norwood supported a host of small stores where merchants in ostensibly mild and friendly competition made a decent living. In addition to the two downtown theaters (there was also a third, the Southern, in South Norwood, another place entirely), two taxi stands, three Five-and-Tens, and Parke-Snow's, I count (aided by a look at advertisements from that time) two restaurants, two hardware stores, two banks, two supermarkets (A & P, First National), three fabric and drapery shops, four drugstores, four appliance stores, four specialty food shops, five shoe stores, seven jewelry and gift stores, and eleven places to buy clothes (men's, women's, and/or children's). In the 1950s, of course, there was nothing unique about this Friday-night world of mine. The American town in the middle of the twentieth century had a wholeness and self-sufficiency that seems extraordinary only in retrospect. Such places defined this country, from coast to coast. Norwood had 16,000 people when I was growing up there in the late Forties and early Fifties. The town sits thirteen miles southwest of Boston, to which it was connected during my childhood by several lines of approach: the New York, New Haven & Hartford Railroad; the Dedham, Norwood, and East Walpole bus that delivered us in forty-five minutes to the Forest Hills station of the Massachusetts Transit Authority—the fabled MTA; and a complex series of secondary roads that went by twists and turns through (depending on preference and habit) Westwood, Islington, Dedham, West Roxbury, Roslindale, Jamaica Plain, and on into downtown Boston. These several connections notwithstanding, Norwood in my childhood was not a suburb. It was a separate place, with its own industrial base of tanneries, an ink mill, and two book binderies, and a definite sense of itself or, rather, of several selves. The town had rich layers of cultural identification that today would be labeled "ethnic." Having grown up with these, I mostly took them for granted, but it has since occurred to me that the clarity and depth of the definitions of otherness there rendered them exemplary—even archetypal.

All Norwood was divided into three parts: old-line Yankees, ethnic and immigrant Irish, and the more recent immigrants from Southern and Eastern Europe. As a child, I knew little of the third group, for most of them lived in South Norwood, "the Flats," a wilderness of triple-decker apartment houses separated from the rest of the town, in classic fashion, by the New Haven Railroad tracks. You even had to go down under a railroad bridge to get to what was literal terra incognita to me. But the Yankees and the Irish were a different story. I was pretty sure that I knew what each of those terms stood for. Even as a boy, I could feel the tension between the long-established Yankees, who still ran the place, and the Irish upstarts, who, after all, had been there for only a hundred years. I was naturally curious, in part because, though we didn't talk much about ethnicity, I was conscious of being more Irish than anything else. (When I had asked my mother if Fanning was an English name, she had replied—with a chuckle—"no, Irish.") There were also Germans in our background on my mother's side, about whom I knew a little, and Yankees on my father's, about whom I knew nothing.

Two iconic presences, the Town Hall and St. Catherine of Siena Church, still face each other across Washington Street beyond the Town Square in the heart of Norwood. By age ten, I had figured out that these buildings were public territorial markers for the Yankees and Irish respectively. The Town Hall seems the more imposing of the two—a pseudo-Gothic towered structure of Weymouth seam-faced granite with mullioned windows and a World War I cannon pointing out into the intersection of Washington and Nahatan Streets. I don't recall ever going into the building as a child. The

Figure 1. The Norwood Memorial Municipal Building and St. Catherine of Siena Church at Washington and Nahatan Streets. From Bryant F. Tolles, *Norwood: The Centennial History of a Massachusetts Town* (Norwood: Norwood Printing Co., 1973). Courtesy of Bryant F. Tolles.

church, which we attended every Sunday, has an English Gothic facade of gray Roman brick with yellowish limestone trim. In what looks to be a gesture of self-regard, the statue of St. Catherine has her back to the street. She is looking up the wide stone steps at the three sets of wooden front doors. St. Catherine's was a pretty well-heeled, predominantly Irish parish that included a thriving parochial school, grades K through 8, which we did not attend.

These obvious symbols of Yankee state and Irish church were not defining for me, however. I was instead intrigued by two secondary sites that were dramatically opposed in social and historical weight. Though I had no such idea at the time, nor for many years thereafter, finding roots and reasons for this jarring, incongruous pairing was to become a continuing occupation of my adult working life as a student of immigration and ethnicity.

In my mind, the heart of Yankee Norwood was a five-foot boulder of rough-hewn granite planted right smack in front of the Morrill Memorial Library on lower Walpole Street. As these were the years when I discovered books in a big way, I walked past that rock two or three times a week. For me, it was Norwood's equivalent of Plymouth Rock, and I can still recite from memory the two sentences inscribed on its mottled gray face: "Near this spot on April 19, 1775, Captain Aaron Guild left plow in furrow, oxen standing, and departed for the Battle of Lexington. He arrived in time to fire upon the retreating British." Here was History with a capital "H," earnest, eventful, awe-inspiring. During the American Revolution, what was now our town had been the South Parish of Dedham, one of the oldest towns in the state, incorporated in 1636. Norwood seceded from it in 1872, by which time the Irish diaspora triggered by flight from the Great Famine of the late 1840s had already transformed the demography of eastern Massachusetts. South Dedham/Norwood was one of the places most dramatically affected.

In the 1950s, my sense of the Irish character of Norwood could not have been more different from my idea of the town's Yankee heritage. As a child, I saw the local Irish genius loci centered not in St. Catherine's church but in a small, low, two-story clapboard building with peeling gray paint that was tucked between the town jail and the Electric Light Company, one block off Washington Street. A short flight of wooden steps led to a cramped front porch that was wedged up under a corrugated iron roof. To a stranger in town, it could have been the private home of some down-and-outer, for there was no sign advertising what went on inside. But the door was often open, and from the sidewalk we kids could see the corner of a plain deal bar and one or two hunched, shadowy male figures. This was "the Irish Heaven," or simply, "The Heaven." It was a barroom—more accurately, a pub, though I certainly didn't grasp that distinction at the time. One of Norwood's two tanneries, Winslow Brothers & Smith, had been right across the street since the nineteenth century, providing a thirsty clientele for several generations. There had been fierce industrial strikes at this tannery in 1933, 1938, and 1949, after which the factory was shut down.

What I could discern inside "The Heaven" was a haze of pipe and cigarette smoke and a glimpse of a dartboard, and I could just make out the sporadic thunk of darts and clinking of glasses. There was also a low hum of conversation, some of it in the unfamiliar rhythms of a foreign tongue. I knew the language was Irish, but I had no idea how extraordinary it was to be hearing it, here and occasionally on the downtown Norwood streets. Actually, we had a few Irish words at home as well—*gamal* for the creator of an embarrassing public spectacle, *amadán* for "clumsy oaf" (used whenever my brother or I spilled something messy), and *tóin* (pronounced "thoon") for backside, the area upon which punishment for the other two was to be applied. These had been passed down from my mother's mother, born Johanna Frances McAuliffe in Whitechurch, County Cork, in 1879. I've since heard from my friend the Gaelic scholar Maureen Murphy that Norwood was a popular destination for chain migration (neighbors following neighbors) from the villages along the Irish-speaking south Connemara coast. When she was there learning the language in the mid-1960s, Maureen would ask people if they'd ever been to Dublin, and sometimes the reply would be *Ní raibh mé chomh fada sin, ach bhí mé i Norwood* ("I haven't been that far, but I've been to Norwood").

Thanks to another scholar-friend, Phil O'Leary, I've also come to know that Norwood in general and the Irish Heaven specifically were well known to the most accomplished writer of fiction in the Irish language of the mid-twentieth century—Máirtín Ó Cadhain. It's very likely that on some of those afternoons when I was standing outside, he was in The Heaven speaking Irish with friends and relations. Born in 1906 at Cnocán Glas near Spiddal on the Connemara coast, Ó Cadhain was of the people, as he put it in one story, "whose guardian angel was the American trunk, whose guiding star was the exile ship, whose Red Sea was the Atlantic." And in the same story he describes a Connemara girl "nurtured on American lore from infancy. South Boston, Norwood, Butte, Montana, Minnesota, California, plucked chords in her imagination more distinctly than did Dublin, Belfast, Wexford, or even places only a few miles out on the Plain beyond Brightcity" (his name for the city of Galway). Moreover, Norwood also appears 12in Ó Cadhain's 1949 masterpiece *Cré na Cille* ("Churchyard Clay"), the first great novel in Irish, which consists of the Connemara graveyard conversations of a whole townland's worth of deceased local people. In it, a formidable character is the ninety-year-old matriarch Baba Paudeen, whose immigration to "that bitter bee-hive" of "Big Brian's family in Norwood" is one of the novel's key events. I'm afraid, however, that the exotic linguistic, literary, and ethnographic allure of the Irish Heaven was no conscious part of my perception as a ten-year-old in 1952. No, I saw it as shabby, clandestine, and literally outlandish.

We never went near the place as a family. Barrooms were anathema to my father, and I only found out why sometime after he died, when my mother told me that when he was a child, his father would take him to downtown Norwood and tell him to wait outside a "store" while he did some "business." The store was always a barroom. My father would stand there alone for an hour or more at a time. I could picture him when my mother told the story, and I can see him now—a little boy scuffing his feet and wiping his nose, trying to puzzle out where he might belong in the post–World War I passing scene.

Eventually, I realized that neither Aaron Guild's rock nor the Irish Heaven was an accurate, encompassing symbol. I came to recognize that the Norwood geography of my childhood was built on stereotypes, a word not yet in my vocabulary in those years, and a concept not much in the foreground generally on the seemingly smooth surface of American culture in the Fifties. But of course the Yankees were not as solid, chiseled, and undislodgeably established as Aaron Guild's monument, and of course the Irish were not as back-street, closeted, and shady as the Irish Heaven seemed to be. Even at ten or eleven, I knew of exceptions to both distorted rules in the form of local disreputable Yankees and successful, upstanding Irish Americans.

I had heard already about two of Norwood's notable Yankee eccentrics. One, Fred Holland Day, had been a leading figure in the Boston version of the decadent Nineties. In 1893 he cofounded Copeland and Day, an influential publishing house in the Arts and Crafts tradition, which produced American editions of works by W. B. Yeats, Oscar Wilde, and the controversial *Yellow Book*, as well as Ralph Adams Cram's *The Decadent* and Stephen Crane's *The Black Riders and Other Lines*. Day was also a pioneering photographer in the Pictorialist movement. His studies of children, immigrants, African Americans, and allegorical subjects were central to the development of photography as a fine art at the turn of the twentieth century. In Norwood, though, he was best known for having posed himself as Christ on the cross and for spending the last twenty years of his life a virtual recluse in his ornate, faux Tudor mansion a short block from downtown. (You could look it up. My sister Patti has written Day's biography, *Through an Uncommon Lens*.)

The other Yankee eccentric, Joseph Ferdinand Gould, Harvard Class of 1911, the son and grandson of prominent local physicians, had set himself up in the Twenties as "Joe Gould," a Greenwich Village bohemian with no fixed address who lived on cadged meals and claimed to be writing *An Oral History of Our Time*, a record of all the conversations he'd ever had. He also said, and would demonstrate on demand, that he could speak the language of seagulls. Joe's friends included Malcolm Cowley, William Saroyan, and E. E. Cummings, who wrote a poem about him that begins, "little joe gould has lost his teeth and doesn't know where / to find them." (I also have almost firsthand knowledge of his character. Auntie Mae, my father's older sister, who had known elementary school classmates of Joe, told me that he was "a pain in the ass," notorious for throwing stones, pulling girls' hair, and spitting on anyone who came into range at recess.)

On the other hand, Irish American successes included a family of doctors whom we knew well and admired tremendously. "Old Doctor O'Toole" (Thomas H. O'Toole, MD) had started his own hospital and built a reputation at the turn of the century as a compassionate general practitioner. His son, "Young Doctor O'Toole," delivered me and my brother and sister, took out my tonsils, and was our family's doctor for thirty years. Moreover, in the wider world of sports celebrity, Norwood also boasted an Irish American native son, "Jumpin' Joe" Dugan, who had been the regular third baseman for the "Murderers' Row" New York Yankee teams in the 1920s. In my childhood, Jumpin' Joe was a lively octogenarian, whose favorite tagline I myself had heard more than once: "On the road, I roomed with Babe Ruth's suitcase. He was always off with some broad."

The interesting point here is that although I knew of these prominent Norwood families, I did not at the time associate them with their ethnicity. When the Yankees deviated from the perceived norm of respectability or the Irish from that of disrepute, I simply didn't see it. Though I identified myself as mostly Irish Catholic, my sense of the local ethnic hierarchy was indistinguishable from that of the least tolerant pew holder in the First Congregational Church. The rheumy old men walking unsteadily along Washington Street, muttering to themselves, were obviously Irish, and that made Yankees of all the upstanding businessmen in blue suits. It was not until later on that I began to break the cultural code that lay behind my counterintuitive blindness to the salient examples of local Yankee oddity and Irish accomplishment.

Walkabout

Even when our family had a car, we walked almost everywhere and measured time in that older, more natural way. Bicycles were for far-flung excursions with friends, but they were much too valuable to be left unattended, so from about age ten I often walked downtown and all over town when there were errands to run. Because of the central location of our house, I walked all twelve years to school—elementary, junior high, and high school. I walked to the library, to the playground, to the movies. This is how I came to know Norwood so well—in the same way my parents had come to know it. Mine was probably the last generation to have that experience. I also had two jobs between ages ten and twenty—paperboy and electric meter reader—which contributed mightily to what became an impressively detailed, street-by-street knowledge of the town.

I didn't realize how much of this geography was still in my head until I found a copy of a book that brought it all back in a rush. This was the *List of Male Persons Twenty Years of Age or Older Liable to be Assessed for a Poll Tax and List of Women Twenty Years of Age or Older residing in the Town of Norwood on January 1, 1954, Together with their respective ages, occupations and nationality, if not citizens of the United States.* For most of 1954 I was eleven, so this particular edition of a very familiar book focused the town of my childhood. We kids used to love to page through the "street list" every year when it arrived in the house, shouting out names, ages, and occupations, to which our parents would reply with hoots of skepticism, especially about the ages of people they knew. Now, some fifty years later, I was amazed at the richness of remembrance evoked. The pages of that town directory brought forth a flood of images of houses and people long forgotten. There were so many shocks of recognition that I decided to count the number of Norwood streets in 1954 where people lived whose names and faces came back to me. That number was 176 out of 254 streets—nearly 70 percent!

My paper route, begun in fifth grade, was a real eye-opener. In this, as in many forays into the wider world, my younger brother Geoffrey was there ahead of me. He had been delivering papers for nearly a year when I signed on with Welch's Newsstand, the local distributor for the *Norwood Messenger* and the six Boston dailies: the *Globe*, the *Herald*, the *Traveller*, the *Record*, the *American*, and the *Christian Science Monitor*. I had an evening route—Geoffrey's was in the morning—and six afternoons a week the bundles of papers were dropped on our driveway by three o'clock. I stuffed them in my shoulder bag and started up Walpole Street. A year later, I also took on a Sunday route that covered much of the same ground and added some new territory as well. I kept the Sunday route all through high school. Because I walked up everyone's front walk and put the papers between the two front doors, this was an early lesson in the unequal distribution of economic resources. The whole range was there. I went right onto Eliot Street, with its row of three-deckers, three apartments to a building. Then left onto Highland, a street of small but single-family homes in one of which lived my third-grade teacher, Miss Kenefick. At the top on the right was the neighborhood's only mansion—the Cox place, one of Norwood's great old homes, complete with ten-foot hedges, a long driveway, and two-story columns. That the Coxes took no papers from me contributed to the mystique of wealth. I assumed that they were too rich to need news in print form. I then proceeded back down Highland Street on the other side and up Eliot again, right onto Crescent Avenue, left on West Street with apartment buildings and single-family homes alternating all the way to the top. I remember one flat-roofed three-decker on West Street where an unmarried woman of forty or so on the third floor came uncomplaining down the two flights every Friday evening with the exact change, a nickel tip, and a question about how I was doing in school. Though I never came later than four o'clock, she was always already in her "housecoat" and curlers, tucked up for the night. Another kind of mystery there.

I then turned left onto Nichols Street and walked past Norwood High School, a long, beautiful brick building with white trim and a columned entrance facade. This "school on the hill" was still several years away for me, but it already loomed with scary promise. The climax of my evening route was Victoria Circle—a sheltered enclave where lush-lawned, landscaped houses clustered around a delicate small park of grass and sculpted greenery. Each house was a gem: a standard white colonial with black shutters framing many-paned windows; a deep-dormered cape with green canvas awnings both cozy and enigmatic; an austere saltbox painted a pale blue I'd never seen anywhere else; a dark beauty shaded by huge, spreading trees and fronted in large stones of gray and muted orange; a long, low ranch-style place with vast, sparkling picture windows and a double front door that was answered—uniquely on my entire route—by a uniformed maid.

These were fairly ordinary New England upper-middle-class homes, no match for the Cox place or for latter-day McMansions in either size or ostentation. But that was part of the allure. We weren't about to move there, but these houses seemed not to be impossibly out of reach. Anyway, I always felt a calm descend when I left the open, often windswept, hilltop stretch of Nichols Street to enter the hushed, protected confines of Victoria Circle. It was easy enough to pretend that I lived there, especially in the dark of winter when I had been walking for over an hour and my feet were cold and wet. So I let myself think that the lamps glowing in the windows, revealing jewellike, dollhouse interiors with that illusory perfection of the partial glimpse, were welcoming me home.

The other location that figures most strongly in my memory of delivering papers is "Westover." Part of the master plan of Norwood's resident visionary, George F. Willett, a successful industrialist whose ideas had shaped the town up through the 1930s, this thousand-acre tract was designed to be "a New England Village of the Twentieth Century," a place, in the gushing prose of Willett's prospectus, where "every home shall have a perfect setting and a protected privacy, in harmonious architectural surroundings, which shall grow more beautiful through succeeding generations." The Depression-era time lag between conception and realization of this ambitious plan had stalled the project for twenty years. We had called the abandoned streets the "Crazy Roads" and ridden bikes around the place, half hoping to get lost. By the late 1950s, however, the "new development" was finally getting under way—though not on the scale Willett had intended—and with it would come Norwood's transformation from a separate entity to a suburb of Boston. The town experienced its greatest population boom at this time, growing by about half, from 16,636 in the 1950 census to 24,898 in 1960. This process took place before my very eyes, as the tangled "Crazy Roads" were christened one by one with legitimate, if implausible, pseudo-British names: Avon, Downing, Buckingham, Churchill. All through my high school years the new ranch and split-level houses went up and were added to my Sunday route. The newcomers—"carpetbaggers," my parents and other Norwood natives called them—were city people with the foreign accents of New York and New Jersey, and they didn't even work in town. They went to Boston on the train that was Norwood's ticket to becoming a bedroom community.

From my newsie's perspective, the most important fact about these folks was their reluctance to get out of bed on Sunday mornings. When they had forgotten to put the money for the paper between their two front doors on Saturday night, I would have to ring the bell and wake them up to collect. Naturally they hated this, fumbling and grumbling week after week: Why couldn't they pay by mail, as they had back in Queens or Newark? Why couldn't they at least pay just once a month? Well, as I explained, Welch's Newsstand simply didn't work that way. I had to collect every week and bring the money, tips included, to the "paper store," where the books were reconciled and I was paid on the spot by John Connolly, a heavy bear of a man with a thatch of white hair whose claim to fame in Norwood was holding the record for the longest engagement to the same woman. (He had been keeping company with Evelyn for thirty-five years with no official consummation in sight.) One by one, we paperboys would cast down our pennies, nickels, dimes, quarters, half-dollars, and crumpled bills before John every Sunday afternoon. He would sweep the treasure toward his barrel chest, separating the coins and filling a sheet of paper with numbers. He then drew a double line and rendered up the figure of our pay. None of us kids had any idea what he was doing—"the figuring" was what he called it—but we were agreed that he was somehow screwing us over, as we always got less than we expected, and no two weeks were ever the same.

My most vivid memory of being a paperboy involves a blizzard. The *Norwood Messenger* came on Thursdays, and I had taken to hauling that day's heavier load in a red steel wagon left over from earlier childhood, the handle of which I had lengthened with a piece of rope. One of those days we were hit with a big snowstorm starting at about one o'clock in the afternoon. This timing was just wrong: school wasn't called off, and the papers got to my house at the usual 3:00 PM. I set off a half-hour later into a welter of snow coming more and more thickly from the darkening sky. The papers were heavy, so I needed the wagon, but the wheels kept jamming with ice as I proceeded slowly along the streets. The route usually took me an hour, but not until 5:30 was I pulling the load out of Victoria Circle, my farthest point from home. My hands and feet were freezing, but I wasn't in the least frightened. The gray-black sky, the great gobs of falling snow, the trees already sheathed in white—all this was beautiful and dangerous, a heroic adventure. When I looked up, there coming toward me on foot was Uncle Joe. This was my father's youngest brother, a handsome, dark-haired, quiet man, then in his mid-thirties, married with two little kids and living right around the corner from us. I knew only two things about him. He had served in World War II in the Pacific, and he had come back to try out a vocation as a Franciscan monk. Worried about my absence in the intensifying storm (nearly a foot of snow had fallen in three hours), my father had called Uncle Joe to help look for me. He came up to me smiling, and took the rope handle of my cart. My father joined us ten minutes later, and we finished the route together.

A year and a half after this event, my uncle dropped dead of a heart attack on a Saturday morning in spring at the age of thirty-eight. This was the first sign that my father's generation of Fannings had weak hearts. Summoned by phone, we all rushed around the corner to find his wife, a daughter of immigrants, screaming in Polish through the house: *"Joe jest martwy! Joe jest martwy!"* On the day of the funeral, I remember pushing myself up into my parents' bedroom because I felt I should tell my father how sorry I was. When I stammered out the words, he turned to the window, unable to reply. Shortly after this, I began to have a recurrent dream that mixed my uncle's failed vocation as a monk with that snowy Thursday and with death. In it, I'm wading through the snow, pulling my wagon full of papers. I am truly lost and starting to panic. I see Uncle Joe ahead of me, beckoning. He's only ten yards off, but I can't close the gap between us. He shakes his head, then turns away and disappears into the swirling whiteness. He's wearing a hood, a black hood, and calling my name.

It was a summer job during college that really established my expertise in the internal geography of Norwood. I became a meter reader for the Electric Light Department, filling in while the regular staff took their vacations, and in this capacity I walked the whole town, street by street and house by house, three or four times over for three summers in a row. At the end of all this, I knew the place inside and out, north, south, east, and west. I carried a flashlight and bulky, metal-covered logbooks that held the monthly readings. The meters were glass globes containing two spinning disks. Between them, a slowly turning row of numbers ticked off the amount of electricity being used. Newer houses had the meters attached outside, but in many cases I knocked on doors and was pointed to the cellar, where the meter perched in some dark corner, purring like a cat. At this point in time, three encounters from that job continue to stand out—one each for beauty, danger, and opéra bouffe.

One sunny summer morning I knocked on the front door of a run-down house on Davis Avenue in my mother's old neighborhood and was greeted by the most beautiful teenaged girl I had ever seen. She smiled a wholly unselfconscious smile and led me back through a dark hall into a small, cluttered kitchen with an old-fashioned slate, two-tub sink and a big, clunky iron stove. The dingy yellow linoleum floor was matched by a yellow formica table, chipped at the edges and piled with newspapers. Around it were sitting three pretty ordinary looking people, who I assumed to be the girl's parents and younger brother. I stumbled down the cellar stairs, read the meter, came back up, and left the house. Nobody walked me out. I recall shaking my head in wonder that no one in that house—including the girl herself—seemed to have any idea how extraordinary she was. I don't remember now what she looked like, other than a vague sense of a roundish face and honey blonde hair, but though I never saw her again, I know that her smile stayed with me for months, maybe years.

My brush with danger was much less unexpected, because I had been warned about this contingency by the regular employees. In those more innocent times, some people left those slanting cellar doors, called bulkheads, unlocked so that the meter reader could do his job without having to knock on the front door every month. Stepping down into one pitch-black cellar I heard a sound that made my blood run cold—the low, throaty growl of a dog. My flashlight picked him out—a Doberman just coming up on his front legs, his eyes shining red. I could see the meter on the wall behind him, but duty failed utterly to call. I backed up and out with all deliberate speed and let down the bulkhead door just in time.

As for comedy, I made one great gaffe that lived on in Light Department legend for at least the duration of my employment there. One afternoon a woman standing on her front porch waved me inside toward what I thought was the door to the cellar. Unfortunately, there were two doors, and the one I opened led to a tiny water closet under the stairs. In it, a second woman was seated on the toilet, perusing a copy of the *Ladies' Home Journal.* (I swear, this detail is engraved in my mind.) She screamed and slammed the door in my face. That meter didn't get read either.

A Polyglot Place

The most useful picture I have found of the transformation of Norwood from a Yankee backwater to the bustling, various town of my childhood comes from an unexpected source—none other than hapless "little joe gould." I had first heard about Joe around the time of his death in August 1957 at the age of sixty-eight, when the local papers ran stories about his Norwood roots and New York bohemian life. The *Norwood Tribune* obituary said that Joe had grown up in the family home at 486 Washington Street in Norwood, attended the Everett School (his spitting goes unmentioned) and Norwood High, and gone on to graduate from Harvard, after which he had done some epic drifting all over North America. He wandered around Canada and then worked on an uncle's farm there for several months. In the summer of 1915 he studied eugenics at a place called the Eugenics Records Office on Long Island. He followed this interest by traveling out to North Dakota in February 1916 to measure the heads of Mandan and Chippewa Indians on two reservations. Joe returned to Norwood in the late spring of 1916, and from there he went down to New York City. Most of the material in the *Tribune* about his subsequent life had been taken from a 1942 essay, "Professor Sea Gull," by the great *New Yorker* writer Joseph Mitchell. Joe Gould had taken a job as a police reporter for the *Evening Mail,* which he quit to go permanently on the bum in the summer of 1917 in order to devote all his time to writing his *Oral History.* It was said to have reached nine million words "scribbled in hundreds of nickel notebooks, which he abandoned in the cellars and closets of his friends." At the time of his death, Joe's magnum opus had not been found.

Figure 2. Joseph Ferdinand "Joe" Gould, 1889–1957. Monochrome watercolor sketch by Charles Fanning, 1972.

Joe Gould had surfaced again for me when Mitchell published a second, and surprising, piece, "Joe Gould's Secret," in 1964. Within a year, the two Gould essays had appeared as a book, *Joe Gould's Secret*, a copy of which I found in a used-book store. Here Mitchell revealed that the *Oral History* had never really existed. All that Joe had produced over the course of the forty New York years, during which this "odd and penniless and unemployable little man" had "ducked and dodged and held on as hard as he could," was hundreds of obsessive reworkings of three or four themes, including "An Infinitude of Bushwa," "The Death of Dr. Clarke Storer Gould" (his father), and "Drunk as a Skunk, or How I Measured the Heads of Fifteen Hundred Indians in Zero Weather." The *Oral History of Our Time* had been a scam, a shtick, a device by which to panhandle—either that or a sincerely held, heartbreaking self-delusion on which was grounded a profoundly dysfunctional existence. Or both. In 2000, Stanley Tucci turned Mitchell's book into a film that features a tour-de-force performance by Ian Holm as Joe. The film highlights a chilling connection between author and subject: though Joseph Mitchell continued to come to work at the *New Yorker* until just before his death in 1996, he never published another essay. Since I began my own writing life, Joe Gould has been a frightening, admonitory figure.

A few years ago, my sister Patti, who has written extensively about our town's history, showed me another, more positive, piece of the puzzle that was Joe Gould. Two years after college, he had published in the *Norwood Messenger* the longest coherent piece of writing he was ever to complete—a nine-part "Racial Survey of Norwood," which appeared in weekly installments between July 5 and October 4, 1913. To my great surprise, Joe's analysis of the town's changing population is both focused and illuminating. It's everything that his *Oral History* in all its forms, real and imagined, is not. The work is soaked in the consciousness of place. Joe begins the series with a telling analogy: "Before starting on a walking trip, it is always well to look at a map to find the main points about the region one is to traverse; and in the same way before we attempt to plod through the various groups of people in this town, it would be well to glance at some sort of a chart which would tell us what we are going into."

The chart he consults is the mid-decade census of the state of Massachusetts from 1875 through 1905, from which emerges a tale of dramatic change. In the first such census after Norwood's creation in 1872, the new town had a population of 1,744, of whom 567 had been born there. Only 316 had come from foreign countries, and 55 of these were English, Scottish, or Canadian. The Irish were already the largest foreign-born group, with 217 immigrants, and there were 35 Germans in town. By 1905, Norwood had 6,731 inhabitants, 4,277 of whom were of foreign birth or parentage. Of these, 2,771 were Irish; 524 were German. In addition, there were natives of some twenty other countries, including Sweden, Finland, Austria, Poland, Italy, France, Syria, and China—as well as "21 colored and 10 [American] Indian inhabitants." There were also 51 Civil War veterans still living in town.

Joe's series title "Racial Survey" is misleading. He follows a popular convention of the day by referring to ethnic groups as though they were separate races, but his articles are in fact remarkably tolerant and welcoming of

Norwood's newcomers, especially in the context of the upsurge of nativism and prejudice against the so-called new immigrants from Southern and Eastern Europe from the 1890s on and the national drumbeat toward immigration restriction that would culminate in the legislative slamming of the Golden Door in the early 1920s. In the matter of his own Yankee ancestors, Joe refuses to dwell on "the eagerness of Aaron Guild to get into the battle of Lexington," "the history of the ancient parish of South Dedham," or "the influence of the old Yankee stock upon local industries and town affairs." He declares instead that "in view of some neglected opportunities, perhaps they did no better than others would have done." Further, he dismisses as irrelevant the Mayflower descendants' "sentimental claim of being a little deeper rooted than others in the national soil," for, "as [Israel] Zangwill points out in his play 'The Melting Pot,' it is not birth but ideals that make the American."

The first immigrant group discussed in the survey is the Irish, who have "always been the largest foreign born element in our population," and Joe's assessment is wholly positive: "The first comers from Erin suffered from several handicaps. Many of them were poor and uneducated. . . . Under these circumstances, the part which the Irish have played in town life has been extremely creditable. Almost from the start of the town they have held offices in local government, and performed their duties well, and many Irish-born and Irish Americans are prominent here in business or professional life." So much for the discouragement of Irish job applications by many in Joe's New England WASP cohort! He goes on to emphasize place names and place lore: "There are three streets in Norwood, Casey street, Lydon street and Curran avenue which are named for Irish families, and there are three districts, Dublin, Galway and Cork City which bear the names of places in Ireland." He notes that the large immigration to Norwood from the south and west of Ireland explains the latter two names, and that in the first case, "the owner of the land gave it the name of Dublin to commemorate a visit he had paid to Ireland." Joe further contends that "these names have always been of assistance to our schoolboys in the study of their geography, and doubtless some have wished when asked to name the chief counties or cities of Ireland that we had more of these districts." He goes on to praise the "efforts which the Irish are making to preserve their best traditions by social organizations," among them the Ancient Order of Hibernians and their Ladies' Auxiliary. He also cites the Norwood Gaelic Club, whose 136 members are committed to "spread[ing] a knowledge of Gaelic," a language that Joe estimates "is certainly understood by nearly a thousand people in town, and probably spoken by nearly half that number." In sum, "this club has a very desirable mission to perform in perpetuating Irish culture, and its activity and enthusiasm are especially timely now that home rule for Ireland is in sight."

Joe's description of Norwood's Germans is also informed and balanced. He begins this section with a sensitive distinction: though we call them all "Germans," the town's "German-speaking people" include Germans, Austrians, and "Switzers." In the group are "about twelve families from Baden, about ten from Prussia, six from Saxony, four from Scheswick-Holstein and three from Wuttemberg." Joe also describes several German American organizations, locating them in the neighborhood then known as "Germantown" and on the same street, Wilson Street, where my mother, Frances Patricia Balduf, was born in 1913. Founded in 1889, Norwood's Turnverein boasted at its peak (around 1900) a membership of 150 people taking classes in gymnastics and the German language. This organization disbanded in 1908 "owing to the apathy of the new generation of Germans," according to Joe. Two ethnic Protestant sects—German Lutherans and German Baptists—also served this small community, holding their Sunday services "every fortnight in the Swedish Lutheran and Swedish Baptist churches respectively."

Joe's survey proceeds over several more installments in the *Messenger* to discuss the "other British" (English, Scots, and Canadians), the Scandinavians (Norwegians, Swedes, and Danes), the French and French Canadians, the Italians, Russians, and Finns. Every article contains the names of kids I went through school with. All feature historical context about reasons for emigration from Europe, lists of organizations that the groups formed in Norwood, and their association with particular neighborhoods. Finally, Joe describes special positive contributions, group by group. The Irish are significantly involved in the cultural and language project of the "Gaelic Revival," which "started in this country, but . . . is now a strong movement in Ireland." In keeping with their passion for music, there are six Germans in the Norwood town band. The determined bilingualism of the Swedes and the French Canadians is an intellectual model for other citizens to emulate. The Swedes encourage the life of the mind by means of the Swedish Literary Society, which meets at the homes of members. The Finnish Socialist Club on Chapel Court spreads its message through its lending library of 300 volumes, and even here, Joe has nothing derogatory to say about political ramifications. He remarks only that in this group, "men and women meet on an equal footing, and among the Finns more than among other people of Norwood the two sexes are socially and intellectually in partnership." This is plenty fair enough, and yet, a few months after the Gould series ran, a *Messenger* editorial early in 1914 warned that "a flood of undesirables from the darker sections of the Old World" were landing on our shores with "no conception of American ideas." Moreover, in January 1920, Norwood was the target of one of the infamous Palmer Raids, which were carried out in twenty-three states without benefit of probable-cause warrants. Twelve Lithuanian immigrants were arrested in town "on suspicion of being 'Reds' or members of the Communist Party," according to the *Messenger*, and the detainees were marched through the streets of Boston in chains.

As Joe Gould pointed out, Norwood's dominant immigrant/ethnic group in 1913 was the Irish. This continued to be the case for the next forty or so years, up through my own childhood. In *Our Own Kind*, his fine, neglected novel of 1946, Edward McSorley describes young Willie McDermott's trip on the train from Providence to Boston with his grandfather, who declares that "it was Irish, all Irish from Mansfield, Norwood right in to Boston and out again to Cambridge, every stick and stone of it." In this, as in much else, my own retrospective sense of the town is corroborated in *The Social Ecology of Metropolitan Boston: 1950* (Boston: Massachusetts Department of Mental Health, 1961) by Frank L. Sweetser of Boston University, a detailed analysis of the 1950 U.S. Census data for eighty-three cities and towns, with a combined population of 2.5 million, which surrounded Boston and Cambridge. Conveniently for me, the data for Norwood is further divided into three census tract districts that correspond roughly to the three parts of the town as I recall them: the Yankees (nearest to the business center), the Irish (north and east, closer to Boston), and the "new immigrants" from Southern and Eastern Europe (in "the Flats" of South Norwood).

Three conclusions emerge from Sweetser's analysis. First of all, with 682 Irish-born inhabitants, Norwood in 1950 was the most Irish town anywhere in the metropolitan area outside the city limits of Boston and Cambridge. Second, Norwood was then still very much a working-class place, with 56.4 percent blue-collar workers among the Yankees, 63.3 percent in the Irish wedge, and a whopping 75 percent in South Norwood. Third, the Flats, where most residents were immigrants and ethnics from Italy, Lithuania, Poland, and Syria, was a profoundly different place and much poorer by all the numbers than anywhere else in town or virtually anywhere else in the Boston area. The percentage of foreign-born for all of metropolitan Boston was 16.2 percent in 1950, and Norwood's Yankee (at 15.9 percent) and Irish (at 16.3 percent) census districts matched this norm. In the Flats, however, the percentage of foreign-born was 29 percent, and very few places outside Boston itself were as high. Also, income was lower in the Flats, the quality of housing was poorer, and the percentage of high school and college graduates was much smaller than anywhere else in Norwood.

Sweetser also computed a summary Social Rank Index using "a composite of a measure of education and a measure of occupational status." Here, on an ascending scale of 0 to 100, the Yankees were at 61, the Irish at 56, and the new immigrants at 30, which was one of the lowest rankings anywhere in metropolitan Boston. Thus, my own smallish town in 1950 provided sharp contrasts between privilege and underprivilege in an ethnic context the likes of which one might not have expected to find outside America's larger cities. And that's pretty much how I remember it.

The foreignness of the Flats was augmented in my childhood by an influx of European immigrants after World War II. We called them "DPs," short for Displaced Persons, and many were from war-ravaged Poland and Lithuania. They didn't all live in the Flats, either. In about 1949 a Lithuanian family, the Ridikases, moved into a second-floor apartment across the street from us. Their two children, Regina and Joe, showed up in my elementary school classroom, where they picked up English with remarkable speed. Joe and I became friends, and the smell of cabbage cooking in the Ridikas kitchen became the essence of the foreign in my mind. It occurs to me now that I was repeating the experience of a nineteenth-century Yankee kid coming into the homes of my Irish and German forebears. In some parts of Norwood, it had taken just about a hundred years for boiling cabbage to become exotic again.

Norwood had become an Irish town quite early. At the time of the Great Hunger of the late 1840s in Ireland, "South Dedham" began to be a significant site of new employment opportunities. The Norfolk County and Boston & Providence Railroads were being built, and many industries were opening up along their routes, among them foundries, ink works, printing mills, tanneries, a furniture factory, and car shops for the trains. Many Famine-generation Irish immigrants came straight off the boats and out to the rapidly developing area. The settlers clustered at the crossroads of Washington Street and Railroad Avenue (the "Dublin" and "Cork City" that Joe Gould reported), and their first benchmark was the establishment of a Catholic parish, St. Catherine of Siena, in 1863. After Norwood became a separate town, chain migration from Ireland continued, much of it from the Irish-speaking villages of South Connemara. Mirroring the national trend

Figure 3. Norwood Gaelic Football Club, 1915. Norwood *Tribune*, April 17, 1958.

among immigrants, by the turn of the century, sons of Irish factory hands were moving on to the growing municipality's public works, police, and fire departments.

Predictably, signs of ethnic respectability soon followed. In 1880 a local chapter of the Ancient Order of Hibernians (AOH) was established "to give aid to widows and orphans, to provide for the sick, and to befriend the stranger." In 1892, St. Catherine's Total Abstinence and Literary Society began meeting. Twenty years later, in 1912, the Irish were comfortable enough in Yankeeland to start up the Gaelic Club that Joe Gould mentions. This very active organization supported Irish freedom from British rule, traditional music and dancing, and the Irish language. They even fielded a Gaelic Football Club, playing matches against other teams around Boston. (Irish friends tell me that this makes sense for Norwood, the immigrant destination of so many young men from the rough terrain of Connemara, where football was preferred to hurling, which required a smoother field.) Again, the names of these Irish founding fathers and mothers are familiar to me as the grandparents and great-grandparents of kids I grew up with: Callahans and Costellos, Flahertys, Kellihers, Kellys, Collinses, and Cotters, and so many more. All of this supports the conclusion that Norwood was for some Irish in the late nineteenth and early twentieth centuries a distinct and definite immigrant destination. Indeed, as late as the 2000 census, fully 37 percent of Norwood's 28,500 residents—10,600 people—claimed Irish ancestry, and in 2002, Máirín Concannon, an immigrant to Norwood from near Spiddal in South Connemara, recorded a CD of songs in Irish sung in the *sean-nós* (old style) tradition.

One corroborating—and unintentionally comic—artifact of Norwood's cultural Irishness is a collection of two dozen poems about the town, *Selected Gems,* self-published in 1917 by Patrick J. Pendergast, who had come as a young child with his parents from County Waterford. He was to have eleven siblings born in Norwood. Even as specimens of autodidactic versifying, Pendergast's poems are pretty awful, and yet they do manage to convey sincere pride in and affection for the town and its Irish Catholics. (I realize that the attribution of sincerity to a poem is akin to saying that an ineffectual person "means well.") The vehicle for Pendergast's paean to Norwood is detailed evocation of place. My childhood self in the 1950s would have understood his celebration of downtown in "The Great White Way," which describes the church-bound Sunday morning "throng" strolling past the Premier theater, the National Bank, the Socony gasoline station, and Hartshorn's Market. This poem ends with an arresting metaphorical memento mori: "Now when you are leaving Norwood forever more to stay, / In a wooden boat for an overcoat you'll sail the great white way."

Pendergast's poem "Willet's [*sic*] Pond" begins with the route—right past my mother's house, and the precursor in reverse of our Friday night journeying—that people took to get there: "When ever you're in Norwood and you recreation seek / Step upon a Walpole car, get off at Wilson Street. / And now I can assure you the time you'd ne'er regret, / When you look upon that new made Pond named after George Willet." This was still the "New Pond" in my childhood, and Pendergast waxes eloquent about its genesis: "You can talk of Winnepesaukee and the Isles that there abound / For no where in this Country can their equal be found / But they were made by nature and are covered with moss, / George Willet's Pond was formed by man with the tip cart and the horse." In other poems, Pendergast celebrates the swimming pool, bowling alley, and cinder track of the "Civic Association," the "Village Hall on Broadway," and the "Piano Supply Company," where he got his own organ repaired.

Pendergast wrote enough conventionally pietistic poems about Catholicism to make his religion a major theme of the collection. However clumsy, these constitute a strong statement of belonging in the milieu of Yankee Protestant New England. Here place is again central, for he describes several area churches, among them his home parish of St. Catherine's in Norwood ("On Easter morn it's my delight to rise and cross the track / And in St. Catherine's receive [communion] from the hands of Father McCormack"); St. Mary's in Dedham, where "The granite came from Westwood; from the Quarry there close by"; and Gate of Heaven in South Boston, "the finest church in all the land," where, miraculously, "crystal bulbs did light supply," creating a scene that "I'll never forget till the day I die." There is also stock praise of the old country in poems such as "Dear Ireland, Now Thy Praise I'll Sing" ("I'll sing thy praises everywhere / Because my mother came from there") and "Robert Emmet" ("martyr slain / Thought Ireland's freedom to proclaim"). And Irish nationalist local color is the subject of "Hibernians' Lecture," which describes an AOH meeting in Norwood's Columbia Hall, transformed for the event by a stage curtain on which are painted "Tara's harp" and "St. Patrick with his mitre and his crozier in his hand."

Townlands

The idea of the townland struck me as fascinating when I heard the term during my first visit to Ireland, during the summer of 1973. This backpacking solo venture was the reward I bestowed on myself for having finished my dissertation, and one of the highlights was spending several days on the family farm of John and Nora Twomey and their four children in the rough, jagged hills of east Kerry. Cousins of a Boston friend, the Twomeys were wonderfully hospitable, giving bed and board to a stranger and answering all manner of dumb questions about their ways of living, including what the place was called and why. From halfway up a steeply pitched hayfield one beautiful July evening, John Twomey pointed out the neighboring townlands, explaining that these were the oldest and still the most useful locating names in this or any other district of the island. Theirs was "Gortlahard," and I took it back to the states as the first word of their functional postal address: "Gortlahard, Kilgarvan [the nearest town], County Kerry, Ireland." John told me that *gort* was Irish for "field," and that consequently it appeared in the names of many townlands, and that *ladhar* meant a dividing point, a fork, in a road or river. Thus Gortlahard meant the fields at the fork.

I've come back to this, some thirty years later, by way of finding the townlands from which some of my own family came out to America. I now know that the townland is the smallest geographical unit of land on the island of Ireland in the oldest surviving taxation and census documents. In 1861, the pioneering geographer William Reeves counted 62,205 of them. The average acreage per townland by county ranges from a high of 457 acres in County Down to a low of 172 in Monaghan, and Reeves concluded that the difference between these two extremes has to do with "the civil peculiarities of the districts, while in the possession of the *original inhabitants*." (The italics are mine.) This is one more indicator of the great antiquity of the system and the townland names. Indeed, Reeves cited the earliest notation "representing the characteristics of a primitive townland" as "an Irish memorandum in the Book of Armagh, written before the year 800." More recent scholarship counts nearly 67,000 townlands and brings the system back to the *trica cet* (literally "thirty 100s") and *bally betagh* ("place of hospitality")—ancient demarcations in Irish law tracts that date at least as far back as the 600s. The average size of a townland in Ireland comes in at a very humane, controllable amount of space: 326.4 acres.

Not so long ago, townlands did in fact contain "towns." These were clusters, or *clachan*, of a dozen to fifty or sixty cabins of mostly blood-related families. Here small communities of farmers worked the land by the old open field or "rundale" system, whereby an unfenced patchwork quilt of arable "strips" (the "infield") radiated out from the cabins to poorer boundary land reserved for pasturage (the "outfield"). This was by necessity cooperative farming, with shared labor in cultivation, harvest, and the raising of livestock. As a distinctive byproduct, these rundale communities fostered the traditional arts of dance, music, and storytelling. The world of the *clachan*-centered townland was shattered by the Great Hunger. But the townlands remain. As names in the old language, still alive as landmarks, postal addresses, and deeds of title across every Irish county, they are powerful, vestigial memory banks. Having followed a circuitous route with many wrong turns (to be retraced presently in these pages), I now know that the old-country farms of my Irish forebears were in the townlands of Urbalkirk in County Monaghan and Coolowen in County Cork.

I've seen these places laid out on maps of surpassing detail, accuracy, and beauty—in fact, a cartography lover's dream. And thereby hangs another tale. The first maps of Ireland with any degree of islandwide accuracy were those made by and for Elizabethan colonial officials in the mid-seventeenth century. These never showed lands below the level of "barony," a unit of area introduced as an aid to the colonization process, roughly corresponding to the "cantred" (or "hundred") in England. These early maps ignored even Ireland's counties, which, according to historian J. H. Andrews, the mapmakers believed were "too poor, economically and socially, and too ineffectually governed" to warrant attention. It took nearly 200 years for the ills of British colonial mapmaking in Ireland to be redressed. But this was accomplished with a vengeance when, in 1824, the Duke of Wellington, then the British prime minister, authorized the first Ordnance Survey of Ireland, in aid of valuation for local taxes, to make maps on the breathtaking scale of six inches to one mile. To put this prodigiously detailed project in perspective, a single-sheet map of the whole island at that scale would cover half a football field. (Set in a remote townland of County Donegal, Brian Friel's play *Translations* (1980) brought knowledge of the Ordnance Survey to a wide audience for the first time.) It remains the most painful of ironies that the years in which the Survey was being carried out, 1833 to 1846, coincided with the storm gathering toward the Famine. While the land was being scrutinized with an unprecedented passion for topographic accuracy, the people living on and by that land were staggering toward a devastating collision of exploding population and crop failure.

My friend and colleague Ed O'Day told me that the Newberry Library in Chicago had the whole gorgeous run—it turns out to be 1,994 sheets—of what J. H. Andrews termed the "paper landscape" of Ireland. And so I now have had the pleasure of hefting the actual four-foot by three-foot Ordnance Survey volumes for Monaghan and Cork off the cart in the high-ceilinged Newberry Map Room, and turning the luxurious, thick pages on which are engraved the lineaments of my family's townlands. Moreover, I was delighted to discover that the maps for both Urbalkirk and Coolowen contain even the lines of the individual farm fields. (In the early stages of the project, there had been debate about this incredibly painstaking level of detail, and not all the maps had benefited from the decision to include what the brilliant cartographer and environmental essayist Tim Robinson has lovingly called "the crackle-glaze of field boundaries.") To be sure, in the engraved final maps the individual fields were not named. However, it remains a measure of the depth of the spirit of place in Ireland that they could have been: we know that the Gaelic scholar John O'Donovan tramped the country for the Ordnance Survey in the 1830s collecting place lore, and that among the fruits of his labor were the "Field-name Books," several thousand small handwritten volumes, tied up in bundles and stored in the Survey Offices in Dublin.

Dindshenchas *of Norwood*

The Irish have always been deeply concerned with the history and elucidation of specific localities and landmarks. One of their oldest and most persistent forms of knowledge has been *dindshenchas*, which means place lore or tradition about places. (The word combines *dind*, literally "shelter," and *shenchus*, narrative or story.) In the oral tradition, this was the province of the *fili*, or poets, and, along with heroic tales and legends, this body of material began to be written down by Christian monks in the sixth century. In fact, place lore looms large in the heroic material itself, including *Táin Bó Cúailnge* ("The Cattle Raid of Cooley"), the most complete of the surviving sagas in the Ulster Cycle about Queen Maeve, King Conchobar, and the hero Cuchulain; *Lebor Gabala Erenn* ("The Book of Invasions of Ireland"), Ireland's pseudo-historical creation story; and *Acallam na Senórach* ("Tales of the Elders of Ireland"), the oldest extant compilation of the stories of Finn Mac Cool and his warrior band, the Fianna.

From the ninth century on, many separate poems containing place lore began to be written down as well. These were brought together in the eleventh and twelfth centuries into one large compilation, the *Metrical Dindshenchas*, in which are gathered some 300 poems, many with prose synopses, each purporting to explain the etymology and history of a place in Ireland. The writers drew on many sources, among them heroic tales and local folkloric traditions, and some of the poems seem plainly to have been pseudo-etymologies and stories invented to explain preexisting names. The "places" include all manner of topographic features, large and small, from mountains, glens, rivers, lakes, islands, bogs, and plains to hills, ridges, caves, fords, wells, and fields. Also included are archaeological sites, both pre-Christian (passage-graves, cairns, ring-forts, standing stones, dolmens), and early Christian (monastic foundations, churches, and burial grounds). One of the most famous of these poems contains the first recorded survey of the royal hill of Tara with its formidable mix of pre-Celtic, Celtic, and Christian monuments, forts, graves, and mounds.

A still indispensable latter-day guide into this absorbing field is Patrick Weston Joyce's three-volume *Origin and History of Irish Names of Places* (Dublin: McGlashan & Gill, 1869). Joyce begins with a sense of wonder: "This great name system, begun thousands of years ago by the first wave of population that reached our island, was continued unceasingly from age to age, till it embraced the minutest features of the country in its intricate net-work; and such as it sprang forth from the minds of our ancestors, it exists almost unchanged to this day." He concludes that "the great body of our townland and other names are at least several hundred years old," and that names of pagan origin can be traced as far back as 300 B.C. Indexed both by the names and their "root-words," *Irish Names of Places* is divided into three large parts: "Names of Historical and Legendary Origin," "Names Commemorating Artificial Structures," and "Names Descriptive of Physical Features." Joyce's book is a fine, rambling hodgepodge, and it makes great bedtime reading.

Ingrained reverence for the spirit of place accompanied the many thousands of post-Famine immigrants who left homes in rural Ireland for new lives in urban America. A theme of my own work in this field has been the idea that this transported legacy was an essential aid in the ultimately successful, though traumatic, conversion of farmers to city folk. That completed dissertation which I was celebrating in Ireland in 1973 was about Chicago journalist Finley Peter Dunne (1867–1936), the first voice of literary genius to emerge in Irish America. Dunne created the first memorable Irish character in American literature, the aging immigrant bartender Martin J. Dooley, and the first fully realized ethnic neighborhood, Bridgeport on Chicago's South Side. Created as weekly newspaper columns in the 1890s, the "Mr. Dooley" pieces taken together evoke a whole community, and what makes it cohere is place and place lore. Mr. Dooley defines all movement in relation to the "r-red bridge," which joins Bridgeport to the rest of the city where Halsted Street crosses the south branch of the Chicago River. "Archey Road," his local name for Archer Avenue, is a lively main street extending from Dooley's saloon to his rival Schwartzmeister's establishment "down the way" to "Father Kelly's church" to the political capital of the neighborhood, "Finucane's Hall." Questions of social status hinge on the proximity of one's home to the gas house and the rolling mills (at Archer and Ashland Avenues) or to the waters of Healey's Slough, a swampy Chicago River runoff. Thus firmly located in the imagination, Mr. Dooley's Bridgeport blossoms as a believable ethnic subculture with its own customs and ceremonies, a social hierarchy rooted in ancestry, family, and occupation, and a shared perspective on the world.

Certainly, the town of Norwood in my youth was full to bursting with place lore. Furthermore, I now realize that my friends and I were participants in the ongoing, universal human project of making necessary surveyor's maps of the places where we lived. Here's one salient example. Beginning in junior high, when we could go out for an hour or so after supper, the neighborhood kids gathered nightly on the corner of Walpole Street and Phillips Avenue, just half a block from my house. This was the site of a tiny strip of businesses that included a drugstore with soda fountain and a mailbox. By the time we were in high school, my friends and I had given

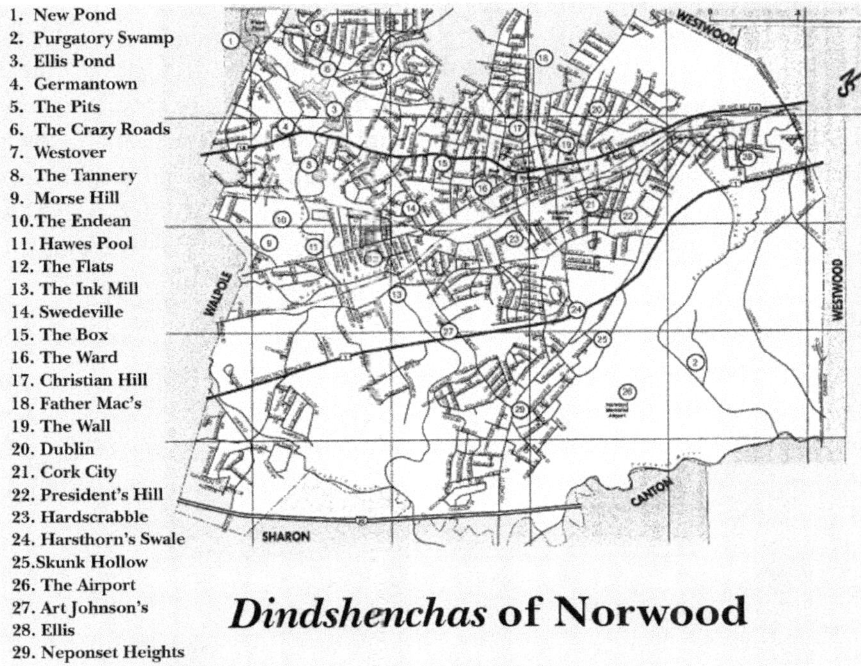

Figure 4. *Dindshenchas* of Norwood by Charles Fanning, 2007.

our place a name. It was "the Box" and we were "the Box Boys." Our main rivals in playground and pickup sports were "the Wall Boys," who hung out at "the Wall" surrounding the Shattuck School several blocks away. The Box Boys were a sort of parody and self-parody. No one took us seriously as a gang. We wouldn't have thought to fall afoul of the police, we were terrified of girls, and most of us were serious students with ambitions to attend college. The Wall Boys were much rougher, prone to getting into trouble that we considered big at the time, and precociously involved with cars and the opposite sex. Also, they were much better athletes and regularly cleaned our clocks in baseball, touch football, and kick-the-can. The point is that these place names and their connotations became widely known around the town. We had created a piece of Norwood's *dindshenchas*.

When I came to understand this, I began to write out and map the place names that my friends and our families had used to negotiate the town that was our world in the 1950s. Prompted since by conversations with many others, the names that I am now able to summon, along with the Box and the Wall, are New Pond, Purgatory Swamp, Ellis Pond, Germantown, the Pits, the Crazy Roads, Westover, the Tannery, Morse Hill, the Endean,

Hawes Pool, the Flats, Swedeville, the Ward, Christian Hill, Father Mac's, Dublin, Cork City, President's Hill, Hardscrabble, Hartshorn's Swale, Skunk Hollow, Ellis, the Airport, Neponset Heights, Art Johnson's, and "Down Behind the Ink Mill." There are twenty-nine in all. In a town that measures 6,712 acres, this works out to one place name for every 231.5 acres. As this is the size of many an Irish townland, I'm inclined to see a connection.

2

My Father's Chapter

> And then there came into my heart a very great love for my father and I thought it was very much braver to spend a life doing what you really do not want rather than selfishly following forever your own dreams and inclinations.
>
> —Alistair MacLeod, "The Boat"

The picture I'm looking at is a schoolroom shot. Everyone in the class must have had one taken. There's a blackboard behind the boy with what looks like a poem chalked on it. He's wearing a coat that's too big for him, double-breasted and rumpled, and a clumsily knotted tie. He's holding an opened book with both hands. His hair is carelessly combed, and a cowlick falls just above his right eye. There's a fresh-faced openness and innocence, a touching vulnerability, about him. This is my father, Charles Frederick Fanning, at ten or eleven. The picture is mounted in a colored postcard frame that folds twice for mailing, "copyright 1916 by T. C. Willson." On the left side, from which the photograph looks out in an oval frame, is a school facade with open door and three steps. A boy and girl are skipping into the foreground. Both are well dressed, the girl in an orange pinafore, the boy in a classic blue-and-white sailor blouse, red tie, high socks, and knickers. He's carrying two books and a plaid cap. Over all is the poetic gloss: "With lessons over / We're in Clover / Run and Shout / School is out." On the right side are a solidly middle-aged, middle-class couple sitting before a cheery fire. The woman has a collar and cuffs of white lace and a book in her lap. The man sits in a wing chair, wearing a smoking jacket and slippers, with a pipe in his mouth. The smoke from pipe and fire swirl up to form a frame for an imagined red schoolhouse with a wooden pump before it. The caption reads: "And to dream the Old dreams over Is a luxury divine, / When my truant fancies Wander to those Old School Days of mine." Though he may not have known it at the time, the picture marks my father's educational valediction. He left school after sixth grade and never went back.

In the parlance current in my New England youth, there was a whole lot

Figure 5. Postcard with insert photo of Charles F. Fanning, c. 1919.

of "mixed marriage" between Protestants and Catholics in my father's family. The potentially troublesome contradictions were dramatically doubled in that his parents were *each* half Irish and half Yankee. Typically, much less information is out there about the Irish parts. To some extent, the disparity is due to the difficulty of tracing nineteenth-century Irish Catholic antecedents, most of whom would have been small tenant farmers or farm laborers before emigrating. To this challenge can be added the daunting Massachusetts context of Irish Catholic genealogical self-deprecation (until recently, that is) in the face of all those Mayflower legatees, Founding Fathers, Colonial Dames, and Daughters of the American Revolution, with their governing passion for energetic self-aggrandizement through family history. My father's mother, Mary Ann Frances Shedd, was born in New Brunswick in 1877 to an Irish Canadian mother, Bridget Kerrigan, and a Yankee father, Frank Shedd. My father's father, Charles Winslow Fanning, born in 1876 in Dedham, Massachusetts, had a Yankee mother, Sarah Rebecca Radcliffe, and an Irish American father, John Fanning. About the Kerrigans and Fannings back in Ireland, I have been able to discover nothing before the nineteenth century. For the Yankees, on the other hand, there is a veritable cornucopia of names, dates, and nuggets of history stretching way, way back. About the two main families, the Shedds and Drapers, whole books have been published—self-published, to be sure, but books nonetheless. Most of this is very recent news to me—a measure of how little it mattered to my upbringing, by which time any vestiges of Yankee clout were long gone—but I am now able to trace direct lines from my great-grandparents, Frank Shedd and Sarah Radcliffe, for twenty and thirteen generations respectively, back to the British counties of Suffolk and Yorkshire.

Shedds and Drapers

The Shedds came from Suffolk and Essex, just northeast of London and the home counties of over half of the 25,000 Puritans who came to New England before 1650. An unbroken line goes back twenty generations to John Schedde, born about 1390 in Sudbury, Suffolk, who followed the trade of woolen cloth refiner, or "fuller." The family prospered, and by 1524 his descendant John Shedd (born in 1480) was the richest man in his parish, excluding only the lords of two manors. This John had moved south into Essex, where the family stayed put for seven generations until about 1640, when young Daniel Shed, aged twenty, took off for America. He showed up in the town records of the newly established Puritan settlement of Braintree, Massachusetts, south of Boston, in 1642. There he married in 1646 and leased a 120-acre spit of land on the Fore River in Weymouth that came to be known as Shed's Neck.

In 1658, Daniel Shed left Braintree with his wife Mary and seven children for the greener, cheaper, but more dangerous pastures of Billerica, north of Boston, where he was able to buy a twenty-three-acre plot of land. The danger came from Indians. The earnest family history *Daniel Shed Genealogy* (published for the Shedd Family Association, Boston, 1921), which is my source for all this, declares: "Friendly as seemed those whose dusky forms were often seen at their own firesides and who had in a measure embraced Christianity and civilization . . . still the settlers watched them closely to guard against any treachery and to gain some hint of impending attack from the less friendly tribes farther back." Daniel's son Zechariah grew up in Billerica and got some firsthand violent experience of the Indians in 1675 through "service in the garrison house at Chelmsford in King Philip's War," the bloody conflict in which 3,000 Native Americans and 1,000 colonists were killed and a dozen settlements laid waste. Zechariah came home to Billerica and went on to start a family that suffered a catastrophe worthy of Nathaniel Hawthorne's imagination. On August 1, 1692, they were attacked by Indians who "killed the wife (aged about 36) and the eldest and youngest child; none were taken captive. Zechariah Shed's family then consisted of five children, of whom Hannah aged thirteen and Agnes a child of two years were slain."

Subsequently, Zechariah married twice more and had eleven more children, one of whom, Ebenezer (born in 1695), moved down to Charlestown and had a successful career as a housewright and land speculator. His claim to a historical footnote came when he was married to Abigail Ireland (the daughter, colorfully, of Abraham Ireland and Abigail Greenland) in 1722 by Chief Justice Samuel Sewall, better known as the judge who made a public apology for his role in the 1692 Salem witchcraft trials. (Sewall's extensive diaries were to be a key influence on Hawthorne's fiction.) The youngest child of Ebenezer and Abigail was Zechariah Shed, born in 1744 in Charlestown and named for his grandfather. It is he who will put my daughter Ellen into the Daughters of the American Revolution (DAR), should she ever want to go there. Owner of a large farm near Mount Auburn Cemetery in Cambridge, this second Zechariah was a Minute Man at the Battle of Lexington on the nineteenth of April in '75, serving shoulder to shoulder, I presume, with South Dedham's Aaron Guild. He was also on the spot, providing "a large wagon load of bundled hay" for the fortifications, when General Washington took Dorchester Heights in March 1776.

As the Sheds marched into the nineteenth century, reclaiming their second final "d" along the way, our direct line led to John Franklin Shedd, born in Medford, Massachusetts, in 1833, trained as an "iron moulder," and notable in three ways. He was the first Shedd (or Shed) to marry an Irishwoman: the immigrant Margaret Mary Gately, in Roxbury in 1851. He served for three years in the American Civil War as an engineer's assistant in the Union Navy. And shortly after that war he deserted his wife and seven children and was never heard from again. The *Daniel Shed Genealogy* is silent on any connection between Irishness and desertion, but something similar will happen again in our family a bit further on and much closer to home for me.

The first child of this unfortunate union was Francis ("Frank") Shedd, born in Roxbury on October 5, 1852. Ignoring his parents' troubles, he, too, married a woman of Irish background—and, it appears, a divorcée as well. Agnes Bridget Kerrigan had been a "two-boater," a term of vague disapprobation that was still current when I was growing up in Norwood. Her parents, Miles Patrick and Bridget Kerrigan, had been Irish immigrants to St. John, New Brunswick, probably in the 1830s, when several Kerrigans showed up there. Born in St. John in 1850, Bridget probably took her second boat down to Maine as a young adult to get work. There she married an Englishman named Booth and had two children, James and Charles, born in Maine in 1869 and 1871. When this marriage failed, Bridget returned to St. John. At some point, she left her boys there with the Kerrigans and took a third boat down to Massachusetts, where she met and married Frank Shedd in Dedham on August 4, 1875. Their first child, Frank Jr., was born six weeks later on September 19.

Four more children followed, all but one born in the Hyde Park section of Boston, where they had settled. The second child (and only daughter) was my grandmother—Mary Ann Frances Shedd. She was born in St. John, New Brunswick, on October 8, 1877, and baptized there at Our Lady of the Assumption Roman Catholic Church on October 14. (Perhaps they were back visiting the Booth boys. Perhaps Bridget simply wanted to have the child in her home place.) In the 1900 census, the Shedd family of six is living in Hyde Park. Frank Shedd is a day laborer, his wife keeps the house, her son Charles Booth, aged twenty-eight, is a machinist. Three other children are at home: Frederick, fifteen, John, seventeen, and Mary, twenty-two and working as a laundress. And here, at last, is the connection with my grandfather Charles Winslow Fanning, who also worked in a laundry—the Norwood Laundry, to be specific—a business which he eventually co-owned and, ultimately, lost. I'm assuming that Mary Shedd's job was in the same place, as her brother Fred also went to work there as a truck driver early in the new century.

In 1900 my grandfather Fanning, listed in the census as a "laundryman," was living in Dedham, Massachusetts, with *his* grandmother, Sophia Draper Radcliffe. Within her double-barreled Yankee name lies a second genealogical tale. Our immigrant Draper ancestor was James. Born in 1618 at Heptonstall Vicarage, Halifax, in the West Riding of Yorkshire, James Draper had followed his father Thomas into the weaving trade. (In Heptonstall today, there is still a Draper Lane.) The family traces back for two more generations to James's great-grandfather, John Draper, for whom we have this family's oldest date, that of his death on May 21, 1561, at the Priory of Heptonstall. On April 21, 1646, his twenty-eighth birthday, the weaver James Draper married a local girl, Miriam Stansfield, aged twenty, the daughter of a blacksmith, Gideon Stansfield, who was also known as "Standfast." As James and Miriam had already had their first child, a daughter, on February 7, 1646, it is safe to assume that her father stood fast behind the idea that this marriage ought to take place. Within a year, the newlyweds and their child were on their way to America. Accompanying them was Miriam's ten-year-old sister, Abigail, who found a husband in Boston six years later. Serious religiosity seems also to have taken root here, for Draper family history declares that "from his exceedingly strict piety [James the immigrant] was known in his day as 'James the Puritan,' and thus is still known to genealogists and historians. He was the owner of several looms, and followed his trade of clothier in this country."

James and Miriam built a substantial house in Roxbury, Massachusetts Bay Colony, near the Dedham town line on the Post Road (renamed and still known as Centre Street) between Boston and Providence. (I have seen photographs of the place, an imposing three-story saltbox that stood until 1870, when it was destroyed by a fire. At that time, according to the local paper, the final inhabitant, Mrs. Emma Draper Tate, had been boarding cats there in the summers to make expenses.) The first New World Drapers had eight more children, all born in Roxbury and Dedham.

"James the Puritan" died in Roxbury in July 1697. A last bizarre event (again, worthy of Hawthorne) followed eight months later, when his first-born son James died on April 30, 1698, "from an injury sustained in wrestling on a May day," according to one of the family histories. It appears that, following "the English custom," a Maypole had been set up on the Roxbury common, "about which wrestling, pitching quoits and other games were kept up. On such a day a person appeared, claiming to be champion of the ring, challenging any who might choose to enter the ring with him. A number accepted, but he threw them all with so much ease that there was no one left to compete with him." Along came James Draper, aged forty-four and "in the prime of life." Persuaded to enter the ring despite the protests of his wife, James bested the champion easily. However, "the cry of 'unfair' was set up, and he tried him again, and at the word, the stranger was once more laid on his back by the stalwart James. But in doing this a second time he broke a sinew in his leg, from which he never recovered. He was carried back to his house, but was never able to go out again." And there's another gloomy echo here. Like the Zechariah Shed whose family was murdered by Indians, this second James Draper was a veteran of King Philip's War, during which he had attained the rank of sergeant. So, I find two ancestors who fought in the "Indian killer" campaign of 1675 and went on to suffer calamities. The sins of the fathers?

Of James and Miriam's nine children, our ancester Jonathan was the youngest, born in 1670. He married Sarah Jackson from Newton around

1700 and set up as a farmer and a tavernkeeper in the family home on the Boston Post Road. The sixth child of Jonathan and Sarah was Moses Draper, born in Roxbury in 1721. This Moses married Mary Aldis Allen, a widow, in 1743, and their first child (of six), also named Moses Draper, was born in 1744. His career doubly ensures my daughter's eligibility for the DAR, because he also fought in the American Revolution. He became *Colonel* Moses Draper. (Lest we forget, Aaron Guild was only a captain.) In fact, this Moses started as a second lieutenant in the First Roxbury Company of Minute Men at the Battle of Lexington, where he already outranked the family's other revolutionary veteran, Zechariah Shed. Moses became a captain at Bunker Hill, served in the federal force during Shays' Rebellion, and was made an honorific colonel in retirement.

Better yet in the credentialing department, the colonel's mother, Mary Aldis Draper, was a legendary figure who became the patron saint of the West Roxbury branch of the DAR, which bore her name until it went out of business a few years ago. She also had a swimming pool and a park named for her, and the DAR put up a Mary Draper Memorial fountain in the garden of what is now the West Roxbury branch of the Boston Public Library. Her stirring story appears in several Draper family histories. After her husband's death in January 1775, Mary continued to live in the Draper homestead in Roxbury In *The Drapers in America* (New York: J. Polhemus, 1892), Thomas Waln-Morgan Draper provides the rationale for Mary Draper's patriotic canonization:

> When, in response to the appeal of the Massachusetts Committee of Safety, minute-men and militia from all parts of New England began to collect about Boston, this patriotic woman fired her three great brick ovens, and, assisted by her daughter Kate, kept a table spread in front of her house with bread and cheese and great tubs of cider for the hungry soldiers who passed her door. During the siege of Boston, [she] melted all her pewter pans and dishes to obtain material for bullets, and molded the bullets herself. She made coats for the men from her own homespun, and cut up her sheets, her blankets, and even her own petticoats, to make clothing for the soldiers.

As a child, I had actually heard a version of this story from my grandfather Fanning. He had it right except that he thought Mary was a Radcliffe, not a Draper, and he said the bullets were silver. Whenever this would come up, my mother—neither a Fanning nor a Yankee, as she was quick to point out—would chuckle mordantly and cite one of her favorite maxims: "Faraway cows have long horns." I'm amazed that the story is substantially true.

I am almost done bringing it all down to my grandfather's time. These genealogies were so hard to untangle—and the job would have been impossible without a lot of help, notably from my cousins Francis and Margaret Fanning—that I feel compelled to finish it up. So. Colonel Moses Draper married Grace Hyde of Dedham in 1770, and they *also* had a son named Moses, born in 1774, just before the war broke out. This third eighteenth-century Moses Draper grew up to marry Sarah Gurney in 1796. The third of their four children was Benjamin Jackson Gurney Draper, born in Roxbury in 1800. Benjamin married Hannah Burrill in Dedham in 1825. One of their six daughters, born on February 7, 1828, was my great-great-grandmother, Sophia Ann Draper. There were to be no sons, so this was the end of the Draper surname line where my family is concerned. The bodies of twenty-nine of these Drapers, from James and Miriam on through to the late nineteenth century, rest in the Westerly Burial Ground on Centre Street in what is now West Roxbury. Laid out in 1685 near the old family homestead, this small cemetery—it's now sandwiched among shops and strip malls—remains the genius loci of Draper family history.

Though she died in 1900, Sophia Ann Draper has a palpable connection to my own life. She wasn't only my grandfather's grandmother. She raised him. At age twenty on July 3, 1848, in Dedham, Sophia married a young man with another formidable Yankee name—Winslow Radcliff. Or Radcliffe. (Like the second "d" in Shedd, this family's final "e" comes and goes throughout the written record. It does appear on all their gravestones.) Sadly, Winslow's life was deeply troubled and his death appalling. His tragedy is the subject of my next chapter. Winslow and Sophia Draper Radcliff(e) had four children: Benjamin Draper, born in 1850, Sarah Rebecca, born in 1854, Albert Winslow, born in 1857, and Frank Edward, born in 1860. Sarah was my great-grandmother.

Simply by the reckoning of what she survived, Sophia Draper Radcliffe had to have been a woman of great courage and strength. Money was an issue at least since 1870, when the U.S. Census finds the Radcliffes running a boarding-house—there were four unrelated people living with them—in their home on Washington Street in Dedham. During one terrible week in April 1874, Sophia's husband died and her first-born son, Benjamin, attempted suicide. In 1881, there were three terrible blows. In February, her two-week-old granddaughter, Hattie Frances, died. (Because she is buried

Figure 6. Sophia Ann Draper Radcliffe.

with him, I assume that Hattie was the child of Sophia's unmarried youngest son, Frank.) In May, Benjamin Radcliffe died at age thirty. In November, Frank Radcliffe died at age twenty. (His headstone contains these verses: "When blooming youth is snatched away / By death's resistless hand / Our hearts the mournful tribute pay / Which pity must demand.") Perhaps there were too many deaths for Westerly to handle, for all these Radcliffes lie in Dedham's Protestant burial ground, Brookdale Cemetery, where Sophia had bought a large plot in 1881. Another terrible shock came three years later. In the 1880 census, the tenants of the widow Radcliffe had included her daughter Sarah, Sarah's husband, John Fanning, and their four-year-old son, my grandfather, Charles Winslow Fanning. But then, on August 7, 1884, two weeks after her thirtieth birthday, Sarah Radcliffe Fanning died, leaving her husband and their eight-year-old only child. Finally, sometime in the late 1880s, John Fanning abandoned his son and everyone else in Massachusetts and disappeared into the West. I was the descendant who found him there, over 100 years later.

Catching Up with Walking John

My great-grandfather was long gone by 1890, and as far as my generation of the family knew until a few years ago, he was never heard from again while alive. We had heard that John Fanning had died around 1950 in St. Louis, Missouri, and that an obituary and picture had made its way back east. All of this made pretty good sense, especially because we still had the picture. Propped up in front of me as I write this, it shows a very old man in a light fedora with wisps of white hair sticking out over his ears. He's wearing a threadbare, rumpled, striped suit, the pants hiked up well above the waistline, and a buttoned white shirt with no tie. His hands, poking out noticeably from the ill-fitting jacket sleeves, are large and gnarled, and the fingers are very long. He has the unmistakable aquiline Fanning nose, and there may or may not be a small mustache tucked under it. Narrow-shouldered, frail, and with a wary, distrustful gaze, he is picking his way along a city street. There are store windows stuffed with merchandise behind him, and to his left a woman carrying packages and a purse has just come out of a doorway. There seems to be no connection between them. Because of this picture and his history of desertion, our family always referred to John Fanning as "Walking John."

Born in Needham, Massachusetts, on July 5, 1854, he was the oldest of the seven children of the Famine-generation immigrants Phillip and Margaret Bohan Fanning, both of whom had left Ireland in 1851. (These Irish Fannings have their own chapter.) Because he was the first member of my family of Fannings to be born in the United States, and because I had moved to St. Louis in 1991, I made a special effort to track him down. I looked hard and long at St. Louis and Missouri records—street directories, obituaries and documentation of deaths, the U.S. Census—and found nothing. The breakthrough was my cousin Margaret's discovery of a copy of the will made by Walking John's father, the immigrant Phillip Fanning, on November 1, 1892. In this document "John Fanning, son" is said to be living in "East St. Louis, *Illinois*." (His father left him $10.) With this new information, I went through the same search, hard and long again, of East St. Louis and Illinois records. Again, nothing. At this point—it was in the early spring of 2003—I concluded that John had indeed walked entirely out of our family's history.

A week or two later, I was venting my frustration about this seeming dead end to Ed O'Day. He mentioned casually that maybe I should check the Illinois Records and Archives Depository—IRAD—which held vital records for the sixteen southernmost counties of the state, including East

Figure 7. John Fanning, last known photograph, c. early 1940s.

St. Louis. And where was IRAD? Why, on the campus of Southern Illinois University at Carbondale, where I had been teaching since 1993. The archives were in a blue-metal building on McLafferty Road, a five-minute drive from my house. Ed also told me that sometimes the IRAD folks could do a preliminary search on the basis of a telephone request. So I called and asked for any information on John Fanning of East Louis who died around

1950. In two hours I got a call back: "I think we may have found your man." When I arrived at IRAD five minutes later, there, on the screen of the microfilm reader, was the probate estate record of an East St. Louis resident who had died on October 24, 1946, at the age of ninety-two. His name was John F. Dunham, "alias John Fanning." No wonder I hadn't found him. He had changed his name. The helpful history grad student on duty in the archive, Pat Nunley, explained that the only reason he popped out at all was that the state of Illinois had kept a "Cross Reference List" of aliases found on probate records. That was the only place anywhere in IRAD's files where the name John Fanning appeared, and it pointed to Box 858, case 000085, microfilm roll 204, wherein was contained the record of probate for "John F. Dunham, deceased." Shaking my head in wonder that the haystack had yielded me this needle, I turned eagerly to the microfilm reader.

The images were distressingly fuzzy. Hard to read at best, impossible to make out at worst, the pages as they rolled past seemed to me a figure for the man, my shadowy ancestor, whose economic life they summarized. I could see that the record was large and tangled, and that the key issue was the assumption of the debts that "John F. Dunham, alias John Fanning" had left. The recipient of this dubious legacy was my grandfather, "his son, Charles Fanning, defendant herein, as his only heir at law." Through a lawyer, my grandfather had courteously declined responsibility for his father's debts, and an East St. Louis bank had "seized and possessed" whatever properties remained. This closed the probate case.

Given my IRAD discovery, I was now able to find three more pieces of the puzzle of Walking John Fanning: an obituary, his will, and his death certificate. In a newspaper I hadn't known existed, the *East St. Louis Journal,* for Friday, October 25, 1946, was an obituary with the headline "J. F. DUNHAM DEAD; WAS 92." Its three short paragraphs hold all there is ever likely to be in the way of solid information about the last years of our family's mystery man:

> *John F. Dunham, 92, resident of East St. Louis for 50 years, died at 6:50 p.m. Thursday in his home at 1627 Parsons avenue after an illness of six months.*
>
> *He had been retired for 15 years and last was employed by the Huschle Coal Co. He is survived by a son Charles Dunham.*
>
> *Private funeral services will be held at 10:30 a.m. Saturday in the Robins chapel with burial in Mount Hope cemetery.*

This, then, was the obituary that had come to my grandfather in Norwood. Small wonder, given his father's name change and the assumption that he too was a Dunham, that Charles W. Fanning chose not to preserve the clipping.

Pat Nunley at IRAD had also suggested that, having found my great-grandfather's new name, I ought to check with St. Clair County, in which East St. Louis is located, for possible additional information. Expecting nothing to augment the already startling revelations, I phoned the courthouse in Belleville. "Well," the voice said, "we do have a will for John F. Dunham." This document turned out to be a bitter piece of John's story, one that illustrates the depth of his alienation. Two-thirds of a typewritten page long, it begins, "I, John F. Dunham, of the City of East St. Louis, County of St. Clair and State of Illinois, being of sound mind and memory, do make, publish and declare this to be my last Will and Testament." It calls first, with unintended irony, for immediate payment of "all my just debts and funeral expenses." After this, declares John, "I give, devise and bequeath to Joe Fanning, of Norfolk, Virginia, all the residue of my estate, of every kind and character, whether real, personal or mixed."

At first, I was mildly surprised by this beneficiary, who turns out to be John's youngest sibling, Phillip Joseph Fanning. Born in 1870, Joe had been given the name of an older brother who was drowned near their Needham home at age eleven in 1868. As a young man, this second Joe had lost a hand while trying to jump onto a moving train. Perhaps, I thought, it was that accident that got him into his older brother's will. And yet, when I saw that the will was dated March 8, 1922, I was shocked. If he knew his brother Joe was living in Virginia, I realized, then John Fanning must still have been in some kind of touch with his Massachusetts family at that relatively late date. Thus, John probably also knew about the more recent tragedy that had befallen the family of his own only child, Charles, who had been widowed and left with five small children just four years earlier. And if John Fanning had this knowledge, how very profound must have been the gulf that had opened between him and the Fannings in Massachusetts. Here was a wound so deep that when he made his will in 1922, this lost soul was able to overlook his son's time of great trouble, itself an echo of John's own loss of his wife thirty-three years before.

Forever Mt. Hope

John F. Dunham's death certificate arrives in the mail from the Illinois State Archive in Springfield on Saturday, July 26, 2003. Included are his last occupation—"common laborer"—his death date, and the notice of interment in Mt. Hope Cemetery in the city of Belleville, Illinois. On the phone to Belleville information on the following Monday, July 28, at nine AM, I am told that there is only one possible listing: "Forever Mt. Hope Cemetery and Funeral Service." I promptly call, and a cheery voice answers, "Forever Mt. Hope. How may I help you?" And lo—in five minutes time, a second voice, no less upbeat, has informed me that a man known as John F. Dunham was indeed laid to rest on October 26, 1946, in the cemetery formerly known as Mt. Hope, but now sporting the prefix, "Forever." He gives me directions from Carbondale and says he'll provide a map of the site for me as well. In less than two hours and 100 miles I find myself in front of a large, splashy sign proclaiming "Forever Mt. Hope" on West Main Street, Belleville, just over the East St. Louis line. After my long and frustrating search, it seems nearly miraculous that I have finally found the place where my great-grandfather's half-century ramble came to an end.

Here I am, then, driving into a thickly wooded cemetery complex on a partly cloudy morning in July. Maybe it's the pull of family history, but for some reason I am vaguely apprehensive as I stop the car in front of a bland, white rectangular building with a few faux columns spaced across the front. But now the telephone voice has become Fred, a friendly man in shirtsleeves and striped tie who sports a bushy white mustache. His card reads "Family Service Counselor," and he does indeed have a map for me. Fred invites me to take a look around the place. He says that Forever Enterprises is a national organization which began in California with a flagship operation the name of which (I am not making this up) is "Hollywood Forever." Their specialty is taking over down-at-heels cemeteries and bringing them "back up to speed." In other words—mine, not Fred's—the Forever folks resurrect moribund graveyards! Fred tells me that when they took over a mere eighteen months ago, Mt. Hope had pretty much gone to seed. Yet now I am looking at a thoroughly contemporary, one-stop "Funeral Home/ Memorial Office," which had opened just the previous November. Handing me a glossy brochure, he explains that the operation includes "Live Webcast of Funeral Services," "Forever LifeStories" of the deceased logged in at "forevernetwork.com," and perpetual care of graves, complete with "the finest silk and satin flowers." This is a lot more information than I need, but it occurs to me that people in search of lost relatives must be one of the few conduits to new business in the cemetery trade, so I don't mind the spiel. Also, Fred has kindly offered to take me out to John's grave, even though, as he tells me, there's a funeral scheduled for this afternoon.

We step between the columns into a morning still overcast and with the leaden sky now spitting rain. Fred hands me the map. Most of the names of the various sections of the place are abstractions: Peace, Devotion, Communion, Faith, Hope, and Love. A few are geographical: Illinois, Belleville. One is historical, and that's where we are headed. "The Garden of Lincoln" is where we will find my great-grandfather. We hop into Fred's car and drive up a short rise into the cemetery proper. Bisecting Faith and Belleville, we take a right at Communion, a left at Hope, and come to the top of a short, steep hill that looks down into a vale—signposted "Lincoln." The site is really quite lovely. Evergreen trees frame the thinly graveled road that winds down to a cul de sac—there's no walking out of this one, John—bordered by large, closely packed maples and redbuds.

At the bottom a small jitney comes up behind us, and we are joined by Dave, a middle-aged groundskeeper in muddy boots and overalls. Fred explains that Dave may be able to help us find the site, as he has worked here since long before the takeover by Forever. It could be a challenge, he says, his voice lowering, as there is no record of any stone. On the spot, I feel a pang of sympathy for this man on whose grave I will surely be the first blood relative to stand. Given the coordinates—Section O, Row X2, Space 34—Dave starts up toward the line of trees. I notice that the four or five rows of gravestones are progressively less grand, though none is particularly large or elaborate. The penultimate row contains one-foot markers, raised six inches at most, and with only names and dates on them. The back row looks empty. No stones of any kind are in sight. But Dave walks in from the end about six long strides, kicks at the ground with his boot, and says, "Here it is. Thirty-four." He scrapes away more dirt and grass, and I see a squarish piece of rock, about four inches wide, with a barely visible number carved into it. Dave says that many of these burials took place before the law required concrete vaults. (Here a slight entrepreneurial ripple crosses Fred's face.) Without the vaults, the graves often settle and sink and these minimal markers are lost forever. We are lucky, says Dave, to have found this one.

A few minutes later I am on my way back to Carbondale—with Fred's card, a handful of Forever brochures, a Diet Coke, and three sugar cookies from the pile already stacked on a plate for this afternoon's service. On the way home, I do the math on Walking John and discover that next July will be the 150th anniversary of his birth back in Needham. Maybe, I think, we can get a stone put up by then, one with his real name on it, the name he left behind in Massachusetts. It's something to think about. At any rate, I have found him, the first of my surname family born on American soil. I have been to the place where he ended up.

POSTSCRIPT: When I did get around to having a proper marker put on my great-grandfather's grave, Mt. Hope had changed a lot. Contrary to the promise of its name, the Forever Corporation was long gone from Belleville, having sold the cemetery to an outfit called Mid-America Growth and Development in 2005. Mid-America, in turn, had run afoul of the law by allegedly misplacing more than $300,000 that had been paid into prearranged burial accounts between 2005 and July 2008. Litigation was still ongoing when I arranged with Weiss Monuments of Belleville to place a simple granite marker with the inscription "John Fanning, July 5, 1854–October 24, 1946." I did this on April 29, 2009, and realized only after hanging up the phone that it was my own father's 100th birthday.

Walking East St. Louis

But why did John walk away? And why did he never come back home? The 1880 U.S. Census reveals that he had worked as a house painter in his wife's hometown of Dedham, Massachusetts. I now also know, by having gone back to the records equipped with the name "John F. Dunham," that he continued at that trade in Illinois and that he lived out his long life in East St. Louis boardinghouses. In addition, the IRAD probate records confirm that he never remarried. He was out there—or, rather, out *here,* as I should now say, being myself a transplant to the Midwest—for over fifty years: through two World Wars, the great Depression, and the births of five grandchildren and a half-dozen great-grandchildren, of whom I am one. As far as my generation knows, he never once called or wrote home. "Heart mysteries there," as W. B. Yeats says. Since getting all this information together, I have worked out a number of implications about John Fanning that bring me as close as I'm likely to get to explaining his fateful decision. All are weighted down with trouble and sorrow.

In the first place, the fact of their "mixed marriage" was, to put it mildly, seriously problematic in late nineteenth-century Boston—especially as this was a union between Yankee Congregationalists and Irish Catholics, the two groups whose mutual detestation had been building since the flood of Irish refugees from the Great Hunger of the late 1840s transformed forever the Puritan "city on a hill." Even worse, Sarah's mother was not just a Yankee but a Draper from Dedham. That she was now running a boardinghouse may well have exacerbated Sophia's disapproval of her daughter's marriage to an Irish Catholic. None are more conscious of family standing than those whose place on the ladder is slipping. By the same token, Walking John's father, Phillip Fanning, was not just an Irish Catholic but a Catholic from County Monaghan in Ulster, the only Irish province where, thanks to the seventeenth-century plantations, Protestants were a demographic majority as well as the ruling class. To be an Ulster Catholic was to be doubly bound—by population as well as politics—and doubly stubborn in the faith. Not surprisingly, family lore has it that Walking John's latter-day estrangement from all of us was rooted in his parents' great displeasure at the marriage of their son—their first, and first American-born child—to a Protestant. To make matters worse, John and Sarah were married not by a priest but by a minister, William G. Babcock of Boston. Both were twenty-one, and the wedding took place in November 1875, seventeen months after the sudden death of Sarah's unfortunate father, Winslow Radcliff.

The next trouble-laden item about Walking John's marriage comes by way of simple arithmetic. My grandfather was born on February 22, 1876, less than four months after his parents' marriage. Surely, the impulsion of Sarah's pregnancy had cast a further pall over this match. What follows then is a complication similar to that surrounding my own father's middle name. (Onomastic indecision appears to run in the family.) On his birth certificate, filed belatedly on January 17, 1877, nearly a year after he was born, my grandfather is "Charles *L.* Fanning." Nor was this the last word on his name. At some point, maybe not even officially—who knows?—he became Charles *Winslow* Fanning. I've come up with two theories about the delayed bestowal of the Winslow name. By keeping alive the first name of her recently deceased father, Sarah Radcliff Fanning may have been attempting to bless his memory. Either that, or the change was her mother's idea, perhaps enacted after Sarah's death and John's desertion, as a way to neutralize her grandson's Irishness.

The last sad circumstance is Sarah Radcliff Fanning's woefully short life. She was just thirty when she died on August 7, 1884, leaving her husband and eight-year-old son. I believe that the very manner of her death was damning for John Fanning's relationship with his wife's family. Sarah died of "phthisis," tuberculosis of the lungs. In point of fact, given the overcrowded, unsanitary conditions in which they were forced to live, many thousands of Irish immigrants and ethnics died of TB—"consumption" was its graphic common name—in nineteenth-century New England. There were so many victims that it became known as "the Irish disease."

Surely, the Dedham Drapers were aware of this stigma of social shame. Indeed, for Sophia Draper Radcliff, it could well have been the twisting of the knife in the wound of her only daughter's early death. Here was the climactic upshot of having married an Irishman and a Catholic!

The earliest Illinois record I have found for John F. Dunham puts him in East St. Louis in 1891, which is when a city directory lists a boarder, "Dunham John, painter, Lotta av and Wienman Place." By 1910 he was boarding in the house of Leona Lurwald, a German immigrant widow with three children, at 1800 Weiman Avenue. In 1920, at age sixty-three and still a house painter, John was living alone in a rented house at 1920 St. Clair Avenue. He stayed there at least through 1930. In 1924 his occupation was "paper-hanger," and in 1928, "laborer." John's last workplace, Rudolf Huschle's Coal and Ice Company, was right next door at 1922 St. Clair. (The Huschles, first-generation German Americans, lived down the street at 1914 St. Clair. After prohibition ended, Rudolf switched from coal to beer distribution from the same site.) By 1934, John Dunham had left St. Clair Avenue. He surfaces again in a 1945 directory as "retired" and living alone in a rented house at 1627 Parsons Avenue. This is the address on his 1946 death certificate, which also states—erroneously—that he had been living there for "30 years." The probate documents from IRAD provided additional nuggets of information. Somehow over the years, John had managed to acquire two pieces of property, one on Exchange Avenue and one on Wienman Place. At the time of his death, both were rented "month to month": a four-room frame dwelling on Exchange to Frank and Ethel Bartlett, and a three-room house to Ida Stoehr on Wienman. Because John had paid no taxes on these properties for many years, they were sold to help reduce his outstanding debts.

A map of East St. Louis established that all these places, John Fanning's home turf for fifty-five years, are within a three-block square. Thus equipped with clear coordinates, I made a visit to my great-grandfather's old neighborhood in search of place lore in July 2004. East St. Louis, Illinois, has changed a lot in the half-century since John's death, and not for the better. Today, it is one of America's most unfortunate cities, with an infrastructure not just crumbling but devastated. Profoundly abandoned by all and sundry powers that be, its mostly African American population has a catastrophic unemployment rate. Since the completion in the early 1970s of Interstate Highways 64, 55, and 255, no one who hasn't wanted to go there has had to drive on its ragged, pot-holed streets or seen up close its ruined buildings and weed-choked lots. I've sailed blithely over the place in my car hundreds of times on the way to or from St. Louis since we moved to the Midwest in the early nineties. Until finding out that my ancestor had lived and died there, I had almost never looked down.

For as long as I've been crisscrossing Interstate 64, my cultural marker for East St. Louis has been a derelict factory tower of weather-blasted gray stone that squats forbiddingly just off the highway to the north. By far the tallest structure for miles in either direction, it's an empty-eyed hulk of a place, a frightening memento mori for the all-but-forgotten city whose presence it announces. Today, July 5, it's eleven in the morning when I approach East St. Louis. The skies have been getting darker and darker with flashes of lightning, and just as I begin looking for the Baugh Avenue exit, which leads directly into John's old neighborhood, one of those sudden and awesomely violent Midwest summer rains comes pelting down. It's lighter up ahead in St. Louis, and I pull over onto the shoulder and stop to wait it out. I want to be able to *see* those streets when I get there. After ten minutes the downpour lets up to a slow, steady rain, and again I'm off. In just a few minutes more I roll off the highway at the correct exit and I am there. I look to the east down Parsons Avenue and—my God—there's my landmark gray tower, just three blocks ahead at the dead end of the street! I hadn't noticed it earlier because of the rain.

In a flash, the meaning of a familiar reference point has been utterly transformed. From this moment on, the ruined tower stands for my ancestor's self-imposed exile. It must have been a salient landmark in John Fanning's East St. Louis life—a working factory no doubt, and the place of employment for many in this neighborhood. (A few days later I find out, thanks to the kindness of two members of the East St. Louis Public Library staff, who actually drive out to the site on their lunch hour to verify the location, that this was the Como Feeds mill.) I see also that there's a disused railroad bed running north-south past the gray tower. The old maps I've consulted identify it as the Southern Belt Railroad. As well, the new St. Louis-to-Belleville Metro-Link light rail follows an older east-west railroad line through this neighborhood. It's clear that this place used to be a complicated, functioning mixture of homes and industry. What's left is one more reminder of my ancestor's early years here, when East St. Louis had the second largest stockyards complex in the United States (after Chicago), as well as thriving steel and aluminum mills and various subsidiary operations.

But now I find myself on the streets my ancestor walked for fifty years. I stop the car at the corner of Eighteenth Street and Weiman Avenue. All the old houses are gone. I'm surprised to be in the middle of what looks to be a recent development of neat, attractive, low-rise duplex houses in shades of beige and gray. The lawns are trimmed, flowers bloom under windows, and there's a park with brightly colored slides and swings on the corner opposite the duplex at 1800 Weiman, the site of the house where John boarded with the Lurwalds. I see that Exchange Avenue to the north and Parsons to the south are the same. Row after row of these duplexes. It's a sign of hope for East St. Louis, but I'm disappointed that this part of John's neighborhood has been erased entirely. Now, I cross the Metro-Link roadbed and find that the site of 1627 Parsons, where my great-grandfather died, is a parking lot enclosed by a wrought-iron fence between two of the duplexes.

I've about given up on finding any specific vestiges of my great-grandfather's Midwest life. But there's one more street to check. Two blocks south of Parsons is St. Clair Avenue, where Walking John lived and worked for Huschle Coal in the 1920s. I have to drive down Eighteenth Street under Interstate 64 to get there, and now I find that the highway marks the end of the duplexes. It looks as though St. Clair Avenue has been left to its own devices. Certainly, the first building I see is the real thing. Though it hasn't been used for years, I'm guessing that this used to be a tavern. It's a substantial two-story place on the corner of Eighteenth Street with large windows fronting on St. Clair and a pleasing crenellated design built into the brick facade. The wooden front door is generously wide and also sports decorative trim of carved blocks. As in many Midwest taverns, the doorway is cut diagonally across the northeast front corner of the building, providing a triangle of shelter from the elements and an invitation to enter. Heading east on St. Clair, I find next a few ramshackle small houses across the south side of the 1800 block. These are still inhabited, and my excitement grows as I approach the next block—John's block.

But here again I'm out of luck. First comes an abandoned gas station, its street number—1916—scrawled a yard high on the front of the building. After this, there is only a double vacant lot followed by the Southern Belt railroad tracks and then Twentieth Street. Still and all, this empty space is certainly where my ancestor lived and worked. Huschle Coal must have been next to the tracks, and a crumbling cement walk next door points up into the weeds where John's rented house at 1920 St. Clair once stood. I park the car and walk back along the cracked and heaving asphalt of St. Clair Avenue from the site of my great-grandfather's second-to-last home to the boarded-up tavern. I then retrace my steps to stand in front of the crumbling walk at 1920. Turning back to my car, I realize that this is as close as I am going to get to walking in my great-grandfather's shoes.

And yet, a few days later I find that a bit more of John Fanning's lost world is retrievable. I check again in the East St. Louis city directories. Sure enough, in 1924 the corner building at Eighteenth and St. Clair was listed as "Felix Hatcher, drinks." (Yes, prohibition was still on, but I have no doubt that drinks there were. This was, after all, East St. Louis, a wide-open town if ever there was one.) I also find that the same corner was the living center of the neighborhood, with George Rolek's Grocery and Meat Market and Maurice Isbill's Restaurant right across the street from Hatcher's. I have at least found what were for ten or fifteen years John Fanning's cardinal points of home, work, sustenance, and recreation. It's not much to go on, but it's going to have to do.

I have made this pilgrimage because I wanted to imagine my great-grandfather's East St. Louis life—especially because knowledge of it came so close to being gone forever. And yes, I can picture him now, if barely, in my mind's eye. I see the solitary, grizzled figure in that surviving photograph. He's finishing up for the day at the Coal Company, then stopping next door at his house to wash up, then ambling slowly down St. Clair to Hatcher's for a drink. He's got plenty of time. The smells wafting from Como Feeds permeate the air. Some nights he buys a steak at Rolek's to cook at home. Some nights he walks into Isbill's modest eating house for a sit-down supper. I do not know how often his thoughts turn to Massachusetts—to Sarah Radcliffe, his long-dead Yankee wife, to Charles Winslow, his abandoned only child (but not his heir), to the five grandchildren he'll never see, one of whom is my father. Nor do I know how well or how badly he gets along in this solitary life he has chosen so far from home. I find myself hoping that he has some friends, some fun, some satisfying works and days. And I want to believe that he could not have lived out his long, strange exile without having come to a measure of release through contrition and the passage of time from the pain of remorse. Rest in peace, old man.

Grampy

And so my grandfather was raised by his grandmother, Sophia Draper Radcliffe, in her boardinghouse on Washington Street in Dedham. That she continued to struggle to make ends meet is clear from Sophia's petition in

1890 to reinstate her late husband's Civil War pension of $8.00 per month. This document asserts that "she is without other means of support than her own manual labor and has been so situated since her husband's death." Sophia died of liver disease on October 8, 1900, at the age of seventy-two. The death certificate states that she had been ill for six months. Her occupation was listed as "Kept her own house." In the will made five days before she died, Sophia's heirs were her last living child, Albert Winslow Radcliffe, and her three grandchildren, George and Walter Radcliffe and Charles Winslow Fanning. Her son Albert and grandson Charles each received $65, which was the sum total of Sophia's personal estate after expenses. Albert Radcliffe got most of his mother's furniture and also "the use and improvement of my lot of meadow land [ten acres] in West Roxbury." Albert's sons George and Walter got "all my real estate owned by me at my decease"—that is, the Washington Street house. And finally, "I give to my grandson, Charles W. Fanning, my chamber set, the bedding, carpet, and four rugs in my room, the map of Oxford, and all other furniture belonging to his mother." Why did he get so little? I have to assume that although she had raised my grandfather from childhood, Sophia was influenced in the execution of her will by the sins of his errant father. No one in our family has any idea what "the map of Oxford" could have meant, and I can't imagine that it provided my grandfather with anything in the way of useful place lore or direction on the tough road that lay ahead. But I half believe that giving my grandfather her "chamber set" was a vindictive Yankee witticism on Sophia's part, her way of protecting him—but barely—from the destitution suggested by the old saying, "He doesn't have a pot to piss in."

Around the time of his grandmother's death, Charles Winslow Fanning met Mary Ann Frances Shedd at the Norwood Laundry and commenced their steamy courtship. They had many things in common: the workplace, roots in Dedham, mixed Yankee and Irish lineage, and a number of similar sorrows—desertions, displacements, early deaths. When they actually got married isn't known. (It's the only key event for which no one has found documentation, and I sometimes wonder if this marriage happened at all.) Charles and Mary Ann went on to have five children, the first, Mary Frances, named for her mother, on October 21, 1907. My father was born on April 29, 1909. There was a naming problem, however. On his birth certificate, he is Charles *Edward* Fanning, and I've wondered, with a measure of romantic chutzpah, whether this was a reference to Charles Edward Stuart, "Bonnie Prince Charlie," the last hope of the eighteenth-century Scottish Jacobites against the English. It could have been a nod to his mother's native

New Brunswick, the immigrant destination of so many Scots after their ultimate defeat at Culloden in 1745. In any case, my father was "bonnie" for only ten days. He was baptized Charles Frederick, for his uncle and godfather Freddy Shedd, on May 9, 1909. Three more children followed: John Phillip, born December 20, 1911; Frank Edward, born April 15, 1913; and Joseph James, born March 9, 1917.

The laundry business seems to have been going fairly well in those years. In the 1910 census, my grandfather, living at 185 Railroad Avenue (the heart of Irish Norwood), is listed as "Proprietor Laundry," and in 1911 a local advertisement declares that "C. W. Fanning and R. A. Mandeville" are running the place:

The Norwood Laundry

THE LAUNDRY THAT IS DIFFERENT

Our Custom Work is unexcelled

Family Work by the Basket

Visitors are always welcome. Cor. Washington St. and Railroad Avenue.

Everything changed on Sunday, April 7, 1918—at four in the afternoon, according to my grandfather's last surviving friend, who died a few years ago. A week later, the *Norwood Messenger* reported that "Mrs. Mary Fanning, wife of Charles W. Fanning, died Sunday at the Norwood hospital after a short illness of pneumonia. . . . Her pleasant disposition and attractive personality won her a large circle of friends by whom she will be sadly missed. Besides her husband she is survived by five young children, and much sympathy is felt for the bereaved family." Mary Ann Frances Shedd Fanning was forty years old. My father was eight years old, the same age that his father had been when *his* mother died. As another historical footnote, my grandmother's illness was probably part of the spring wave of an influenza virus that returned in the fall of 1918 as the "Spanish Flu." This catastrophic pandemic caused over 500,000 deaths in the United States and 20 to 30 million deaths worldwide. Most victims, like Mary Ann, were previously healthy adults between the ages of twenty and forty.

When I think of the Fanning family in the succeeding years, James Joyce's tableau in *A Portrait of the Artist as a Young Man* of the younger brothers and sisters of Stephen Dedalus comes to mind. As they sit around a kitchen table littered with crusts of bread and puddles of tea singing "Oft in the Stilly

Figure 8. My grandmother Mary Shedd Fanning with her children, Charles and Mary.

Night," Stephen "listen[s] with pain of spirit to the overtone of weariness behind their frail fresh innocent voices. Even before they set out on life's journey they seemed weary already of the way." Here, though, the melancholy is mitigated because the scene contributes to Stephen's epiphany about his own life, which leads to his decision not to enter the priesthood: "He smiled to think that it was this disorder, the misrule and confusion of his father's house and the stagnation of vegetable life, which was to win the day in his soul."

Certainly, there was plenty of disorder and confusion in the Fanning household through the 1920s. A further shock came when the Norwood Laundry building caught fire at four in the morning of March 5, 1920. The *Messenger* reported, "There are three tenements upstairs occupied by C. W. Fanning and family, Mrs. M. Webb and family and Mrs. Clara Tingley and family, in all fourteen persons. These were awakened by the smoke, and many of them had to make their escape through the windows. The firemen placed ladders, and Patrolman Snow and a detail of the firemen assisted the people down the ladders to safety. They were cared for in nearby houses." The "very smoky fire" wasn't brought under control until 7:48 AM. But since the fire centered in the attic and roof, the building was saved, and the laundry reopened two weeks later. How terrifying this must have been for my grandfather and his five children. Small wonder that he and his four oldest missed the 1920 U.S. Census entirely. Only the youngest child, Joseph, got counted. He was two years old and living with his uncle and aunt, Freddy and Eliza Shedd, on Lenox Street in Norwood.

A little over a year later, in June 1921, at age twelve, my father finished his last school year—grade six—and went to work. One small trove of evidence has turned up suggesting what life was like for his family in those years. I have from my grandfather's effects two small pocket notebooks and two check registers. I can't recall how or where I got these cracked and battered artifacts, but, having now looked at them closely for the first time, I am struck by how informative and moving these random shards of the family record are.

The first notebook has a black imitation leather cover, embossed with gold lettering identifying it as a gift from the Phoenix Printing Company of Milwaukee, makers of shirt envelopes, handkerchief cases, and collar bands for the laundry business. It's undated, but the handwriting is my grandfather's. I place it after his wife's death because the light blue, graph-hatched pages contain a number of grocery lists on which the repeating items are butter, lard, eggs, and apples. Other purchases include roast beef, lamb, potatoes, sugar, and candy. Columns of figures being added or subtracted are scrawled all over these pages. My grandfather records one large item: a "medical cabinet" purchased for $5 from F. H. Clark, whose pharmacy stood just across the street from the Laundry. The second small notebook—it's red and measures only three by five inches—contains the actual cash-flow records of the Norwood Laundry from October 1921 through December 1922. I don't know how complete these are, but the fiscal news is definitely not good. There are four categories for money coming in weekly:

"H., P., West., Wal." My guess is that the first two stand for Hand wash and Press, and the others, for Westwood and Walpole, towns also served by the laundry. On October 1, 1921, the laundry account contains $150.35. The gross intake week by week is between $100 and $150, the payroll is usually about $100, and the rest gets split between cash kept on hand (averaging about $10) and a deposit to the laundry's bank account, from which purchases of materials (soda, potash) and payments for utilities get made. On December 29, 1922, the account contains $156.31. If this is the whole picture, then the net profit of the business over the fifteen months was $5.96.

The two checkbooks register my grandfather's personal transactions from June 8, 1921, when his balance was $415.10, through March 22, 1924, with $53.72 left in the account. He never wrote more than three checks a month, but the record is still revealing. By far the largest expense during this three-year period is $330, paid in three installments to the Norwood Monumental Works for his wife's headstone. There are payments to E. H. Grant for rent of the apartment above the laundry, to which the family returned at some point after the fire. Recurring checks go to the milkman, the gas company, and a coal dealer. The checkbooks also reveal a number of family illnesses—predictable certainly, with all those children at home. By evidence of the entries, the sickest was "Frankie," who turned eight in April 1921. For his care, the Norwood Hospital received two checks that year—$3.00 in August and $1.45 in October. There is also a steady stream of checks written to individuals. These are labeled "loan" or "borrow," and, given the overall state of the family's finances, I assume that they are repayments by my grandfather of personal loans made to him. Most are between $5 and $25. The largest is $40.

In 1930 the whole family reappears in the census, living at 108 Central Street (one block away on the same street as the Irish Heaven). In what is clearly a demotion, my grandfather is now listed as "Assistant Manager" of the laundry. His daughter Mary, twenty-two, is a "graduate nurse" on private duty, and my father, Charles Frederick, twenty, is working as a "welder's helper." I have no idea how he got to this trade, but it could not have been an easy road.

All in all, there is nothing earth-shattering in these few documents. The faded hen scratches in my grandfather's hand constitute cryptic evidence of a family in serious economic trouble a full decade ahead of the Great Depression. Clearly, the Twenties failed to roar in the Fanning household. It occurs to me now that when my brother and sister and I were growing up, there were many opportunities for my father to deliver a form of the sermon in which a parent contrasts his own early experiences with his children's easier life in order to emphasize the inappropriateness of a child's reluctance to perform a chore or accept denial of a request. In our family, there was certainly a normal amount of that reluctance, but we never got the sermon. Not once. I believe that for my father the memories were too painful to resurrect.

By all accounts available to me, the most impressive thing about Charles Winslow Fanning was his middle name. The details are vague, but I know that after leaving the laundry, he went on to work, with little success, at a number of jobs, among them selling dry goods and running a gas station. Though he was my only living grandparent, I have few solid memories of "Grampy," as we called him. When we lived on Winslow Avenue during my first three years of elementary school, he and Auntie Mae, in her early forties but firmly established as a spinster charged with the care of her father, were living just around the corner from us. We didn't see them all that often. However, when we moved to 145 Walpole Street in 1951, they moved with us—literally—and for several months we saw them all the time. The Walpole Street house was my parents' first—and only—experience of home ownership, made possible by the pooling of resources with my grandfather and aunt. This was a two-family house, and the plan called for Grampy and Auntie Mae to move into the smaller apartment, 143 Walpole, as soon as the tenants we had inherited from the previous owner could find another place to live. They were a crusty old Yankee couple, the Cobbs, and it took them quite a while to find a suitable apartment. Meanwhile, the four of us—my father and mother, my brother Geoffrey and I—found ourselves jammed together into one front bedroom for what seemed an eternity.

There was one benefit to the Cobbs' prolonged stay. Every once in a while they would invite us over at 5:30 in the afternoon to watch while the tiny, flickering screen of the first television set we had ever seen mutated from the concentric circles and high-pitched monotone of the test pattern to the face and then the voice of Howdy Doody. I recall that as a veteran of the radio, with its constant and varied imaginative challenges, I was not especially impressed by the slapstick cavorting of Buffalo Bob, Clarabell, Phineas T. Bluster, and the eponymous freckled star himself. Still, I had a crush on the teenaged female lead, Princess SummerFallWinterSpring (was it all one word?), and I have retained her real name along with the residual skip of the heart that used to accompany my view of it on the show's credits: Judy Tyler. Probably I've remembered her because, when I was in high school, she died in a car crash at age twenty-three, shortly after finishing what might have been her breakthrough movie, *Jailhouse Rock* with Elvis Presley.

During the long months of our three-generational family proximity, my brother and I observed the occasional visits to Grampy of "Mr. Zig" (short for Ziergiebel), one of his old cronies from way back, a short, squat man with a face like a boxer (the dog, that is), who, like my grandfather, wore suspenders and a tie on a daily basis. Mr. Zig also smoked foul-smelling cigars as the two old friends sat in the "sun parlor," the unheated but glassed-in porch—warm on sunny winter days, open to breezes in the summer—that had become Grampy's unofficial living room. They would talk and chuckle in the late morning sun, pouring occasional shots of whiskey from a flat brown bottle, while Grampy's scruffy old flea-ridden dog "Butch" panted at their feet. My brother reminds me that Grampy was always more talkative after Mr. Zig left. Butch, who smelled awful to us too, plodded along behind his master everywhere. It looked for a while as though he would live forever, but he died after being hit by a car on Walpole Street.

When the Cobbs finally left, Grampy and Auntie Mae moved next door, but they still came to Sunday dinner pretty often. I recall that during one of those meals my grandfather declared to the assembled family that he was proud of me. I don't know what I had done—this had to have been in fifth grade or earlier, and my grades weren't all that great. The occasion might have been the completion of one of the plasticene clay models that absorbed a lot of my attention in those years. In any case, the compliment pleased me no end, and gave me a sense of having contributed something to the larger Fanning family. A similar feeling accompanied the afternoon, also a Sunday, when Grampy, my father, and I posed in the driveway for a picture of the three Charles Fannings. Grampy told me that I was the oldest son of an oldest son of an oldest son, though he didn't say what that distinction entitled me to.

At school the next day, I shared all this with my best friend, whose full name was Daniel Edward Callahan the Third. Dan, who always knew how to get my goat, pointed out that I was still only a "Junior." Hmm, I thought. This was Grampy's fault. I could have been a "Third" *and* a Winslow. That would have been terrific, because we were attending the *Winslow* School, and before Walpole Street our family had been living on *Winslow* Avenue. Here was an indication that I might have in my background a smidgeon of retrievable old New England prestige. But my mother explained that my father's family was in no way connected with those Winslows, whose patriarch was a founder of Winslow Brothers and Smith Tannery, a bellwether

Figure 9. Three generations of Fannings, c. 1952.

industry in Norwood since the nineteenth century. Still, Dan Callahan needn't have known that. Had I been Charles Winslow Fanning the Third—well then, I could easily have claimed blue-blooded grandeur *du temps perdu*. But "Frederick"—what a dumb name. Where had that come from anyway? (I was informed that the name came from Freddy Shedd, my father's uncle and godfather.)

Grampy died of coronary thrombosis at the age of seventy-seven on

Sunday, September 20, 1953. He was waked at home, which was beginning to be a rare occurrence in Norwood, even among the Irish. The hours of the wake were listed as 2:00 to 5:00 and 7:00 to 10:00 on Tuesday, but it seemed that every few minutes from noontime on I heard the bell ring next door as I sat in our parlor, separated only by a wall from the room where Grampy was laid out. Auntie Mae had invited me to come over to "see" my grandfather, but I was ten and too frightened at the prospect. My parents did not insist. Still, I was mightily curious, and so I sneaked around the house from the side yard and peered into the small bow window of the parlor of 143. All I saw were some flowers, the heads of a few standing people, and the top side of the raised coffin lid, a deep, dark brown slab of wood, as shiny as our dining table top.

The funeral service was also held at home—on Wednesday at 2:00 in the afternoon. I was able to avoid this too, by offering (cleverly, I thought) to stay on our side of the house with my brother and sister, but I did slip out to stand on our front porch against the wall to watch his four sons and two other men carry Grampy's coffin down the narrow walk to the waiting hearse. There were enough images from these two glimpses to force the occasion into my dreams for the next several months. There's one last detail as well. Grampy's obituary in the local paper yields an informative coda to his uneven course. It looks as though his grandmother, Sophia Draper Radcliffe, had the last word on the conveyance from this life of the soul of Charles Winslow Fanning. Officiating at his funeral was the Reverend Percy Back of the First Baptist Church.

The Crazy Roads

The town of Norwood was hit early and hard by the Great Depression. In November 1930 an Emergency Committee was charged with making a survey of the unemployed. As reported in the *Norwood Messenger,* they found that already many breadwinners had been out of work for upward of nine months. A committee spokesperson "had it on good authority that local physicians are looking forward to an increase in many diseases this winter because of malnutrition." In December the committee used funds that the town had raised—one source was an "Unemployment Dance" at the Armory—or borrowed from banks to create temporary public works jobs for 260 people. Only married men with dependents were eligible for the jobs, which included laying sewer and water pipe extensions, cleaning highways and culverts, building sidewalks, cutting brush, trimming trees, spreading creosote on gypsy moth cocoons, and maintaining the town's Highland Cemetery. By mid-December 1930, 290 men were employed on these projects, most for three days a week, but so many were still out of work that a new call went out for "permanent or temporary help from factories or individuals who may have vacancies to be filled, or extra work to be done." In the midst of this crisis, town officials were "exceedingly pleased" to receive a letter praising their efforts from "President Hoover's Federal Committee on Unemployment."

There is no doubt that my father was unemployed in the early 1930s. In a 1931 Norwood directory, he is listed as having "no occupation." Moreover, if he had had a job, he wouldn't have been allowed to join the Civilian Conservation Corps, which was mandated in the spring of 1933 as part of the first package of FDR's New Deal legislation to alleviate unemployment. By then, "Chick" had become Dad's permanent nickname, and it is Chick Fanning whom I imagine signing up for the CCC shortly after its formation. The plan called for the enlistment of young men into military-style camps, mostly in parks and preserves all over the United States, where they would work on forestry, fire prevention, flood control, and construction projects, while also taking night courses toward high school diplomas and job training. To be eligible, candidates had to be male American citizens, unemployed, free of venereal disease, and owning "three serviceable teeth, top and bottom." Wages were set at $30 a month, $25 of which had to be sent home to families. When the program ended in 1942, over three million young American men had been put to work in hundreds of camps, coast to coast. Since he first told me about "the corps," I've been interested in the CCC as the one concrete link between my father's hard start in life and the larger history of America during the Depression.

Discovering my father's connection to the place we kids called the "Crazy Roads" provoked my earliest curiosity about the lives of my parents and led to my first, tentative linking of family history to the wider world. It made me realize how very little I knew about him, even though he and my mother had been born and raised in Norwood, where I was also growing up.

On hot July mornings in the early 1950s, my friends and I would ride our bikes out Nichols Street, away from town, past two boarded-up, never-lived-in houses—the first and last of George Willett's long-stalled Westover project. Half a mile farther on, we would turn onto an unmarked asphalt road, hidden by encroaching greenery, which went straight for fifty yards, and then forked left and right. Scraggly, new-growth, twenty-year-old trees and thick clumps of thorny bushes and weeds jostled one another for light. We would skid our bikes quickly into the left-hand turning, and immediately we were out of the known world. As the hum of crickets grew louder, the road suddenly forked again, and we found ourselves inside a maze. Here were the Crazy Roads, private, enigmatic, and creepy. There seemed to be miles and miles of them, twisting back on themselves, intersecting and springing out like the snakes with their own tails in their mouths that create the interlacing knots in Celtic illuminated manuscripts. But the aim here was not the celebratory mimicry of God's intricate designs. Rather, as was clear to us even as children, these roads were a plain, sheer waste of energy and time. Profoundly disturbing about this place was not only the scary likelihood of getting lost among the swervings and criss-crosses and the scruffy, random, unchecked tangles but also the tangible, mute evidence here that adults too could screw up badly and permanently.

I recall the first time I did get lost there. Riding in ahead of my friends with foolhardy boldness, in ten minutes and several turns I was disoriented and beginning to panic. Spotting a treeless, open area ahead to my left, I assumed with great relief that I had reached the outside world of Nichols Street again. Instead, I found myself in a desert landscape, a circular flat plain, wider than a football field is long, studded with huge boulders and surrounded by twenty-foot cliffs of loose sand. Two burned-out 1940s black sedans sat on their rims in the center. At once, I recognized this as a legendary Norwood place that I hadn't been sure even existed—the Old Sand Pit. This was where high school boys with their parents' cars were said to drink and make out with their girlfriends. Here, by the lights of my pre–Vatican II Catholic tutelage, was the palpable evidence of Sin (with a capital "S"). All around were piles of beer cans and the blackened remains of scattered bonfires. As well, I discovered for the first time artifacts that were the height of the forbidden—discarded girlie magazines in their early Fifties format of black-and-white nude figures with eyes masked by sinister black rectangles. Small wonder that this proscribed and threatening place soon began to appear in my preadolescent dreams and reveries.

There was a further, personally disquieting dimension to the site as well when my father told me that the sand pit had been gouged out when the roads were being built and the sand used as the main ingredient in the asphalt surface. He knew about this, he explained, because he had helped to build the Crazy Roads. They had been a project of the CCC. I still feel saddened whenever I think about this fact of Dad's biography. It seems to me, in perhaps romanticized retrospect, that this was where he lost his own way

Figure 10. *A Road in the Making*. Civilian Conservation Corps, October 16, 1935. Library of Congress, Prints and Photographs Division (LOT 6302 F, neg. #1002).

in the world. Having turned twenty-four in April 1933, he had been out of school and in the workforce for twelve years. He must have had a great number of odd, temporary, discouraging jobs already behind him. Finally, he was taken on by the CCC to do pick-and-shovel, essentially meaningless work, building roads to nowhere for minimum wage. Often I've imagined what it must have been like for him out there in a hot, summer sun, digging out rocks and slashing brush, shoveling sand into the asphalt maker, spreading the black goo over the tamped-down, leveled surface. Arduous labor, and without even the secondhand recompense of contributing to the logic that any road ought to have—making it easier to get from one place to another. Where was the promise in that?

Much later, I learned of an analogue from nineteenth-century Ireland—the "Famine roads" created under the halfhearted public works relief efforts devised by the British government during the Great Hunger, by which the starving native Irish could be provided the money to buy food without experiencing the dangerous precedent of getting something for nothing. I've seen one such road in the County Clare limestone wilderness known as the Burren, a stone route through a land of stone: rocks and boulders organized and piled with such care that, mortarless, they still form a distinguishable roadbed 150 years later. This road also goes nowhere. It begins on a high plateau above the sparkling western sea and ends in the middle of what W. B. Yeats called "cold Clare rock and Galway rock and thorn." The abrupt termination marks either the cutting-off of public money or the last debilitation of the walking scarecrows who were doing the work.

I have managed to construct one positive association with the Crazy Roads: like the Famine roads in Ireland, they were built to last. They remained well-drained and passable throughout my childhood and beyond, and when I was in high school, they became the base network for building houses that eventually helped turn Norwood into a suburb of Boston. However illogically, I have come to connect the workmanship that went into the Crazy Roads with my later understanding of my father's pride in doing as good a job as possible, all along the way. His full-time job for the last twenty-five years of his life was as a building custodian for the Norwood public schools. He was often praised for the way he kept his school building, and one college summer I worked beside him for two weeks and saw first-hand the scrupulousness of his labor. Room by room through the dog days of August—and there were thirty classrooms in the Norwood Junior High School—he was down on his knees, scrubbing the year's worth of dirt and shoe marks from baseboards, the ephemeral spotlessness of which no one else was ever going to get close enough to notice.

Checking the Building

The time line I have constructed of my father's working life has many gaps. I don't know how long he was with the CCC, or what else he went on to do in the 1930s. The only inkling I've had into how he managed in those years came when an old acquaintance of his told me that in his teens and twenties, "Chick Fanning used to fight like hell." I do know, however, that by the end of the decade, he and his youngest brother, Joe, were helping to run a Texaco gas station at the corner of Walpole and Wilson Streets in Norwood. The station, which may have been leased to my grandfather, who was by then a long way from the laundry business, was on the edge of the neighborhood that was known as Germantown because of the concentration there of German immigrants and their children. One of those local families was that of Edward Balduf, a widower with five daughters. The second youngest, Frances Patricia, known as "Pat," became my mother. She and my father married on April 19, 1941, and moved in with my grandfather

Balduf, who was in declining health. After his death, they moved out to an apartment. I was born on November 11, 1942, my brother Geoffrey on February 15, 1945, and my sister Patti on September 14, 1951.

Thanks to his training in the previous decade, my father had secured wartime employment as a welder at Bethlehem Steel's Fore River Shipyard in Quincy. This was a huge operation, employing 32,000 by the end of the war. Fore River produced more naval tonnage than any other American yard: tankers, cruisers, destroyers, tank landing ships (LSTs), the battleship USS *Massachusetts* (launched in May 1942), and four aircraft carriers (three in 1943 and one in 1944). Dad was thirty-two when Pearl Harbor was bombed by the Japanese on December 7, 1941, which put him well above the desirable upper age limit of twenty-six for draftees under the Selective Service Act of 1940 and its amendments. That, along with his employment in the defense industry and the fact that he was married, kept him out of the armed services during the war. But his two youngest brothers were both in the military. Frank, twenty-eight when the war began, went through the Italian campaign in the U.S. Army. In 1944, he endured and survived the murderous four-month stalemate at the Anzio beachhead south of Rome. Joe, twenty-four, joined the U.S. Navy and served in the Central Pacific campaign for the Marshall and Mariana Islands in 1944 and 1945.

My father and his four siblings all lived out their lives in Norwood. I don't believe any of them gave much thought to going elsewhere. This was the place. This was home. Mary—Auntie Mae—continued as a nurse, on private duty and then working with the elderly at the Victoria Rest Haven. Phil became a bartender. Back from the war, and after extensive rehabilitation from the Anzio experience, Frank got a job in the Department of Public Works on the rubbish truck. Joe also became a custodian, though not right away. Also affected by the war, he had considered entering a monastic brotherhood but ultimately chose a home and family.

After the war, Dad left the shipyard as soon as he could. Construction welding paid very well, but he had suffered headaches and nausea caused by breathing in the gas of the welding torch in the enclosed space of a ship's hold. So, Dad found work as a building custodian for the Norwood Public Schools. It was a civil service job and steady, but the pay was low, and he soon began supplementing his income by working as a waiter for Holman's Catering, a local Norwood company. Though hard work, waiting on table was also a kind of recreation for my father. It was clear that he enjoyed the hustle and camaraderie of the winter banquet circuit and the summer round of clambakes. As kids, we would wait eagerly for his return from a "bake" with a paper bag of leftover "steamers"—steamed clams—which we would reboil, open, and eat with bowls of drawn butter over newspapers spread out on the kitchen table. On lucky nights, there would even be a lobster or two, which made us precocious experts in the culinary challenge of fresh "lobbies." Later on, my brother Geoffrey, who worked through high school and college for the same catering outfit, discovered that on the job our father was a noted wit, full of subtle, humorous perspective on Norwood and the world. Here was a glimpse of someone I almost didn't recognize.

When Geoffrey and I were in elementary school, our father's job of building custodian held something of a mystique for us. On Sunday mornings, our mother took us to the seven o'clock Mass. Dad stayed home with our baby sister, as he had with us in our younger years, though he was never much of a church-goer anyway. After we got home, if we hadn't acted up too much, he would take us with him on his weekend patrol of the junior high. We looked forward eagerly to this Sunday ritual, which was a lot more fun than Mass in any case. We called it "checking the building." It was for us the height of excitement to enter the boiler room by the back door and to proceed over a suspended metal floor that clanged beneath our sneakers. We looked out over the two enormous boilers, muffled in white-stuccoed asbestos coats on which were stuck dials and gauges and big iron doors. One of Dad's hardest jobs was climbing inside the boilers once every summer to clean them out. My friend Terry Winch reminded me of this in a poem about his father, also a school custodian, who would emerge from the same task "black / with soot that took days to wash off." Dad's least favorite job, however, repeated time and again all winter long, was shoveling out the school after snow storms. Often the snow came down overnight, and he would rise and go out at four in the morning to get the walks done before school.

On our Sunday visits we went down a set of metal stairs, scary because they had no risers, to the concrete subbasement floor below. Here, in the stairwell, was Dad's "office"—an old teacher's desk with a rusty gooseneck lamp, some charts and papers, receipts for school supplies that had been shipped in, a calendar, pencils, an ashtray. Spread out from here, all around us, were the exotica of our father's domain: all manner of equipment either waiting to be junked or lined up to be fixed: file cabinets, toilet bowls, desks and chairs, blackboards, map stands. Then past the boilers—flat-out roaring in the heart of winter, even on Sunday, ticking ominously at other times—and up onto a jerry-built wooden landing whose big steel door swung open into the junior high wood-and-metal-working shop, which held another cluster of wonders: table saws, drill presses, lathes, and a locked cage in the corner full of pristine pieces of wood—pine of course, but also some beautiful boards of oak, cherry, and walnut.

From there, we were released into the bowels of the school itself. While Dad walked slowly around, humming and jingling his huge ring of keys, trying, opening, and relocking doors, Geoffrey and I climbed the wide stairways to the upper floors of the three-story building. We walked the echoing dark hallways, the only light spilling in from the clear-glass transoms of the classrooms. We would pretend to be stalking the "bad guys," and it was still close enough to the war that they were mostly Germans and "Japs," with just a smattering of North Koreans and Chinese, our early 1950s bogeymen. Eventually, we got brave enough to split up and play a two-person version of hide-and-seek, sometimes really managing to scare one another.

Then there was the gym—a pretty good-sized one, with a raised stage on one side of the basketball court and a balcony of seats on the other. This was where the school had assemblies and theatricals as well as basketball games, and also where Norwood held its town meetings two or three times a year. My brother and I would swing on the horse and parallel bars, and we were allowed to go in under the balcony to the rabbit-warren office of the phys. ed. teacher (which smelled of his cigars) and get out basketballs for shooting and two-man dodge-ball. The stage had a heavy red curtain, which we would open and close by pulling on thick ropes. We had special knowledge of what was underneath as well. Three sets of latched doors in the front of the stage opened to wooden chutes through which the folding chairs were passed out onto the gym floor for assemblies, then handed back in and down to be stored in a long, low room lit by bare bulbs. Sometimes this hadn't been done on Friday afternoon, and my brother and I would help my father clear the gym for Monday's phys. ed. classes. We folded the chairs one by one, carried them over to the opened doors, and slung them noisily down the chute to Dad's waiting hands. This was a real and important job, our first. Oh, everything about those Sunday mornings was thrilling, magical—and imbued with my father's proud, proprietary air. We kids could see that he was in charge of this complex, living organism, that it was he who kept it breathing.

Four Stories

I am thinking of defining events for my sense of my father. One of these involves maps and a journey. During my childhood, we took very few trips and never as a complete family. One reason was that for long stretches we didn't have a car. The height of adventure involving the outside world was a day trip to Boston on the train during my father's summer vacation, and even this didn't happen every year. We took our de facto parochialism pretty much for granted, and it wasn't until I went off to college and met people who had been lots of places that our situation seemed at all out of the ordinary. But the point wasn't really driven home until one weekend in the middle of November 1966, when my father and I set off in his car for upstate New York to attend my brother's last college football game. Always an outstanding athlete, Geoffrey was finishing up his career as a four-year starter both ways, offensive center and defensive line-backer, for Bridgewater State College in southeastern Massachusetts. He was also the team's cocaptain. The day was bleak and gray with a threat of snow hanging in the air as we set out on the Massachusetts Turnpike. By the time we crossed the state line onto the New York State Thruway, flurries had started, and it snowed off and on all the way to Rochester, where we had a room in the same cheap hotel where the team was staying.

My brother remembers that it was called the Cadillac Hotel. Our room had basic twin beds with thin blankets, faded beige walls and a cracked ceiling, and a window that gave onto an airshaft. In college, as the student manager of an athletic team, I had ridden buses, even flown, to university towns all over the Northeast, and since then, I had been across the country and back from an ill-fated but eventful graduate-school experience at the University of California, Berkeley. So I was singularly unimpressed by this excursion. On the other hand, as soon as we debarked at the hotel, I could see that Dad was as excited as I had ever seen him. He had brought the road map up to our room, and as soon as we had put down our bags—his was an old leather suitcase with outside straps that I had never seen before—he spread out the map, picked up the phone, and called home. Tracing the route with his finger, he named off the towns one by one to my mother on the other end of the line. As he went on to explain that we had driven over 400 miles, it suddenly dawned on me that this was for him a very big deal. He was farther away from Norwood than he had ever been before.

After dinner with the team in the hotel's seedy dining room, Dad went back up to the room, and I took a walk around the block. There was a small drug and sundries shop in the lobby, and I picked up some gum and hard candy for the return trip. When I got back to our room, he was asleep. Next day, the game took place against Brockport State College, a few miles outside of Rochester. Like many of the Bridgewater State games that year, it wasn't much of a contest. The two teams churned the overnight snow to mud, and more snow fell through all four quarters. My brother recalls that the final score was Brockport 28, Bridgewater 7. I remember Geoffrey standing there near the goal line in the falling snow, his college career now over, with many more losses than wins. But our whole family had loved coming to his games, and I couldn't have been prouder if it had been the Rose Bowl in Pasadena. By the time the game ended at 3:30 it was nearly dark, and the snow had begun to accumulate. When Dad and I got to the car, he suggested that I drive. This surprised me until I saw in his eyes that he was reluctant to get out on the big highway in a snowstorm so far from home. I had never seen him frightened before. So I drove. It snowed hard all the way, and the trip took nine hours instead of seven. When we pulled into our driveway, Dad thanked me.

A second story surrounds the point in the mid-1950s when we realized at home that something was up involving Dad and the school department. Four or five of his fellow custodians began coming to our house on weekday evenings—three times in the course of a month. Any such gathering was news, as we were not, to put it mildly, a very social family. Relatives did come around—aunts and uncles, a cousin or two in tow—but not often. About the only previous precedents of repetitive, extrafamilial meetings were the mildly bibulous visits of Mr. Zig to my grandfather. Thus, when some of the other custodians started showing up, my brother and I became curious. It was our mother who told us that they were starting a local of the Massachusetts Municipal Employees Union. She explained that in the custodians' view the Norwood public school system was a well-established dictatorship when it came to school assignments, definition of duties, allocation of overtime, promotions, and pay raises. I have no doubt that my father was the brightest of the bunch by a pretty long stretch. The others I can remember seemed just to shuffle quietly by, pushing their brooms in the school halls. Many were veterans of World War II, and some were known to have problems with "nerves" or alcohol. There had been stories of flat brown bottles and solo song recitals in the boiler room of my own elementary school. In short, the custodians en masse were a vulnerable, easily bullied group.

The union was my father's baby, though, and he pushed it through. I imagine that this was especially hard work, because he was such a loner. He hated organizations and had belonged to none. And yet he made this union happen. The superintendent of schools was not happy with this result, and he exacted a nasty retribution in the form of writing into their first contract the provision that the custodians would have to wear uniforms of matching gray shirts and pants—which they would have to buy—with (the real kicker) their names sewn on over the shirt pocket. Their first names. This last my father refused to do. We could tell that he hated the idea of having to wear a uniform at all, and of course he was well aware of the potential for wise remarks from junior high kids created by having immediate, visual access to the janitor's first name. I believe that the superintendent understood this and that he reveled in the idea. In the end, there was a compromise. Instead of "Chick," or even "Charles," his shirt said "Mr. Fanning." I've always hated uniforms too, including the expectation—much relaxed now, but still the custom of the country when I started out in the mid-Sixties—of wearing a tie and jacket to teach. I know this animosity traces back to my father's experience, the ramifications of which I understood pretty well at the time, though, characteristically, he never discussed it. Here, as in most areas of family life, my mother was the interpreter.

I'm sure the union helped to improve working conditions in a number of ways, though it certainly didn't generate a lot of extra cash for the custodians. In 1966, my first full-time teaching job paid $8,000 a year, and that was $3,000 more than my father ever earned from the school department. The one substantive financial bonus from this labor-organizing venture that I saw came shortly after Dad's death. One rainy morning, I drove my mother into the heart of Roxbury, then well along in its transformation from an Irish to an African American ghetto. There, in a basement office in an old brick building on a corner, she signed for and received my father's death benefit check from the Mass. Municipal Employees. The amount was $2,000, hardly enough to pay the undertaker.

I was back in Norwood a few months ago, and because my sister still lives in our old house on Walpole Street, I was able to make some measurements about which I'd been wondering for years. These relate to a third event that I see as defining in my father's life. One spring when I was in junior high, we began to smell something bad in and around the "back bathroom," a small room with toilet just off the kitchen. As the weather got warmer, the smell got worse, and after a few days, having first made sure that the source was not outside the house, my father investigated. This was not an easy task. He had to go "down cellar" (our term for the descent), where behind the stairs there is a crawl space, the only access to the back bathroom sewer line. That hole is four feet off the ground and no more than three feet in diameter at its widest point. It goes back under our dining room and kitchen and stops under the back bathroom toilet. The distance is thirty-five feet.

What my father found there was a huge pile of human waste that had been building since sometime the previous winter when the pipe connecting the toilet to the town sewer line had ruptured. Moreover, the force of continual flushing had coated the walls for several feet back toward the cellar hole. There was only one thing to be done. He was going to have to crawl down that thirty-five foot tunnel pushing a bucket ahead of him, fill it, then crawl out again backwards, scrape the stuff into a barrel, and crawl back in for more. Then he had to pack handfuls of lime into the dirt walls and floor at the far end. Then he had to measure and cut new pipe, push it down the tunnel, and hook it up. He had to do all this while lying flat on his stomach with his arms out ahead of his face. From start to finish, the job took three weeks of night and weekend work. To fight off the stench, he soaked a handkerchief in vinegar and tied it around his nose and mouth. As a school custodian, my father's workdays were full of dirty lavatories and plugged-up toilets, and I am sure that this noisome chore seemed to him a particularly unfair judgment from the household gods. At the time, though, like everything else he did at home, we all took it for granted that he would meet this challenge. Taciturn most of the time anyway, Dad was stonily silent all the way through to the end of the job.

The fourth story is the earliest. When I was five, Dad took me downtown on a Saturday afternoon to get my first haircut at Eddie Armour's Barbershop. Before this, I had accompanied him a few times for his haircuts, but I had no idea of what was going to happen until Eddie swooped down and lifted me into the big, ornately metal-backed chair, cracked a sheet out straight, and wrapped it around me. Eddie was a formidable man, a stocky and muscular navy veteran of World War II with a big blue anchor tattooed on his forearm and an always smoldering cigar. I panicked on the spot and started to whimper and flail my arms to fend off the buzzing electric clippers. After three or four passes at my head, Eddie shrugged and gave up. Dad and I rode home in silence. When we got into the kitchen, he was shaking with anger, and it looked like he was about to hit me with his open hand. My mother came between us, asserting that it wasn't that big a deal. It was just that I had been surprised, and wasn't I also getting over a cold? With more warning, I would certainly get my hair cut, wouldn't I? She calmed us both down, and the following week I got my first professional haircut without incident. It wasn't until sometime in high school that I figured out why my father had been so mad. The haircut had been my first test of conduct outside the home in his adult Norwood world. And I, his firstborn and namesake, had flunked. I hadn't acted properly. The subject never came up again, but from what I now know about his family and upbringing, I think I've got it right. Such a display of self-indulgent behavior would have been unthinkable during Dad's childhood, especially after his mother's death.

May 10, 1971

My father was a quiet man, just under six feet tall, straight-backed, with a beautiful head of hair (his one conceit), the standard Fanning aquiline nose (he called it "roamin," his pun for "Roman"), and lightish blue eyes. Handsome, even distinguished-looking, he was, in later years at least, certainly not satisfied with his life. Dad was very intelligent, especially in math—he often helped with my homework right up through senior year in high school—and he was extremely gifted mechanically. But he was well and truly stuck in an occupation that most of the outside world dismissed as low-status and dead-end. He had a wife and three children, and I would guess that he was stalled from taking chances on improving his lot by these facts of life and also by his memories of the significant failures in his family and in the larger boom-and-bust American society in which he had grown up. His father had lost the Norwood Laundry in the 1920s. The national economy had crashed in the 1930s. Unemployed for long stretches in his teens and twenties, he had finally made good money during World War II, but in a job that made him ill. Civil service in the form of custodial work for the Norwood public schools was a lifeline which he must have grasped eagerly. And he held on tight—but at what cost, he certainly never let me know. Since I first heard it, Robert Lowell's mordant line about *his* father has kept coming back to me as sadly appropriate in my family, too, though a decade later: "In his forties, Father's soul went underground." I looked at my father and wanted to hear more, much more, about who he was and what he felt and understood. We never had any such talk.

Because of his own mother and grandmother, my father was well acquainted from an early age with death in the family. Still, his father had made it to seventy-seven, and his grandfather, Walking John Fanning, had lived into his nineties, and so it was a great shock when Joe Fanning, my father's youngest sibling, dropped dead of a heart attack in September 1956 at age thirty-nine. Eight years after that, their brother Phil's heart gave out in July 1964. Phil was fifty-two, two and a half years younger than Dad, and I recall that at the time, some people thought at first it was Chick who had died. A few years later on, my father's legs began to bother him, a significant liability for a custodian and waiter. The pain was diagnosed as due to poor circulation, and in the spring of 1970 a surgeon removed two veins, cleaned them out, and put them back in Dad's legs. I was in Chicago doing dissertation research at that time, and when I called him up, we had one of our longest conversations ever, as he explained the operation in detail and told me how serious it had been. I think this was his first stay in a hospital. I know it was his last. At this point, Dad gave up smoking, after God knows how many years, which had to have been a very hard thing for him to do. (I can't forget that for most of his adult life, the magazine ads had been full of testimonials from doctors with packs of Camels in the pockets of their white coats.) Given the weight of all this family death and illness, I'm not surprised that Dad got more and more withdrawn and cranky. I can imagine him in those years silently assessing his own life and coming up short when faced with what he had and hadn't accomplished.

The last year of my father's life began with a disaster at work. On Saturday evening, January 23, 1971, the third floor and part of the second floor of the Norwood Junior High School were destroyed by fire. The event (with a picture) made the front page of the *Boston Sunday Advertiser,* which reported that "as flames burned on the top floor of the school, two custodial employees, John Maleiko and Charles Fanning, entered the basement with firefighters and helped turn off gas and oil lines." Seventeen towns and the city of Boston sent equipment and men to fight the blaze, and twelve firefighters were injured before it was brought under control. Thursday's *Messenger* reported that "there were mixed emotions in the crowd that gathered at the scene. Some youngsters were observed with tears in their eyes while others romped gleefully about." The cause was arson. Investigators found that shortly before eight o'clock on Saturday evening, three separate fires had been set in the building. The damage estimate was $2 million, and no arrests were ever made. After Dad's death four months later, several townspeople who had known him told our family that the fire had taken the heart out of him. I wasn't living at home then, but I'm sure this was true. How could it not have been? The building of which he was custodian had been deliberately and ruinously sullied.

My father's death in May 1971 was sudden and unexpected. The context was especially strange. The banquet honoring Norwood High School's undefeated, league-champion 1970–71 ice hockey team had been trumpeted for weeks. In those days, the Bay State League was always one of the toughest in the hockey hotbed of eastern Massachusetts, and that year's team was being talked about in the local press as "the most successful hockey team in Norwood history." A fund drive to support the gala had been on for some time, and tickets were for sale all over town. To honor the team, the coaches of Bay State League rival towns Dedham, Walpole, Milton, and Needham were invited, and the featured speaker was to be Jack Kelley, one of New England's most famous coaches, whose Boston University team had just won the NCAA national hockey championship. The *Messenger* ran a full-page celebratory advertisement, paid for by donations, on May 7, and the banquet went off on schedule at the newly renovated American Legion Hall in Medfield, on Monday, May 10. Three days later, the paper was full of the great event. There was a glowing front-page story, and a detailed inside report took up all of local sportswriter Frank Wall's column. What was missing from all this hoopla—though missing, to be sure, only from our family's perspective—was the news of my father's death, which had occurred at the hockey banquet. The Norwood firm of Timothy's Catering (Holman's successor), for which he was then working his second job of waiter, had served the food. As we got the story, my father had just carried a load of dishes into the kitchen when he collapsed with a massive coronary attack. He was dead before he hit the floor.

I do believe that previous to his last years, there had been a rewarding integrity and balance to my father's life for a good long time. His family made him happy. He took pride and was respected in his work as a custodian. He enjoyed waiting on table. He kept our house dry, warm, and running smoothly. He loved fixing things, a fact of which I am reminded every time I pick up one of the few tools of his that I still own: a couple of saws and screwdrivers, a pick from the Ellis Pond Ice Company. Though the business ends of these are rusty, their wooden handles are burnished to a silken sheen, lovely to the touch. I know that our heartlessly throwaway society—we pitch out perfectly good machines that need only a tweak or two to mend—would have confused and dismayed him no end.

I recall that shortly after he died, I replied to someone who asked, "What was your father like?" that, "I didn't know him all that well, but he was very good at washing his hands." At the time, I thought to myself that this was a pretty odd thing to say, but now I see that it unlocks a powerful truth about Dad. I observed this ritual daily for many years. He would come home from work at 3:30 or 4:00 in the afternoon and go straight to the kitchen sink. Rolling his sleeves way up, he soaped his arms to above the elbow and scrubbed away with hot, hot water for a good five minutes. Then he turned back around, wiping his arms and hands with a dish towel, and smiling. Another image has just surfaced that strikes me as similarly telling. When we kids were all home at the same time in the summer, Dad would walk up the street from the junior high at lunch time, and as he turned into our driveway, he would whistle—a two-note song repeated three times that told us he was home. The gist of his life when it was going well was a quiet, authoritative presence, but it's clear to me that toward the end he lost that centered wholeness. The deaths of two brothers, his own health problems, the junior high fire—all contributed to erode his sense of significant toil. I believe that he could no longer find enough on the positive side of the ledger to zero out these negatives. Maybe he was just too tired. After all, when he died at sixty-two, Dad had been out in the working world for fifty years.

My favorite memory of my father is of a weekday afternoon that recurred day after day throughout my childhood. Dad would come home from work, wash his hands, and go upstairs to my parents' bedroom with a big pile of newspapers. Of the four or five Boston dailies in the early Fifties, we got the morning *Post* and the evening *Globe*. On Thursdays there were two competing Norwood weeklies as well, the *Messenger* and the *Tribune*. Dad would stretch out on his bed with all those papers and I would climb up beside him to look at the funnies and the sports pages. Before he dozed off, we would do puzzles together—sometimes the crossword, but more often the "Twistagram." You got two letters to start, then a series of tricky definitions of words of three, four, five, six, and seven letters, which required using the previous letters plus one new letter each time. The result was a pyramid of words that were also thematically connected. The answer was available on another page of the same paper, which made the activity much more fun than the crossword, for whose answers we had to wait twenty-four hours. Dad was very good at these puzzles. To this day, every time I lie down with the paper, the luxurious feeling of stretching out and the sound and smell of crinkling newsprint bring me back to those quiet afternoons. I couldn't have known it then, but at those times, my father and I were as close as we were ever going to be.

Our home life was full of evidence of my father's many skills. I do not recall a single instance when a tradesman crossed our threshold to do a job of work. This was fortunate as we pretty much lived from paycheck to paycheck, and could not have afforded many such visits. Certainly, we had no fewer domestic nuts-and-bolts crises than any other New England family of five living in a house built before 1875, but Dad handled them all. He did the plumbing, wiring, and appliance repair. He fixed the broken windows.

He scraped and hung wallpaper. He painted whatever needed painting, inside and out, and he put the shingles on the roof.

Nor did we support Norwood's automotive repair industry. My father never owned a new car, but he kept our fitful parade of clunkers running by not only changing the oil, filters, and plugs but also performing major surgery when necessary on the radiator, brakes, transmission, and engine. Whatever needed doing, he did it. In fact, he must have saved the Norwood public schools many thousands of dollars over the years. In this, at least, he was well suited to his job.

It now occurs to me that I last saw my father in this role. He was working on his car out in the garage late on a warm Sunday evening in May 1971. I had been home for the weekend and was about to drive back to my apartment in Cambridge. It was 8:45 and not quite dark yet when I called out "Goodnight, Dad." He came to the open garage door wiping his hands on a rag, waved, and said, "Goodnight, Charles." And that was it. The next night was the hockey banquet.

One of his favorite expressions, always delivered with self-deprecating wryness, was "Jack of all trades, master of none." But to us, he was master of the whole physical world.

3

Young Winslow Radcliff

After a few days of holiday we commenced anew the peaceful labors of the life of a citizen, and cares of business and family have gradually dimmed the memory of the scenes we have endeavored to record, until they seem like impossible dreams, save, perhaps, to those whose broken frames or impaired health connect the present with the past.

—*History of the Thirty-Fifth Regiment Massachusetts Volunteers, 1862–1865*

When I consider the small but misery-laden body of information available about my Yankee ancestor who fought in the Civil War, Nathaniel Hawthorne's powerful story "Young Goodman Brown" comes to mind. *Young Goodman Brown came forth, at sunset, into the street of Salem village, but put his head back, after crossing the threshold, to exchange a parting kiss with his young wife.* Her name is Faith. Just three months wed, the young man looks back with regret, resolving never to leave her again after just this one night away. Plunging into the dark forest, he meets first a man of fifty, carrying a staff *which bore the likeness of a great black snake,* who urges him on, claiming close acquaintance with Brown's family: *I helped your grandfather, the constable, when he lashed the Quaker woman so smartly through the streets of Salem. And it was I that brought your father a pitch-pine knot, kindled at my own heart, to set fire to an Indian village, in King Philip's war.* This is Satan, and he guides the newlywed into *the heart of the dark wilderness, still rushing onward, with the instinct that guides mortal man to evil.* This inverted pilgrim's progress is marked by a cacophony of voices that direct Goodman Brown to a clearing where all of the most admired members of the Salem community gather to celebrate the baptism into evil of the young man and his Faith. *Now are ye undeceived!* proclaims the dark presiding figure. *Evil is the nature of mankind. Evil must be your only happiness. Welcome, again, my children, to the communion of your race!* Hawthorne suggests that all this may only have been *a wild dream of a witch-meeting.* And yet, the result is the same either way. The following morning, Young Goodman Brown returns to his village, irretrievably embittered and deranged.

In his second inaugural address on March 4, 1865, President Lincoln sought to place within God's plan for the United States both the curse of "American Slavery" and the will to remove that curse, even if the war were to continue "until all the wealth piled by the bond-man's two hundred and fifty years of unrequited toil shall be sunk, and until every drop of blood drawn with the lash shall be paid by another drawn with the sword." He prayed that the reunited states could achieve a world in which the heavy burden of the aftermath of civil war was acknowledged and shared out: "With malice toward none, with charity for all; with firmness in the right, as God gives us to see the right, let us strive on to finish the work we are in; to bind up the nation's wounds; to care for him who shall have borne the battle, and for his widow, and his orphan—to do all which may achieve and cherish a just, and a lasting peace, among ourselves, and with all nations." Like Hawthorne's young good man, thousands upon thousands of callow volunteers went out from their quiet villages to serve on both sides of the conflict. "Never such innocence, / Never before or since, / As changed itself to past / Without a word," as Philip Larkin says of World War I. For many, the time and space between naiveté and knowledge were hardly greater than Goodman Brown's single night in the forest. Nor was their return to families and communities then on the uncomprehending other side of a gulf of nightmare any less difficult. Sadly, the binding and care, the lasting peace of Lincoln's prayer, were to elude many returning veterans, among them my great-great-grandfather Winslow Radcliff, for whom a dark vision like Hawthorne's was to win the day.

Born in New Hampshire in 1823, Winslow had made his way south to Massachusetts, where he wooed and won Sophia Ann Draper. When they married on July 3, 1848, Sophia was twenty and Winslow was twenty-five and working at the trade of "fuller," shrinking and thickening cloth. Winslow joined the Thirty-fifth Massachusetts Volunteer Infantry Regiment on August 5, 1862, and was assigned to Company I. The pressing question for me is, why did he volunteer? Here was a man in his late thirties with a wife and four children between the ages of eleven years and twenty months. He was by then put down as a "railroad employee," which ought to have been steady and substantial work, and I doubt that money was an issue. In fact, the proffered bounty for enlistment in the Massachusetts Thirty-fifth was not large enough to appeal to most family men. The "inducements" were "$25 bounty in advance; also, $13, one month's pay in advance; $12 per month State aid; and $75 bounty at close of war." Moreover, Winslow may have lied about his age. In the roster of Company I, he is listed as thirty-four, but the figures on his marriage and death certificates make him thirty-nine in August 1862 and thus one of the oldest soldiers in the unit.

For a generation, especially in New England, support for the abolitionist cause had been building steadily, and the South's secession had sealed and steeled the resolve of thousands. Thus, conviction alone may have motivated Winslow Radcliff's enlistment—especially as just one month earlier, on July 2, President Lincoln had called urgently for "300,000 men for three years." Having looked further, however, again with the invaluable spadework done by my sister and cousins, I now see a probable further impulsion from inside Winslow's family. I just can't imagine that the Drapers of Dedham would ever have let him forget their illustrious Revolutionary War pedigree, featuring Colonel Moses Draper and his sainted mother, Mary. As one of six children, all girls, born to Hannah and Benjamin Draper, Winslow's wife Sophia had no brothers in the Union Army, but Draper cousins galore answered the call to service. There are no less than thirty-six Drapers, from Algernon to William, in the roster of Civil War soldiers from Massachusetts, and two of them, Private Frank W. And Sergeant James A., were in Company D of the Thirty-fifth Regiment.

There's more: the Drapers must have known the single most embarrassing fact about their son-in-law. He was illegitimate. Various records reveal that Winslow was born somewhere in New Hampshire to an unacknowledged father and a mother, Ann, whose surname was, depending on the document, *either* Winslow *or* Radcliff. Consequently, I believe that Winslow Radcliff's embarrassing family history added to the pressure from his wife's family to prove his mettle in this time of extreme threat to the Union, in whose creation the Drapers had played so big a part. In any case, the decision to enlist would cost Winslow dearly. Ahead of him lay Antietam, Fredericksburg, Vicksburg, madness, and suicide.

As he left no written record of his experience, a chorus of other voices must speak about Winslow Radcliff's war and its aftermath. Diving into this material was a reminder, like that provided by Ken Burns's famous TV series, of the expressive ease of so many who were affected by the conflict. How well they wrote. How unselfconsciously eloquent and evocative are their narratives and letters. I read somewhere that more has been written about the Civil War than about everything else in American history—combined. My search for Winslow Radcliff bore out dramatically the vastness and richness of the resources.

Company I

The Thirty-fifth Massachusetts was organized at Worcester on August 1, 1862, and Company I was fully subscribed with the statutory complement of 101 soldiers by the middle of the month. It was called the "Second Dedham Company" because sixty-five of the officers and men were from that town. The next largest numbers were sixteen soldiers from Weston and ten from Needham. (The "First Dedham Company" had been Company F of the Eighteenth Massachusetts Volunteers. Formed a year earlier in April 1861, the Eighteenth had joined the Army of the Potomac in August and gone on to fight in the Peninsula Campaign and beyond.)

Many of the names of Second Dedham Company volunteers are familiar to me from people and places of my youth in Norwood, which was then still part of Dedham. (It broke off in 1872.) Reflecting the area's two dominant groups, these are Yankee names (Ellis, Fisher, Hartshorn), and Irish names (Curran, Hogan, O'Connell, Phalan, Sullivan). The youngest to join was seventeen-year-old Daniel Adams, a farmer from Weston, and three men were forty-five at the time of enlistment: John Monnaghan, a Needham laborer, David Phalan, a Dedham laborer; and William Wilcutt, a Needham farmer. All told, nineteen were under twenty when they signed up, fifty-four were in their twenties, eighteen in their thirties, and seven in their forties. (Three had no age listed.) Their captain, Bostonian Sidney Willard (Harvard College Class of 1852), and first lieutenant, John Lathrop from Dedham, were lawyers. One sergeant, John D. Cobb of Dedham, was an 1861 graduate of Harvard and a law student. There were also four clerks and two other students. However, as the *Dedham Gazette* of August 23, 1862, explained, "The company is mainly composed of farmers and mechanics, men inured to toil, and consequently well fitted not only to endure the privations of the camp, but to do hard fighting in the field. They may safely be relied upon to do their whole duty." And there were, in fact, nineteen farmers, seventeen laborers, eleven cabinetmakers, seven mechanics (that is, skilled workers or artisans of various sorts), six carpenters, four spinners, four teamsters, and one or two each from other trades, among them blacksmith, wheelwright, weaver, cooper, hatter, printer, and inkmaker.

I have found four voices from Winslow Radcliff's own Company I that speak directly in letters and a diary of their experiences in the Civil War. Far from ghostly abstractions, these were real people, sharing their immediate impressions of the war with loved ones back home. John Lathrop, the twenty-seven-year-old Dedham lawyer who entered as Company I's first lieutenant, was much admired in the town; his friends sent him off to war with gifts of a sword, sash, and revolver, and he sent back letters from the front to the local paper, the *Dedham Gazette.* Promoted to captain after the death in action of Sidney Willard, Lathrop was discharged for disability in November 1863. John D. Cobb, twenty-two, who came in as one of four sergeants, rose to first lieutenant, acting adjutant, and finally captain, mustering out of service at war's end without having been wounded. Henry W. Tisdale, twenty-five, a clerk from the West Dedham neighborhood of Mill Village, also came into Company I as a sergeant. Wounded severely in the regiment's first battle, South Mountain, in mid-September of 1862, he spent five months recovering and returned to the front in February 1863. Tisdale was taken prisoner in May 1864 and confined in four separate prisons, including Andersonville, for the duration of the war. The fourth resurrected voice (and my favorite) is that of ordinary soldier Fisher A. Cleaveland. Listed as a mechanic and one of Company I's oldest volunteers at age forty-three, Private Cleaveland had come the farthest of anyone to join up, being a native of East Freetown, a tiny farming community north of New Bedford in far southeastern Massachusetts. Wounded in September 1862, he rejoined the company the following February, which is when his surviving letters to his wife and children begin. He served for the rest of the war and was mustered out a corporal.

In letters and diary entries, these four men describe the time of service they shared in Company I of the Massachusetts Thirty-fifth with my great-great-grandfather, who left no words of his own on this or any other subject. Added detail can be found in the official *History of the Thirty-Fifth Regiment Massachusetts Volunteers, 1862–1865*, published in 1884 by "A Committee of the Regimental Association." (As Company I's representative on this committee was Dedham's John Cobb, his voice carries over here as well.) These voices convey the unprecedented challenges to body, mind, and spirit faced by those who fought in the Civil War and help us understand how so many, including my ancestor, were broken on that wheel.

Winslow Radcliff's War

The final statistics for Company I of the Thirty-fifth Massachusetts are grim. Only forty-five of the original 101 soldiers were mustered out with the regiment on June 9, 1865, "having had the honor," in the words of John Cobb, "to represent the loyal people of Dedham under McClellan, Burnside,

Hooker, Grant, Sherman, Foster, Slocum, and Meade, in Virginia, Kentucky, Mississippi, and Tennessee." Twenty-four members, almost one quarter, had died—twenty of battle wounds and four of fever during the brutally hot summer of 1863 in the South. Twenty-eight more had been wounded but survived. Twenty-seven had been discharged earlier because of disability or illness.

There was no quicker, ruder, or more violent awakening into the realities of this war than that experienced by the Thirty-fifth Massachusetts Volunteers. In mid-August of 1862 they gathered at the army training camp in Lynnfield and received their weapons. "Being now fully armed and equipped," notes the regimental *History*, "it was supposed that a few days at least of camp duty and drill would be allowed before active service." Instead, the demand for troops for the Army of the Potomac was so great that "much to the disappointment of the men and grief of their friends, orders were received to proceed immediately to the front, and the regiment started accordingly on the twenty-second of August—Friday." Three weeks later, the Thirty-fifth was in action at the Battle of South Mountain. Three days after that, they were on the field at Antietam.

The earliest voice from Company I is that of Henry Tisdale, an earnest, even stodgy, twenty-five-year-old from West Dedham who struggles on every page of his diary to reconcile his ideal of Christian duty with the realities of the war.

From the Diary of Henry W. Tisdale, July 30, 1862

The past 22 days have been busy and eventful ones to me. Thursday, July 10th, enlisted as a volunteer in the service of the U.S. Soon after the President's call for the 300,000 volunteers felt it my duty to be one of them, feel it as much a christian as a political duty, and feel that every citizen ought to feel it so. . . . I have been busy packing my effects and preparing my camp equipage. Tomorrow go to camp at Lynnfield.

From the Tisdale Diary, August 20, 1862

Went to Uncle William's in forenoon and bid Carrie goodbye. At 11 a.m. left for camp bidding adieu to the folks perhaps forever. My heart was too full to speak as I bid them goodbye. There were many, many things I wished to say to them and which I fully intended to, but kept putting them off through the morning and when the hour for departure came, I could not control myself to do it. Now perhaps I may never speak to them again. O God if it may be thy will, grant that we may meet in heaven through the merits of thy son, Jesus. Amen. Cried near half the way to camp. Rode to Readville to take the cars with S. R. Baker. There are five of us from West Dedham in Company I: S. R. Baker, E. A. Roberts, Geo. E. Whiting and David Sullivan. As the day is closing think of those from whom I have parted.

From the Tisdale Diary, August 22, 1862

At near 11 a.m. left Lynnfield enroute for the front or seat of war. There was a long train of us and one could not help feeling a sort of pride to be steaming along thinking of the great work we were going to do. "We Are Coming Father Abraham, 300,000 More" was our song, as I hummed it over could not keep the tears from my eyes as I thought of home, left perhaps forever.

From the Tisdale Diary, August 31, 1862

Sabbath. Changed our camp ground about half a mile and are now near Fort Coccoran, have a fine view of the Potomac and a portion of the city of Washington. Have had some little drill the past few days. New troops are arriving every day and camping about us. Evidence multiplies that stirring times are about us and reports of hard fighting, as going on near the old Bull Run battle ground. A portion of McClellan's army marched by our camp today. They looked worn and weary, their soiled and worn uniforms and tattered flags presenting a strong contrast to our new and clean attire and trappings. Somehow felt ashamed of my new uniform, and wished that I could with them show the marks of honorable service.

From the Tisdale Diary, September 14, 1862

On the march since the 10th off and on and are now camped near Middletown, M'd. According to reports we are attached to Reno's Division of Gen. Burnside's 9th Corps. Was some little fighting yesterday between our advanced parts of the army and the rebels under Stonewall Jackson near Frederick, MD. The country through which we have passed very fine in natural scenery, interspersed with fine farms and woodland, the latter more of a true forest style than our Northern woods, having much less underbrush and rocks, and the wood much larger. Passed through two or three small villages; these and the farm dwellings and buildings we have passed are far from equaling in style or taste those of the North, showing many of them in a dilapidated appearance, and far more whitewash than paint. One feels already the taint of slavery upon the land in the somehow thriftless and want of enterprising look of the country. Our march through Frederick, MD yesterday and by moonlight, over the hills and beyond it was very fine. The scenery from these hills delightful. This morning was opened with the booming of cannon and during the day thus far troops have been passing by our camp in one continued stream. Hard to feel it the Sabbath. Prospects of our getting into action before night multiply causing a sort of feverish excitement to come over me. Help me my heavenly Father to do my duty in thy fear and for glory for Christ's sake, Amen.

Letter from Captain John Lathrop to the *Dedham Gazette*
from Camp near Harper's Ferry, September 17, 1862

We left camp at Middletown Sunday afternoon, about 2 o'clock, and marched three or four miles to the battlefield. As we approached, we met the wounded being carried to the rear in numbers. We formed in line in a cornfield, threw off our blankets, and prepared for action. We were first ordered into a wood, to disperse the rebels who were concealed there. As we approached, some shots were fired and returned. One of my men, Henry Tisdale, was here shot in the thigh by a wounded rebel, but was not very badly wounded. The wood was very dense, and it was almost impossible to force our way through. In, however, we went, as well as we could, but the men were soon separated, and when I got out, no more than half of my company was with me, the rest being with Lieut. Hill. The other companies were in the same condition—officers separated from their men and men from each other. As yet we knew nothing of the plan of battle or what we were expected to do. When we emerged from the roads we were ordered into a field where the rest of the brigade were drawn up in line of battle by regiments, our regiment being in the rear. I had not got my company into line, when the firing commenced. I ordered my men to lie down. They did so, and returned the fire. When the firing was over, I attempted to reform my men, when I was ordered to take them into the woods behind, and form them there. This I did, and had just got them into line when a murderous volley was poured into us by the rebels. Two of my men were struck. The bullets whistled over our heads singing like very demons. We were soon ordered out of the woods to the road, to keep the rebels from flanking us. Here we lay for over an hour, the bullets whistling over our heads. About eight o'clock the firing ceased, and we camped for the night on the field. I had then only fourteen men of my company with me, and both of my Lieutenants were missing. The other companies were in about the same condition. . . .

About three o'clock I got back to the field, and turned in under a rebel blanket. We gained a great victory. The next morning dead rebels were in every direction. In the road where we were that night were over fifty. We could not move without stepping on them. The fields and roads around were filled with bodies, and knapsacks, haversacks, guns and all such things. Such a sight I never beheld. There we remained until afternoon, and then the order was forward. We marched until after dark, and turned in in a ploughed field. The next morning—yesterday—a battery opened upon our camp. Several shells struck near us, and others went over our heads. Seven or eight men were killed—one in a regiment directly in front of ours had his leg taken off.

From the Tisdale Diary, October 29, 1862

Some six weeks have passed away since writing. They have been eventful ones to me, full of God's providential goodness and mercy. A good deal of the time have been unable to write and the remaining time have been indisposed to it.

At near 4 p.m. September 14th our brigade was ordered to the front, a rough march of some 4 miles brought us to the scene of conflict, climbing steep hills, some almost mountains crossing rough fields through corn fields and some of the way at double quick. On our way meeting many wounded being carried to the rear and as we neared the battle ground here and there a dead body was to be seen. At little after 5 p.m. were upon the ground where the booming of artillery the screaming of shot and shell and rattling of musketry told us we were mid the stern realities of actual battle. The sight of the wounded sent a kind of chill over me but in the main feelings of curiosity and wonder at the scene about me took hold of my mind.

Were drawn up in the line of battle in a cornfield and then advanced through a sort of wooden field to a thick wood where we met the rebels or a few scattering ones for their main body was on the retreat. In entering the wood came upon a large number of rebel dead lying in a ravine, presenting a sad and sickening sight. They were making an advance upon our lines, but when crossing the ravine, were met by a volley from the 17th Michigan which so thinned their ranks that on that part of their line they made a precipitate retreat. Just after we entered the wood was wounded by a rifle ball passing through my left leg just opposite the thigh bone. As the ball struck me it gave me a shock which led me to feel at first that the bone must have been struck and shattered and for a moment did not dare to move for fear it was so. Found on moving that the bone was not injured and that I had only a flesh wound which relieved my mind and thankfulness to God that I was not maimed or dangerously hurt came. Think that the shot must have been fired by some straggling rebel or sharpshooter in a tree as we had not yet got up to within reach of the rebel lines.

Found myself in a few moments growing weak and tying my towel above the wound to stop its bleeding tried to make for the rear where the surgeons were. As I was limping off a wounded rebel who was sitting against a tree called me and asked me if I did not have something to eat, exhibiting a loaf and going to him I opened my knife to cut off a slice when he placed his hands before his face exclaiming "Don't kill me" and begging me to put up the knife and not to hurt him. Assuring him I had no intention of hurting him I spoke with him a little. Found he had a family in Ga. that he was badly wounded and was anxious to have me remain with him and help him off. But found I was growing weaker from loss of blood and that the surging to and fro the troops about us made it a dangerous place so limping and crawling was obliged to leave him and move for the rear. Soon came across some men detailed to look out for the wounded who placed me in a blanket and took me to the rear to the surgeon.

Antietam

The *History of the Thirty-Fifth Massachusetts* summed up the Battle of Antietam on September 17, 1862, with stark conciseness: "It had been an afternoon in the valley of death." In the aftermath, "as one man expressed it, 'patriotism was played out,' meaning that the hurrah-boys spirit had evaporated. We had seen the slain of the Confederates on South Mountain and our own dead at Antietam, and the grave fact that we had engaged to be, and had become, slayers of our fellowmen stared us in the face, without the glamour of flash oratory and colored lights about it." Certainly, no one disputes the importance or the horror of Antietam. Historian James M. McPherson published the book *Crossroads of Freedom* (2002) to assert that "Antietam was arguably, as Karl Marx and Walter Taylor believed, *the* event of the war." His narrative begins with arresting statistics:

Despite the ghastly events of September 11, 2001, another September day 139 years earlier remains the bloodiest single day in American history. The 6,300 to 6,500 Union and Confederate soldiers killed and mortally wounded near the Maryland village of Sharpsburg on September 17, 1862, were more than twice the number of fatalities suffered in the terrorist attacks on the World Trade Center and the Pentagon on September 11, 2001. Another 15,000 men wounded in the battle of Antietam would recover, but many of them would never again walk on two legs or work with two arms. The number of casualties at Antietam was four times greater than American casualties at the Normandy beaches on June 6, 1944. More American soldiers died at Sharpsburg (the Confederate name for the battle) than died in combat in all the other wars fought by this country in the nineteenth century *combined*: the War of 1812, the Mexican-American War, the Spanish-American War, and all the Indian wars.

Letter from Captain John Lathrop to the *Dedham Gazette*, September 18, 1862

We had a severe fight yesterday, our regiment suffered terribly—nearly all the officers were wounded. I escaped without a scratch. To-day we shall probably have to stand it again.

18th, 4 P.M.—We have been drawn up in line of battle all day, but there has been no firing on either side as yet. Each wants reinforcements. For an hour yesterday, we were drawn up on a hill with a battery on our right. Our position was a very commanding one. The battle field was but a short distance below. We could see every shot from our battery strike, and also not a few of the shots from the rebel battery strike near us. Then the order came to go forward. Down the hill we went, and formed on the line of a creek, the rebels being on the opposite side. After this we crossed a bridge which was taken by our side, and formed on the brow of a hill. Here we lay all afternoon, with the balls singing and screeching over us, until about 5 P.M., when we were ordered to forward. We had first to ascend a hill, and then go down at the double quick for some forty or fifty rods. All this time the regiment was exposed to the heavy fire of the rebels—shot and shell and bullets were pouring into us. At the bottom of the hill we formed behind a rail fence, the rebels being behind a stone wall some two hundred feet distant. We stood here about an hour, when our ammunition giving out, and no more being at hand, and no reinforcements sent to our relief, we retired to the brow of the hill. Just previous to this I had gone part way up the hill to see Capt. King, who was acting as Major, to get permission to send for ammunition, but I could not find him. I then commenced to take the cartridges from the dead and wounded, and to tie up wounds as best I could, when I saw the regiment leaving. I was, at the time, near the top of the hill, and had just got the leg of a man tied up, when a ball struck him in the other leg. The balls flew around like hail, and I was covered with the dirt as I stooped over the wounded man. I escaped unhurt.

The regiment is fearfully cut up. In the fight on Sunday our Colonel was wounded. Yesterday our Lieut. Colonel and nearly all the officers were wounded. The major was not with us. There were but three Captains left—Cheever, Andrews and myself. My escape is a miracle.

Patrick Walsh from Needham

The abruptness of the end of innocence in Company I emerges in the story of the brief life of one soldier, Patrick Walsh, whose experience also hits close to home for the Fanning family. Thirty-eight years old and a tailor by trade when he enlisted as a private, Walsh had been an Irish immigrant to Needham, Massachusetts, as had my great-great grandfather, Phillip Fanning, who came over in 1851 and was forty-four in 1862. They could well have known each other. In the *History of the Thirty-Fifth,* Walsh comes into view when the Massachusetts regiment is on the steamboat *Bay State* between Fall River and Jersey City on the night of August 22–23, 1862, en route to the seat of war.

Company I chronicler John Cobb recalled how "one Walsh, an old marine, with wits enlivened by whiskey, gave to the wakeful ones a spirited free exhibition of the bayonet drill, dancing about and whirling his rifle, bayonet fixed, over the sleepers" spread out on the ship's deck. (And here, once again, is the familiar Irish bibulous figure of fun, as described by a Yankee observer.) On the morning of the Battle of South Mountain, Sunday, September 14, Cobb again saw "the irrepressible Walsh," return from a foraging expedition in a nearby village "with a tea-kettle and cabbage—of course he was a tailor as well as a marine—and set to work boiling the vegetable." Interrupted by the order to fall in, "Walsh had not time to cook his cabbage; so he slung it, kettle and all, to his belt, in hopes of a chance to finish it." Company I approached the fighting at about 3:30 in the afternoon "upon a sunken road in which lay many dead and wounded Confederates. A few scattering shots from the forest in front saluted our appearance in the field. The momentary halt gave Walsh an opportunity to deposit his precious kettle in the corner of the wall, he now looking for warmer work. . . . That little scene among the trees, with the dead and wounded, their cadaverous faces and pale gray clothing, arms thrown up for mercy, and the little cloud of smoke dissipating above, left a vivid impression."

What follows is a picture of great confusion, contradictory orders, and heavy casualties. The commanding officer of the Thirty-fifth, Colonel Edward A. Wild, had his arm shot off almost immediately, and at day's end the regiment had lost 25 wounded and 9 men dead. Among these was twenty-six-year-old Private George F. Whiting from Dedham, who failed to survive the amputation of his leg. His was the first death in Company I. Three others were wounded, all from Dedham, including Henry Tisdale. The unhurt survivors were forced to spend the chilly night on the battlefield, and, says Cobb, "in the morning some made a breakfast upon the small round biscuit with which the haversacks of the dead Confederates about us were filled; others preferred to go hungry rather than do anything which seemed like robbing the dead. Whether Walsh recovered his kettle of cabbage was never reported."

Three mornings later and just a few miles farther west came Antietam, where the casualties in the Thirty-fifth were 150 wounded and 69 dead. In Company I, 11 men were wounded and 6 died. The regiment's *History* reports that after the battle, "men found their clothing and equipments bored by bullets in every conceivable way. He was the exception who had not some curiosity of the kind to exhibit. One man found a bullet hole through the flesh of his thigh, which he was not aware of in the excitement until he went to the creek to wash. Thrilling accounts were given of the deaths of the fallen, or of adventures in the fight." To this summary description, John Cobb adds that "Walsh, the man with the tea kettle, lay dead by the rail fence with the other noble fellows." Patrick Walsh was buried on the field.

Fredericksburg

After the great battle, the troops of the Thirty-fifth Massachusetts remained in camp at Antietam Creek until the end of October 1862, at which time they recrossed the Potomac River and marched down the east side of the

Blue Ridge Mountains in support of the Union cavalry. Their most significant fighting here was at Sulphur Springs, Virginia, on November 15, after which they marched to the vicinity of the little town of Fredericksburg, Virginia, where they went on picket and guard duty until the next disastrous engagement with the Confederate Army. McPherson's judgment of the Battle of Fredericksburg on December 13, 1862, is unequivocal: "When the early twilight finally turned to darkness the Union army had suffered one of its worst defeats of the war. Nearly 13,000 Federals were casualties—about the same number as at Antietam—most of them in front of the stone wall at the base of Marye's Heights. Fighting on the defensive behind good cover, the Confederates suffered fewer than 5,000 casualties. . . . Fredericksburg brought home the horrors of war to northerners more vividly, perhaps, than any previous battle."

Here was the worst case yet of valiant troops sacrificed to bungled orders from their generals. As part of the foolhardy, suicidal uphill thrust toward the well-defended Heights behind the town, the soldiers of the Thirty-fifth Massachusetts were among those mowed down like ripe corn before the scythe: 10 were killed outright and 60 wounded. As for Company I, their own Sidney Willard, thirty-one, now commander of the entire regiment, was killed, as were Lieutenant William Hill, twenty-nine, Corporal John McKew, twenty-two, and Private George Bunker, twenty. Many more from the company were wounded. Following the six-hour battle the Thirty-fifth endured an additional unrelieved twenty-eight hours of picket duty in the frozen mud.

Letter from John D. Cobb, December 26, 1862

In camp near Fredericksburg, Va.

Friend G.——

. . . The eleventh of this month commenced one of the most terrible battles which has been fought during this war. All day long the roar of cannon was terrific, and sounded like continuous bursts of thunder. We, the 35th, were then supporting a battery about four miles from the brigade camp. We marched that day about ten miles, back and forth, with the mud over our ankles. You can bet that we were a used-up set of boys. Just before sundown they succeeded in laying the pontoon bridges, and early Friday morning our brigade crossed and camped on the bank of the river, in front of the log houses used by the rebel sharpshooters, while our troops were crossing. We staid there all day and night, and lived high, in flour,

molasses, corned beef, found in the houses in the city. I think that the boys ransacked every house in the city. They broke open the safes in the banks, and abstracted the contents, and they broke into jewellers' shops, and paraded the streets with all manner of household utensils. The city was completely riddled with shot from our batteries. One splendid house had twenty-one shot-holes through it, and some were almost torn in pieces.

Saturday the big row came off. It commenced just outside the city at the foot of a range of hills, and nearly all day the solid shot, shell, grape, canister and minie balls fell as thick as hail stones in a storm. Just before we went into the fight I was sitting in the window of a house, when a shell came screeching and tearing through the house, and passed out within two and a half feet of my head, filling my eyes with mortar dust, &c. It struck in the street without bursting, and, glancing along, just grazed Sergeant Fiske's elbow, as he reclined in the street. It was rather uncomfortably nigh, but I noticed all hands kept their sitting, as we did not fear a repetition of the affair. In the fight, our boys did splendidly, and fought hard to drive the rebels from their intrenchments, but every effort proved unavailing, and the ground was covered with dead and wounded. I saw a solid shot strike one poor fellow in the bowels, cutting him nearly in two, and tearing off the leg of a member of Co. K, dashed it against the fence, and passed on its way. I lay within six feet of them at the time, and many who were nearer were spattered all over with fragments of flesh and blood. It was awful, but nobody seemed to mind it, the excitement was so great. After dark we withdrew from the field and slept in houses in the city. We were so near the rebel batteries that the reports of the guns and those of the shells, when they burst, seemed almost together. Sunday night our brigade was sent out on picket. and we laid for 28 long hours in the mud, with no covering, our guns in our hands, and not a man lifted his head a foot from the ground without having a bullet whiz uncomfortably near it. It was terrible, I tell you. I didn't move from my position but twice during the whole time. About 12 o'clock on Monday night we were relieved and marched across the bridge to our old camp, where we arrived about three in the morning, tired and completely used up. During the night all of our forces were withdrawing[,] the pontoons taken away, and when the rebels woke up in the morning they had the whole thing to themselves.

It is reported, and generally believed, that our whole division is to be sent to Alexandria. God grant that we may! Our wounded have all been sent to Washington, and all from Co. I are doing well. All of us have been pretty well, but all say that they wish somebody in Dedham thought enough of us to come and see us. No one has been to see Co. I, while nearly every other company has some friend to see them nearly all the time. Hoping soon to be at home all right, and with love to all inquiring friends, I am your friend, C.

A letter in the *Dedham Gazette* on January 3, 1863, contains a grim summation of the war so far for the Thirty-fifth: "The noble and gallant 35th regiment that four months ago left the Old Bay State with 1000 men, to-day only numbers 282 privates and 72 sergeants and corporals for duty; total enlisted men in camp for duty, 354. We have 107 non-commissioned officers and privates detached for extra duty, teamsters, nurses, &c., so that we have a total of 461 enlisted men on duty. To-day we have only 2 Captains and 4 Lieutenants in command of companies." The writer also reports that at Fredericksburg, "Major Willard fell as he was leading the regiment into the thickest of the fight. His last words to the men were, 'Come on boys; remember South Mountain and Antietam!' And well did they remember those terrible battles, and many a rebel fell under their fire."

Private Fisher Cleaveland

Here begin excerpts from the letters, extraordinary in their humanity and quiet heroism, of Private Fisher A. Cleaveland, a forty-three-year-old mechanic from East Freetown, Massachusetts, to his wife, Jane, and his children, Jennie, Hattie, and Henry. Wounded at Antietam, Cleaveland spent five months in a hospital. He rejoined Company I in February 1863 at their winter encampment near Newport News, Virginia.

Letter from Fisher A. Cleaveland, Newport News, Va., February 25, 1863

Dear Daughters I rec'd your letter last Monday night and was very glad to hear that you all were well I left the Distributing Camp wednesday night in a steamer for this place thursday night we anchored at the mouth of the Potomac and staid until the next morning a boat came alongside loaded with oysters they sold them all out to the soldiers aboard at 50 cts per bushel or 10 cts for a water pailful so that we had oysters for supper we eat them raw with a little pepper on them the river is from 2 to 6 miles wide and it is a very pleasant sail in good weather it rained and was foggy this day the next day we crossed the bay to fortress Monroe arrived at 3 PM . . . I found the boys well and hearty they looked a great deal better than I expected they never expected to see me again as they heard that I had lost my hand then my arm and finally that I was dead there is 61 men in my Co now besides the officers it is the second Co as to size in the regt Lieut Col Carruth and Adjt Wales arrived at camp on Saturday the soldiers were very glad to see them back as they have now got somebody to lead them and look out for them the Lieut Col has sent for all the men that are absent from the regt that are able to come back

Letter from Fisher A. Cleaveland, Newport News, March 3, 1863

Dear Daughters . . . The Capt has put me in assistant cook so that I have an easy time of it there is 61 men to cook for we have 2 men detailed to bring water every day we have to cut up our wood for cooking 2 of our Co are teamsters so that we have 63 men in our Co in Camp besides commissioned officers it is the largest Co in the regt there has been 81 men killed died of their wounds and of disease from Aug 22 to the first of Jan in our regt there is 460 men in camp now

Letter from Fisher A. Cleaveland, Newport News, March 22, 1863

Dear Daughter I rec'd yours of the 16th last night and had got about tired of looking for a letter as I have not rec'd any for 8 or 9 days before tell your mother she must do as she thinks best about the hay if there is any left there will not be any corn fodder to keep the cow on another winter we have had a snow storm here it began last Thursday morning and snowed until Saturday morning the snow was wet and about a foot deep on a level it rained Saturday to day is pleasant the snow is about gone and the ground will be about dry tonight. . . . my hand ached and was so numb with the cold that I told them that I was a fair weather cook and they must get some else to cook while it was so cold and stormy it was rather hard work to keep warm in the tents but we wraped up in our blankets drank warm coffee and kept pretty comfortable you can judge as to the room we have as our tents are not more than 8 foot square and 5 men to a tent we have to be pretty accomadating to each other to get along we are under marching orders now as understand our Lieut told me yesterday for Tennesee by the way of Baltimore and then by railroad there is a report to day that we are a going either to Newbern or Port Royal

Letter from Fisher A. Cleaveland, Camp of the 35 Regt near Winchester, Ky., May 14, 1863

Dear Jennie . . . my feet were very sore I had 4 large blisters on one foot but it is about well now new Shoes done it my health is very good I am glad to hear that you have got a good teacher you must try to improve as much as possible this term tell Henry and Hattie they must try to learn as fast as they can Henry must let me know how the sheep get along and how the rye looks and how the planting gets along I wish to know who lives in Mrs Spooner house I am glad that the money came safe as there has been a great deal lost sending but none from this regt. . . . how does the corn hold out and potatoes did you have hay enough to keep the cow out what is Mr Brown a doing do you get any Money or things of him how do you get along for wood now

Coming through Carbondale

Another of those startling connections with the past, the encircling loops that ensnare and connect us to family and cultural history, came when I read in the *History of the Thirty-Fifth* how the recuperating regiment moved west by rail in the spring of 1863, and then south to the sieges of Vicksburg and Jackson, Mississippi. The regiment set out in boxcars from Baltimore. After one bone-jarring night packed forty to a car, "in the morning the men found that riding upon the car-tops was as comfortable as within, barring the cinders and tunnels, and certainly better for viewing the scenery, for cattle do not require windows in their cars. Those were merry times, passing through the towns, the boys on top shouting and waving caps and flags, the citizens rushing to doors and windows to respond, small children astonished out of their wits, dogs barking, horses frightened, and a lively time generally." The word came that the Thirty-fifth was being lent to General Grant to add force to the siege of Vicksburg, and their journey by rail led from Cincinnati through Indiana and across the Wabash River at Vincennes into Illinois, where "warm greetings were extended to the troops by the inhabitants all along the route."

Then comes the next leg of the trip: "At Sandoval we changed direction from due west to south, taking the Illinois Central Railroad. . . . At Centralia, in the evening, pans of hot beef-steaks were passed into the cars, and devoured as ravenously as by the animals in a menagerie. . . . In the morning of June 7, we were at the jumping off place—Cairo—disembarking from the cars upon the levee, at the mouth of the Ohio." I live these days in the university town of Carbondale, Illinois, three blocks from the Illinois Central tracks that still connect Centralia and Cairo. And so, I find that my great-great-grandfather Winslow Radcliff rode through this place with his regiment during the night of June 6–7 in the year 1863. Not only that, but, following a most eventful summer in the South, he came back the same way, passing again through Carbondale during the night of August 12–13. The regimental historian says: "If we were a hard-looking set when we first passed this way, we were a deal rougher returning; but our welcome along the road was more hearty than ever; even the coarsest food of every-day life, offered along the way, was luxury after such a campaign." I cross those Illinois Central tracks several times a day, and, looking up and down the arrow-straight cut, I often think of Winslow and the men of Company I, so many of whom I now know by name, as they must have looked waving from the roofs of the boxcars on their brief holiday from hell.

At Cairo, on their way south, the Massachusetts soldiers transferred to the steamer *Imperial*, which took them down the Mississippi to Sherman's Landing, from which, on June 14, "downstream, looking south-east, lay in plain view the buildings of the city of Vicksburg." Acting only as backup, the Thirty-fifth saw no action during the siege, but they were on hand on July 4 when the triumphant Union Army under General Grant entered the city. Once more Company I and the rest of the regiment were witnesses to a crucial turning point, for, in James McPherson's view, "the capture of Vicksburg was the most important northern strategic victory of the war, perhaps meriting Grant's later assertion that 'the fate of the Confederacy was sealed when Vicksburg fell.'"

Before backtracking north in August, the Thirty-fifth Massachusetts went on to participate in the siege of Jackson, and to endure extremely harsh weather. As the regiment's *History* puts it, "The men affirm that they never, before nor since, experienced such torrid heat." On the march through Mississippi, "weak men, overcome, threw themselves down by the roadside in desperation; strong men fell, and lay struggling and frothing at the mouth; the ambulances and wagons were filled with the helpless. Those days cost the regiment more good men than a battle." These conditions certainly exacerbated the suffering of those already afflicted with wounds and disease. Seven members of the Thirty-fifth died of malarial fever in July and August, including, from Company I, Privates David Phalan, forty-five, of Dedham and Samuel Wright, thirty-eight, of Needham. After arriving back in Cincinnati in mid-August of 1863, the Thirty-fifth marched south through Kentucky and over the Cumberland Gap. They went on to take part in the siege of Knoxville and other operations in East Tennessee in the winter and spring of 1863–64.

The voices of Fisher Cleaveland and John Cobb chronicle the remainder of the time, beginning with their journey west enroute to Vicksburg, during which Private Winslow Radcliff was with the regiment.

Letter from Fisher A. Cleaveland, Cairo Ill., June 7, 1863

Dear Wife . . . we arrived at Nickolasville [Kentucky] at 4 PM having marched 32 miles in 22 hours from the time that we broke camp Wednesday night the road was very dry and dusty and the day very warm so that we sweat our dress coats through and were what I should call a dirty looking sett we took the Cars here for Cincinnati at 8 arrived there at 10 Friday morning we got a dinner or rather a supper here at the Sanitary Commission rooms at 4 PM of Coffee fried Ham pickles and soft bread and a hungry sett of us as you ever saw as we had no regular meal before that day we had a treat whilest on the side walk a Dedham man that lives in Cincinnati bought 2 boxes of Oranges 1 box was divided amongst our Co we than gave each man in the regt one a piece as far as they would go from Stanford Ky to here is about 150 miles we left here at 6 PM in the cars on the Ohio and Missippi railroad we stoped at Seymour 87 miles from Cinci and got Coffee our next stopping place was Vinncennes and got Coffee and soft bread we crossed the bridge here into Ill 148 miles from Cin–, we changed cars at Sandover 280 mile from Cin we rode 6 miles and stoped at Centralia and had a slice of beef Steak and a cup of Coffee brought into us in the car we rode all night and arrived at 5 this morning having marched some 40 miles and rode 516 miles in the cars since Wednesday night we shall take the steamer to day or tomorrow either for Memphis or Vicksburg . . . this [Cairo] is a small place of some 3 thousand inhabitants at junction of the Ohio and Missippi rivers if Vicksburg is not taken before we get there we shall probably see some fighting

Letter from Fisher A. Cleaveland, Memphis, Tenn.,
June 11, 1863, on board the steamer *Imperial*

Dear Wife We arrived here and were paid off last night for 2 months or up to the first of May I have sent 22 dollars some which will come the same as the last I sent we left Cairo Monday at 6 PM ran about 20 miles when the steamer ran onto a sand bar and did not get of until 6 the next morning passed Hickman Tenn about 9½ AM about 1 PM we stopped 4 miles above New Madrid on the Missouri side of the river we stopped an hour went on shore . . . we expect to leave here this afternoon for Vicksburg about 400 miles from here we shall not get there before Sunday I think at least and we may get fired on to and delayed before we get there about 30 thousand men have already been sent down to reinforce Grant . . . I shall write to Ormond when I get to Vicksburg I wish that you would send the Standard and write as often as you can as I beleive I have not rec'd but 2 letters from you since I left home tell the children that I have not forgot them or the neighbors either but I do not feel as if there was much that would be interesting to write about I shall put in a few shells in this I must now close so good bye for the present and be sure and not work to hard as I do not beleive it is your duty to make yourself a slave for your children but make them help you as they can save you a great many steps so that you can go out and enjoy yourself

Letter from John D. Cobb, near Jackson, Miss., July 15, 1863

Dear Father:—As a mail is about to leave camp, after a long interval, I take the opportunity to let you know of my welfare and whereabouts. I wrote to you last from the rear of Vicksburg, July 3d. I wrote in the morning, and of course was not able to give out the great and glorious news of the surrender which took place, as I understand, on that evening. . . . At night, rather unexpectedly, we received orders to pack up and start after Johnson, who was supposed to have retreated towards this place. . . .

The country here is much more level than about Vicksburg, is heavily wooded, and water is only obtained from cisterns and hollows where the rain has been collected. We have the hottest weather I ever experienced. One day the thermometer is reported to have stood at 114 deg. in the shade. What marching in closed ranks over a dusty road is I leave you to imagine. While I write the perspiration makes my hand so wet that I daub the paper all over with marks, as you see, and which you must excuse under the circumstances. Many of our boys have been sun-struck. . . .

All the Company are doing well at present. We lost a Lieutenant, Act [ing] Quart[ermaster], by the fall of a tree struck by lightning. Give my love to all, and tell them we are doing our best to finish the war, and come home to enjoy peace with you. With much love to you, my ever dear father, I sign myself your son, J. D. Cobb

Letter from Fisher A. Cleaveland, Milldale, two miles from Snyder Bluff, Miss., July 26, 1863

Dear Daughter . . . we marched until 7 P M and then encamped when we started at 4 our regt had some 200 men in ¾ of an hour we had not more than 50 left it was the hottest marching that I ever saw we had but 4 officers left Lieut Col Mitchell of the 51st NY who has commanded us since our Col was sunstruck so was the adjt Capt Parks Capt Pratt and some other officers and some 20 or 30 men we have had some 60 men in our regt sunstruck since the 4th of July but one has died of it yet other regts have suffered about as much there is the most men sick and haveing sores that I ever saw I had a boil on my knee and 3 around it I had my knapsack carried and made out to keep up we started on our march from our camp 1 mile from the Big Black river at 4 P M we had just crossed it when it began to rain in 3 minutes the most of the men were wet through where there was no water before in that time there was brooks a running as large as pond brook in the spring we kept on a marching until 10 when we encamped for the night it was the hardest marching that I ever saw the mud and water was shoe deep and slippery some the men tumbled down and were a pretty looking sett of fellows if we did not look out we were in the water ½ way up to our knees

Letter from Fisher A. Cleaveland, Milldale, Miss., August 2, 1863

Dear Wife . . . there is more sickness in the regt than ever before as to boils there is no end to them in the Corps those that have them are not sick when I got into camp I could hardly go in 4 days I had it opened and got ½ a tea cup of matter out of it I have had poulticed ever since it has got so near well that I can walk pretty well I caught cold the night that we crossed the big black as we had a thunder shower and got wet through but it is now about well I feel better than I have for 2 months we do not know when we shall leave as we have been a waiting for transports the last 10 days and there is none at the landing now but I hope we shall get out of this State soon for if we do not there will more die by sickness in this Corps than if we had been in a tough battle one of our Co died and was buried last thursday there is not a day but there is several funerals we know by hearing the volleys fired over thier graves

Letter from Fisher A. Cleaveland, Paris, Ky., August 23, 1863

To Jennie Dear Daughter Our regt arrived here last night on a wagon train from Covington . . . we marched 16 miles before we came up with the train there was but 220 of us that are fitt for duty in the regt the rest are sick and carried off to the hospitals we started Wednesday morning at 5 there was but 30 waggon that stoped and 10 that brought our baggage we al rode which is rather easier than marching but it is not the easiest seat in the world to ride on our knapsack in a baggage wagon we got terribly shook up before we got here we stoped at Crittendon and encamped we came 11 miles to day I had a tuch of the chills here it took me at 2½ PM I had been a sweating and began to feel rather chilly I put on vest and dress coat and buttoned them up I then took my India rubber and carried it out spread in the sun and laid down on it but it did no good as I would shake some and felt as cold as ever it lasted 1½ hours when I was sick at my stomach

Among those who were "sick and carried off to the hospitals" was my ancestor, Winslow Radcliff, for whom the shooting war ended here. Fisher Cleaveland remained with the Thirty-fifth Massachusetts for the march into East Tennessee and beyond. Here are excerpts from two more of his letters:

Letter from Fisher A. Cleaveland, camp near
Crab Orchard, Ky. September 12, 1863

To Jennie Dear Daughter . . . I have to go to the surgeon 3 times a day after medicine but you need not think that I am sick as I shall probably have to go some time yet as he gives me what he calls a small dose but it answers every purpose my apetite is very good all the trouble is due to craveing I am glad to hear that those trees bear and that Apples are plenty at home you must look and try to dry for I shall want some dried Apple pies when I get home as I expect to be at home in the spring I told the boys some 6 weeks ago that I expected to be home in season to plant the garden in the spring and I see nothing yet to alter my mind as to fighting it is about played out with rebs in these parts we may have to into battle again but I think it very doubtful but sometimes I think I had about lives go into battle as to do so much hard marching there is times when we fare hard and are all tired out that we feel as if we had as lives fight as not it makes feel kind of reckless at such times I should almost pity any force of an equal number that were obliged to fight us

Letter from Fisher A. Cleaveland, camp of the Army of East Tenn, 19 miles northeast from Knoxville, December 19, 1863

To Jennie Dear Daughter . . . we have been besieged in Knoxville 18 days since I wrote I was out in front as skirmisher 7 days in that time and our regt made 2 charges in that time it lost 2 men killed one belonged to our Co and 4 men wounded and 2 taken prisoners the rebs had rather the hot end of the poker that time they charged our own works and undertook to take Benjamins battery but they could not come in they had 319 men killed right out and some 5 to 6 hundred men wounded and taken prisoner our loss was 26 killed and wounded . . . our regt has had the hardest time for the last 2 months that it has had since it came out one bullet struck my cap if it had gon ½ an inch lower it would have struck my head however I do not believe that the ball is cast to kill me

This conviction, happily, was borne out. Fisher Cleaveland survived to the war's end and was one of the 45 of the original 101 members of Company I to be mustered out on June 9, 1865. His last letter home to East Freetown is dated April 30, 1865. In it, he tells his daughter Jennie to "tell [his son] Henry to get all the manure ready to plant as I may be at home in season to do the most of it."

"Disability One Half"

Though seriously ill since Fredericksburg, Winslow Radcliff had remained with his regiment through the sweltering summer of 1863 in Mississippi, and then as they marched north and east for 700 miles to Paris, Kentucky. There, according to his discharge papers, he left his compatriots and was sent to the field hospital in Dennison, Ohio, where he arrived on August 26. His discharge states that "Private Winslow Radcliff" was ultimately sent home from the military hospital at Portsmouth Grove, Rhode Island, on November 19, 1863, suffering from "Phthisis Pulmonalis [tuberculosis of the lungs] contracted during the battle of Fredericksburg in December 1862." After that battle, the document continues, he "did duty with his Regiment more or less up to August last when he was sent to Camp Dennison Hospital, O[hio]. Has done no duty since. Unfit for Invalid Corps. Disability one half (½)." Winslow had also been diagnosed with "Chronic Dysentery," which was unabated from August to his discharge in November. He had been through the Battles of South Mountain, Antietam, and

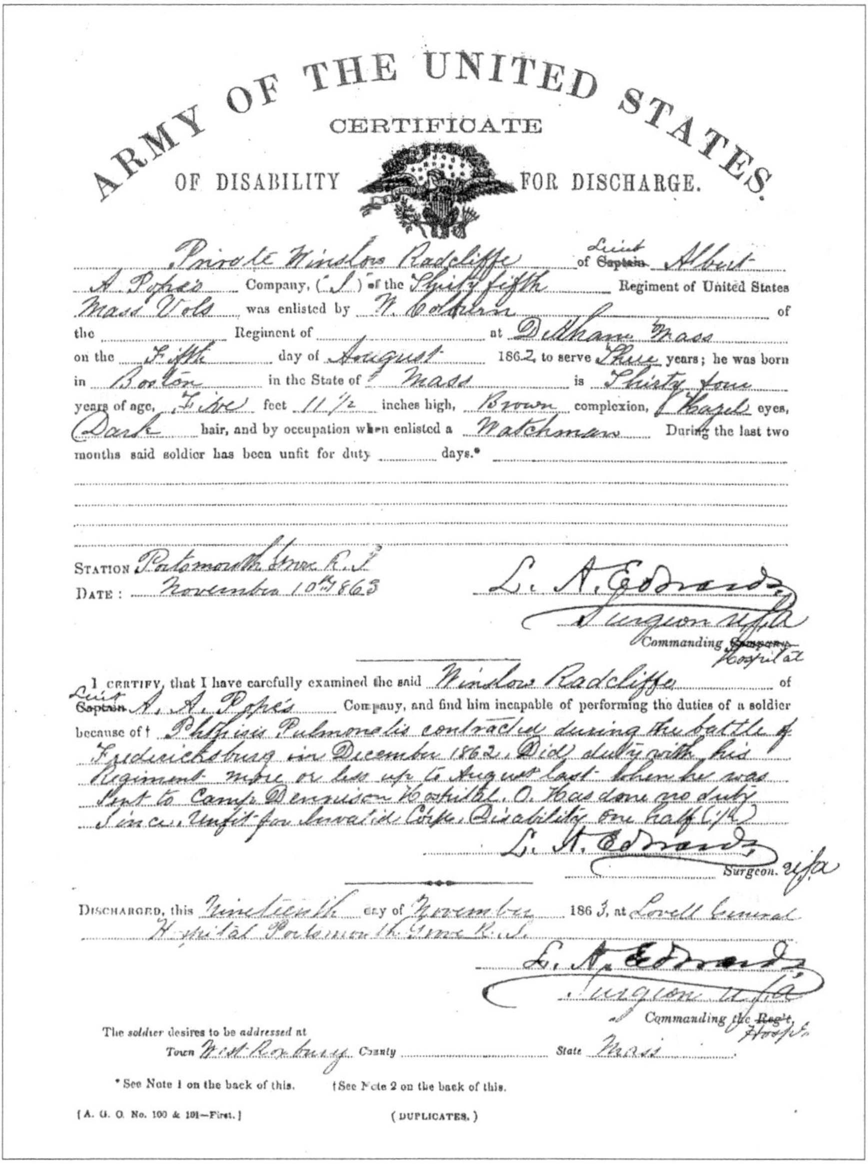

ARMY OF THE UNITED STATES

CERTIFICATE

OF DISABILITY FOR DISCHARGE.

Private Winslow Radcliffe of ~~Captain~~ Lieut Albert A. Pope's Company, (I) of the Thirty fifth Regiment of United States Mass Vols was enlisted by N. Colburn of the Regiment of at Dedham Mass on the Fifth day of August 1862, to serve Three years; he was born in Boston in the State of Mass is Thirty four years of age, Five feet 11 1/2 inches high, Brown complexion, Hazel eyes, Dark hair, and by occupation when enlisted a Watchman. During the last two months said soldier has been unfit for duty days.*

STATION Portsmouth Grove R.I.

DATE: November 10th 1863

L. A. Edwards

Surgeon U.S.A.

Commanding ~~Surgeon~~ Hospital

I CERTIFY, that I have carefully examined the said Winslow Radcliffe of ~~Captain~~ Lieut A. A. Pope's Company, and find him incapable of performing the duties of a soldier because of† Phthisis Pulmonalis contracted during the battle of Fredericksburg in December 1862. Did duty with his Regiment more or less up to August last when he was sent to Camp Dennison Hospital O. Has done no duty since. Unfit for Invalid Corps. Disability one half (1/2)

L. A. Edwards

Surgeon. U.S.A.

DISCHARGED, this Nineteenth day of November 1863, at Lovell General Hospital Portsmouth Grove R.I.

L. A. Edwards

Surgeon U.S.A.

Commanding the ~~Reg't~~ Hosp'l.

The soldier desires to be addressed at

Town West Roxbury County State Mass

* See Note 1 on the back of this. † See Note 2 on the back of this.

[A. G. O. No. 100 & 101—First.] (DUPLICATES.)

Figure 11. Winslow Radcliff's *Certificate of Disability for Discharge* from the Union Army, November 19, 1863. Courtesy of Margaret Fanning.

Fredericksburg, the sieges of Vicksburg and Jackson, and the marching summer of 1863. After returning home, he got back his old job as a watchman for the railroad, and his income was supplemented by a pension of $8 per month as a disabled veteran. But subsequent events prove that he never recovered from the war.

In the late 1860s and beyond, there was much discussion about the effects of the Civil War upon those who had fought it. One set of answers from Massachusetts officialdom is a stunning example of whitewash and wishful thinking worthy of our latter-day political spin doctors. It was the bright idea of Massachusetts Adjutant-General William Schouler to send off the following query to the municipal officers of every town in the state in December 1865: "Gentlemen,—As a matter of public interest, I am endeavoring to ascertain what proportion, if any, of the returned soldiers belonging to your town have been guilty of any crime since their return home; or whether their habits have been better, or worse, than they were before they entered the army." Schouler allowed as how "my opinion is that, as a body, they are as good men now as they were when they enlisted in the service of their country," and it is hardly surprising that the gathered results dramatically corroborated his preconceived view. All but eleven of Massachusetts cities and towns replied, and of the 324 responses, 203 found no visible change in the veterans, 113 detected "social and moral improvement," and only eight "testified to the contrary, although," the compiler felt compelled to add, "in very various degrees and sometimes on trivial points." The town of Dedham, home to so many in Company I, reported no measurable change. Several surrounding towns, however, logged in on the sunny side, among them Needham ("My opinion is that they are better men than they were before they entered the service"), along with Sharon, Dover, Weston, Medfield, Franklin, Stoughton, and Lincoln, where, "so far as my observation extends, they have returned home vastly improved in personal appearance and gentlemanly manners and bearing, and thus better fitted for the duties of citizens."

This halcyon perspective suggests that there was little enough support around the village greens of the Bay State for the many returned veterans—and Winslow Radcliff was certainly among them—for whom postwar reality was quite other. As resounding counterweight to the Schouler view, we have, of course, the evidence of thousands of pictures, letters, narratives, and histories from which the full enormity of the experience of this war emerges. Eric Dean's 1997 monograph, *Shook Over Hell: Post-Traumatic Stress, Vietnam, and the Civil War* (Cambridge: Harvard

University Press, 1997), is especially useful to an understanding of what befell my ancestor and so many others. After studying the medical records of Union Army veterans who spent time in Indiana's central state insane asylum after the war, Dean concluded that virtually all these men suffered from the malady that was identified only after Vietnam as post-traumatic stress disorder (PTSD). He points out that "thousands and thousands of Civil War veterans were wracked with pain for the rest of their lives from the consequences of malaria, typhoid, rheumatism, camp fevers, and epidemic diseases, unrelenting gastrointestinal pain and discomfort, and agonizing pain from poorly performed operations on gunshot wounds, from which bone fragments would work their way out ten and twenty years after the war—all of this in addition to the psychological complications of warfare, such as flashbacks, nightmares, survivor guilt, and the like." Dean finds that among the prevalent physiological causes of acute PTSD in the "Indiana sample" were stomach pain and diarrhea from chronic dysentery, and the abuse of opium in relieving tubercular coughing. Unlocalized anxiety and dread, depression, cognitive disorder, and suicidal tendencies were the common accompanying psychological symptoms. Indeed, 51 percent of the 291 men whose records he studied "either attempted or completed suicide, or were regarded in some measure as 'suicidal' at the time of their [asylum] commitment."

Winslow Radcliff left the Union Army suffering from dysentery and tuberculosis, according to his discharge papers, which also describe him as "Five feet 11½ inches high, Brown complexion, Hazel eyes, Dark hair." He left no letters, and the only example of his handwriting that survives is a signature of ownership in a family Bible. There is, however, one photograph. In it, Winslow is gaunt and hollow-cheeked, with thinning hair. Extraordinary in a formal portrait, which this obviously is, his visage is scowling, suspicious, shifty-eyed, distraught. He looks hunted and haunted. There are left to us also two articles from local newspapers that report his suicide at age fifty-one on April 7, 1874—nine years almost to the day after Lee's surrender at Appomattox Courthouse. One chilling detail suggests what those years must have been like: he had tried to kill himself seven times before. As countless chronicles make clear, Winslow's hard fate was far from uncommon among his generation of Civil War veterans. His life and sad end are part of a pervasive tapestry of pain that connects our family to the most traumatic era in American history. Here, then, are the public words that were my great-great-grandfather's only testimonial.

Figure 12. Winslow Radcliff after the war. Courtesy of Francis Fanning.

Attleborough Chronicle, Saturday, April 11, 1874

Winslow Radcliff committed suicide at his home last Tuesday. Early in the morning it was found that he had been eating opium and drinking rum all through the night. All appearance of life had gone. Physicians were called and by their assistance about the middle of the afternoon he was for a few moments aroused from his stupor but he soon relapsed into unconsciousness and died about 4 o'clock. Mr. Radcliff had been employed in taking care of the depot at North Attleboro. He had lately been discharged from his situation which was partially the cause of his act, although he had on seven previous occasions attempted to take his own life. He had a wife living in Dedham where his home was. He also had a son who lived with him in North Attleboro and who was also in the employ of the Branch Railroad. The sudden and strange death of his father so completely deranged the mind of the son that on Wednesday night he also attempted suicide in the same manner as his father. The close attention of physicians and friends prevented the fatal results. In the case of the father's death the evidence was so conclusive that Coroner A. M. Sperry rightly deemed an inquest unnecessary. The funeral services were observed on Thursday.

Dedham Transcript, Saturday, April 11, 1874

RASH ATTEMPT AT SUICIDE—The neighborhood of Church Street in this village was thrown into a state of considerable excitement on Wednesday night and Thursday morning by the fact that a young man named Benjamin Radcliffe, whose father lay dead in the house on that thoroughfare from suicide committed in Attleboro', had made an attempt upon his life by the same means—poison. Dr. Mansfield was called, but no stomach-pump being at hand, it was decided to save his life by keeping the patient awake by walking him about the streets, which was done during the whole night. This project was successful, and the son was able to attend the funeral of his father which took place on Thursday afternoon. The drug was supposed to be laudanum or opium, and the mental shock caused by his father's rash action is assigned as a reason. The father was buried in West Roxbury.

And that was where my sister and I found him, in an isolated spot at the rear of the tiny Westerly Burial Ground in West Roxbury. His wife Sophia's poverty probably dictated the fact that a place was found for Winslow there in Draper heaven. She and their children have their own plot several miles away in Dedham. The volunteer sexton at Westerly was excited to find out about Winslow from us. He had been looking for information about this non-Draper interloper for years. Listing a bit to the right, Winslow's small stone is one of the unadorned, standard-issue markers that were put up after the war by the Grand Army of the Republic veterans organization. It reads:

WINSLOW RADCLIFFE

CO. I

35TH MASS. INF.

There is nothing else on the stone. A small, bleached-out American flag drags on the grass to the side.

Figure 13. Winslow Radcliff's grave, Westerly Burial Ground, West Roxbury, Massachusetts. Photograph by Charles Fanning.

Again, Hawthorne comes to mind: *But alas! It was a dream of evil omen for young Goodman Brown. A stern, a sad, a darkly meditative, a distrustful, if not a desperate man, did he become, from the night of that fearful dream. . . . Often, awaking suddenly at midnight, he shrank from the bosom of Faith, and at morning or eventide, when the family knelt down at prayer, he scowled, and muttered to himself, and gazed sternly at his wife, and turned away. And when he had lived long, and was borne to his grave, a hoary corpse, . . . they carved no hopeful verse upon his tombstone; for his dying hour was gloom.*

4

Mapping Monaghan

> Scattered over the hills, tribal
> And placenames, uncultivated pearls.
> No rock or ruin, *dún* or dolmen
> But showed memory defying cruelty
> Through an image-encrusted name.
>
> —John Montague, "A Lost Tradition"

All students of Irish genealogy know that journeying back into the nineteenth century is not easy. In June 1922 the Irish Civil War began with the bombing by provisional Irish government forces of Dublin's Four Courts building, a beautiful Georgian landmark on the River Liffey which had been occupied by members of the un-disbanded Irish Republican Army. These IRA men were opponents of the treaty that had ended the Irish Revolution in December 1921 but provided for the partition of the island into the Irish Free State and the Northern Ireland statelet: six Ulster counties still under British rule. An unforeseen result of this violent event was the destruction of most original Irish census schedules. Quite literally, the historical record of millions of individuals who had lived, worked, and died in Ireland was obliterated in a flash. The bits and pieces that survived the firestorm in the Public Records Office reveal that since the early nineteenth century, this record had been kept with awesome detail, which included religion, ages, occupations, marital status of children, cause of death of decedents, and literacy in English. The terrible loss to history of the burning of the Four Courts left extant only two wholesale surveys of the population of Ireland in the nineteenth century. These are the *Tithe Applotment Books*, tallied between 1823 and 1838, and *Griffith's Valuation*, made between 1848 and 1864. Both were created as aids to the levying of taxes, or "tithes," which were paid by the predominantly Catholic tenants to support the Church of Ireland (Protestant) ministers in their home areas.

Not long ago, I found that most of the information we had about our

Fanning immigrant ancestor was wrong. We thought he had come to the United States as a small child, in about 1830, from the northern Ireland city of Belfast. The revised version came from his naturalization records, which I hadn't known existed until they popped up in the papers of a second or third cousin. These revealed that Phillip Fanning, born on August 14, 1828, in the mid-Ulster county of Monaghan, travelled to New York City from Liverpool as a young adult of twenty-two on March 14, 1851. He came as one of 413 passengers on the *Queen of the West*, a clipper built not long before for the immigrant trade and well enough appointed to indicate sufficient available money for a relatively comfortable passage. Just over two years later, on May 26, 1853, Phillip Fanning, listing his occupation as "laborer," was married in Roxbury, Massachusetts, by the Reverend P. O'Beirne to Margaret of many last names—variously recorded over the years as Bohan, Bowen, Bourne, Boughan, and Brigham—also a native of Ireland. She had arrived in New York, also at the age of twenty-two but accompanied by her mother, on the *Columbus* on February 17, 1851. These newlyweds went against the tide of many fellow immigrants by leaving the city for the rural community of Needham, Massachusetts, where Phillip set up as a farmer. They had seven surviving children over the next fifteen years. Their first child, born in Needham in 1854, was my great-grandfather, "Walking John" Fanning.

Phillip Fanning's parents were John Fanning and Elizabeth Ann Bradford, both of whom lived their entire lives in Ireland. (Phillip was later to follow established Ulster onomastic practice in naming two of his children, John and Elizabeth, for their grandparents.) The *Griffith's Valuation* of County Monaghan was done in 1860, and at that point, ten years after the Great Famine, there were only three Fannings listed in the whole county, if the usually accurate "Householders' Index" is to be credited. All were in the civil parish of Monaghan, which radiates from Monaghan town, north central in the county. This was certainly the place to start, especially as two of the three were named John. In 1860, the first John Fanning was renting plot 33 of the "Park street Intersects" in the town of Monaghan itself. Although the house, yard, and small garden included no measureable acreage, the holding was valued at a not inconsiderable £26. The other Monaghan listing for a John Fanning was a small plot of just over five acres in the townland of Knockaturly, which lies three miles south of Monaghan town. This holding included no buildings, and it was valued at only £3, 5 shillings. After discussing the evidence with genealogists in America and Ireland, I am convinced that these two John Fannings were the same man. The Knockaturly plot was probably the old home place back before the Great Famine of the late 1840s. For reasons that are not far to seek, John Fanning could have left this place, letting the buildings fall down, in order to seek a better life in town as a shopkeeper or craftsman. The third Monaghan Fanning named in *Griffith's* was Patrick, who was renting a six-acre plot valued at under £6 in Urbalkirk, the next townland east of Knockaturly.

I next moved backward to that earlier slice of daylight into nineteenth-century Irish rural culture—the *Tithe Applotment Books*. It came as no surprise that there were more Fannings being counted on the ground of County Monaghan at that point in time. Obviously, there were more members of every family everywhere in pre-Famine Ireland. In contrast to the three (or two) Fannings in the entire county in *Griffith's* (all of them in the one civil parish of Monaghan), the Tithe Book for Monaghan parish alone (obviously the place to look, given the information in *Griffith's*) contained nine possible names. Because of the exigencies of spelling in the early nineteenth century, there were no exact "Fannings" but three variants: Fannen, Fannon, and Fannin. These nine renters appeared in seven separate townlands, five of which are within four miles of Monaghan town. The largest holding by far was sixteen acres. The others ranged from nine down to five. Not much to build on here in the years of increasing deprivation leading up to the Famine.

Because their names will not likely appear elsewhere, I cite them all—by townland, with acreage and total valuation:

At Ardaghey Kill, Edward and Phill Fannin & Margret Fannin, renting 7 acres, valued at £7, no shillings, 2 pence.

At Cornamunady, Pat Fannon, renting 5 acres, valued at £7, no shillings, 6 pence.

At Dancinear, Patrick Fannen, renting 16 acres, valued at £24, 5 shillings, 9 pence.

At Lisseraw, James Fannen, renting 9 acres, valued at £11, 19 shillings, 10 pence.

At Knockaturly, Francis Fannon, renting 6 acres, valued at £4, 16 shillings, 2 pence.

At Sheetrim, Pat Fannen, renting 7 acres, valued at £7, 19 shillings, 2 pence.

At Urbilkerk, John Fannin, renting 6 acres, valued at £5, 12 shillings, 8 pence.

The Monaghan *Tithe Book* is dated 12 December 1826, which is less than two years before the birth in that county of my immigrant ancestor Phillip to John and Elizabeth Fanning. Furthermore, in that book only one tenant named John is listed for the civil parish of Monaghan. Therefore, I claim this John Fannin, small farmer at Urbilkerk, parish of Monaghan, county of Monaghan, province of Ulster, as my great-great-great grandfather. It is my corollary assumption that by the *Griffith's Valuation* year of 1860, John Fannin's six-acre farm in the townland (now spelled "Urbalkirk") had passed to Patrick (now spelled "Fanning"), presumably the eldest son remaining at home.

Approaching Urbalkirk

Linguistically, the name of this townland itself conveys the dual heritage of the North of Ireland, combining *urbal,* the Old Irish noun for "tail," as in the tail of an animal, and the Scots *kirk,* for "church." So, it means "the tail of a church." The shape of Urbalkirk may somewhat resemble a smashed-down, slightly curving tail, although to me it looks more like a top-heavy, lopsided turnip. Not surprisingly, taxation of Ireland by England had prompted the earliest recorded mentions of the townland by name. It was already on the books as "Veblekirke" on the first attempt at an Irish census in 1659, in which were counted four people, all of them Irish, as liable for a special poll tax. (For the whole of Monaghan parish, the numbers were 32 English and 101 Irish. The context was the wholesale Ulster land confiscations of the seventeenth century and the confusion that surrounded the restoration of Charles II to the throne.)

With characteristic graciousness, the Newberry Library made me a copy of Ordnance Survey sheet number 13 for County Monaghan, published in 1835, which includes Urbalkirk and environs. To get closer to the ground sense of the place, I then had a copy shop enlarge Urbalkirk to a two-foot square, which I laid out on my cellar workbench. Using colored pencils, I outlined the townland and its larger roads in red, then shaded and stippled in green and brown the areas designated as bog and wasteland. There were a lot of these, reinforcing my sense of County Monaghan as a boggy, rocky, uneven landscape, not well suited for agriculture. (The name itself, *Muineachán,* means "a place abounding in little hills.") I have since found an original sheet of the 1836 "Index to the Townland Survey of the County of Monaghan," which served as a title page and key to the thirty-four

Ordnance Survey sheets covering the entire county. This is an extremely detailed map in its own right, containing black dots for hundreds of buildings, and it now hangs on the wall beside my desk, where, with the aid of a magnifying glass, I can get lost in it at will.

I've had some fun poking around in the *dindshenchas* of Monaghan, especially where the vocation of writing is concerned. It turns out that one of the most famous places there in the earliest recorded times was the monastery at Druim Sneachta (meaning "ridge of snows"). The spot, now Drumsnat, is less than five miles northwest of Urbalkirk, and, in a bit of a stretch, I can see the tail of my family's townland actually pointing in that direction. The monastery was founded before the year 600 by Saint Mo Lua, a native of County Limerick who was selected by Saint Comhghal for special training at Bangor on the northeast coast of Ulster. Advised not to found a monastery in his own "country," perhaps through fear of not having his prophecy honored there, he set out for Monaghan "with a few monks and five cows." According to historian James Kenney, the monastery at Druim Sneachta was the source of "the oldest secular [Irish] manuscript of which we have genuine knowledge," the *Book of Drumsnat* (*Cín Dromma-Snechta*), "which may have been as old as the first half of the eighth century." The original is lost, but transcriptions made from it in the later Middle Ages show that it was a collection of the old heroic texts. Among these is one of the earliest narratives of the material that was later organized as *Táin Bó Cúailnge*.

Monaghan is also the home place of Ireland's first great modern writer from a rural background, Patrick Kavanagh, who was born in 1904 in the townland of Mucker, parish of Iniskeen, in the far south of the county. In prose and verse both, he describes growing up among small, hardscrabble farms of five or six acres (like that of my ancestors) where the land was watery, rocky, and unproductive but also inspiring in its beauty: "Walking through the meadow in summer was a great excitement. The simple, fantastic beauty of ordinary things growing—marsh-marigolds, dandelions, thistles and grass." Kavanagh's faith in the inexhaustible value of the local is pervasive in his work. I share wholeheartedly the faith he declares: "Oddly enough the village, though only a mile from my birthplace, was always outside the orbit of my most intimate interests. To know fully even one field or one lane is a lifetime's experience. In the world of poetic experience it is depth that counts and not width. A gap in a hedge, a smooth rock surfacing a narrow lane, a view of a woody meadow, the stream at the junction of four small fields—these are as much as a man can fully experience."

Copies of the Ordnance Survey (OS) maps, keyed to the family-holding numbers in *Griffith's Valuation*, are kept in Ireland's Valuation Office on Lower Abbey Street in Dublin. With the maps are the handwritten books recording all transactions involving the land from the time of *Griffith's* on up. In other words, these maps and records are still very much in use—which surprised me when I first learned of it, though it shouldn't have. Similarly old and sometimes older artifacts are the tools of the real estate trade in American towns and counties as well, as anyone who has had to have a title search done—and gasped at the cost—knows. But the fact that the landholding of my Irish ancestors could be pinpointed so accurately, and might still be identifiable as a discrete chunk, was, again, an exciting prospect. I took this final step in the research journey during a trip to Dublin a few years ago.

In the 1860 *Griffith's Valuation* for the townland of Urbalkirk, the six-acre holding of Patrick Fanning is listed as number 1 of 29 separate parcels of land. All the holdings are small, and the average is under ten acres. The entire townland contains 271 acres, 3 rods, and 30 perches. Moreover, the same numbers were in force in the land-record ledgers. Patrick Fanning's six-acre plot was number 1 of 29 separate listings in the earliest entry for Urbalkirk, which was dated 1 February 1864. When hauled out and placed carefully beside me in the Valuation Office, these books were as impressively bulky as the Ordnance Survey maps. And here, section by section and ledger by ledger, my Irish family's land transactions marched through the years. The records were really quite beautiful, handwritten in different colored inks for the various entries on each separate page, and they put me in mind of the cryptic codes in the Mississippi family ledgers that held so many revelations for Isaac McCaslin in William Faulkner's great novella "The Bear." The capstone came when the attendant brought out the accompanying map—a sheet of OS 13 covered over with small figures and notations. On it I found number 1 for Urbalkirk—a small plot in the far northwest corner of the townland. There it was. What a thrill to put my finger on the very spot from which the Fanning family patriarch had come out to America!

The first change in the ledger entries came in 1883, when the "Reps" (meaning representatives) of Patrick Fanning took over. This gave me the year of Patrick's death and made me wonder if the Monaghan native Patrick Fanning, age twenty-two, who joined the Royal Irish Constabulary in 1886 (a fact found in another search by my cousin Margaret) had been his son, giving up on the land. In any case, the holding was in some disarray for the

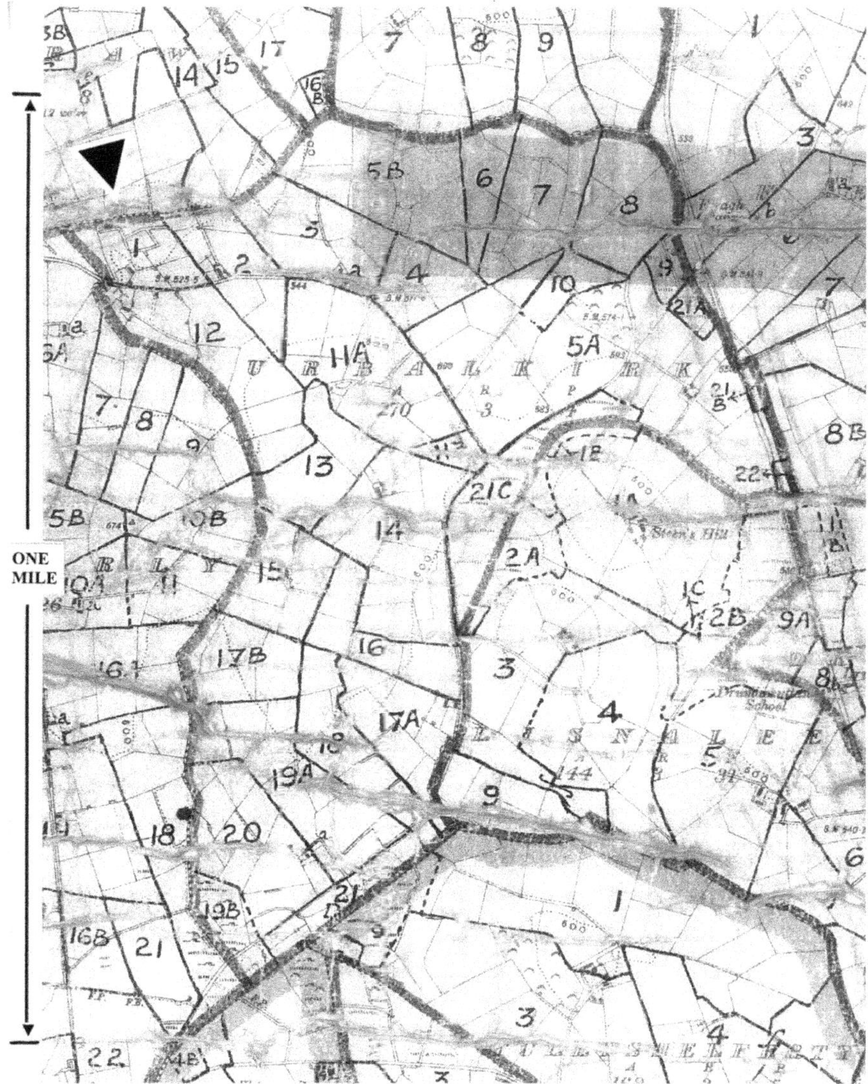

Figure 14. Government Valuation Map (detail), Townland of Urbalkirk, County Monaghan. Valuation Office, Dublin 1, Ireland. The Fanning holding is number 1 in the northwest corner of the townland.

following twenty-five years, as no single family member emerged until the reps of Patrick gave over to a new John Fanning in 1908. Perhaps a grandson of Patrick, this John brought back the oldest original name we have: John Fannin, the father of Phillip the immigrant, who had been on the land at the time of the Tithe Applotment survey in 1826. Then came the vital historical entry: "In Fee L. A. P.," dated 1909. This was the year when John Fanning "bought" the holding on which his family had farmed for at least a hundred years, and probably much longer. "L. A. P." means that it was a Land Act Purchase, under the terms of the quietly revolutionary British legislation that culminated in the Wyndham Act of 1903, whereby the massive transfer of ownership back to the people had been made possible by means of 100 percent mortgages to the tenants, combined with bonuses to the landlords for selling. By 1909, this was a common enough occurrence that a red rubber stamp was used to mark the plot-by-plot transactions.

In the near-century of ledgers from 1909 to 2002, I found just two more key entries. Mrs. John Fanning became the "In Fee L. A. P." owner in 1923, a date that probably marks her husband's death, and in 1966 the holding was sold to one Felix McKenna, which gave me the date when the Fannings left their land. From 1826 to 1966, the Fanning plot (number 1 in the townland of Urbalkirk, parish of Monaghan, County of Monaghan) had remained at the same size of just over 6 acres and the same valuation of under £6.

Meet the Westenras

One of my favorite books when I was about seven was that early Dr. Seuss classic *The 500 Hats of Bartholomew Cubbins,* which opens with two graphic contrasting perspectives on the same territory. From his mountaintop palace, King Derwin of Didd looks down on his subjects, "first, over the spires of the noblemen's castles, across the broad roofs of the rich men's mansions, then over the little houses of the townsfolk, to the huts of the farmers far off in the fields." The narrator declares, "It was a mighty view and it made King Derwin feel mighty important." From the doorway of his hut on the edge of a cranberry bog, the small boy of the title sees "exactly the same view," but he sees it "backward," with the result that "it was a mighty view, but it made Bartholomew Cubbins feel mighty small."

The adventure begins when Bartholomew goes to town on a Saturday morning with a basket of cranberries to sell. He's wearing his only hat, "an old one that had belonged to his father and his father's father before him." When King Derwin's sparkling entourage rolls by, Bartholomew naturally takes off his hat, only to find that, magically, another has taken its place on his head. Infuriated at the insult, the king orders the "impudent trickster's" removal to his castle for punishment. Hats keep flying off the boy's head all the way to the castle, and no one can figure out what is happening. Stupidly, if reluctantly, the king decides to execute Bartholomew for insubordination, and he is led to the highest turret of the castle to be pushed off. (Every time I read the book, I was appalled anew by this decision.) As they climb the winding stair, Bartholomew desperately takes off hat after hat. But now comes a striking change: hat number 451 (the king's record keeper has been keeping track) has two feathers in it, whereas the original and its 449 followers had had only one. From here, the hats get progressively more elaborate, until Bartholomew steps out on the battlement wearing number 500, "the most beautiful hat that had ever been seen in the Kingdom of Didd." On the spot, the king buys the hat from Bartholomew for 500 pieces of gold and sends him home. It is clear that only Derwin's vanity has spared the boy. When the hat is removed, Bartholomew feels "the cool evening breezes blow through his hair." At long last, his head is bare, and he shouts, "Look, Your Majesty! *Look!*" The king replies, "No! *You* look at *me!*"

I hadn't thought about this book for years, but when I began to imagine what life was like for my ancestors in pre-Famine Ireland, it all came back. I now remember that Dr. Seuss's book had bothered me because there was no satisfactory redress of wrongs at the end. Although *The 500 Hats* had appeared in the deep Depression year of 1938, the good doctor had hedged his bets. The peasant boy Cubbins went back to his bog, albeit with a bag of gold, and the king remained, preening, on his throne. Nothing essential had changed about the feudal system in the Kingdom of Didd. Furthermore, *The 500 Hats* had corroborated the layout of my town of Norwood, which had a number of stately mansions, each labeled with a notable Yankee family name—Day, Shattuck, Rich, Winslow (that name again), Cushing, Plimpton, Morrill, Forbes—while the rest of us lived in modest anonymity. So, in an echo of my earliest realization about social and economic inequalities, I have come to look at the Fannings of Urbalkirk as the Cubbinses, with the part of Bartholomew taken by my great-great-grandfather Phillip, who turned seventeen in August 1845 when the first word of a failed potato crop was spreading across Ireland. Similarly, King Derwin and company become the family Westenra, who were lords of all they surveyed across County Monaghan in the nineteenth century.

In fact and by British law, the entire townland of Urbalkirk, along with a big chunk of the rest of north-central Monaghan, was "owned" by the Westenras, the descendants of three Dutch brothers who had come over from Holland at the time of the restoration of King Charles II and become "free denizens" of Ireland by Act of Parliament in 1662. The vast majority of Irish farms were "rented" by mostly Catholic tenants from mostly

Figure 15. Rossmore Castle from the Lake. From Lord Rossmore, *Things I Can Tell* (London: E. Nash, 1912).

Protestant landlords whose ownership had been established during the wholesale confiscations and redistribution of Irish land that had taken place in the seventeenth century. By the time of the Fanning tenantry, the Westenra patriarch was the Honorable Warner William Westenra, a member of the Irish parliament in the late eighteenth century who became an Irish member of the British parliament when the Act of Union went into effect on January 1, 1801. By the close of that year, Westenra had been created the first Lord Rossmore—most likely his reward for helping to vote his own parliament out of existence. According to the Irish volume of *Burke's Guide to Country Houses*, it was the second Lord Rossmore who in 1827 built the first "range" of Rossmore Park, a "castle of great size and complexity; partly Tudor-Gothic." Over the following two decades, there was a lot of tinkering with the castle, wherein lies an interesting tale.

About twenty miles south of Rossmore Park is an even larger seat, Lough Fea, the Irish estate of the Shirley family, which had owned vast tracts in the south of Monaghan since the marriage of Sir Henry Shirley to the daughter of the Earl of Essex, the Lord Lieutenant of Ireland in 1599 and a sometime favorite of Queen Elizabeth I. The Shirleys had been thoroughgoing absentee landlords for over 200 years until about 1827, when Mr. E. J. Shirley, Esquire, began to build his own "Tudor-Gothic" castle on a beautiful site overlooking the lake. Until then, he had camped out during his very occasional visits to Ireland at his lakeside "cottage," which had twenty-seven bedrooms. An 1835 surveying source notes that work was continuing on Shirley's "extensive mansion . . . of cut freestone and in the Elizabethan style," and that "a great quantity of beautifully carved oak has been brought over from Holland at a considerable expense for the purpose of paneling the library and dining-room. One specimen, the Crucifixion, is admirably executed." For some reason, maybe because they both began building at the same time, Mr. Shirley and Lord Rossmore "vied with one another," as *Burke's Guide* puts it, "as to which of them could build the bigger room." To this end, Rossmore enlarged his drawing room five times, only to lose the contest when Shirley added on a "vast and baronial" great hall "with a lofty hammer-beam roof, a minstrels' gallery and an arcade at first floor level." Undoubtedly, the Westenras were consoled by the fact that the family owned two castles, for adjoining Rossmore Park was Camla Vale, a large, late Georgian house bought early in the nineteenth century by Lord Rossmore's brother Henry.

Much more can be learned about these folks, for *Burke's Guide* also explains that "in the later Victorian and Edwardian days, Rossmore was noted for its gaiety; the then (5th) Lord Rossmore, known as 'Derry,' being one of the brighter sparks of the Prince of Wales's set, and author of some lively memoirs called *Things I Can Tell*." Published in London and New York in 1912, this book has its smug title emblazoned in gold script across a dark green front cover which also features in gold the name "Rossmore," signed with flamboyant assurance, and underlined twice. *Things I Can Tell* provides a detailed picture of Monaghan life from the perspective of King Derwin. It's a classic portrait of a certain type of pampered, callous, insouciant Anglo-Irish aristocrat. Born in 1853, two years after Phillip Fanning left County Monaghan for America, Derrick Warner William Westenra, fifth Baron Rossmore, peers out in his frontispiece photo with a stern, even gaze. He is a portly figure, white-haired and white-ascoted, with a subtly dandyish close-trimmed mustache curled up at the tips and the small, pronounced exclamation mark of a tufted goatee just under his lower lip.

"Derry" Westenra opens by explaining that he decided to write a memoir because so many of his friends deplored the idea. In retaliation, "I herewith proceed to gossip to my heart's content." It is fair to say that the book does illustrate the life plan declared unashamedly by its author: "I found myself in the year I retired from the Guards the owner of a fine property and a good income. I had likewise excellent health and the Irishman's capacity to enjoy life, so it is small wonder that I threw myself into the pursuit of pleasure and determined to have a thorough good time." The year was

1876. Derrick Westenra was twenty-three and two years past his anointing as fifth Lord Rossmore.

Derry's memoir is a parade of anecdotes issuing from Rossmore Castle: childhood cockfights, badger-drawing, and general horsing around giving way to adolescent pranking at school (Sandhurst), a brief brush with the military (Ninth Lancers and First Life Guards, where duty consisted of riding around on horses and dressing up for parties), and then on to the fully adult activities of wine, women, song, foxhunting, bird shooting, steeplechasing, horse racing, dinner parties, club life, excursions to South Africa and Australia, women, and wine. Lest the wrong impression be left by so many references to "the amusing side of insobriety," Derry lets the record show that "imbibing in the country never seems to be so harmful as tippling in town, and we were used to rough nights which did not, however, interfere in any way with our early rising and thoroughly enjoying a day's hunting or shooting." Having contracted gout as a young man, he proudly reports that "the late Lord Winchelsea" told him that nobody deserved it more. Derry also got married (in 1882 to Mittie Naylor, daughter of British gentry) and produced offspring, but the references to his immediate family are few, scattered, and offhand. We aren't even told how many kids he had or what their names were.

Derry seems amazingly unengaged by history, either familial or national. Of his grandfather, Warner William Westenra, the second baron, we learn only that he "was a great believer in Catholic emancipation," that his wife was a Catholic—*Burke's Peerage,* not Derry, tells us that she was Mary Anne Walsh of Walsh Park, County Tipperary—and that he was often drunk while a student at Trinity College Dublin. As to the lay of the Monaghan land, Derry says that "our neighbours round Rossmore were delightful people and we managed to have some very good times." These included the Cootes of Bellamont Forest, Lord and Lady Dartry, the Lucas-Scudamores of Castle Shane, Lord Francis Hope (he of the "Hope diamond") of Castle Blaney, Sir John and Lady Constance Leslie of Glaslough House, and "the Shirleys of Loughfea, the largest landowners in the county of Monaghan," whose building contest with the second baron also goes unreported here. As predicted by the mention in *Burke's* of Derry's honored place in the rollicking "set" of Queen Victoria's long-deferred heir, Bertie, the Prince of Wales, the memoir is indeed full of loving references to HRH's considerate nature, sense of humor, keen memory, and tactfulness.

Like everything else about his birth, upbringing, and place in the world, Derry took his Orange politics entirely for granted. Although the years of his tenure as fifth Baron Rossmore were wildly eventful for Irish nationalism, there are but three notable references to his engagement with political matters in the entire book. First, he tells us that as "a brat of a boy," he joined the Monaghan Militia. Second, as a young man he almost fought a duel with "an Irishman whose name is well known as a writer," following a heated debate on the merits of Gladstone's 1886 bill for Irish home rule. Third, there was what Derry refers to as "the Roslea Incident, . . . the only occasion when I have ever loomed largely in the public eye." This event took place in 1882, while he was serving both as a Resident Magistrate and as "co-Grand Master of the loyal Orangemen of Monaghan." Having been warned that agitators for land reform "intended to invade our neighbourhood" to hold a gathering at Roslea—an east Fermanagh village on the Monaghan border—Derry called "a small influential meeting when it was determined to hold a counter-demonstration at the same hour and on the same day that the rebel meeting was to take place." In the event, Derry led 2,000 men from Clones to Roslea, where they held a peaceful Unionist rally "only a hedge and a ditch" from the so-called rebels. Derry allows that "no further notice would have been taken of the meetings at Roslea if I had not considered it my duty to write to all the principal English newspapers to warn their readers what was going on in Ulster, and stated that it would mean bloodshed one day." This initiative of patriotic self-publicity earned the fifth Lord Rossmore his fifteen minutes of fame. He got a banquet at the Rotunda in Dublin, a celebratory meeting in the Ulster Hall, Belfast, and—who could ask for more?—a caricature in *Punch*.

Although he mentions the 1882 Phoenix Park murders of British Government Officials and the all-round "bad times," Derry fails to point out just how much political activity there was in his part of Ireland. In fact, Monaghan was a significant center of agitation from the early years of the Land War. The Monaghan Tenants' Defence Association dated from 1872, and the Irish National Land League, from its founding in 1879, was quite active in the county. Concerted effort by the tenantry resulted in the defeat of local Tory M.P.s Sir John Leslie and Sewallis Evelyn Shirley in the 1880 general election, which solidified the power in parliament of the Irish party under the leadership of Charles Stewart Parnell. And yet there is no mention of Parnell or the Land League's Michael Davitt in these pages, much less of Captain Boycott, the estate agent from nearby Mayo whose name entered the language, thanks to successful tenant organizing against landlords at this time.

Judging from his memoir, Derry Westenra wasn't much interested in the Catholic tenantry of Monaghan either—even though, I feel obliged to say, his life of ease was balanced on their backs. Still and all, the Cubbinses of his world figure in a few telling anecdotes. There is nothing of noblesse oblige here to relieve what can only be described as pervasive, amused condescension. This tone is established early in his book with a thinly veiled reference to landlord/tenant procreative dalliance. Derry reports that the Westenras have "an old-established stammer which appears at intervals in successive generations." His father had it "rather badly, and other Westenras must have been afflicted with it too, for it has been observed that quite a number of the old tenant farmers who lived round Rossmore used to have a similar impediment." In the same vein is the offensive mention of a horse-racing crony, "the late Lord Vivian," who was banned from weekends at the home of a mutual friend because "he couldn't stand the worry of [Vivian's] visits, as the maid who brought up his guest's early cup of tea had usually to leave her situation later owing to family reasons."

Similar anecdotes illustrative of relations between the Grand Dukes and the Cubbinses include the one about the "old beggar woman whose appearance so annoyed [Lady Pilkington's] dog that it promptly bit the mendicant." Placated with ten shillings from the "kind-hearted" noblewoman, the beggar fell on her knees in the road and prayed to "the blessed Saints to persuade the crathur to bite me on the other leg!" Also good for a mean-spirited laugh is the story of Derry's boon companion, the "kind-hearted and open-handed" British aristocrat "Chicken" Hartopp, captain in the Tenth Hussars, owner of an Irish estate, devoted huntsman, and "a personal friend" of the Prince of Wales. It seems that while serving as Master of Fox Hounds in the south of Ireland, Hartopp became so annoyed at the demands of a certain beggar for assistance that he threatened to "dynamite him." Derry reports that "the man, who was legless, used to push himself about in a go-cart with the aid of two sticks." After one importunity too many, "Chicken promptly took away his sticks, tied an empty tin case underneath the go-cart and informed him that within ten minutes he would be blown up." Despite the beggar's cries, Hartopp "kept the game up" for eight minutes, after which "he untied the canister and returned the sticks to the man, who left the neighborhood as though he were pursued by the seven devils." What a good time for all.

So much for Derrick W. W. Westenra and his set. Derry died in January 1921, shortly before his sixty-eighth birthday. His son William succeeded him to the peerage. As for Rossmore Castle, the last word again comes from *Burke's Guide to Country Houses*: "Post World War II, the castle became severely infested with dry-rot, and was abandoned by sixth Lord Rossmore in favor of Camla Vale. Now demolished." Camla was sold in 1962 and also subsequently torn down. *Sic transit gloria mundi*—sometimes.

Conditions on the Ground

In the meantime, small-farming tenants of the Barons Rossmore such as the bog-dwelling Fannings (peat rather than cranberry) had held on by their fingernails through those leanest of lean years of the earlier nineteenth century. My immigrant ancestor Phillip Fanning was born, presumably at Urbalkirk, in August 1828, the year after Rossmore Park and Shirley's Lough Fea began to go up. Thus, his childhood and adolescence were spent Bartholomew Cubbins–style, in the shadow of these massive architectural projects and also of inexorably worsening destitution in his own home place. There had been at least two other serious famines in the county earlier in the century—in 1817, accompanied by an epidemic of typhus, and in 1821. As it happens, there's a good deal of information available about just how poor many in Monaghan were in the years leading up to the Great Hunger. Unprecedented in scope, the Duke of Wellington's Ordnance Survey plan had also included the writing of parish-by-parish "Memoirs" to expand and classify the wealth of material being obtained by the surveyors. The categories included Natural Features, Natural History, Modern Topography (public buildings, schools, churches, gentlemen's seats), Ancient Topography (forts, dolmens, other ruins), Social Economy (dispensary and school reports, the poor, habits of the people), and Productive Economy (trades, occupations, fairs, crops, grazing). The Memoir project ran through the decade of the 1830s, only to be stopped (as a superfluous expense) by the government of Sir Robert Peel. Only the northern half of the country had been completed, and the results lay unpublished until the 1990s, when forty volumes were co-issued by the Institute of Irish Studies at the Queen's University of Belfast and the Royal Irish Academy. The editors of this admirable venture rightly termed the Memoirs "a nineteenth-century Domesday book" and "a uniquely detailed source for the story of the northern half of Ireland immediately before the Great Famine."

The Memoirs for County Monaghan were taken down in the middle to late 1830s. Unfortunately, the one for the civil parish of Monaghan, which contains the townland of Urbalkirk, is one of the skimpiest. Done in April 1838, it contains the fact that the parish runs six by six miles at the extremities and contains 13,547 acres, 26 of them under water. There is a bare enumeration of hills, lakes, rivers, climate, crops (wheat, oats, flax, and potatoes "set in April and dug in October and November"), a "Weather Journal" for 1 February to 10 April (lots of rain and six days of snow in February), and under "Productive Economy" only a single mill—operated by tenant James Hanna in Aghantamy townland, "diameter of water wheel 14 feet." A lot of information about the lay of this land appears, however, in the Memoirs of four contiguous parishes for which detailed notes were written.

It's clear, first of all, that this was predominantly Catholic country. The Catholic chapels were much bigger and better attended than the churches of Wesleyans, Presbyterians, and the Church of Ireland. The largest, a chapel in Drumdesco townland, Tydavnet parish, had a capacity of 1,800 and a "general attendance" of 1,400. Two others "accommodate[d]" 1,000. Furthermore, the masters of seven of the fourteen national schools visited by the Ordnance Survey team in these four parishes were themselves Catholics, which certainly indicates demographic power in the mid-1830s. This had been the situation countywide since at least the late eighteenth century, when 64 percent of Monaghan's population had been Catholic. During debate about the partition of Ulster in the early 1920s, the Catholic majority was still so large that Monaghan was never seriously considered for inclusion in the Northern Ireland statelet.

The Ordnance Survey Memoirs describe the fairs that were the chief highlight of rural social and economic life in the 1830s. In Tydavnet, a parish northwest and twice the size of Monaghan parish, the monthly fair featured trade in cattle, pigs, and sheep, along with "huxters who retail callicoes, printed and plain coarse linens, stockings and socks, and a bad description of hardware, cutlery, brushes and combs." More detail is supplied by William Carleton (1794–1869), the first voice of literary genius to emerge from Ireland's Catholic tenantry, who described a Monaghan fair in the early nineteenth century in his story "The Fair of Emyvale." Featuring everything from "pitch-and-toss to manslaughter" and faction fights "on a large and comprehensive scale," this north Monaghan fair was "a moving mass of animation, and occasionally of uproar; the latter produced by the shouting of men and the bellowings of startled cattle, as the parties conducting them came into contact with each other while passing in the street." At day's end, Carleton continues, "the young of both sexes, might be observed, in connexion with their friends and relatives, to devote more of their time to pleasure and conviviality."

"Straggling," "irregular," "poor," and "unclean" are adjectives that the Memoirs apply to villages of twenty-five and thirty thatched cabins throughout north and central County Monaghan, and a summary description (in January 1835) of the parish of Currin, ten miles southwest of Monaghan parish, is typical of Ordnance Survey reactions to the whole county: "A glance at the wretched hovels, scantily covered with straw, surrounded and almost entombed in mire, which everywhere present themselves throughout the parish, sufficiently testify that the total absence of all activity in industry is one source of the wretchedness and misery which almost overwhelms the land." As for diet, "potatoes and buttermilk constitute their chief and almost only source of subsistence." Though butcher meat, butter, and "well-fed pigs" were observed, none of these were consumed by the locals, for "all are transported to make up the rent, and nothing remains but the light, gay and cheerful spirits of the emaciated frames of a half-starved population."

Medical reports in the Memoirs are especially disturbing. Richard Maffett, M.D., surgeon at the dispensary of Emyvale, just ten miles north of the townland of Urbalkirk, reveals (for 1836 and 1837) a "fearful amount" of typhoid fever "of the most afflicting nature, from 3 to 6 [family members] being frequently ill at the same time. This melancholy fact is chiefly attributable to: the destitute state of the people; the want of proper clothing and nourishment calculated to sustain the friends of the patients in their incumbent duties at the bedside; and to that terrific practice which prevails to such an extravagant excess (from absolute necessity), association with the diseased during the day in the same apartment and rest during the night in the same bed." Moreover, in the same period Dr. Maffett treated "upwards of 70 cases of smallpox . . . , and very few out of this number had been vaccinated at any period during their lives." All told, abroad among the people of this parish, Dr. Maffett found "absolute distress and wretchedness." The Memoir also explains how the health system was funded. Area landlords made yearly subscriptions to the dispensary and received "2 visiting tickets and 10 tickets of recommendation . . . for each guinea" paid in. "Tenants of those landed proprietors who have not subscribed to the funds of the dispensary shall not be entitled to medical advice for attendance from the dispensary." In 1837, there were twenty-eight subscribers. Most paid £1, 1 shilling. Dr. Maffett was open for business on Mondays and Thursdays from ten to two at Emyvale.

Derrick Westenra makes no mention of the calamitous events in his county in which had been rooted the land agitation of the 1870s and 1880s that he experienced. Apparently, local memories of the Famine did not fall into the category of "Things I Can Tell." In point of fact, however, County

Monaghan had been much affected. Certainly, the Great Hunger of the late 1840s was the catastrophic engine for wholesale, revolutionary change in the nature of rural Ireland and for the virtual creation of urban Irish America. Between 1845 and 1851, the population of the island decreased from a conservatively estimated 8.5 million to 6.5 million. Over a million people died of starvation and related diseases, and over a million emigrated. Despite the loss of the census records of individual families in the Four Courts fire, there are available detailed statistics that were published in the decennial census books and elsewhere. (One wishes that some part of the exemplary zeal for measurement on the part of the British government in Ireland in the nineteenth century could have been transferred to a desire to keep Irish people alive by feeding them.) These statistics are lately being used to great effect, thanks to the new historical work inspired by the 150th anniversary of the Great Hunger over the years 1995 to 2001.

The population figures show that for an agrarian society, Ireland before the Famine was a very crowded place. Just before disaster struck in 1845, the average density countrywide was at least 47 people for every 100 acres of land. In the so-called Congested Districts it was much larger. (As earlier mention of the rundale system has indicated, this was very different from the American idea of the large, self-contained farm run by an isolated nuclear family.) And County Monaghan was among the most congested places in Ireland—according to the 1841 census figures, the third most densely populated rural county, averaging 58 to 60 persons per 100 acres. Worse yet, in the most crowded parts of the southern baronies of Farney and Dartry, where lay the Shirley estates, the density was over 200 persons per 100 acres. By the time famine struck in late 1845 and 1846, all these populations would have been greater still.

The potato blight appeared early in County Monaghan. The first notice of trouble came in the fall of 1845, and by spring 1846 there was considerable rot in several areas, including around Monaghan town among the tenants of Lord Rossmore, where smallholders reported that they had no seed to plant a new crop. Another indicator of trouble was theft of grain from a meal store in Monaghan town that same spring, one of the first such examples of societal breakdown in Ireland. In March 1846, government reports listed Monaghan as one of the six most blighted counties, with over 40 percent of the crops affected. Disaster followed disaster from here on through to the end of the decade.

Consequently, the population loss in Monaghan due to Famine deaths and emigration was one of the most severe in Ireland. In the six years from

1845 to 1851, the county lost nearly 67,000 people, as the population plummeted from 208,400 (a figure extrapolated from the 1841 census) to 141,800. Monaghan suffered the third greatest percentage loss of rural population in Ireland. Only Roscommon and Mayo lost greater percentages of their people. Furthermore, the estimated annual rate of what in Famine studies has come to be called "excess mortality" (deaths due to famine conditions rather than natural causes) in County Monaghan from 1846 through 1851 was 28 per 1,000 people. County Mayo was first, at 58 per 1,000, which is reason enough for a tag line that developed in response to the question "Where are your people from?" To which the reply became "Mayo, God help us."

By and large, rates of excess mortality in and emigration from Irish counties were inversely proportionate during the Famine years. That is, people died who hadn't the resources to leave. But in North Connacht and South Ulster, including Monaghan, both rates were high, which meant that societal upheaval was at its greatest. Tenth among Ireland's thirty-two counties in excess mortality, Monaghan was eighth in emigration rate. The first figure had mostly to do with the large number of very small tenant farms and the quality of life thereon. When the Famine began in 1845, over half of recorded tenant farming families in the county lived on five acres or less. Only four Irish counties had a higher percentage of these smallest holdings—Mayo, Roscommon, Galway, and Sligo, the places that would be most devastated.

The second figure, high emigration, was related to a couple of other factors. Because of the collapse of the linen trade as a cottage industry, these same counties of North Connacht and South Ulster had experienced heavy emigration in the three decades *before* 1845, and one result was a flow of "remittances" from America to subsidize a continued exodus. In addition, some of these counties, including Monaghan, housed large numbers of tenants whose holdings were valued at £4 to £6. Whereas landlords were required to pay the entire poor rate on holdings valued at £4 or less, tenants who just missed this cutoff line were both poor (though not quite destitute) *and* enjoined to pay taxes. During the crisis years, many would have cashed in their last bits of capital and left the country, or at least been forced to send off their children.

The figures for all of Ireland emphasize a huge decrease in the number of very small landholdings as a direct result of the Great Hunger. The number of persons holding one acre or less—the lowest of the low in tenantry legally on the books and taxable—went from 135,300 in 1845 to 37,700 in 1851. Similarly, the number of persons holding between one and five acres went from 182,000 in 1845 to 84,000 in 1851. Indeed, this change was revolutionary. Encouraged rather than resisted by the powers that were, this dramatic shift also reinforced the desire of the Irish landlord class to turn out the small tenants—who were increasingly a social nuisance and an economic drag on profitability—and to turn the land from tillage to pasture. The countrywide decrease of nearly 200,000 leases of five acres or less in six years is also a cohort of people many of whom swelled the statistic of excess mortality, as they lacked the means to leave the country.

There were also many thousands of Famine victims who never turned up on the official rolls of the tenantry because they held no leases and paid no taxes of any kind. These were cottiers (those granted the space to throw up a mud cabin and till a small plot on someone else's holding), or "conacre men" (whose families lived in even flimsier huts for a portion of the year, from which they were seasonally turned out to seek employment elsewhere), or itinerant beggars upon the roads with no habitation of any kind. For obvious reasons, many of these people didn't make the census either. Harvard's John Kelleher, my friend and mentor in Irish Studies, has said that "they were too humble for counting"—which is why the population of Ireland on the eve of the Famine was probably closer to 9 million than to the verifiable 8.5 million. This teeming underclass of cottier, conacre, and beggar families was virtually wiped out between 1845 and 1851.

With their passion for detail, the government census collectors also provided a focused survey of the quality of habitation countrywide, divided into four categories. In ascending order, fourth-class housing was "all mud cabins having only one room"; third-class was "a better description of cottage, still built of mud, but varying from two to four rooms and [containing] windows"; second-class meant "a good farm house" of stone with several windows. First-class houses, mostly in towns and cities, were very substantial, often of two stories. The 1835 Ordnance Survey Memoir for one central Monaghan parish described typical *third*-class mud houses: "divided into three apartments, seldom exceed 1 storey high, furnished occasionally with small glass windows, but often without them, an earthen floor with no ceiling and universally thatched with straw. One extremity appropriated as a bedroom for the family, the opposite end for the cattle and the centre a kitchen and dining room for the whole household." Overall, "nothing can surpass the filth and dirtiness of these cabins and the enclosures around them. . . . Families are numerous and the children swarm around the cabins."

In County Monaghan in 1841, 99,800 people (about half the population) had lived in third-class houses. Another 54,700 (more than a quarter of the population) had been counted as living in the very worst—one-room, fourth-class—hovels. In 1851 the percentage of third-class dwellings in Monaghan was up slightly, to 56 percent (housing 80,100 of the much depleted overall population), and the percentage of fourth-class cabins had plunged to 7 percent (housing 10,400 people). In this figure is a strong correlation with the decline in the number of landless cottiers and laborers, whose homes these had been. (Over all of Ireland, the percentage of people living in fourth-class houses in rural districts dropped from 40 percent in 1841 to 14 percent in 1851.)

Still and all, these various measures do not begin to register the thousands of temporary undertenants and squatters in the complex, teeming hierarchy of the poor on the land. In Famine-generation Ireland, the misery intensified. These were people designated, in one enumeration of those evicted from a Monaghan estate in 1835, as "undertenant of a hovel," or one "got in as a weekly tenant under a temporary tenant for a year," or one who "lived in gripe of a ditch under road . . . never paid rent." These descriptions and statistics should also act as a corrective to the way we may look at the domestic stone ruins that dot the Irish countryside today. Even if we move beyond their picturesqueness as photo opportunities to see them as somehow connected to the Great Hunger, these crumbling walls do not begin to tell the story. What we see today are what's left of good homes on relatively successful farms. The vast majority of Monaghan's—and Ireland's—houses before the Famine were third and fourth-class mud buildings, and those telling signs of rural population density and squalor are simply no longer there. There were over one million separate inhabited houses in Ireland counted in the census of 1841. Ten years later, there were 282,000 fewer houses on the ground.

Other occasional surveys done in nineteenth-century Ireland fill in the quotidien picture even more. A general survey of nutrition by county, made in 1836 when my great-great-grandfather, Phillip Fanning, was eight years old, showed that everyone in County Monaghan ate potatoes; 20 to 40 percent of the people ate oatmeal; 20 percent drank milk regularly, 45 percent occasionally, and 35 percent not at all; less than 20 percent ate eggs or bacon; 5 percent ate fish regularly and 15 percent occasionally; and only 5 percent ate any butter. In this almost entirely agricultural place, that was the diet. Period. Contained in these data was a clear blueprint for the disaster that hit ten years later, and yet, having collected these statistics, British officialdom in Ireland took no action.

Again, only the statisticians rose to the occasion when the great catastrophe hit. During the Famine itself, cause-of-death statistics were collected by county for two years—1847 and 1849. Monaghan people died, in percentages not very different from those elsewhere in Ireland, of dropsy, marasmus (or "wasting"), literal starvation, consumption (or tuberculosis), smallpox, and fever (which was the greatest killer throughout the Famine years). Monaghan, however, was in the category of heaviest percentages of deaths from the diarrheal diseases (dysentery and diarrhea) and from measles, of which there was a protracted epidemic in the county. The figures available for organized, government-sponsored relief, such as it was, are another measure of destitution. For the Monaghan Poor Law Union (north central in the county, including Monaghan town and the townland of Urbalkirk), the numbers seeking workhouse relief were among the greatest in Ireland. And yet, though they helped, the workhouses were also sites of concentrated sickness and death throughout the land, and the Monaghan workhouse mortality rate for the week ending April 3, 1847, was the second highest of any Poor Law Union in all of Ireland.

A second measure was the distribution by the Poor Law Unions of free soup. Legislation calling for government-operated soup kitchens in Ireland passed the British parliament in February 1847. The first soup kitchens were up and running in mid-March, but by mid-May one-third of the electoral divisions where soup was mandated had yet to distribute any. The scheme reached its peak during the first week of July 1847, when three million people per day—a third of Ireland's total population—were fed free soup. County Monaghan was much dependent on these soup kitchens, and during that week the Monaghan Poor Law Union distributed soup daily to perhaps as many as 25 percent of the people living there. Yet just two months later, in September 1847, the government soup kitchens were shut down all over the country. People continued to starve and die for nearly three more years, but the kitchens never reopened, even though £530,000 of the monies appropriated for soup had not been spent. There was no more damning evidence of English refusal to respond adequately to the humanitarian crisis.

All told, the Fanning family's townland of Urbalkirk seems to have been a fair microcosm of the situation in rural Ireland, both county- and countrywide, in the 1840s. The townlands around Monaghan town—and Urbalkirk lies three miles south—were notable for their population density, number of smallholdings, and poor housing. In the 1841 census, the area had a density of 60 to 69 people per 100 acres. Over one-quarter of the holdings were less than five acres. Half the houses were third-class, and one-third were fourth-class. (This left 16 percent second-class houses, most of these in the town of Monaghan, and 1 percent first-class—including, of course, Rossmore Park and Camla Vale.) And yet many of these small farms were valued at just above the £4 cutoff that would have absolved the tenants of paying the Poor Law rates. In November 1847, the government called in soldiers to help collect the rates in the Monaghan Poor Law Union, and many tenants sold off what they could and fled. Moreover, between 1848 and 1851, the greatest liquidation of holdings of five acres or less in the county—500 tenancies lost—took place in this same swatch of north central Monaghan.

The collapse of the local cotton and linen industries was another exacerbating problem. Many landless cottiers in Monaghan had depended heavily for sustaining income on spinning and weaving in their cabins. But in the years before the Famine, the cotton industry went entirely over to factories in Lancashire, and the linen industry was shifting rapidly to newly industrializing Belfast. In the 1841 census, 24,700 women and 3,400 men were counted as employed spinners and weavers in County Monaghan. In 1851, the numbers had dropped to 2,300 and 1,300. The death of this cottage industry was also particularly felt in Monaghan town and its environs.

In the pre-Famine national census of 1841, the population of Urbalkirk was counted at 129 people living in twenty-three houses. The post-Famine count in 1851 was nineteen inhabited houses and 80 people, a dramatic decrease of 49 people, one of whom was my ancestor, Phillip Fanning. Nine years later, *Griffith's Valuation* found fifteen tenant families and three landless subtenants living in eighteen cabins. In 1860, *Griffith's* assessed the total value of the land and buildings of the townland of Urbalkirk at £188—about 14 shillings for each of the 271 acres. At this point, the Fanning holding was as poor a place as ever, for the acreage and valuation had remained almost unchanged since the *Tithe Applotment Book* forty-four years earlier, having gone from 6 acres, 1 rod, 31 perches (valued at £5, 12 shillings, 8 pence) to 6 acres, 3 rods, 25 perches (valued at £5, 15 shillings, no pence). Here is where John and Elizabeth Bradford Fanning of the townland of Urbalkirk got stuck. Because their profitless farm was valued at over £4, they were legally bound to pay the Poor Law rates as well as the tithe for support of the Protestant Church of Ireland. In that harrowing time and place, there must have been other exigencies as well. And so, off went their son Phillip to Liverpool, New York, and then Boston in the spring of 1851. The decision to emigrate may have been made easier for the Fannings because a person or family could reasonably walk to the ports of Dundalk or Newry (twenty or thirty miles from the middle of the county), and thence take ship for Liverpool.

Witnesses

A top-down view of Monaghan at the time of the Famine is that of Anglo-Irish land agent W. Steuart Trench, author of a memoir, *Realities of Irish Life*, published in 1868, with illustrations by his son, J. Townsend Trench. The aim was "to give the English public some idea of the difficulties which occasionally beset the path of an Irish landlord or agent who is desirous to improve the district in which he is interested." Trench seems to have been something of a roving troubleshooter, taking over several estates and bringing them through the troubled times. He spent two years (1843–45) as agent on the vast estates of the Shirley family and the Marquis of Bath, which encompassed the entire barony of Farney in south Monaghan. (Urbalkirk is about twelve miles north of the Farney border.) To alleviate the pressure of numbers, Trench set up a scheme of assisted emigration to send some tenants to America. He then went south to County Kerry, where he started a similar plan on the Kenmare estates of Lord Lansdowne. In 1851 he returned to Monaghan as agent for the Marquis of Bath, and in 1857 he went south again to run Lord Digby's estates in King's County. By Trench's account, County Monaghan was a hotbed of what he insists on calling "Ribbonism," harking back to the eighteenth-century generic term for land agitation by tenants against landlords.

In March 1843, Trench arrived in Carrickmacross to administer the Shirley and Bath estates. He was greeted by bonfires "on almost every hill" over some 20,000 acres, lighted by the tenantry to celebrate the death of the land agent who preceded him. In subsequent weeks, he witnessed a number of other disturbing events. On April 3, 1843, 10,000 men gathered on the main street of Carrickmacross demanding reduction of their rents. Standing on a chair, Trench answered that he "believed Mr. Shirley was a most kind and indulgent landlord; and that after the fullest and most mature consideration he had come to the conclusion that no reduction of rent was necessary." Further, "I said that I hoped by better management, and more careful husbandry, they would yet find that they could pay their rents without any serious distress." At this point, a strong voice shouted out, "'*Down on your knees, boys!* We will ask him once more upon our knees!' And to my hor-

Figure 16. J. Townsend Trench, "The Message. 'Down on your knees boys!' shouted the same voice, 'we will ask him once more upon our knees.'" From W. Steuart Trench, *Realities of Irish Life* (London: Longmans, Green, and Company, 1868).

ror and amazement the vast crowd, almost all at least who were in my immediate vicinity, dropped suddenly on their knees, and another dead silence ensued." (The younger Trench chose to illustrate this melancholy event.)

Trench also describes battles between process servers and "Molly Maguires" with blackened faces and women's clothes, the incarceration of defaulting tenants in the Gaol at Monaghan town, and mob violence at Magheracloone, where a volley of stones was met with police rifle fire and several tenants were wounded and one killed. Returning to Monaghan and the Bath estates at the heel of the Great Hunger in 1851, Trench found that the county was still "very seriously disturbed." He chronicles three murders of estate agents during 1850 and 1851 along the Monaghan-Armagh border and relates that his own life was threatened on several occasions. This is hardly surprising given that his job was to start collecting again from nearly destitute Famine survivors, many of whom, as Trench puts it disapprovingly, "had not paid any rent whatever for periods varying from two to six years." These were people at the extreme end of their endurance who had seen relatives and friends die all around them.

In the case of one of these estate-agent murders, the Westenras again enter the picture. Trench describes having enlisted the aid of Lord Rossmore—this would have been the father of fun-loving Derry—in convincing the authorities to allow him to offer a pardon to one of the condemned "Ribbon conspirators" in exchange for the man's informing on others of the seditious "Farney boys." Trench's jailhouse meeting with the man proved fruitless, and he was publicly executed in 1852 along with another conspirator at the Gaol in Monaghan town. According to Trench, this spectacle did much to quell agrarian disturbances in the county, as "the whole tone of the estate had altered; industry and activity took the place of apathy and indolence. . . . [A] wholesome acknowledgment of the power of the law pervaded the mass of the population."

As to the Great Hunger, for which his estimate—as late as 1868—is only 200,000 deaths in all of Ireland, Trench has a ready explanation: "No restraint whatever had been put upon the system of subdivision of land. Boys and girls intermarried unchecked, each at the age of seventeen or eighteen, without thinking it necessary to make any provision whatever for their future subsistence, beyond a shed to lie down in, and a small plot of land whereon to grow potatoes." Declaring with irony that "the Celt in all his purity had been allowed to increase and multiply," Trench cites the census of 1841 as having counted "something upward of 44,107 souls" in the barony of Farney, existing on 41,567 acres. Thus, "there was *more than one human being for every Irish acre of land in the barony* [his italics]. . . . Such were the masses with whom we had now to deal." And yet, lest the owners and managers be blamed, Trench complains that "if any landlord or agent is determined to resist this system [of subdivision and subletting], and to evict those who in spite of all remonstrances and entreaties persist in this pernicious course—though the plot of land be scarcely sufficient to feed a goat, and the hut be of the most degraded class—he is attacked with a virulence and bitterness of hostility." Nowhere does Trench suggest just what the people, if prevented from subletting and squatting, were supposed to do to keep themselves alive.

In fact, for agents and landlords like Trench and Lords Rossmore and Bath, the Famine was widely seen as something of a blessing. All shared the opinion of a surveyor on the Shirley estate, who had declared as early as 1814 that there could be no significant profits "without entirely sweeping off the present population and replacing it by real farmers. . . . An entire change of system should take place." As if to corroborate this view, Trench finds 1,600 happy tenants on the 24,000-acre Bath estate—for an average holding of fifteen acres—upon his return to Monaghan in May 1865 on the occasion of the first visit—ever—of the Marquis of Bath to his Irish lands. Here, "as published in a local journal, and afford[ing] a true record of the change of feeling which had taken place upon the property, between 1852 and 1865," Trench's narrative takes a sharp turn toward Dr. Seuss's Kingdom of Didd. On the great day, "the quaint old town of Carrickmacross" was full of "triumphal arches, floating banners, and gay streamers," and "the principal buildings and houses, as well as those belonging to the humble classes, were decked out with laurels and evergreens." Greeted by a band and his loudly cheering tenantry, Lord Bath proceeded to "the spacious Market Hall," where "a throne was erected, and superb carpets were strewn on the floor." There, a spokesman for the tenants gave a speech of effusive welcome and thanks that "we have experienced from your lordship and your ancestors much kindly consideration," and that "your lordship, though absent, has not been unmindful that 'property has its duties as well as its rights.'" And so on. And so forth.

Historian Patrick Duffy has studied the estate records of E. J. Shirley, Esquire, the largest landowner in Monaghan and Lord Rossmore's rival in the competition to build the biggest room. In 1841 the 25,000-acre Shirley estate housed over 18,000 tenants, and nearly 3,000 were landless cottiers, many of them undertenants at more than one remove. It was the trouble caused by such subdivision that land agent Trench railed against, and his scheme of assisted emigration was meant to address the problem. During the Famine years, some 1,500 Shirley tenants went to America by this means, sometimes followed by unsubsidized, chain-migrating neighbors. The number of emigrants, however, in no way tallies with the overall attrition of people from this estate. Outright evictions increased as the situation worsened in 1847 and beyond. In September 1849, for example, 245 Shirley tenant families (1,225 people) were evicted by bailiffs. By 1851, through a combination of emigrations, evictions, and deaths, half the Shirley townlands had lost over half their population, and there were 8,000 fewer people living on the estate than ten years earlier.

In a survey made after his appointment as land agent for Shirley in 1843, Trench had reported that "even in Ireland it has never fallen my lot to witness destitution to the same degree and over such a large extent as I have seen it on this property." There were "many tenants' houses where there are neither windows, bedsteads, tables nor chairs, and hundreds destitute of one or more of these comforts." Evidence of such inhumane extremities is contained in the boxes of petitions in the Shirley papers from tenants to their landlord. Duffy explains that "from the early 1840s a great many sought relief in the form of concessions on rent arrears, for example, or help in times of sickness. One common request was for blankets, a reflection of particularly extreme poverty and a universal indicator of want, especially among the landless in wintertime." In February 1844, Anne McEneaney, tenant on two acres, asked for a blanket for her son, lying "on his death-bed." In December 1844, Francis McCabe reported that "between himself, his wife and two children they have not one pound of day or night woolen covering, and are nearly famished with cold." In January 1845, the widow Catherine Martin declared that, her husband having died under a useless blanket, she hoped "that your honour will give her some covering to shade her feeble bones from the acute cold of the present season." I do wonder how Mr. Shirley, Esquire, received the petition of Owen Fitzpatrick that he be allowed to keep a landless laborer on his smallholding in 1844. Perhaps the famous builder of Lough Fea was able to excuse the evils of subdivision for once, because Fitzpatrick said that he had built a house for his cottier, "roofed with timber before your honour prohibited."

One more gathering of eyewitness testimonies is a manuscript book recording inquests in the north of Monaghan during the Famine years. From his study of this text, historian Brian Ó Mórdha concludes, "The first thing we can learn is that Monaghan suffered as severely as any other part of the country, and that in the county no area would appear to have escaped." Further, "Monaghan escaped war but having got its famine could not hope to escape the plague and in the latter half of 1846 we find both fever and dysentery rampant in the county." The local situation also mirrored the national in those most affected: "Starvation was widespread and affected the majority of the people, but . . . two classes were particularly hard hit, indeed one might venture to say, practically wiped out; these were the cottiers and the beggars. The cottiers, having but a plot of potatoes to give them food and a pig or two to pay the rent, . . . had nothing with which to fight starvation when the blight struck; even the pig had to go when the potatoes failed." The Monaghan beggars "had a well organized itinerary" of "houses in which they could spend the night. Frequently we find references to the fact that the deceased—a beggar—was 'making' for some place." But now, most cabin doors were shut against the poverty-stricken, and inquests provide "a glimpse of an old custom dying hard and of a people's natural charity . . . receiving its death blow during the Famine."

In the manuscript, one priest observes that in the spring and summer of

"Black '47," "the number of deaths in this parish average at present between seven and eight each day." Examples are detailed and painful. The February 1847 inquest of cottier Patt Murphy of Drumcrew (the name of the victim's townland always appears) reveals that "the bed clothes of the deceased was an old single blanket and when the weather was wet the rain fell on them when lying in bed." His daughter Alley stated that "often their diet was broth made of boiled turnips with meal and water. . . . There were two days in which they had one meal of food. . . . When there was much down-rain deceased would lie on some straw on the floor." The March 1847 inquest of cottier Pat McCabe of Greaghletterkepple explains that he and his fever-ridden family were reduced to living "at the back of a ditch," near which his body was found "lying in an open field, with no covering except his usual tattered dress. At a short distance from the body of the deceased sat deceased's wife, with her child exposed to the inclemency of the weather, having no other covering but their clothes which were of the worst description, beside her. Witness saw a little milk but no food." Bernard Kelly of Koolnacart "died by the roadside in Aughalisk" in June 1847. "He was in extreme destitution—extremely filthy and swarming with vermin—and that the neighbours considered he was ill of yellow fever was the cause none offered to take him into their houses."

In March 1847, Mary Ann McDermott of Cladone died on the side of the road between Kileevan and Clones, where she had gone to beg a cup of meal. Her daughter Catherine, "aged about eleven years," explained that "for the past four months her mother has . . . had no mode of living but by begging, supporting herself by the charity she received. . . . During the past fortnight deceased had no food whatever for herself and two children save a little gruel at night, the meal to make which she collected during the day." The coroner's verdict was unambiguous: "It appeared, upon examination of the body, deceased had some greens of a bad quality in her stomach and a small quantity of raw turnips in her bowels insufficient to sustain life." The gruel (also called stirabout or porridge) with which the poorest of Monaghan's poor attempted to stay alive is described in this inquest book as having consisted of "meal and water mixed into gruel and thickened with boiled nettles," or "broth made of boiled turnips with meal and water," or "a drink of meal and water." Ó Mórdha remarks that "we can see the sense of frustration felt by many such persons [giving inquest evidence] when they saw their people dying in hundreds around them and they realised they could not help them."

Several of the inquests also suggest to Ó Mórdha that by early 1847, "already emigration had started," and that "some people set out hopefully to emigrate with but little money for the journey. They obviously just headed for a seaport and hoped for the best." One of these was Michael Nugent of Lisceveny, who died "on his way possibly to Dundalk, in order to emigrate to America." Another was Thomas Kure, "who died after falling, through exhaustion, into a roadside pool of water" in the townland of Cladone. His young son stated that "they were on their way to Scotland. It took them four days to reach Clones as they were 'subsisting by small grains of meals given them on the road but which was not half enough for them.'" The Fannings were better off than these unfortunates, but such stories of great misery had certainly been abroad in the land when young Phillip was making up his mind to leave. The maps of the Ordnance Survey reveal that the townlands where many of these people lived and died—Drumcrew, Greaghletterkepple, Koolnakart, Cladone, Drumnavail, Lisceveny—are all within ten miles of Urbalkirk.

A Village in Clare

It's December 1, 1999, the start of the last month of the last year of the sesquicentennial of the Great Hunger, and I am hiking up a steep, rutted, zigzag hill, going slantwise across the face of one of the solid limestone humps of which the 100 square miles of the Burren in north Clare are fashioned. This morning I talked to a local historian who told me how to find the ruins of an entire village that was abandoned during the Famine. He sent me south on the coast road, itself built up during the Famine, around Black Head to the village of Fanore. It occurred to me while driving that this must have been one of the few public-works Famine roads that actually went anywhere. Most, as I recalled in connecting them with the Crazy Roads of my childhood, went from nowhere to nowhere. Following the directions given, I turned my rental car east, away from the ocean, and drove past St. Patrick's Church on a narrow road that follows the Caher River, little more than a stream really, into the heart of the Burren. I was told to drive for two miles, then to look for a disused chapel from the penal times. This I was able to find. Then parking the car, I headed up the looming hill on the north side of the road.

I am in Formoyle East, one of the thousands of townlands where there's no longer a town. The hike begins easily enough. I follow a newly made road leading to a house that is under construction—a substantial two-story, definitely first-class habitation by the nineteenth-century census standard. There's a big picture window and even a garage. It's probably a summer second home for someone for whom the Celtic Tiger of new prosperity is roaring. After this, it's pretty rough going, for the Burren landscape opens out again—virtually all rock, some smooth, some tumbled about, some formed into dozens of stone walls that snake back and forth across the incline. Three-quarters of the way to what I think is the top, I pass five cows sheltering in the lee of a six-foot stone wall. Above this, the hill ahead seems to go up and up, no end in sight, and no Famine village. Then I see it. To the west across a deep-cut valley of rocks, on the brow of the next hill, is the outline of a cluster of stone gable ends, highlighted against the far-off sparkling sea. With binoculars, I make out a dozen or more roofless ghost houses, and among them clumps of rock and earth that used to be fireplaces, hearths, doorframes, windows. There are no trees, no sounds.

Almost immediately, the weather comes down—it's been threatening all afternoon—with gusts of wind and big splatters of rain. I realize that I can't get over there today, for it's getting dark as well. Never mind. While picking my way back down to the safety of my car—a saving splash of red that comes in sight within ten minutes—I try to imagine what it was like to live in those cabins. Even in the best of times, whenever those might have been, it must always have been a cold, wet, windy, exposed, and desolate place. And then, to have been starved out. I realize at once that the true metaphor is the one I've just experienced. I mean, not getting there. I mean, seeing the place from the next hill over. Had I made the proper ascent and stood among those ruins, I would not have gotten any closer to what the people of Formoyle East endured. All that is far beyond me. Even with the mass of detail I've gathered about the Famine in Ireland and County Monaghan, even with the rain now pelting down, I'll never shake off the comforting blanket of tourism and buried time that covers the scene.

5

My Mother's Chapter

Softly, in the dusk, a woman is singing to me;
Taking me back down the vista of years, till I see
A child sitting under the piano, in the boom of the tingling strings
And pressing the small, poised feet of a mother who smiles as she sings.

—D. H. Lawrence, "Piano"

I've always loved D. H. Lawrence's poem "Piano," but I didn't know why until I started to think back to my childhood. I realized then that the poem echoed one of my earliest memories. I am playing with blocks—ABCs in primary colors—on the yellow linoleum kitchen floor of our family's apartment in Norwood. As we left that place in the summer of 1947, I was no older than four. I am sitting under the ironing board on which my mother is ironing shirts for my father. I feel the thump of the iron and smell the crisp, clean smell of hot metal on dampened cloth. The radio is on and Mum is singing along with a song. The radio was always on. The steady flow of news, music, soap operas, and baseball games kept her generation of "homemakers" company. As for those songs my mother sang along with, the ones she really liked, I now realize that there was a ground note of sadness running through most of them. Why was this? World War II, with its myriad deaths and dislocations, had just ended. Before it, there had been the Great Depression, affecting many in her large extended family of tradesmen and laborers. Also, the decade of the Thirties had begun with her mother's death and closed with her father's, after a long illness. And both of these events had significantly diverted Mum's dreams of how her adult life ought to have been getting under way.

The songs that had come out of the war registered the enforced, threat-filled absences that went on for years: "We'll meet again, don't know where, don't know when, / But I know we'll meet again, some sunny day. / Keep smiling through, just like you always do, / 'Til the blue skies drive the dark clouds far away." One of her favorites was a song of military sacrifice: "There's a Star-Spangled Banner waving somewhere / In a distant land so many miles away. / Only Uncle Sam's great heroes get to go there / Where I wish that I could also live some day." She would put something extra into the litany of heroes—"I'd see Lincoln, Custer, Washington and Perry, / And Nathan Hale and Colin Kelly, too." Her voice would shake with emotion when she sang "Colin Kelly," and she explained to me that he was a young man who had stayed at the controls of his doomed plane until his crew could bail out and it was too late for him to escape.

Other songs had in common a wistfulness of missed connections, stalled relationships, loneliness. But I notice now that in those my mother sang most often the feelings were likely to be oblique, off-center, deflected by buffering and sometimes humorous conventions. "Little Sir Echo" ("How do you do?") turns out to be talking to himself: "You're a nice little fellow / I know by your voice / But you're always so far away (away)." And in "Playmate," the context for a similar refusal of contact is a child's pretence: "Playmate, I cannot play with you / My dolly has the flu / Boo hoo hoo hoo." Another favorite was "Red Wing," which tells of star-crossed American Indian lovers out on the prairie—a long way from Norwood: "Now, the moon shines tonight on pretty Red Wing / The breeze is sighing, the night bird's crying, / For afar 'neath his star her brave is sleeping, / While Red Wing's weeping her heart away." All of this music was my initial exposure to rhythm, rhyme, and melody—to poetry, that is. There and then I realized that emotion could be bottled mnemonically and decanted at will.

Germans

In the nineteenth century, more people came to the United States from Germany than from any other place. In the peak decade of the 1880s, 1.5 million Germans took the chance of an American fresh start. More came from the southwest than any other part of Germany—first from the Palatinate in the central Rhine valley, then farther south from the provinces of Baden and Württemberg and the Black Forest (*Schwartzwald*). For all of these, the River Rhine was the conduit to America by way of the North Sea ports of Rotterdam, Bremen, and Hamburg. The vast majority of German immigrants came to the Middle Atlantic states and the Midwest. In 1890, New England was home to only 2 percent of America's German-born residents. The census counted only 10,362 Germans in Boston, whereas

New York City had over 200,000 and Chicago, 161,000. Most German immigrants had come for the Promised Land's standard assurance of increased social and economic opportunity to counter overpopulation and status immobility in Europe. Many came as already constituted family groups whose breadwinners tended to be literate, skilled craftsmen and laborers. In the mid-nineteenth century, people also left to escape political repression and the relentless demand for military service provoked by campaigns that culminated in the creation of the German Empire in 1871.

Though in the minority who chose New England as their destination, my mother's German ancestors fit this profile in other respects. Here, Joe Gould's 1913 "Racial Survey of Norwood" for the local paper is a solid gold source for me. In his article on the town's Germans, Joe remarks that "quite a history of military Germany could be gathered" from the memories of Norwood's many German veterans. One of these had served in three European wars in the 1860s. Another had participated in the earlier turbulence inside Germany during 1848 and 1849. This man from the province of Baden turns out to be my own great-great-grandfather, Lawrence Kuld, about whom I had previously known almost nothing:

> In 1848, a revolutionary wave swept over the smaller states of Germany and was ruthlessly suppressed by Austria and Prussia, so that many German refugees came to this country thereafter. Lawrence Kuld, the oldest German in Norwood, whose eighty-sixth birthday was yesterday (Friday) [August 1, 1913] was one of the fugitives. He was in Artillery Division No. 3 of Baden, and when this force was defeated in 1848, he had several narrow escapes from capture, and as he came in a roundabout way, he did not reach this country until 1852. He lived for many years in the "German block" on Walpole street, and he worked for fifty-eight years in the tannery, and still seems hale and hearty.

Lawrence Kuld died seven months later, on February 13, 1914. At least he missed the guns of August.

Kuld had been born near Karlsruhe, the capital of the Grand Duchy of Baden, in 1826. A few miles east of the Rhine, Karlsruhe is twenty miles northeast of Baden-Baden, the site of underground hot springs (whence its name) and a famous summer watering hole for European royalty throughout the nineteenth century. The province of Baden had been a hotbed of radical liberalism in Germany since the early nineteenth century. Harvest failures in 1816 and 1817 combined with increased discrimination against the many southern Catholics, so that the base of disaffected citizens included farmers, craftsmen, and the lower middle class. One of only two German states to get its own constitution in 1818, Baden became a place where the liberal press and public meetings to air grievances flourished. And there continued to be plenty of grievances. In the late 1840s the situation reached crisis proportions. A full-scale famine that hit the south in 1847 was due to a conjunction of elements similar to that affecting Ireland at the same time: a blighted potato crop for several years running, rapid population growth, further subdivision of already small holdings, and continued collection of feudal dues by the aristocracy and the church, "owners" of the land that the peasantry farmed. The tithes exacted were 10 percent of the harvest plus as much as three months of labor, and evictions from the land often followed inability to pay.

In the European revolutionary year of 1848, mass meetings and agitations proliferated. Much heartened by the overthrow of the July Kingdom in France in February 1848, a "March Movement" of rioting and disruption of local governments spread across Germany. This was especially intense in Baden, where the leaders included Friedrich Hecker, Gustave Struve, and Lorenz Brentano, later viewed as heroes of German freedom. It was in this climate that Karl Marx published the *Communist Manifesto* in London in February. In March, he moved to the city of Cologne on the Rhine, near where the action was. A contemporary observer of revolutionary activity in early 1848 declared, "Along side Paris, attention turned above all to Karlsruhe, Mannheim and Heidelberg." By early 1849, threatened aristocratic rulers in many parts of Germany were desperate enough to call on their militaristic, empire-building neighbors, the Prussians, who were only too happy to march in and squelch democratic dissent in Saxony, the Ruhr area, and the Palatinate.

In Baden, a significant early success of the liberal movement had been the abolition of all feudal dues in April 1848. Thus encouraged, the province remained so volatile that the term "Baden Revolution" came into currency. Throughout the latter part of 1848 and on into 1849, "People's Clubs" sprang up everywhere. Though pledged to Leopold, the Grand Duke of Baden, many soldiers in the province's 15,000-man standing army sided with the liberals. Some proved their sympathies by joining local People's Clubs, and on May 10, 1849, the entire garrison of 5,000 troops stationed at Rastatt, just twelve miles southwest of Karlsruhe and the site of a magnificent ducal palace and a fortress holding political prisoners, rose up against the duke. Spokesmen for the Rastatt garrison announced in a public meeting that each army company had become a People's Club. Three days later the garrison at Karlsruhe did the same thing. Twenty-one-year-old Lawrence Kuld of Artillery Divison No. 3 of Baden was one of these rebel soldiers.

A congress of deputies elected by the People's Clubs was meeting in nearby Offenburg, and when representatives from the garrisons arrived wearing green oak branches entwined on their shakos, the gathering erupted in joyful celebration. With the army joined to the cause, it seemed that victory was possible. Led by Mannheim lawyer Lorenz Brentano, the Offenburg congress elected a permanent State Committee to conduct the business of the People's Clubs of Baden. At this point, Grand Duke Leopold fled across the Rhine to Alsace with his family. Upon hearing of this, Brentano and the other leaders of the movement met in the marketplace at Rastatt and declared that the State Committee was now the provisional government of the province of Baden, and on June 3, 1849, the citizens of Baden cast 180,000 votes to elect eighty deputies to a new Constituent Assembly. No other German province got this far on the road to representative government.

The Grand Duke proceeded to call in the Prussians to put down the uprising and regain power. Abetted by the railroads, imperial and Prussian armies totaling 60,000 men were soon advancing on Baden from the north. Theirs was a ruthless, scorched-earth operation. With no more than 20,000 men in the field, the Badenese were easily defeated in a series of brutal actions. After the climactic engagement at Waghäusel on June 21, the remaining insurgents, numbering fewer than 13,000, marched to Rastatt to make a final stand. In his report on the state of his fighting force at this point, the Badenese commander said that "at the roll call half the army was missing, had gone astray, been destroyed, lost. . . . A third of the horsemen have gone over to the enemy, a third of the infantry have surreptitiously returned to their homes, as have also two thirds of the national guard. Only the artillery remains steadfast, complete, and full of zeal."

The Badenese lined up on the banks of the River Murg outside Rastatt. Some were singing the "Marseillaise." Beginning on June 29, the Prussian onslaught overwhelmed them in short order. Six thousand of the insurgent soldiers retreated into the fortress at Rastatt, while the rest of the survivors fled and scattered out over the countryside. Artilleryman Kuld was likely one of these lucky ones. The rebels trapped in the fortress held out for nearly a month, but the Baden Revolution ended with their unconditional surrender on July 23, 1849. In victory, the Prussians were merciless. Every tenth prisoner in the fortress was shot. Drumhead courts martial were set up at which dozens of the insurgent leaders were executed and buried in unmarked mass graves. Hundreds more received long prison terms. These bloody events lodged in the folk memory of the people for generations. The "Badenese Lullaby" begins:

> Sleep, my child, sleep quietly,
> There's a Prussian outside the door.
> He's killed your father
> And made your mother poor.
> And if you don't sleep peacefully and quietly
> He'll come and close your eyes.
> Sleep, my child, sleep quietly,
> There's a Prussian outside the door.

I was excited to come upon this heartening piece of my mother's family history—an ancestor who fought on the side of liberalism against the conservative, militaristic forces out of Prussia whose victories ultimately led to Otto Von Bismarck's Second Reich, which was, in turn, to serve as precedent and model for Adolph Hitler. In the summer of 2006, I visited Rastatt and found that one wing of the Grand Duke's still splendid baroque palace has become a museum and archive—the Memorial Center for Liberation Movements in German History. Open since 1974, and with a strong focus on the 1848–49 revolution, this remarkable place also houses many reminders of German "freedom fighters" from other eras. There are biographies, with pictures and artifacts, of German supporters of the French Revolution, nineteenth-century "exiles" to the United States, some of whom fought in the American Civil War, heroic opponents of the National Socialist regime of 1933–45, among them the "White Rose" student defectors from Hitler Youth in Munich, and resistance fighters in Communist East Germany after World War II. The climactic exhibit is a big chunk of the Berlin Wall, a twenty-foot-high, graffiti-laden exclamation point to the museum's overall theme.

After the defeat at Rastatt, emigration was the choice of many. It is estimated that 80,000 people left Baden almost immediately—one in eighteen of the provincial population of 1.5 million. Huge rafts, 100 by 300 meters, carried wood down the Rhine from the Black Forest to the North Sea ports. Now, whole villages, as many as 600 people, rode these rafts on top of the load on their way to America. The trip could take three months, and it was

Figure 17. The Baldufs in Rastatt, Baden, c. 1865. (Back) Julius, Peter. (Front) Mary Anna (mother), Anna, Fritz, Peter (father). Photograph by F. P. Luber, Rastatt.

no picnic. What must it have been like, floating north on the great river, taking in a passing scene of often breathtaking beauty, studded with markers of eventful history? On either side, a haze of steep cliffs or gentle hills covered in greenery; small towns, just like those that had been abandoned, with steeples poking toward the blue sky and little sandy beaches. On either side, medieval monasteries and fairytale castles, some in picturesque ruin, others still flying papal or ducal flags. Here were the famously romantic symbols of church and state, *kloster* and *schloss*, transformed for these emigrating families into grim reminders that neither spiritual nor temporal power had done anything to keep them in their homes—quite the opposite, in fact.

As he told Joe Gould, Lawrence Kuld was on the run for over two years and in danger of capture several times, yet he stayed in Baden long enough to marry a woman named Frances (her last name is lost) and to bring their first child, Louisa Agatha, my great-grandmother, into the world in the spa town of Baden-Baden on August 27, 1851. A year later, these three arrived in the United States. It may have been training as a tanner that brought Lawrence Kuld to Winslow Brothers on Endicott Street in Norwood, Massachusetts. At any rate, he liked the place well enough to work there for nearly sixty years. He and Frances had four more children, three girls and a boy, all raised in Norwood.

As a young woman, Louisa Agatha Kuld met another German immigrant from an all too familiar place in her home province: Julius Franz Balduf, born on August 7, 1848, in the insurrectionist city of Rastatt. His mother may well have sung him to sleep as an infant with the "Badenese Lullaby." Julius was one of the four children of Mary Anna Goeleige and Peter Balduf. I have a picture of this handsome family of six, taken by a professional photographer, F. P. Luber of Rastatt. It's quite the rare item in my collection—the only photo I've ever seen of any family members taken in the European home place. The three boys and one girl appear to be in their early to late teens, so it's probably the late 1850s or early 1860s. The Baldufs look solidly middle class, with ties, jackets, vests, and lots of buttons. They must have been doing well to have had this picture taken.

All three boys, Peter, Julius, and Frederick (known as Fritz), left for the United States at about the same time, the mid-1860s, and for the same reason: to avoid being drafted into Bismarck's Prussian-led armies. Their sister, Anna, remained at home. Emigration from Baden and the rest of southern Germany had continued apace all through the 1850s, which was a time of extreme conservative reaction following the movement toward social emancipation that had marked the heady months before the surrender at Rastatt. Constitutional rights and universal suffrage were rescinded; the church-state concordat, a central police system, and press censorship were restored; and many functions that had been assumed by local governments were abrogated. Also, militarist flag-waving flourished toward the end of the decade, thanks to deepening crises on three fronts: continued bad relations between Prussia and Austria, the threat of war with France, and a dispute with Denmark over sovereignty in Schleswig-Holstein. In September 1862, Bismarck became minister-president of Prussia, and the die was cast for an aggressive, empire-building foreign policy.

In Baden, there was a three-year conscription for privates to fight in the army of the Grand Duke, which, of course, was pledged to the Prussian cause. Three short wars followed in quick succession: Prussia against Denmark in 1864, against Austria in 1866, and against France in 1870. (One of Joe Gould's Norwood informants had been unlucky enough to serve in all three.) Prussia won them all—handily. When the smoke cleared, Denmark had been ejected from Schleswig-Holstein, Austria was cast out on its own, and Prussia had officially annexed several smaller German states, including Baden. In addition, the French capitulation after six months of lackluster fighting provoked a new upsurge of pan-Germanic patriotism. The result was the unification of Germany on January 1, 1871, into Bismarck's Second Reich, with the Prussian King William I as titular head of the empire.

By this point, all three Balduf boys were safely in Massachusetts. Julius had arrived in about 1865 at age seventeen. It has come down through the family that he paid for his passage by working as a ship's steward on a "salt boat," whatever that was. He, too, found employment at Winslow Brothers Tannery in Norwood, where he ultimately put in fifty-four years, rising to the position of foreman in the "pickle cellar." What an island of calm the towns of eastern Massachusetts must have been for the Kulds, Baldufs, and other German immigrants after the pelting storms of early life in a most troubled part of Europe in a most troubled time.

Having come from Rastatt, in flight from the Prussians, and now working in the tannery, young Julius Balduf must have had a lot to talk about with Lawrence Kuld. Maybe the older man brought him home to dinner. In any case, Julius and Lawrence's daughter, Louisa, fell in love. They were married at ages twenty-five and twenty-two on July 7, 1874. The newlyweds settled in "Germantown" on Wilson Street, which was only a brisk walk from the tannery but out of range of its smells. This neighborhood became a typical German American enclave, close-knit and self-contained, with several church and social groups. Still going strong when Joe Gould wrote in 1913 was the *Arbeiter-Kranken-und-Versterllasse*, or Workmen's Sick and Dead Benefit Fund, a "mutual benefit" insurance and social club that had been launched in 1898. Their headquarters, Arbeiter Hall, had been built in 1901. This I still recognized, for Workmen's Hall had been a landmark in our family's history. It was just up Wilson Street from the house in which my mother was born and raised. We heard a lot about the place, and it was still in use during my childhood and beyond. A scrap of recovered news from the local paper conveys my mother's connection there well into young adulthood. In December 1939, she and two of her sisters are listed in the Norwood paper as members of the executive board of the

Figure 18. Lawrence Kuld (seated at front far left) and the Balduf family in Norwood. My grandfather Edward Everett Balduf is standing on the far right. In front of Louisa and Julius Balduf is a framed picture of their son George, who died at age 3 in 1888.

Workmen's Sick and Death Benefit, which is planning "a joint Christmas party" with the Wilson Improvement Association, to be held at Workmen's Hall. "All children of the district and children of members are invited."

Julius Balduf became a true immigrant patriarch, but he had had some trouble of his own along the way. His brother Peter had gone another, though still typically German, route in the New World by opening a saloon—on West Third Street in South Boston—and the story is told that Julius became his brother's best customer for a while in the 1870s. He was, however, so valued an employee at the tannery that Winslow Brothers paid to send him away to dry out, and the cure worked. His foreman's position carried high status and was well enough paid that he was able to acquire a substantial amount of land along Wilson Street. He built a big, rambling house at number 71. He and his wife needed the room, for they went on to have twelve children between 1874 and 1894, ten of whom lived to adulthood. (George died of diptheria at age three in 1888 and Elsie May died of a burst appendix in 1907 at fifteen.) Several of the Balduf children followed their father into the tannery.

Julius also put up and operated a bowling alley on his Wilson Street property. Mum told me about this when I was five or six, and I asked her to show me where this place, which sounded utterly mysterious, had been. During one of our excursions to Wilson Street, she led me and my brother into a dense growth of pine, where we found a long rectangle of rocks—the outline of the building. I stepped through the break in the wall marking the doorway and paced the length of the big room. As the tall grass swished against my bare legs—it was summertime—I tried to imagine people I'd never met, the family and friends of a long-deceased great-grandfather, playing this game called bowling, which I'd also never seen anyone do. Somehow, I associated this activity with their having been Germans. This all came back to me in junior high when I read about the phantom crew of little men bowling in the Catskills in Washington Irving's "Rip Van Winkle." The association spurred me to lead a contingent of friends on our bikes to the site of Balduf's Bowling Alley. I couldn't find the foundation line of rocks—I think because a new house had gone up nearby—but that just added to the allure of the place, which had become ghostly too.

Born on April 18, 1879, the fourth child of Julius and Louisa Kuld Balduf was given the very American name of Edward Everett Balduf. He would become my mother's father. (Another son, born in 1892, was called Grover Cleveland.) In the 1900 census, Edward is twenty-one, living at home, and working as a "printing press feeder." He had chosen to make his living not in tanning but in another industry that was just taking off in Norwood—the printing of books. In the 1890s two big firms opened for business in town: the Norwood Press and the Plimpton Press. My grandfather Balduf went into "Plimpton's," which expanded rapidly through the 1910s, at its peak turning out 50,000 volumes a day.

Both presses were still in operation when I was in college in the early 1960s, and, as it happened, both were of interest to me. When I discovered the Irish poet W. B. Yeats as a college freshman, I noticed that his *Collected Poems,* though published by Macmillan in New York, had actually been printed at the Norwood Press. Here was something local to be proud of, and I pointed it out immediately to my roommate. (He wasn't much impressed.) Also, the summer after freshman year, I followed my grandfather's footsteps by going to work on the three-to-eleven shift at Plimpton's. It was 1961, and one of the books rolling off the presses was Edwin O'Connor's novel *The Edge of Sadness*. One of my jobs was to haul big dollies of these books from the room where a cadre of permanent employees, all of them women, had clothed them in jackets. I would inch these precarious piles onto a freight elevator, and then ride them down to the loading dock. Only once did I make the fatal miscalculation of pulling the elevator rope before the dolly was fully on the platform. Hundreds of O'Connor novels spilled out and all that were bruised even slightly went off to the discard heap. I was dressed down by my supervisor but also rewarded: he gave me one of the damaged copies. The book is still in my library, and I prize its random, retrospective symbolism, as I have gone on to spend most of my scholarly life reading and writing about the literature of Irish immigration and ethnicity to which O'Connor's books have contributed so much.

Strong Farmers

I'm sure he brought books home as well, but Edward Balduf did a lot better than that. He found his wife at Plimpton's. Johanna Frances McAuliffe, my only immigrant grandparent, had been born at Number 15 Kerry Hall in the city and county of Cork on December 5, 1879, the second of the eight children of John J. McAuliffe and Anne Marie Hurley, who had met and married in the Boston area. (Born about 1860, John was an Irish immigrant, having come to America as a young man, but Anne was born in Canton, Massachusetts, in 1863, the daughter of immigrants Dennis Hurley, a laborer, and Margaret Kelliher Hurley.) According to the family story, "Hannah," as Johanna became known, was born in Ireland only because her parents were back visiting to settle an estate. Because of this accident, I was able to obtain an Irish passport, available, after a rigorous procedure of documentation, to the grandchildren of immigrants. It's a lovely thing to have.

On the evidence given to me in his nineties by my grandmother's last surviving sibling, Henry "Ted" McAuliffe, their father had come from "Whitechurch" in County Cork. I found that there was only one such place—the civil parish of Whitechurch (in Irish, *Teampall Geal* and Anglicized as "Temple Gall"), which lies about five miles north of Cork City. John J. McAuliffe died in Norwood in April 1924 at age sixty-four, and his death certificate lists his parents as James McAuliffe and Joanna Dunlea, both from Ireland. When I checked at the National Library of Ireland, *Griffith's Valuation* for Whitechurch, completed in 1853, listed six McAuliffes, but only one James. So here he was, my Irish great-great-grandfather on my mother's side. These are the parallel figures to my father's ancestors, the Fannins and Fannings of Urbalkirk, County Monaghan.

The two families were very different, however. This James McAuliffe was living in the townland of Coolowen (in Irish, *Cúil Eoghan,* "Owen's Corner"), which lies two miles south of the village of Whitechurch and three miles north of the city of Cork. He seems to have been doing well enough to have had an estate worth settling in 1879. In 1853 the entire townland covered 1,033 acres, and James McAuliffe was renting 178 of them in three separate plots. He also had two subtenants, Michael Walsh and Mary Fitzgerald, renting houses from him. The valuation of the whole was over £111. Thus, James was what's known in Ireland as a "strong farmer"—established, prosperous, a dominant figure in Coolowen townland and society at large. Backing up to the one available earlier source, I found that in the *Tithe Applotment Book* for "Temple Gall," completed on January 9, 1826, McAuliffes showed up in three townlands west and south of the village of Whitechurch. All appear to have been strong farmers:

In Droumgariffe, Daniel McAuliffe rents 84 acres, valued at £60.

In Gorteenastooka, John McAuliffe rents 61 acres, valued at £42.

In Coolowen, Daniel McAuliffe rents 106 acres, valued at £112.

In Coolowen, Cornelius McAuliffe rents 116 acres, valued at £105.

In 1826, Coolowen encompassed 898 acres in total, and the two McAuliffes there held 222 acres, nearly a quarter of the whole townland. Actually, "Daniel" is written over "Cornelius," which suggests that the latter originally held both plots, and that Daniel and James were his sons. (*Griffith's* corroborates this, as Daniel is still on the books there.) So, the McAuliffes were historically a strong family of strong farmers. Even their name has a powerful ring to it, for *Mac Amhlaoibh* means "Son of Olaf," and thus goes back to the Viking invaders.

Their land was good as well. North Cork's relatively rich soil was planted more in grains than potatoes, and there was decent pasturage for dairy cows. The people there were altogether better situated than many to weather the Great Famine—especially those who farmed the larger holdings. Coolowen was a long way from the meager six-acre holding of the Fannings up in Monaghan. In 1851, Phillip Fanning had come to America from a greatly impoverished part of a greatly distressed country. John McAuliffe arrived a generation later, after Irish society had reconstituted itself, much to the benefit of the strong farmers who had come through the Famine relatively unscathed. Chances are that he came to the United States of his own volition and with money in his pockets. In keeping with his county of origin, John settled in Norwood's Cork City neighborhood. When he died in

1924, his residence was 277 Railroad Avenue, only a block from my grandfather Fanning and the Norwood Laundry. My mother had very little information about her grandfather's work life, but there were hints that he had been something of a ne'er-do-well. His death certificate says he was an "engineer," but of what and where, nobody seems to know. My grandmother's 1879 Irish birth certificate declares him to be a "porter." There is also talk of service as a "seaman" somewhere along the line. In any case, John appears to have bumped through life in fairly nondescript and undistinguished ways. It's impossible to get a fix on him.

Though it's badly cracked down the middle, one of my favorite photographs from our family's scrapbooks is that of a slip of a girl standing at her work station at the Plimpton Press. There's a matronly woman watching her back and others behind them. Hannah McAuliffe is surrounded by piles and piles of paper—shades of my own accident on the job sixty-odd years later, maybe in the same room! But Hannah looks much too vigilant to upset any of these applecarts. Entirely ready for work, she's wearing a long-sleeved dress and apron, her hair is pulled back, and she's holding a pencil. She also appears cautious, uncertain, eager to please. She's pretty but she may not know it. Whenever I see this picture, I think of an early Yeats poem—it was probably rolling off the line at the rival Norwood Press right about this time—in which the speaker describes a quiet country girl:

She carries in the candles,
And lights the curtained room,
Shy in the doorway
And shy in the gloom;

And shy as a rabbit,
Helpful and shy.
To an isle in the water
With her would I fly.

I like to think that Edward Balduf felt something like this when he spotted Hannah McAuliffe. Their Plimpton's courtship was followed by marriage on June 10, 1903. He was twenty-four and she, twenty-three. Edward was an up-and-comer at the press, and soon he was promoted to a position of foreman. The young couple went on to build a beautiful big house on land provided by Julius Balduf and right next door—at 57 Wilson Street. Here my mother, Frances Patricia, was born on October 11, 1913, the second youngest of the five Balduf girls.

Figure 19. My grandmother "Hannah" McAuliffe at the Plimpton Press.

It had to have been a great place to grow up. Even beyond the stamp of German ethnicity, Wilson Street had unique attributes that stirred prideful *dindshenchas* in my mother and her friends. For example, the neighborhood once had its own hospital. Mum pointed out the site to us whenever we walked around up there. It looked like any other house, but number 95 had been the Wilson Street Hospital—with inpatient care, a nursery, and even an operating room—from about 1900 to the mid-teens, when the Norwood Hospital opened on Washington Street in the center of town. The attending physician at the neighborhood hospital had been the legendary Old Doctor O'Toole, who had delivered Mum and her sisters. The direct line to his son, who was our family doctor, added to the mystique of the street.

The neighborhood also had its own pond. Part of George Willett's plan for the town, a substantial body of water bearing his name had been created on low-lying farm land in 1912 by damming Germany Brook. A new public bathing beach opened just up the street in the summer of 1916, when Mum was two and a half. She and her friends must have felt the place had been made just for them, and in talking about "New Pond"—the name by which it was still known in the 1950s and beyond—she never lost that proprietorial air. Whenever we went there as kids, she would point out where the various bathhouses and concession stands had been in the beach area over the years. Mum was not pleased when this personal sacred site was sold off by the town. The buyer was the Catholic Archdiocese of Boston, which hauled away the sand and put up a new church, St. Timothy's. This was a marker of Norwood's expanding population, but the religious connection did little to soften my mother's sense of egregious encroachment. These new people might be Catholics, but they were still carpetbaggers.

All of this seems idyllic, especially when compared with my father's motherless, seminomadic childhood in and around downtown Norwood. (I don't believe the Fannings ever owned a house.) And yet, there's a dark side to my mother's story as well. The First World War, the "Great War," brought the rudest of awakenings to Norwood's—and the nation's—German American communities. After this watershed, the citizens of the Wilson Street neighborhood must have regrouped with a disillusioned intensity rooted in the deep, dynastic wounds of nativist prejudice against them.

A Basket of Rocks

The sinking of the passenger ship *Lusitania* on May 7, 1915, by a German submarine provoked a strong reaction of anti-German emotion in the United States. It increased in force and finally broke in a whirlwind of intolerant rhetoric and vicious behavior after President Woodrow Wilson declared war in April 1917. In *Bonds of Loyalty: German Americans and World War I* (1974), historian Frederick C. Luebke concludes that the way had been prepared for such reactions by well established WASP perceptions of "this numerous and proud people. American Germans were often difficult to understand; they seemed separatistic or clannish. Their very success in the American environment made them appear as a threat." Nativist sentiment ran deep. Many Americans had come to dislike their German neighbors intensely, and for these the war in Europe was the catalyst for bad behavior.

I am struck by the similarities between the blatant intolerance of 1917–18 and feelings unleashed in America after the terrorist attacks of September 11, 2001. In both situations, simplistic calls to take sides and exhortations to act proliferated, and those in authority all the way to the top stoked irrational fears. In 1917, propaganda was institutionalized in George Creel's Committee on Public Information, created by presidential executive order. Everywhere, there were prohibitions proposed against playing German music, publishing German books and newspapers, and teaching the language in the schools. Half the states passed some such legislation. People, neighborhoods, and entire towns changed their names to expunge associations with Germany. There were several book burnings, as well. Vandals attacked the homes and businesses of German Americans in many parts of the country, and some immigrants were tarred and feathered.

There was even a lynching, which took place in southern Illinois, where I now live and am writing this. On the evening of April 4, 1918, Robert Prager, a native of Dresden who had come to America at age nineteen in 1905 to work as a coal miner, was taken by a mob from a jail in Collinsville, just across the Mississippi River from St. Louis, where he had been locked up for his own protection. An early supporter of Wilson's war effort, Prager had even tried unsuccessfully to join the U.S. Navy. Subsequently, he had gotten a reputation as a loudmouth with socialist leanings. He had also lost an eye along the way, which, some believed, gave him the look of a spy. This was enough to get him hanged from a tree. In May 1918, eleven men went to trial for Prager's murder. The proceeding lasted three days, and the jury voted to acquit after deliberating for forty-five minutes. All this got banner newspaper coverage all over the United States. Certainly, news of the Prager lynching reached the Germantown neighborhood in Norwood.

Indeed, Massachusetts had not been a bastion of tolerance in those inflamed times. Already notorious for his anti-immigration positions, that grand old WASP Senator Henry Cabot Lodge declared that "disloyalists" ought to be given over to military tribunals: "Try them by court martial and shoot them" was his helpful suggestion. In July 1917 the venerable *Atlantic Monthly* published an essay indiscriminately attacking all of America's German-language newspapers and magazines. German-born Dr.

Karl Muck, the respected conductor of the Boston Symphony Orchestra, was hounded and vilified for months. (Among his sins was playing too much German music.) In March 1918 he was arrested by federal officers and interned as a threat to public safety. Finally, in an eerie presage of the beyond-satiric 2003 menu change in the cafeterias of the U.S. House of Representatives from "french fries" to "freedom fries," a doctor in Attleboro, Massachusetts, proposed changing the name of German measles to "Liberty measles."

The barrage of animosities, local and national, toward Germans helps explain why my mother and her sisters were reluctant as children to explore their father's background, even though they lived in a German American neighborhood. The benighted climate of the times had stifled any sort of ethnic curiosity among the Baldufs and millions like them. And then, of course, one very short generation later came Adolf Hitler and the Third Reich. As Luebke states, "It is another irony of the history of the Germans in America that the Nazi era coincided with the very time when they could have been expected to revive the study of their past and, incidentally, to regain the self-confidence lost during World War I."

There was hardly more encouragement for the Balduf girls to investigate their mother's Irish background. With the approach of World War I, all European ethnic identifications (other than ties to England) became positively unsavory in the eyes of many Americans. In 1914 President Wilson had made his famous "hyphenated Americans" speech at the unveiling of a monument to Commodore John Barry, whom Wilson praised as "an Irishman [whose] heart crossed the Atlantic with him," unlike "some Americans" who "need hyphens in their names, because only part of them has come over." Wilson and Theodore Roosevelt became the leading spokesmen in the hue and cry over "divided loyalties" which intensified with United States entry into the war in 1917.

Moreover, the timing of the Easter Rising in Dublin in April 1916 was viewed as shameful to many and rank treachery to more than a few American observers. This unsuccessful but symbolically weighty opening to the Irish Revolution had ended with 3,000 casualties and the British execution of the sixteen leaders of the rising as traitors in time of war. Hostilities in Ireland continued through World War I and beyond, and ended with great bitterness. The treaty signed in December 1921 to end the revolution created the problematic partition of Northern Ireland and the Irish Free State, which, in turn, led to the heartbreak of civil war for two more years. To many, if not most, Irish Americans, these "Troubles" in the old country constituted a shameful coda, which they failed to understand and preferred to disregard.

The result of the tangle of historical embarrassments was a wariness in families such as my mother's about acknowledging, much less valuing, German or Irish ethnicity. There were a few, a very few, German phrases that she taught us: *dummkopf* was one, the equivalent on her father's side of her mother's *amadán* in Irish. And the expression that accused someone of being crazy, always made us laugh: *"Du bist verrückt, mein Herr!"* But that was really about it. Mum had aunts and uncles and cousins galore on both sides of her family, spread all over the town of Norwood, and I'm fairly sure there wasn't much of anything recognizable as "ethnic" about their lives. The same was true on my father's side. After all, his father, Charles Winslow Fanning, had been abandoned by *his* Irish Catholic father, Walking John, and raised by his Yankee Protestant grandmother, Sophia Draper Radcliffe. So much for ethnic pride. In those days, people still remembered the pain that assimilation had cost, and many were still struggling to make their way. They would have judged attempts to define their families as Irish or German as, at best, frivolous and, at worst, asking for trouble.

My mother did share with us one memory of the cost of being identified as German during World War I. In the run-up to America's entry into the war, the town of Norwood had held a "Preparedness Parade" and organized a General Committee for Public Safety, both in March 1917. After Wilson signed the declaration of war on April 6, the General Committee had gone on to sponsor paramilitary drills, organize food and clothing drives, and set up a mechanism for disseminating war-related information in the event of an attack on the home front. There was even a subcommittee known (chillingly) as "Night Riders," a group of local young men who were deputized, armed, and sent out after dark in automobiles to "guard" the town's public and industrial buildings against sabotage. Here was a recipe for abuse of power, and I know from several sources that quite a few Norwood Germans of my mother's generation were harassed and humiliated through the war years and beyond. The story she told us must also have been one of her earliest memories. There was a custom around town that on May Day, friends and neighbors would leave baskets of spring flowers on one another's doorsteps. Mum recalled that on May 1, 1917, when she was three and a half years old, she opened the front door and found on the mat a basket of rocks.

Wilson Street

As she moved toward adulthood, my mother's experience of hearth and home at 57 Wilson Street became troubled. Her parents' deaths had each had a profound practical effect that involved the house in such a way as to augment natural grief. There her mother had contracted the intestinal cancer from which she died on February 1, 1930, at age fifty. This was Pat Balduf's junior year in high school, and her dreams of going on to college and becoming a teacher were stalled and ultimately relinquished. Because her three older sisters were married and gone, only she and her younger sister Peggy were still at home As the eldest daughter, Pat's job became "taking care of Pa."

My mother's report cards for grades seven through twelve were still on file at Norwood High School when I checked a few years ago. I'm looking now at a photocopy of her entire record, which fits on one handwritten page. In junior high, Pat Balduf had a fair number of absences, including one whole marking period missed "due to illness" in seventh grade in the winter of 1925–26. Perhaps because her mother was sick, Pat's yearly grade for "Effort" went from A in seventh grade to C in ninth, but the latter was also the year she signed up for both Latin I and Ancient History as electives. In high school, she missed very few days, even during her mother's last illness. She took English and Social Studies all the way through. She finished second-year Latin and also took two years of Spanish, Bookkeeping, and Freehand Drawing, and one year each of Cooking, Practical Arts, and Public Speaking. She dropped only one course ever—Chemistry, in senior year, after receiving a 60 for the second marking period. Mostly, she got Bs, with a scattering of As and Cs.

This record is ordinary enough, but because it belonged to my mother, several memories that she shared with me about her schooling are bubbling up now, more than seventy-five years after she graduated from high school on June 9, 1931. I know that she liked school a lot, especially English and learning poems by heart. I know that it had been adventurous of her to take Latin and Ancient History in ninth grade, and that success in these challenging subjects—final grades of 80 and 85—had gotten her thinking about becoming a teacher. (She told me this when, thirty years after she did it, I signed up for the same two classes for my ninth grade year at the same school.) I also know that she had hated Public Speaking and that the most practical of the Practical Arts for her had been sewing.

After graduating, Pat Balduf lived out the 1930s with her father and sister at 57 Wilson, with all the crises of town and national life during the Depression playing out around her. And there, her father also got sick—suffering a stroke and then being diagnosed with congestive heart failure. His illness and the gathering storm toward World War II were the backdrop of Pat Balduf's courtship and marriage to Chick Fanning. In the years after high school, Pat walked by the Texaco station on the corner of Wilson and Walpole Streets at least twice a day. She also stood there to catch the bus to downtown Norwood. Chick and his youngest brother Joe worked at the station, and one day contact was made. Dad had known who this girl was because his friends Bobby Sinclaire and Warren Young delivered heating oil to the Baldufs. When she got home, my mother remembers having said to her younger sister, Peggy, "You know who said hello to me? That *old* Fanning guy."

They were married on April 19, 1941, and the photos taken that day suggest a muted, low-key event. My parents-to-be are standing beside the house on Wilson Street, which is where their small reception was held. There's no tuxedo and no wedding gown. Chick has on a dark suit and Pat wears a skirt and jacket and a wide-brimmed hat. After a weekend wedding trip to New Hampshire, the newlyweds moved in with the Baldufs and continued to care for Mum's father. Dad had picked up some nursing skills in the CCC, and he helped out by giving his new father-in-law bed baths.

Edward Balduf's final illness coincided with the sickening plunge into madness of his parents' homeland. He would have had painful memories of the First World War and the indignities that accompanied it in his young manhood, as well as knowledge of his own father's flight to avoid service in the Prussian military machine in the 1860s. And now this. As Edward's health declined, the news from Germany got worse and worse. First, the keys to the secular kingdom were given over without a struggle to a former Austrian tramp who was emerging as a consummate huckster, sneak-thief, double-crosser, bully, and sadist with increasingly dangerous delusions of grandeur. In February 1933 came the Reichstag fire—silly in the obviousness of its deception but purely appalling in the aftermath of brutality and murder that clearly signaled what was to come. Then followed a terrifying blizzard of catastrophes: the Rhineland reoccupied in March 1936; Austria annexed in the *Anschluss* of March 1938; Chamberlain's abandonment of Czechoslovakia in October 1938; and the massive pogroms of November 9, *Kristallnacht*. Then *Blitzkrieg* in Poland and the declaration of war against Germany by England and France in September 1939. Paris fell to the Germans on June 14, 1940, and the London *blitz* proceeded from September 1940 into May 1941. And on and on.

In the last months of his life, Edward would have read about the first American casualties of undeclared war against Germany—eleven sailors killed when the U.S. destroyer *Kearny* was torpedoed by a U-boat while protecting a convoy on October 17, 1941, and 100 men lost in the sinking by torpedoes of a second destroyer, the *Reuben James*, on October 31. That autumn he would also have heard of the early successes in Germany's drive into Russia, which marked the widest territorial sweep of Hitler's dominance over Europe. Edward did not live to see that Hitler's lunatic hubris in going east would prove to be the downfall of the Third Reich. He was, however, a witness to Pearl Harbor, December 7, 1941, and the American declaration of war against Japan the next day. And he would have heard that on December 11, Hitler had rushed to declare war against the United States with a crazed and rambling address to the puppet Reichstag legislators in Berlin in which he attacked FDR as an international criminal controlled by "the full diabolical meanness of Jewry."

Edward Balduf died two and a half weeks later, on December 30, 1941. He was sixty-two. My mother, her name misspelled as "Francis," is listed as next of kin on his death certificate. Edward could not have known how the war would come out or what it would cost. Chief among the horrors he was spared was knowledge of the Holocaust, knowledge that might have included the familial irony that one of history's greatest mass murderers had come from the same home place as Edward's father and mother. The son of a local shopkeeper, Rudolf Franz Hoess had been born in 1900 in the town of Baden-Baden. He joined the National Socialist Party in 1922, served prison time for murdering an opponent of the Nazis in a fit of zeal, and was out of jail in time to join Heinrich Himmler's S.S. in 1933. Assigned to Dachau, one of the first concentration camps, in 1934, Hoess was rewarded for excellence in this line of work with appointment early in 1940 as *Kommandant* of the new camp at Auschwitz in Poland, and he helped design and then supervised the gas chambers and crematoria, which were fully operative by fall 1941. At his Nuremberg trial he boasted of responsibility for 2.5 million deaths. He was hanged at Auschwitz in April 1947.

Immediately after her father's death, my mother was dealt several blows from inside her own family. One sister came up with a suspect will naming her and her husband as estate executors. Another sister's husband brought a truck to 57 Wilson one afternoon when no one was home and took away some of the best china and furnishings, including the rug on the floor of my mother's bedroom. It's not clear whether my parents ever had an option to buy the house or to keep living there, but they ended up moving out, and one of the older Balduf sisters took possession with her husband. I never heard these stories directly, but at some point Mum told them to my sister. When Patti asked whether there were any hard feelings or repercussions, Mum said only that in those days family members just accepted things and went on with their lives. I do believe, though, that after these wounding losses, the goal of home ownership meant more to her than it would have under less difficult circumstances.

For the most part, my mother avoided 57 Wilson Street. During my childhood, we made very few visits to her sister's family there. Usually, we went up once a year, in the summertime, for a picnic lunch in the pine-shaded back yard. We never stayed long, and if we went inside, it was only to use the bathroom or get a drink of water. No "traipsing around" (a favorite phrase of Mum's) was allowed, and we never got above the first floor. My only memory of the place is of a spacious kitchen, in one corner of which was a narrow back stair to the second floor. Ahead and to the left, I could discern the outlines of a glistening table and chairs in the dining room, but that was all. Thus, there were few opportunities—and these seldom taken—for my mother to reminisce about what it had been like growing up in that house.

We didn't go to New Pond very often either. Instead, we would go on picnics to Ellis Pond, a smaller and older body of water, which had no bathing beach. Ellis was fairly close to the houses of my childhood, and sometimes we walked there of a Saturday afternoon in summer. We carried our picnic food and towels in a little red wagon that my brother Geoffrey and I would take turns pulling. My parents knew a narrow path through the woods off Nichols Street that ended in a small, grassy glade, shaded by overhanging trees. As soon as we arrived, my father would place the bottles of ginger ale and orangeade carefully in the water. We'd spread out a khaki army blanket, then walk around a bit, exploring the woods on both sides of the clearing. The blanket was scratchy, but soon enough the sun made it warm enough for dozing off. Sometimes Dad would strip branches from nearby willow bushes, then tie on pieces of white string we had brought along and attach lumps of bread to the free end of the line so that Geoffrey and I could "fish." Without hooks, we had no hope of landing anything, but all the fun was in seeing the minnows and small fry bob the line and eat the bread. The grass came right up to the water's edge, and we would sit on the bank with our pants rolled up and our feet in the water and watch the fish, zigzagging dragonflies, and the water lapping against the shore, the tops of the waves farther out winking in the sun like silver coins. The place was at the end of a small inlet, and if anyone else was on Ellis Pond those afternoons, we couldn't see them. Even in midsummer it was relatively cool there—quiet, too, except for the shrill din of insects and the occasional calling bird. It was a lovely spot, and ours alone. As with Yeats, "stand[ing] on the roadway, or on the pavements gray" while remembering his "Lake Isle of Inisfree," whenever I think of Ellis Pond, "peace comes dropping slow."

A few months after my grandfather Balduf's death and the ensuing domestic upheavals, my parents moved into the second-floor apartment at 30 Lincoln Street in another part of Norwood. All of our houses were still standing when I last checked, early in 2006, and this one is quite small, just two windows wide with a postage-stamp front lawn. Lincoln Street is closer to the center of town than Wilson Street, but it wasn't on any bus lines, and Mum must have felt pretty well dislocated there, especially as she had only ever lived in the one house before. The war was everywhere, of course, saturating the consciousness through newspapers and magazines, the radio, and conversations all day long. Two of my father's brothers and many of my parents' cousins went off to Europe and the Pacific before it was over. About this time, Dad got his job welding battleship hulls at Fore River Shipyard, which meant he was away all day long. And though he was a few years older than most who were joining up, it wasn't at all clear, despite his work, that he was going to be spared active duty. Nobody knew. On top of all this, my mother discovered in the spring of 1942 that she was pregnant. I was born on November 11—the day in 1918 that the Armistice was signed ending the previous generation's war against Germany. Given so many changes and anxieties, it's hardly surprising that, as she told me once, my mother started to feel "funny" shortly after my birth. The form this feeling took was that she had a hard time leaving the house. When she would get out the stroller and start walking me down the street toward nearby Shattuck Park, she said, "I would feel smaller and smaller, and be afraid I was going to disappear." I don't know how long this condition lasted, or how severe it was.

Toward the end of World War II, our family, expanded to four with the birth of my brother Geoffrey, made what looks to have been a very strange move—to a second-floor apartment at 56 Wilson Street, directly across from the big white house on the hill where my mother had grown up. There her mother had died and Pat Balduf's dream of attending college and becoming a teacher had been born and then lost. There she had nursed her father in his last illness. There she had come home one afternoon to discover many of her family's best-loved possessions gone. There her sister and brother-in-

Figure 20. Chick and Pat Fanning with Charles Jr., July 1943.

law were now in residence. What could have spurred this straight-on confrontation with disturbing ghosts that could not yet have been laid to rest? The answer may have been simple—that the new apartment was cheap. This was important, as my father had recently gone from his well-paid, wartime job as a welder to a much smaller salary as a custodian for the Norwood Public Schools. The owners of 56 Wilson were Adolph and Veronica Wiscalis, who lived on the first floor. They had been there since the 1930s, so my mother knew them already. I was aware that there was no love lost between these two and my parents, but I don't know what the bones of contention were. The Wiscalises were Lithuanian immigrants, and he's listed in the street directory as "laborer." It may have been a bitter pill that they had managed something—owning a house—that was beyond my parents at that time. It is clear, in any case, that the location itself invited an underscored line of pain.

We lived in the apartment on Wilson Street when I was two, three, and four years old, from late 1944 until the summer of 1947, and it's the first place I remember. In his wonderful book *The Poetics of Space* (translated by Maria Jolas, 1964), French philosopher Gaston Bachelard sets out to understand "space that has been seized upon by the imagination." A major emphasis is the "poetics of the house," and Bachelard states that "our house is our corner of the world. As has often been said, it is our first universe, a real cosmos in every sense of the word." Furthermore, the "first house," the house of our earliest memories, "has engraved within us the hierarchy of the various functions of inhabiting." Here is where we first make sense of the world by moving through it coherently, to successful ends. In addition, not simply "an embodiment of home," the first house is also "the oneirically definitive house," the prototypic "embodiment of dreams. Each one of its nooks and corners was a resting-place for daydream." It is where we first find and exercise and take pleasure in the imagination. For Bachelard, who was an aesthetician, this is "the chief benefit of the house." That is, "the house shelters daydreaming, the house protects the dreamer, the house allows one to dream in peace."

The kitchen at 56 Wilson Street was where I sat under the ironing board listening to the radio with my mother. Living on the second floor brought both perspective and security. We looked down on the world, seeing it panoramically from windows on all four sides, and at the same time we were protected by height. I would wander from window to window, looking down at the house next door on the left, then the woods behind, then the small park—Wilson Street Playground—on the right, then the street straight ahead. I could see it all, and nobody could see or reach me. Of that home I have four distinct memories, from which, as Bachelard predicts, a lifetime of dreams and daydreams have come. There's one each for fear, for pride, for disruption of the established familial order, and for the mixed blessing of moving away.

I remember hearing a loud, repeating noise one morning. Looking out the front-room window, I saw four workmen just beginning to open up the sidewalk with a jackhammer, picks, and shovels. Mum said they were "town men" from the water department, there to repair a broken main. A little while later, we came out of the house to go for a walk. The men hadn't gotten very far, and were standing around drinking coffee. When we returned in an hour, there was a long, deep ditch where the sidewalk had been. Two of the men were in it, and the jackhammer was making a terrible din. All this noise and digging made me think of the war, and I had some muddled notion about land mines. I was afraid that the diggers would run into one and we'd all be blown up. There was a plank bridge, but I wouldn't step on it, so Mum handed me over to a man who swung me across. Then she stepped over to join me and we went in the house. For weeks, I had nightmares involving variations on bloody disaster.

My second memory is of the morning my mother found a litter of newborn field mice nesting in the ironing board when she opened it up. They were dead, but she recoiled in fright—the first time I'd seen her so disturbed. She couldn't touch them and asked me to pick them up and throw them out the kitchen window into the side yard. I was more than happy to oblige. Here was an important job, and only I could do it. I remember examining the small, pink bodies closely—too closely for my mother's comfort. But I saw their tiny closed eyes, their tiny clenched feet. Then taking them one by one by their tails, I slung them out and away in the direction of the playground. My pride in having done this job knew no bounds. This was a story my mother always told. Somehow, it became a defining anecdote about her firstborn. The point was not my heroic action but my interest in the mice—how I had peered so intently at them. "Peering" became one of our family joke words, applicable to any situation where one of us looked with special closeness at something, anything.

Third, there is the comeuppance that I gave my brother when he was about a year old. I was far less than thrilled to have him around, and one afternoon, when my parents were out of the room, I gave him a clout on the head. Naturally, he let out a yelp. Dad came after me, and I tried to run away. We were in the dining room, and I dashed around the table, then ducked under it. I misgauged my height and the table's, though, and whacked my own forehead—much harder than I had hit Geoffrey, in my view. I mean, it really hurt. I was dizzy and reeling. When Mum said that the big bump on my forehead was a judgment—"See, you're being punished for hitting your brother"—I was distraught with the injustice of it all.

Finally, I remember the summer day when we moved out of the Wilson Street apartment. Dad had borrowed a pickup truck somewhere, and the possibility of rain added just the right edge to the carnival atmosphere. Two of his brothers were there to help, and all day long I watched as our furniture came down the stairs. Then the truck would disappear for an hour and come back empty, only to be loaded up again and driven away again.

Something brand new and important was being accomplished, and the rhythm of the process was satisfying. But it was also disturbing to see the material pieces that had fit together to form our lives suddenly isolated, exposed. Tipped on their sides or upside down to make it out the door and onto the truck, all our tables, chairs, lamps, and beds were rendered strange and vulnerable. Still, I was mostly just very excited. We were leaving Wiscalises'! Better still, we were going to have a whole house to ourselves! What I recall most clearly, and I can still feel it in the soles of my feet and running up my legs, is bouncing up and down on the springs of my own twin bed as it lay on the front porch. I was on my way to somewhere.

There's one other thing about Wilson Street. It was there that my brother and I got the nicknames that stuck with us right on up through high school—and beyond. He was responsible for both. Because my father was known as "Chick," I had started out as "Chicklet." However, when Geoffrey came along and began to talk, he pronounced it "Ticka," and that became the name by which I was known in the immediate family and also among my friends in elementary school. (The name is still with me. My sister calls me "T.") As for Geoffrey, he and my mother had been sitting in the front window watching some town men laying down asphalt. One of them had a limp, and Mum made my brother laugh by chanting "Bumpha—bumpha—bumpha" in time with the man's walk. My brother pronounced this "Buffa," and that was his name from then on.

Winslow Ave

Our next home, 103 Winslow Avenue, was in a better location, from my mother's perspective, but still left a lot to be desired. Not only was this another rental, but it was also part of a Fanning family version of musical houses. My grandfather Fanning had rented 103 for years. My father had lived there before his marriage in 1941. And Grampy and his daughter, Auntie Mae, continued to live there until my uncle Frank came back from the war and used the GI Bill to finance the purchase of a house just around the corner on Walnut Avenue. That was the first house that any of them had owned, and Auntie Mae's salary as a nurse must also have been a key to the deal. So, the Fannings moved out to Walnut Ave, and we took their place at Winslow. It was the summer of 1947. I was four and a half and Geoffrey was two, and we were greeted with unanticipated wonders. First and most exciting, this was a freestanding house, complete with two floors, a cellar, a front porch, and a back yard. Everything was new and bigger and ripe for appropriation. The kitchen was still the nerve center of daily life, but even more so than on Wilson Street, because it had four doorways: to the dining room, the front hall, the pantry, and the back porch. To keep my brother and me in sight and occupied while she was cooking and ironing, Mum devised a game in which we pitched a tent, using a bed sheet draped over the kitchen table and chairs. This was our castle, army bunker, teepee, or cabin in the woods. We filled it with our favorite toys and held out against opposing knights, Nazis, cowboys, or bears. We had the best of both worlds, for all the dangers we imagined were surrounded by supper's comforting smells and the sounds of the radio and Mum's footsteps.

A unique, mysterious feature of the new house was a contraption that my father called "the register." This was an air vent between the upstairs hall and the kitchen, left over from the days when heat for the entire house had come from the kitchen stove. The grate had thin iron shutters, like a venetian blind, which were opened or shut by pushing a knob on one end. It looked directly down on the stove, but by angling a little to one side, I could see the whole kitchen table and part of the sink. What fun this was, especially on the evenings when my parents had guests after I was supposed to be asleep. I would creep out of our bedroom, shuffle on hands and knees to the register, and carefully open the grate. Below me were the tops of the heads of adults. Scraps of conversation and eddies of smoke wafted upward. On the table were a few bottles and glasses of beer, pieces of the newspaper, cigarette packs, sometimes a deck of cards and a cribbage board. I couldn't hear much, nor did I particularly want to. But I was looking down into the part of my parents' world that didn't include me, and that was plenty fascinating—food for much thought and many dreams.

I've recently been teaching Robert Frost again, and his early poem, "An Old Man's Winter Night," reminds me of our bedroom on Winslow Ave. It begins: "All out-of-doors looked darkly in at him / Through the thin frost, almost in separate stars, / That gathers on the pane in empty rooms." Geoffrey and I had the back bedroom, looking out on the yard. The radiator was tiny, and the room got chilly on winter nights. Consequently, the window panes captured frost patterns of wonderfully intricate design. I would imagine that these were crystal mountain ranges, winter's equivalent of the cloud formations that I followed while lying in the grass on summer afternoons. I traced them with my finger, the warmth of which altered the landscapes, rounding off the highest peaks, creating river valleys and lakes. When finished with this dream work, I would sign the window with the letters of my name—C F F—in a cold, wet trail that lasted less than a minute.

It was also great to have our own back yard. As the second-floor tenants, we hadn't ever used the one on Wilson Street. Whenever the weather was warm, "Old Wiscalis," as my parents called him, was out there asleep on a splayed and rickety wooden lawn chair. But now, we could walk out the kitchen door and down three steps into a cozy plot of grass, chain-link fenced and hedged all around. In the spring of 1948, Dad staked out the territory by planting a few rows of tomatoes and cucumbers in a narrow, L-shaped plot, down the right side and around the back. This was the first of his many gardens. And here my brother and I began our first shared sports activity—playing catch with a baseball.

The richest new feature of life outside our house on Winslow Ave was right next door—Farioli's Market, an archetypal corner grocery. Pete and Eddie Farioli were World War II veterans of the Coast Guard and the Navy who had come home to take over the store from their Italian immigrant father. Old Mr. Farioli had moved to Florida but was still around sometimes in the summer. I'd never seen anyone like him before, and so I was always a little afraid if he was behind the counter. Short and round, he had big, owlish glasses that made his eyes look huge. Also, he wore suspenders, spoke with an accent, and always had the stub of a cigar in his mouth. His first name, which I've never seen since, conveyed the essence of the foreign—Torquato.

Geoffrey and I felt that a special relationship at the store came with our proximity to it, but the key was that the Fariolis really liked kids. Pete had enormous patience. He would hover behind the candy counter for long stretches two or three times a week, while I made the agonized decision regarding how best to spend my nickel. He wouldn't just stand there either. He participated in the debate: "Well, Tick, those squirrel nuts *are* good, but the jelly beans are three for a penny." The big problem was that the items I really wanted took the whole nickel at one fell swoop. First and foremost, I loved Necco Wafers. So great was their variety that it was impossible to get bored with those thin, multi-colored disks dusted with white powdered sugar. And boy, could I make them last. It would drive my brother crazy, but I believed, and invariably acted on the belief, that only methodical licking, one disk at a time, could bring out the full vividness of color and flavor. My favorites, all rarities, were cinnamon, licorice, and banana. An added treat came with my learning how to read, for then the New England Confectionery Company rendered up my earliest example, though I didn't know the word, of acronym. The fact that the company name spelled out the product was, to me, the height of cleverness. I couldn't get over it. Anyway, Necco Wafers still act on me like Proust's tea-soaked *madeleine*. Whenever I find them, my Massachusetts childhood comes flooding back. (The last I knew, they were still on the market, but their national distribution leaves a lot to be desired.)

Also, I loved chewing-gum cards of all denominations and genres—Wild West cards, cards from radio shows and movies, basketball, football, hockey, and baseball cards. These also cost five cents for a pack of five cards and a rectangular sheet of gum. Here too, I followed a persnickety ritual that gave my brother fits. Unfolding the gaily colored, waxy wrapper, corner by corner, was a highly dramatic act. Then came the sharp, sweet smell of the gum, intensified as I blew the dusting of sugar from the cards and squeezed out the pictures one by one, as if this were a hand of high-stakes poker. (The idea that now a kid can buy a boxed set of the entire series of cards for any sport at the beginning of a season seems to me, in equal parts, really stupid and really sad.) Predictably—in retrospect—I was a natural packrat and organizer, and I spent hours arranging and juxtaposing events and scenes, teams and players and positions. The Winslow Avenue neighborhood had a lot of kids in it, and trading cards was one of the ways we got to know one another. After trading came the game of "shooting" or "flipping" cards on the concrete against the front steps of someone's house. The card closest to the bottom step won all the cards that had been flipped, unless one achieved a "leaner," a card that stayed standing up against the step, which beat all. We sometimes prepared "waxies," which were special cards coated with candle wax that had been melted in a pan on the kitchen stove. These competitions were intense, making and breaking friendships on a daily basis.

Baseball was Boston's premier sport in those years, and baseball cards were the most important by far. We were then a town of two teams, with the American League Red Sox significantly more popular than the National League Braves. Getting the Ted Williams card was the ne plus ultra in collecting, never achieved by me. But I also had a private pantheon of heroes. I'm not sure why, but my mother loved the Braves, and, consequently, so did I. This was already the team whose games we had listened to on the radio back on Wilson Street, and in 1948, our first full year on Winslow Ave, the Braves won the National League pennant. (They went on to lose the World Series to the Cleveland Indians in six games.) Later on, it was big and terrible news in our house when the Braves left Boston for Milwaukee just one month before the start of the 1953 season. This was the first major-league team relocation in nearly forty years, and they had been at Braves Field on Huntington Avenue since 1915. Henceforth, in our house the name of Lou Perini, Braves owner and construction company czar, was mud. For years, whenever Mum and I would see his name on the cab of a crane at a building site, we would comment on his self-serving treachery. We saw it as adding insult to injury when the *Milwaukee* Braves actually beat the Yankees to win the World Series in 1957.

I enjoyed the badge of uniqueness that went along with being the only kid in my new neighborhood who followed and rooted for the Braves and for whom their cards were the really talismanic ones. The magic names are still with me. There was the legendary pitching duo of right-hander Johnny Sain and the great Hall-of-Fame lefty Warren Spahn. One of my early experiences of the pleasure of rhyme was the mantra of their short-staffed pennant run: "Spahn and Sain and pray for rain." I swear, the Braves players sounded like what they did. There was Del Crandall, the solid, reliable catcher; the crisply competent double-play combination of Eddie Stanky and Alvin Dark; the substantial slugger Bob Elliott at third base. He was my mother's favorite, and when I squeezed his card out of a pack one morning, I went running to show it to her. Maybe because it was already clear that I wasn't going to be much of an athlete, I was partial to the Braves' scrappy jack-of-all-trades, utility infielder Sibby Sisti. His odd moniker—short for Sebastian, according to his baseball card—was also part of the attraction. Slight of build and self-effacing, or so he seemed to me, Sibby hung on for a thirteen-year major-league career with the Braves in Boston and Milwaukee, no mean feat for a lifetime .244 hitter with no permanent spot in the lineup.

It was baseball that made 107 Winslow, the house next door on the left, a special place as well. Here lived Tony Petracca, a musician who gave lessons on the accordion and trumpet and played in small-combo dance bands in Boston. In this line of work, he had befriended a number of baseball players, and often on summer nights these men would come out to Tony's house for parties with their wives and girlfriends. Our back yards were separated by a high, dense hedge, through which I could make out only indistinct shapes and voices. I dreamed of getting an autographed baseball, but we were never invited over. I think my father was too shy to ask. Anyway, these parties were loud, long, late-night affairs, and well after I was in bed and supposed to be asleep, I heard laughter, male and female, the clinking of glass, and strains of accordion music. One night there was even a fight, with raised voices and a couple of squeals. All these players were members of the Red Sox, and my father told me that the guests included three pitchers with reputations as high livers, not to say drunks: Ellis Kinder, a right-hander, and two nutty lefties, Mel Parnell and Maury McDermott. Mum pointed out that the clay feet of these idols supported her preference for the Braves—you'd never catch Warren Spahn, southpaw though he was, in such a situation.

I wonder now, though I never gave it a thought then, what World War II had been like for the Farioli boys. Though it had been over for only two years when we moved to Winslow Ave, no one ever talked about the war, but I do recall hearing at some point that Eddie had seen some very tough action in the Pacific. Maybe that was what made him less approachable than Pete. And yet, it was with Eddie that I formed the stronger connection. I loved comic books, and in buying them at the store, I discovered that Eddie read them too—avidly. At some point we began swapping comics, and we continued doing so right on through my junior high school years. Eddie was eclectic and extremely tolerant in his tastes, and the result was that, in the early years especially, my horizons expanded tremendously—from Walt Disney and *Superman* to *G. I. Joe* and *Tales from the Crypt* and the *Classic Comics* versions of *Treasure Island, Robinson Crusoe,* and *The Count of Monte Christo.* Eddie was also the first adult who took my opinions seriously—except, of course, for my parents and teachers. Because he hadn't the vested interest of these others, our discussions were especially important to me. We critiqued everything about the comics: characters (for realism or grotesquerie, depending on the genre), plots (as plausible, predictable, silly, or appropriate in their twists and turns), art work (ordinary or arresting). The message was clear. Comic books were worth talking about, and so was what I thought of them.

Farioli's Market provided a host of other new vistas as well. A riveting event every couple of weeks was the appearance of "the Bleaching-Water Horse." The first live horse that my brother and I had ever seen, this old nag ambled up to Farioli's curb to deliver bleach and laundry soap that was made somewhere around town. Driven by "an old German" (my mother's label, somehow derived from his battered brown hat), the horse had blinders, a feedbag attached under his nose, and a permanent necklace of buzzing flies. Geoffrey and I were endlessly entertained by this impressively large creature's snorting and stamping and, most of all, by his propensity for peeing at will and dropping huge turds on the street. I also used him to create an image for one of the songs my mother sang around the house: "Put on your old gray bonnet / With the blue ribbon on it / And we'll hitch old Dobbin to the shay; / Through the fields of clover / We'll go down to Dover

/ On our golden wedding day." The old man would carry the big jugs of bleach, two at a time, down the short driveway that was right beside our house, and then down a ramp into Farioli's cellar.

Every day, some tradesman or other would park his truck and heft along this well-worn path yard-high cardboard boxes, wooden crates bursting with green shoots, big clumps of meat wrapped in bloody cheesecloth. From our front porch, I watched with endless fascination the transfer of these goods into the underground heart of the grocery. We were never allowed into this dark sanctum, which looked just as mysterious from its other end, visible when one stood in front of the counter in the store itself. Up the stairs from that basement would come cuts of meat and broccoli in bunches, boxes of cereal and laundry soap, cans of beans, soup, and spaghetti, our gum and candy—all demythologized into individual, family-sized items. Such proximity to the flow and transformation of life's necessary staples, I thought, brought knowledge of how the world works to which most people were not privy. Often in the late afternoons, when the threat of delivery trucks was over for the day, Mum would let me sit on our side of the wall that framed the driveway. There, prompted by piles of empty crates and torn bits of crinkled wrapping paper, I would dream of the faraway places from which all this abundance had come, ending up at Farioli's, right next door to my house. This was for me the equivalent of John Masefield's exotic invocation: "Quinquireme of Nineveh from distant Ophir"

> Rowing home to haven in sunny Palestine,
> With a cargo of ivory,
> And apes and peacocks,
> Sandalwood, cedarwood, and sweet white wine.

Going to Church

Religion belongs here, because it was emphatically my mother's department. I've been trying to figure out why, when I was a kid, so much else in my daily life was more important than Roman Catholicism in any of its forms and observances. My parents were both half Irish and ostensibly Catholic, and yet my childhood lacked the shaping dominance of that dual tradition that features in so many memories of people who grew up when I did. Certainly, the Catholic faith had been mighty low on the list of priorities in my father's family. His mother's death when he was eight had thrown the Fannings onto the meager spiritual resources of Charles Winslow Fanning, who had been raised by his WASP grandmother after *his* Irish Catholic father had left town. I doubt that Grampy and his five kids went to church very often, if at all, and he was buried by a Baptist minister. My mother's family had had stronger ties to Catholicism, but this, too, was through *her* mother's family, the Irish Catholic McAuliffes. Though from heavily Catholic Baden, the Baldufs had been Protestants, and Edward Balduf had made a few waves in his family by converting to marry Hannah. In my mother's memory, her mother seems to have been devout in an old-country way. For example, she kept a bottle of holy water and sprinkled it around the house during thunderstorms, of which she was terrified. Then again, she died when Mum was sixteen, and though I'm sure that the Balduf girls continued to attend Sunday Mass after that, the impetus may well have weakened.

So, there were factors working against wholehearted embrace of Catholicism in both of my parents' family histories. Their crucial decision for me and my siblings was sending us to public school. In the late 1940s, St. Catherine of Siena in Norwood was a thriving, populous, well-to-do parish, with four or five priests in residence at any given time. The pride of the complex was St. Catherine's School, grades K through 8, staffed by a dozen or more nuns, the Sisters of St. Joseph, who lived in an imposing convent on a rise above the school. Why didn't we go there? I get the sense that it was never a serious option. Given their backgrounds, it's hardly surprising that both my parents had attended the public schools. Then again, St. Catherine's charged tuition, which also made it less attractive.

When I was a kid, my father never went to church at all. And that's what we called it, by the way: "going to church," not "going to Mass," perhaps another sign that the ritual lacked gravitas. We went on Sunday mornings with my mother, and it was important enough to her that we were there rain or shine—and we walked when we were between automobiles. We never talked about what went on at St. Catherine's in a spiritual sense, however. That job had been given over to the nuns, but in circumstances that failed to foster very much zeal. As public school kids, we endured the second-class citizenship of CCD (Confraternity of Christian Doctrine) classes, taught on Thursday afternoons by bone-tired, understandably cranky St. Joe sisters who, by our 4:30 starting time, had gone through the full school day with their own properly Catholic (and paying) students.

Given this flawed Thursday-school experience as my only preparation, Sunday Mass—well before the user-friendly changes of Vatican II—provided a weekly dose of extreme ennui. Much prized was the occasional involuntary sneeze from down the row, the louder the better, and my Sunday was made if someone, usually a heavy woman, fainted on the way to communion, swanning in a heap to the floor and bringing the whole operation to a clattering halt. In lieu of such drama, I played silent counting games: how many women wore hats and how many just had handkerchiefs balanced on their hair? (These were the days when women in church had to keep their heads covered. Was this a papal edict, I wondered? When I asked the nun at CCD, she was miffed at the question, replying curtly, "It's a sign of respect.") I also counted the number of males and females in each row, the panes of stained glass across and down the windows, the separate bulbs in the nearest chandelier. None of this availed much, and by the forty-minute mark I was bored to desperation. But ah, the bliss of release at the *Ita missa est* made up for it all as we skipped out the open front doors and down the stone steps into the Sunday morning sunshine.

How I would have welcomed Burns's louse crawling around the brim of a hat in the staid and stuffy Scottish kirk! Alas, he never came, but when I read the poem in junior high, brother, did it make sense, especially because the theme of the pretentious matron brought low, unbenownst to herself, echoed what had been for me the chief lessons of Sunday Mass. These had to do with social hierarchy and ostentation. The Irish had always run St. Catherine's. (See Patrick J. Pendergast's *Selected Gems* of 1917.) The parish complex of church, school, and convent was perched at the crossroads of Norwood's Dublin and Cork City neighborhoods after all, and most of the priests had Irish names—a fact that did not register with me, but I'd say it was clear to my mother, a Balduf girl and native of Germantown. What she did point out to Geoffrey and me was the weekly parade of certain families down the center aisle of the church, dressed to the nines even at the early Masses we attended. From this group came the men who passed the wicker collection baskets on long poles just before and sometimes after communion. ("Today, my brothers and sisters, there will be a second collection for the African missions.") These men wore glistening white shirts, dark ties, and jackets with Knights of Columbus pins in their lapels. Most had jowly, florid faces and shiny hair combed neatly over from one side to the other. Mum said that these folks acted "holier than thou," and she referred to them scornfully as "the Pillars of the Church." I recognized them in one of the few parables that made sense to me in CCD class—that of the Pharisee loudly proclaiming his superiority in the temple, while the sincerely contrite publican simply beats his breast in a corner. (But would the humble really be exalted? The jury was out on that one.)

Speaking of humility, I couldn't fail to notice the men who spent the whole Mass standing in the vestibule, a narrow, stone-floored entrance hall that ran across the back of the church, separated from the main worship space by an oak-paneled wall with small-paned, leaded windows higher than my six- or seven-year-old head. In the winter it was cold out there, and the Mass was barely a murmur, and I wondered why they didn't come in and sit down. Some were decidedly scruffy, even unkempt. They wore loose lumberjack shirts instead of coats and had baggy, bloodshot eyes and hadn't shaved. They coughed a lot, too. It was clear that these guys weren't pillars of anything. They could just about hold themselves up. Most Sundays—for this I envied them—they piled on out of church just after the bell rang for the consecration of the host, at which point, according to my mother, the Mass "counted." This motley vestibule crew gained a touch of legitimacy because there were always a few cops and firemen in uniform there too, catching Mass while on duty but poised for the chase. (The police and fire stations were just across Washington Street, down behind the Town Hall.)

Somehow, the spectacle of parishioners clustering by status at Mass sank in more than what was going on up front at the altar. Also, this phenomenon raised an interesting question: where did the Fannings belong? Neither pillars nor pilloried, where did we fit? The evidence was inconclusive. Most of the time we went to the seven o'clock Mass. Sometimes we went to the eight but never the nine, which the students of St. Catherine's School attended en masse, sitting in pews according to classroom, with a nun at the end of each row. Nor did we ever attend the High Mass at eleven, an elaborate, tony event which, I had heard, went on for well over an hour. (For that relief, much thanks.) Was the choice of early Mass an indicator of low status? There were other indicators that this was the case. Though the pew rent was a quarter, sometimes we put in nickels. We always sat four or five rows from the back of the church and were often joined there by aging Irish immigrants with bad teeth and bad breath. Speaking with brogues and unfashionably dressed, these were friends and relations of my mother's mother. All this suggested to me that we were closer to the publicans than the Pharisees, but I kept this idea to myself.

As I grew older and noticed more, I came to two conclusions. First, our family's "place" in the town was somehow oblique and aslant. My parents saw themselves as off to the side of the social and economic ladder that ran from poverty to privilege. And second, they were not uncomfortable there. I'd say that this was partly because Chick Fanning and Pat Balduf along with all four of their parents had lived virtually their entire lives in Norwood.

They knew in their bones who and where they were. In addition, they were part of the Depression-era culture of acceptance bordering on stoicism. If putting on airs (as in "who do they think they are?") was the first cardinal sin, then presenting oneself as deprived ("hard done by" in my mother's phrase) was the second. Both of my parents had lost their mothers when young. Both had experienced painful troubles within their families. Neither had come near to fulfilling educational or occupational potential. Their dreams had been thwarted in all sorts of ways. And yet I don't remember ever hearing a complaint. Yes, my father's pay as a janitor was low. We never went away on vacation. We didn't eat in restaurants. We didn't get exactly what we wanted for Christmas. Nor did the Fannings belong to any groups—not the K of C, the Elks, the Eagles, or even the Boy Scouts. But as far as my parents were concerned, none of this amounted to a hill of beans—or if it did, we kids never heard about it.

As a direct consequence, my brother and sister and I were blessed with secure and stable childhoods. I don't see the way we lived as anything special for small-town America after World War II, but I do know that things could have been different. This ordinary upbringing was my parents' great gift. I don't know whether it was consciously constructed or not, but I treasure it. In such a childhood, small events were allowed to have large meanings: going next door to Farioli's, on a picnic to Ellis Pond, or downtown on a Friday night. And when a big event came along—embarking on a day trip to Boston, moving from one house to another, starting elementary school—why then, we were ready and able to pay attention, to take it all in.

6

Ars Brevis

The fact is the sweetest dream that labor knows.
My long scythe whispered and left the hay to make.
—Robert Frost, "Mowing"

My short life in art began with small-scale models made of clay inspired by religious, historical, and literary scenes. I had begun fooling about with this stuff around the age of four. On Sunday mornings, when my mother would go downtown to church on her own, leaving my father, my two-year-old brother Geoffrey, and me, making things out of clay was one of our favorite activities. I recall that we began with whales, my father's idea and inspiration, though I don't know why. Shaping hefty chunks of gray or brown clay, smoothing the flanks, sculpting out the mouth and tail, drilling the blowhole with a pencil as finishing flourish: it just felt great to do, and so I began to move on to more ambitious modeling projects of my own.

Strictly speaking, we were working not with real clay but with "plasticine," an artificial substitute that had been developed in the 1890s and used in schools because it remained plastic and didn't dry out so fast. Beyond the generic grays and browns, I discovered at the Five-and-Ten packets of plasticine in bright primary colors, which could be kneaded into a variety of hues just like mixing paints. Equipped with what I soon found was a formidably versatile palette, I began to make miniature tables, beds, appliances, and chairs, and to set them up in shoebox rooms. These were a lot more like the front windows of Callahan's Furniture than the rooms in which we lived, and creating such middle-class domestic dreamscapes became my first self-sustaining hobby.

When I went off to first grade at age five in September 1948, clay modeling became my ticket to extra notice and praise. This was an unexpected development but not unsought, for once in school, I wanted to be marked out as uniquely talented. I wanted very much to be good at something. I'm not sure why, but there it was. There was an additional impetus in that I had trouble seeing the blackboard, even when moved from my alphabetical seat to the front row. This was a kind of attention I didn't want. In second grade I was diagnosed as seriously myopic, and I've worn glasses ever since. I didn't appreciate this distinguishing feature either. However, at Christmastime in first grade, I brought in a freshly minted manger scene, with Mary, Joseph, and the Christ child surrounded by animals in a shoebox tableau. My classmates were intrigued. More important, the teacher, Miss Cataldo, on whom all the boys had a crush, was impressed. She invited the second graders in to look, and my reputation as an artist was established. From then on, I created a host of clay models of buildings, rooms, scenes from history and literature. These got more and more elaborate. Most I brought to school for display and kudos. The irony here was that my flat-out worst subject was penmanship. I was incapable of mastering the Palmer Method. Once in fifth grade, Dan Callahan correctly predicted my grade of "C" in that subject, and I reacted by shoving him into a hedge. To this day, I cannot join more than two letters together. (Without a doubt, this trait is genetic. The handwriting of my brother and sister looks the same.)

In the summers, I continued to make models based on my own ideas and pleasure reading. One of the earliest was a raised relief rendering of Treasure Island based on the book's frontispiece map, which had been drawn by Robert Louis Stevenson himself. The skull-and-crossbones flew from Spyglass Hill, and beneath it was a stockade of popsicle sticks. Overlooking an inlet, Ben Gunn's cave was camouflaged but visible. Up through ninth grade, my last model-making year, the highlights of my plasticine career included the Parthenon to scale with Phidias's lost statue of Athena recovered and reinstalled inside; the Egyptian temple of Karnak, nine feet long and supported by columns decorated with hieroglyphics; and a two-story medieval castle with twelve rooms—including an armory, a throne room, a chapel, and a banquet hall with food on the table—and exterior walls molded stone by stone.

Created in the summer between sixth and seventh grade, my pièce de résistance was the Colosseum at Rome, which prompted my first brush with fame beyond the Winslow School. This model ended up on display in the children's room of the town's public library, and I had a picture and interview in the *Norwood Messenger*. In the background of the picture is a swinging/reversible display board on which is a thumbtacked picture of a boy about my age of eleven. He sits on a stool, hunched over, concentrating on his butterfly collection. Front and center is my Colosseum on a round table. To the left am I, dutifully posed bending toward my creation, echoing the boy in the picture. My fingers are poised over the work, adjusting one of the statues that stand atop the columns circling the arena. I can still recognize myself. Then as now, I have thick glasses with thin rims, nondescript pants, and a long-sleeved, checkered shirt in a sort of tartan pattern, buttoned at the wrists. I'm sporting what was for most of my childhood my signature crewcut, called in those days a "whiffle," which was trimmed up every few weeks at Eddie Armour's barbershop. The look on my face sends me back in a flash to the way making those models made me feel. It's equal parts of calm and concentration, starting in the fingertips and spreading back up the arms and into the mind.

I'm still impressed by this piece, mostly in terms of the absorption in these clay projects that it suggests. My Colosseum was nearly a foot high and three feet in diameter and was mounted on a square of plywood that my father had cut for me at the Junior High. I can't remember whether or not we had a car at the time, but I remember that my friends Dan Callahan and Richie Ross carried the Colosseum down Walpole Street from our house to the library on a beautiful, sky-blue Saturday in July. I marched triumphantly behind them. In the photograph, I count twenty of those statue-crowned columns. The Roman emperor and his entourage sit on a central dais guarded by helmeted centurions with spears and shields. A tapestry emblazoned with a gold laurel wreath hangs down in front of them. To right and left, I can see down two lattice-gated tunnels into the bowels of the building, from which would come animals and gladiators. In the photo, the front-facing side of the model blocks the view, but I remember that I had put real sand on the arena floor and that a fight to the death involving several men was in progress. There were over 300 separate figures in this piece, each three-quarters of an inch high, and I recall making an effort to vary the colors and designs of their robes and togas—mostly to keep from becoming bored. In the prestige seats just above the action are more soldiers along with senators and their families. Above these are the ranks of the Roman populace—in three rows all around the stadium, with a few observers standing behind. It's a full house. When the *Messenger* reporter asked me what would happen to the model after the library exhibition, I answered that I would separate the colors of clay and smoosh them together. Was that going to be a hard thing to do, he wondered? I didn't think so. How else was I to get the material for my next project? In fact, I kept my accumulated clay until the summer between high school and college. By this time, I had two cubic feet of the stuff, and though it had been over three years since I had made a model, I remember that it was really hard to throw it all away. I knew that this was the end of something.

I loved the Sunday comics. I studied them all with rapt attention, indiscriminately and religiously, from the time I started reading right up through high school. Looking at some of the old strips now, I can project back to the roots of the pleasure, visual even more than literal, that I took in them as a child. The pristine, solid colors and uncluttered compositions were my first exposure to art. My favorites were the most complicated: Hal Foster's *Prince Valiant in the Days of King Arthur,* full of meticulously detailed castles and battle scenes, and *Bringing Up Father,* George McManus's kind-hearted satire of Irish America in transition from Brooklyn to the Fifth Avenue *haute bourgeoisie.* Every few weeks, McManus would put Maggie and Jiggs into a panoramic New York scene. He was unbeatable for balancing detail and pattern with freeze-frame clarity. I would happily get lost in these strips, both following the story line and creating my own place in it. Also of interest were the more prosaic and familiar American town lives rendered in Frank King's *Gasoline Alley* and Chic Young's *Blondie,* and I enjoyed the visual soap operas: *Steve Roper, Mary Worth, Judge Parker,* and *Rex Morgan, M.D.* Week-to-week, continuous narrative was key, and, though I read them, I wasn't much engaged with the one-shot comic vignettes of *Mutt and Jeff, Cicero's Cat, The Katzenjammer Kids,* and their ilk.

It was only a step from Foster and McManus to my first exposure to "Art" with a capital "A", which came through a book that I had asked my parents to buy: *Currier and Ives' America, A Panorama of the Mid-Nineteenth Century Scene* (New York: Crown Publishers, 1952), featuring "80 prints in full color." It was a book-club loss leader that I had found advertised in the Sunday paper. I told my parents that the pictures would inspire my art work—and they did. Measuring a hefty twelve by eighteen inches—today it would be called a coffee-table book—it was the largest book I'd ever seen, and it was mine! Though the many house removals I've made as an adult have forced much painful triage of books—always the easiest items to come by and the hardest to move—somehow, this unwieldy, impractical volume is still with me. For the first time in many years—ten? twenty?—I opened *Currier and Ives' America* a few weeks ago. What a flood of memories! Every page was familiar, often down to the small details.

Here the American nineteenth century had been spread out before me in lithographs produced between 1850 and 1880. Idealized visions that were meant to hang on people's walls, the pictures filled my mind and fed my imagination. I pored over *Currier and Ives,* inserting myself into the scenes of town and rural life, walking the summer roads, riding in winter sleighs, stepping over thresholds into warm parlors, hopping aboard the trains poised for departure into the unknown West, peering out of tent flaps at the surrounding wilderness. The book was like the Sunday comics, only more reliable, for it contained scenes both sweeping and intricate to which I could return again and again. These images still have the attraction of an alternative world, one cleaner, less confusing, much more under control than the one we inhabit, and they did in fact inspire many of my clay models.

The standard format of a Currier and Ives print is orchestrated busyness. There is always a lot to look at. Spread across a simple horizontal picture plane are houses, outbuildings, animals, and people engaged in relevant tasks. For example, *An American Homestead Winter* of 1868 has on the left a yard with ducks, chickens, and cows and a farmer standing beside the open door to a barn full of hay. On the right is the handsome, two-story homestead with a woman, no doubt the farmer's wife, in a side doorway. She carries a pail and is about to do something with it. A snow-covered roadway divides the scene at center, and a couple passing through in a two-horse sleigh greet a boy carrying logs, his dog beside him. The background is a stand of lacy-branched, bare trees with a snow-covered hill behind. "The only other sound's the sweep / Of easy wind and downy flake." It was pictures like this that prepared me for Robert Frost's poems in high school.

There were four "Literary Landmarks"—*The Old Oaken Bucket, The Village Blacksmith, The Wayside Inn,* and *The Home of Evangeline.* The last of these inspired another of my early leaps as a clay modeler beyond the annual nativity scene. When we read Longfellow's poem in school, I created a version of Evangeline's cottage in Acadia, complete with diamond-paned windows and surrounded by a horse cart, a wishing well, and a bench for sitting under the weeping willow tree, fashioned of real pine boughs stuck in a clay base.

The Trip to Bountiful

In seventh grade, the world expanded dramatically. My sixth-grade teacher, Mr. Lambert, recognized the potential of my clay models and went out of his way to find me a scholarship to the Saturday morning community classes for children at the Boston Museum of Fine Arts, deep in the city on Huntington Avenue. I had been to Boston but not often, and never alone. This was something completely different. I found myself in September 1954 at age eleven embarked on a fabulous journey, the cultural and geographical adventure of my young life. Mr. Lambert took me in to enroll and showed me how to get there, but after that, I was on my own. I've still got the route firmly in mind.

On Saturday morning at 8:30, I walk downtown to the foot of Walpole Street, where Walpole, Guild, and Washington Streets come together. There I wait for the Eastern Mass Bus, one of our lifelines to the city. The driver's litany at the start of the trip still rings in my ears: "Dedham, Norwood, and East Walpole. Express from Dedham Line to Forest Hills." On the way into the city, I ride through downtown Norwood, Islington, Dedham, and East Dedham, stopping to pick up a passenger or two every few blocks. Then we cross the boundary into the Boston neighborhood of West Roxbury. The name of the road never changes—it's Washington Street all the way—but town changes to city by degrees before my eyes, and I find something new on every trip. Here are scrap yards, body shops, corner groceries, three-decker apartment buildings. One week I notice two rows of gravestones lined up in front of a small frame building where they are made. The next week, I see that the spot actually marks the corner of a cemetery spreading out behind. The names of the neighborhoods are a lot prettier than the places. Roslindale is a scruffy, working-class, mixed home-and-business sort of place. Forest Hills is a desolate stretch of urban industrial landscape, and the station with the same name where I debark is a cavernous, vaulted, two-story wind tunnel, open at both ends for the buses, with the terminus of an MTA elevated line at the top of a set of dingy and battered iron stairs. Stepping down from the bus that is my only link to home, I smell heavy exhaust fumes, hear the screech and slam of the overhead trains, and run my fingers over the pebbly grime that is leached into the stone walls. I am in the city.

Next comes the moment of greatest danger, about which I have nightmares during the week between trips. I don't go upstairs to the el, which would be easy, because it goes only one way. Instead, I have to watch for another bus to make a tricky connection that will take me just around the corner into another pastoral sounding station—the Arborway. If I miss this bus, which has a misleading name (I've forgotten it), then I am really lost. There's also the challenge to my natural shyness of having to ask for a transfer at the end of this two-minute ride. The idea of walking the few hundred yards between the two stations never occurs to me, as Arborway Station is surrounded by a high chain-link fence, and only buses are allowed in. Having achieved this transition—I make it every Saturday, heart pounding, hand clutching my transfer—I am in a grim, windswept asphalt desert containing a train-repair shed, rows and rows of out-of-service buses, and, in the center, a ramshackle circular depot building. It's here that I catch a real trolley car, with electric rod attached to sparking cables overhead. This is the Arborway-Huntington surface line. I swing aboard and am bounced and shunted through the gates and down the middle of the street, back under el tracks and on through Roxbury into the outer limits of Boston's South End.

As the car swings right onto Huntington Avenue, a landmark looms on the left that never fails to send a shiver up my spine. This is a many-windowed, mansard-roofed Victorian pile, guarded by a ten-foot wall of stone with big black wrought-iron gates. A bronze-backed sign nailed to the right-hand wall announces "The New England Home for Little Wanderers"—a lovely name and the most flagrant of the euphemisms that pepper my trip. I have heard of this place already at home, where it is the punch line of a warning that my mother uses to keep order between my brother and me: "If you two don't stop fighting, I'll pack you off to the New England Home for Little Wanderers!" When I report having seen the real place on Huntington Avenue, my mother elaborates the reference with stories of defenseless Catholic kids snared by unscrupulous Protestant asylum staff, never to be heard from again.

This sounded pretty far-fetched at the time, but I've since learned that Mum's take on the place was pretty accurate. Founded in 1865, ostensibly to care for children orphaned by the Civil War, the New England Home had been run by evangelical Methodist "child savers," who were committed to "rescuing" orphans and "victims" of broken homes from the horrors of Roman Catholicism. Historically, the home had been one of nineteenth-century Boston's responses to the unwelcome assault against their model city by thousands of Irish immigrants from the midcentury Famine straight through to World War I. From the earliest years, "orphan trains" organized by the child savers took Boston children, many of them Catholic, from the pernicious city to the pure Protestant air of the Midwest. This work continued and grew in scope well into the twentieth century. The imposing stone pile in Jamaica Plain that my trolley rolled past on Saturday mornings, the third and largest of the institution's sites, had been built to hold 100 children. Already stuffed with Dickens, my mind created images of waifs and runaways, dead-end kids abandoned or gone to the bad, committed first to cold, bare rooms, iron bedsteads, and pinched portions of gruel, then banished forever to the wastelands of Ohio, Indiana, and Illinois.

Now the trolley car follows Huntington Avenue, past newsstands, grocery stores, bars, and another venerable complex, the columned majesty of the Peter Bent Brigham Hospital, until I am deposited at the Museum of Fine Arts. The famed MFA is one of the palaces of Boston's Yankee elite, also known as the Brahmins—a term I will learn before this year is out. I am soon made aware that several other iconic sites are within short walking distance: Mrs. Jack Gardner's Museum, the boggy Fens with their World War II Victory Garden plots, Harvard Medical School, Boston Latin, Horticultural Hall, Symphony Hall, and the New England Conservatory of Music. And yet, even as an inexperienced Norwood boy, I detect a certain dissonance on the ground here in the mid-1950s. Despite the phalanx of Yankee cultural symbols, the neighborhood around the MFA looks to have gone pretty much to seed. Run-down bars and nondescript, shady emporia encroach from all points of the compass, and just down Huntington Avenue is the Boston YMCA, its Christian component eroding toward flophouse status.

One thing is clear. Though the distance is only fifteen miles, I am a world away from Norwood. Such a trip on one's own from town to inner city seems inconceivable now for an American child of eleven or twelve. I was lucky to be a kid when this was still possible, because the entire experience was a matchless gift—a bracing blast of augmented prospects, repeated weekly, and at a time when my senses were as open and receptive as they were ever going to be. My year at the MFA provided crucial encouragement toward the plans that I would make later on—including the idea that even though no one in my family had been to college at all, I could get to Harvard.

My MFA

I would run across Huntington Avenue, dodging the Saturday morning traffic, and up the semicircular drive, past the life-sized bronze statue, high on a pedestal, of an American Indian on horseback, his arms outstretched in supplication. I'd read juvenile fiction and comic books, heard *The Lone Ranger* and other radio westerns, but Cyrus Dallin's *Appeal to the Great Spirit* was my first look at a thoroughly idealized Indian (*pace* Tonto). At that point, I had seen only two "real" Indians, and they had left a very different impression. "Injun Joe" and his wife lived in a shack halfway down the dirt road that separated Norwood's two official sites of lasting abandonment: Highland Cemetery and the town dump. They were ragged, dark-headed, fierce-looking scavengers, reputed to be crazy and violent but probably just harmless lost souls. We kids caught glimpses of them when riding our bikes up that road to the dump. We had been forbidden to go there by our parents, who feared disease, rusty cuts, and worse. Yet there was no fence, and the near edge of the yawning landfill held many fascinating discoveries—costume jewelry, rusty tin toys, curling photographs, curious bottles and cans—which we would bring home and sneak upstairs into our bedrooms.

Dallin's bronze Indian promised a dramatically different class of treasures. Needless to say, the MFA delivered. I would take the stone steps two at a time, then pass beneath four soaring Corinthian columns into the entrance hall. Inside, there was marble everywhere, and I was greeted by a small bust (in tasteful Yankee understatement) labeled "Guy Lowell—Architect—1909" (as in, "the Lowells talk only to the Cabots, and the Cabots talk only to God"). Ahead on the right was an entrance desk past which, as an official Saturday student, I would walk proudly, having neither to pay nor to explain myself. I would then pause to consider—straight ahead—the sweeping, marble staircase to the second floor of the museum. Now came my favorite part. Rejecting the predictable tourist's invitation to the collection proper, I turned sharply to the right, walked ten steps, and pivoted smartly left at a plain-linteled, unmarked doorway. Here was a stone staircase leading down into the bowels of the MFA, where the Saturday art classes met. Every week I hoped that people would notice that I was someone who belonged there and knew where he was going.

Of the actual art instruction that year, I recall very little. I know that we worked mostly in watercolor, and that the teacher encouraged me to relax more, to become freer and more abstract in composition. In the event, verisimilitude, for which I had been receiving praise for my clay models since first grade, was a habit impossible to break. But in the spring my most "relaxed" piece, a watercolor done on marvelously thick, nubbly paper that was itself a revelation, did make it into the final exhibition. I remember that although the piece *was*, strictly speaking, abstract, I had really copied the bright oranges, reds, and yellows of autumn leaves. Still, I was amazed and very proud that a picture I had painted was tacked up on a wall—in the basement, to be sure, but a wall nonetheless—of the Boston Museum of Fine Arts. On the last Saturday of the course, my whole family drove in to see what I had accomplished.

That year, the MFA became my province. Most Saturdays there was time, both before and after class, to explore, and so I was able to discover great art in all its wondrous variety—on my own and as an insider at the museum. I found Monet's haystacks circling the airy rotunda in a blizzard of light and colors through changing seasons and times of day. I found the Dutch seventeenth century. Though far too young to appreciate the depths of character and wisdom in Rembrandt's portraits, I loved the profligate abundance of quotidien marvels with which his contemporaries Jan Steen and Pieter de Hooch had stuffed their genre scenes. The cozy kitchens, the dining-room tables full of crumbly cheeses and bubbling wine glasses, the spotless, shining hallways—all were ideals to which my own shoebox-and-clay rooms could aspire. The iced-over rivers teeming with skaters, both adults trafficking and children at play, of Jan Van Goyen and the Van Ruisdaels, Jacob and Salomon, reminded me of New Pond in winter. I found the spartan legacy of eighteenth-century New England as well. The rigid, uncomfortable-looking colonial furniture and the arrestingly candid "primitive" portraits by itinerant painters had their own chill authority and seemed appropriately displayed in the harshly lighted rabbit warren of the museum's basement galleries.

Three of the discoveries that I made during that MFA year have stuck with me—I think because each held a valuable lesson. Thanks to Yankee sea captains and the collectors who followed them, Boston's Far Eastern collection is one of the greatest in the Western world. In those still and dusty galleries, my eleven- and twelve-year-old Norwood self went missing among the long scrolls that hung on the walls or rolled out for twenty or thirty feet in glass cases. What a feast for the imagination! Tracing the winding rivers and mountain roads, I made up stories about the solitary pilgrims or the small groups meeting by chance on footpaths, in small boats bumping gently together, or in open-air teahouses perched on the sides of beetling crags. Because I was a kid, two of my favorite scrolls, both from the thirteenth century, were atypically action-packed. In the amazing, thirty-foot *Nine Dragons,* the sinuous, smoky denizens of darkness emerge from and blend into a landscape of swirling mists. Somehow they manage to convey both wispy other-worldliness and substantial, ominous threat. *The Burning of the Sanjô Palace,* "one of the great battle pictures of the world," according to an MFA guidebook, embodies its urgent theme of beauty and balance destroyed by war through a mesmerizing juxtaposition of delicate buildings and ravishing flames, of soldiers and civilians caught in a chaotic, deadly dance. Regrettably, neither of these scrolls has been on display during my recent trips to the museum. (A few years ago an MFA guard confided to me, tongue firmly in cheek, "I think they did away with a lot of those scrolls.")

My favorite place in the MFA that year connected those scrolls with my own immediate reality. This was the Japanese Garden. Entering was like walking into a painting. I was fascinated because in this dim, windowless back gallery the MFA had managed to bring the outdoors inside. (This magical feature was lost to younger generations of kids when an outdoor garden replaced it in the 1980s.) The garden was high-ceilinged and cloistered at once, overlooked by a second-floor balcony with a carved wooden railing and hedged in by statues of the Buddha and large folding screens tinged with muted gold. It had a standing pond spanned by a flat stone bridge and stocked with water plants and real fish—fat, shiny carp. It had statues of exotic, lionlike creatures and miniature pagodas placed symmetrically in squares of sand raked into sculpted whorls. It had a stone bench on which, most Saturdays, I would sit for fifteen minutes at a time. Sometimes I pretended to be one of those pilgrims from the scrolls and paintings. Sometimes I was just catching my breath and thinking idly about the Lord knows what. There were two linked lessons here: I liked my own company, and solitude had value.

My other two memorable discoveries were individual American paintings, both from the late nineteenth-century. They demonstrated, each very differently, that kids my own age could end up on the walls of a museum. One rendered children whose lives were impossibly remote from mine. The other echoed my own world.

Gilded-Age Boston's adopted darling son John Singer Sargent was an artist whose utterly confident, fin de siécle painterly flamboyance marked a hundred years of solid Yankee accomplishment since the austere eighteenth century. During my year of lessons, the MFA was preparing for an exhibition called "Sargent's Boston," which was mounted in January 1956 to commemorate the one-hundredth anniversary of the painter's birth. At that point, Sargent had been dead only thirty years, and many Bostonians who had known him were still around. Perhaps it was this flurry of activity that caused the painting that so struck me to be brought to prominent display at a stair head. *The Daughters of Edward Darley Boit* is a monumental seven-by-seven-foot oil of four young Bostonians, painted by Sargent in their Paris apartment in 1882. It's a dramatic composition in which four girls, ages about two to fourteen, occupy a vast living room. The youngest sits on the floor in full light with her doll, while her sisters recede chrono-

Figure 21. The Japanese Garden at the MFA in 1909. Photograph by Baldwin Coolidge. Photograph

logically into a darkening background, the oldest being most in shadow. I found the liquid depth of the internal vista stunning. The only vestige of old New England staidness is the shining wooden floor, itself all but negated by a sumptuous rug on which the baby sits and by two very large blue-and-white Chinese vases which look to be as important as any of the girls. What really got to me about this painting in 1954 was the self-assured, level and leveling gaze of the Boit girls themselves, none of whom seems at all impressed by having been chosen as a subject for a huge picture by the leading portraitist of the Euro-American cultural world. All four, including the baby, radiate a blasé, silver-spoon sophistication that I found breathtaking. Here, rendered with great clarity, was a way I would certainly never be.

In my third MFA discovery, the thrill of the unattainable gave way to its opposite. Winslow Homer's *Boys in a Pasture* came from a place that I recognized right away as familiar. This lovely small oil of 1874 presents two barefoot boys with tattered hats lounging in the grass on a summer's day. I first saw the painting resting on its own easel near the museum's Huntington Avenue entrance to trumpet its purchase in 1953, just before my own time at the museum began. These kids also looked about my age, but now my thought was, this could be me—no, this *is* me—for I had spent countless afternoons stretched out in baseball outfields and my own backyard, idly turning the clouds into islands, peninsular headlands, steep cliffs, and mountain ranges. Much more directly than the Dutch genre scenes, which retained the exoticism of faraway time and place, Homer's picture declared that one of art's great achievements could be to render the glories of the everyday, to let us see how extraordinary the ordinary could be. Coming back to it now, I see that *Boys in a Pasture* embodies the unfettered potential of endless summer days that kids used to take for granted, the great gift of unclocked time and unfettered space in which the imagination runs free. And I continue to wonder how many kids nowadays are allowed that blissful experience of School-Is-Out / Run-and-Shout idleness. So many parents ferry their children from pillar to post all the year round in a relentless drive to equip them for some sort of advantage in schooling and career. In its cartoonish excesses, how dreary this is, and how unfair to the kids. The miracle of Homer's painting is the way he evokes the cool and coppery light of a late afternoon in late summer. The boys have their sleeves rolled all the way down, and it's the knowledge that days like this are numbered that makes the painting so poignant to me now as a viewer well into my sixties.

Following the Emly Shrine

Several years ago, to jog my memory of the MFA in the early 1950s, I paged through old issues of the *Bulletin of the Museum of Fine Arts*. Upon opening the bound volume for 1954, I was surprised to find on its title page the photograph of an extraordinary artifact. The caption read: "Emly Shrine—Anglo-Irish—Eighth Century." I was greatly intrigued. I didn't recall having seen it during my year of grace at the museum, but from my study of early Irish culture, I knew what I was looking at. The piece was a reliquary. Hung around the neck or over the shoulder by a leather strap, it would have held the "relics"—bits of bone or hair—of a Christian saint. The date made it very early and thus, probably, very rare. What, I wondered, had gone on here? The Emly Shrine looked to be an Irish national treasure that had somehow left its country of origin and landed in Boston in 1952, the date of its acquisition by the MFA. How had this happened?

BULLETIN OF THE

MUSEUM OF FINE ARTS

VOL. LII

1954

Fig. 1. Emly Shrine Anglo-Irish Eighth Century
Theodora Wilbour Fund in memory of Charlotte Beebe Wilbour

BOSTON

MASSACHUSETTS

Figure 22. Title page of the MFA *Bulletin* for 1954.

Two further considerations also piqued my interest. First of all, the place name "Emly" brought to mind my favorite entry in the Irish *Annals*, the medieval manuscript collections of dated events from early Irish history. It's an event of the year 947 in the *Annals of Inisfallen*: "*Duilend do nim for altoir nImblecha Ibair ocus in t-én do labrad risna doenib, ocus inganta ile archena isin bliadainse*" (A leaf [descended] from heaven upon the altar of Imlech Ibuir, and a bird spoke to the people; and many other marvels this year). I first read this in Kathleen Hughes's scholarly classic, *The Church in Early Irish Society*, where it seemed lovely, literally miraculous, and perfectly evocative of early Irish Christianity. Tucked into the part of County Tipperary that juts westward into County Limerick, Imlech Ibuir (that is, Emly) was a powerful site in the medieval church. A diocesan seat with its own cathedral, the place was important enough strategically to be burned or plundered at least fifteen times between 845 and 1177.

Second, my love of miniatures came to the fore when I began to look carefully at what was in fact a very small object. The Emly Shrine is a box measuring 4 and 3/16 inches long by 1 and 11/16 inches wide by 3 and 11/16 inches high. Carved from a single block of yew wood, it is shaped like a house with a trapezoidal sloped roof which is the box lid. All the edges are framed with rounded moldings of gilded bronze fastened with small nails. An intricate, stepped pattern of silver lines covers the surface of the walls and roof, spreading concentrically from a regularly spaced series of silver squares, each of which frames a four-part leaf-like design. These interwoven lines of silver are inlaid into the yew wood. Fixed to the surface are three large, circular gold medallions which dominate the design. These are triangulated, with two on the side wall and one on the roof of the little house. Each gold circle contains four inner circles, and each of these is punctuated by cloisonné-inset enamel blocks of alternating yellow and green organized in multiples of eight. All three medallions are blank in the center, but given the overall complexity of the piece, they must have held something wonderful, now lost to the ravages of time. On each end of the roof's bronze ridgepole there perches the head of a fantastic animal whose eye, snout, and mouth are marked out in yellow, green, and red (now faded to brown) cloisonné blocks. These heads exemplify the wild mix of Celtic and Christian design motifs that identify Irish art throughout its golden age of 600–800 A.D. The two heads point inward along the roof line toward, in the center, a tiny house with its own sloped roof that echoes the shape of the shrine itself. This second house is inlaid with a cloisonné grid of twelve yellow and green blocks. As a whole, the piece is breathtaking in its delicate, balanced interplay of colors, lines, and surfaces.

My subsequent digging revealed that the Emly Shrine was indeed a rarity—and something of a mystery as well. I found only four references to it in Irish archaeological literature, the earliest in the 1878 volume, *Christian Inscriptions in the Irish Language*, the magisterial summary of a lifetime's pioneering fieldwork by the eminent antiquarian George Petrie. In describing reliquaries "of the form of the earliest type of church," which is also "that of the ark, handed down from time immemorial," Petrie declares that "the most remarkable examples of such shrines" include but three in Ireland, among them "Lord Emly's shrine." I learned also that before it came to Boston, the shrine had been exhibited publicly only once—at the Great Exhibition of Art and Industry that was held in Dublin from May through October of 1853.

It then occurred to me that I might have seen the piece at least once myself. Mounted by the Irish government to commemorate the American Bicentennial, a spectacular exhibition, *Treasures of Early Irish Art, 1500 B. C. to 1500 A.D.*, had toured the United States from October 1977 through May 1979. The Boston showing had coincided with my first sabbatical as a college professor, some of which I used to take a special course of weekly lectures at the MFA on early Irish art, culminating in early October of 1978 with a private preview of the exhibition. Here were virtually all the greatest examples of Irish culture's flowering: the Ardagh chalice, the Tara brooch, the cross of Cong, the Clonmacnoise crozier, and on and on. Even the Books of Durrow and Kells were there. The exhibition had provoked lively debate over the wisdom of the Irish government in allowing the bedrock artifacts of its heritage out of the country. Nothing like it has happened since. At the time, it was a terrific, fortuitous reinforcement of my growing interest in all things Irish. I had kept the catalogue, and now found that the exhibition had consisted of sixty-nine objects, all but one on loan from the National Museum of Ireland, Trinity College Dublin, and the Royal Irish Academy. That one piece was the Emly Shrine. That's how important it was!

The latest of the four archaeological references had come in 1941 in Joseph Raftery's catalogue, *Christian Art in Ancient Ireland*, which listed "the now well-known 'Monsell of Tervoe' or 'Emly Shrine'" and stated that "the exact locality from which the shrine came is not known, but as it has been in the possession of the Monsell family of Tervoe, Co. Limerick, for some time it may be presumed to have belonged at least to the south of

Ireland." Raftery then located the piece: "Through the kind courtesy and generosity of Commander Edmond Monsell, R.N., the Shrine has been deposited in the National Museum."

How these Monsells obtained the Emly Shrine can be understood in general terms. The greatest disruption to the Irish church since the Viking raids of the late 700s accompanied the Protestant Reformation in the reign of Henry VIII. By decree, most monasteries and churches were destroyed or shuttered and all "chattels" of value confiscated. In 1539 a legislative act ordered Henry's representatives "to investigate, inquire and search where within the said land of Ireland there were any notable images or relics to which the simple people of the said lord the king were wont to assemble superstitiously and as vagrants to walk and roam in pilgrimage, or else to lick, kiss or honour contrary to God's honour." Once gathered, these "divers profane images, pictures and relics" should be "taken into the hand of the lord the king and appraised; and also sold for the use of the lord the king." It's also true that during the Reformation, many Catholic abbots became laicized or went over directly as prelates into the new Protestant Church of Ireland, and they often took ecclesiastical art objects along with them to their new digs. In addition, members of the recently validated Anglo-Irish Protestant nobility did a fair amount of plain stealing of artifacts. It is safe to assume that somewhere in this hurly-burly of shifting allegiances and fortunes, the Emly Shrine went missing from its original ecclesiastical home.

The Monsell family had come from London to County Limerick in 1612 as part of the first land-grabbing "plantation" of Ireland after the Battle of Kinsale. In 1690 they built a notable Irish Big House at Tervoe, Clarina, outside the city of Limerick, and at some unknown point in their progress, they acquired the shrine in question. The Monsells reached their genealogical peak when the then patriarch, William, was created Baron Emly of Tervoe in January 1874. Born in 1812 and educated at Winchester and Oxford, William Monsell went on to an eventful public career—serving as Member of Parliament for County Limerick, Undersecretary of State for the Colonies, Postmaster General, and Vice Chancellor of the Royal University of Ireland. It was he who lent the Emly Shrine to the Great Dublin Exhibition in 1853. Subsequently, he allowed the Royal Irish Academy to keep the shrine on loan until 1872, at which point he took it back.

The Monsell peerage was short-lived, for William's son Thomas was the second and last Baron Emly. He succeeded in 1894 but died in 1932 without leaving a male heir. Thomas Monsell's only child, Mary Olivia Augusta, married Edmond James de Poher de la Poer in 1881. Their son Edmond (1883–1964) became a commander in the Royal Navy. He took Monsell as an additional surname in accordance with his grandfather Thomas's will, and Tervoe House was deeded to him in 1935. It was he who deposited the Emly Shrine in the National Museum of Ireland in 1941, as reported by Raftery. This was likely a World War II precaution, because at some postwar point the Monsells again took the shrine back to Limerick. In 1948, Edmond in turn made the house over to his son, John Humphrey Arnold de Poher de la Poer Monsell, who had been born in 1916, graduated from Sandhurst, and become a career officer in the British Army. John and his family lived at Tervoe for only three years. He moved out in 1951 and sold the Tervoe Estates to the Irish Land Commission. In 1953 he had the house demolished. Meanwhile, as part of the general tidying up, he sold the Emly Shrine to the Boston Museum of Fine Arts in 1952.

There is a bulky folder on the Emly Shrine in the archives of the MFA which provides some clues as to how this extraordinary purchase came about, and also indicates the controversial nature of the transaction. Bringing the Emly Shrine to Huntington Avenue was a high point in the career of the MFA's medieval curator, Georg Swarzenski, who had left Nazi Germany and the directorship of the Municipal Museums of Frankfort in 1937 to take a position in Boston. In collaboration with his son, Hanns, who was affiliated with the Institute for Advanced Study in Princeton, Swarzenski built Boston's medieval collection virtually from scratch. Between them, these two knew virtually every important art collector and broker in Europe.

The intermediary between the Monsells of Tervoe and the MFA was Hector O'Connor of 77 Merrion Square, Dublin, a son of the well-known Irish American sculptor Andrew O'Connor, who had lived out his last years in that house and died there in 1941. In a March 1952 letter to Hanns Swarzenski, Hector O'Connor declares himself "delighted to think that the Boston Museum is taking a serious interest in the shrine. It would be a great pity, I think, for them to miss such an important object. I took your advice and let the solicitor, Mr. Jackson, know that he may receive a communication from the Museum." The MFA file that I was shown contains no details of the ensuing negotiation. The handwritten draft (I have put crossed out words in brackets) of a reply from Hanns Swarzenski to O'Connor, dated November 6, 1952, indicates that the deal has been done.

> My dear O'Connor,
>
> This is just a note to tell you that the Shrine despite its small size has received the greatest admiration, and that we are all very happy that we have it here in our Museum. At your advice, we waited all these months before showing it to the Trustees, but now it will soon be exhibited and published in the Bulletin of the Museum by my father who wrote a beautiful scholarly paper about the piece and its connections with Irish and Anglo-Irish art. Needless to say how grateful I personally am to you and your adviser in procuring the shrine. I [only] hope indeed that nobody in Ireland will resent the purchase and that one will realize that to us this tiny object is the only representation and symbol of Irish art and culture we have in this country, while for you in Ireland it is but one of many examples of your great artistic heritage.
>
> As I am told the Catholic Bishop of Boston unfortunately is not [very] really concerned with artistic matters and so we have not informed him of the purchase and asked him to write to the Papal Nuncio in Dublin to request a formal export license from the Minister of Education. You will remember that Mr. Jackson [and yourself] also thought it [better not to do] unnecessary to do this then and you agreed.

Clearly, the involved parties were aware of potential trouble. The hope that "nobody in Ireland will resent the purchase" is a telling aside. The "Catholic Bishop" to whom Swarzenski refers was Richard J. Cushing, Boston's archbishop since 1944, who would become a cardinal in 1958. A man of great political acumen and strong opinions, Cushing was the son of immigrants from Galway to South Boston, where he had been born and raised. Intensely interested in the affairs of his parents' homeland, he had played a major role in financing the building of a new cathedral in the city of Galway. No one could have doubted that he would have had something to say about the MFA's plan to take the Emly Shrine out of Ireland.

On the other side, sensitivity toward Ireland and Irish America was not the strong suit at the MFA, which was one of the temples of New England Yankeedom. In the early Fifties, the president and vice president of the museum were Ralph Lowell and Henry Lee Shattuck, and the roster of trustees included the names Coolidge, Forbes, Gardner, Paine, Claflin, Aldrich, Bliss, Hallowell, Cutting, and Saltonstall. Indeed, the old MFA issues of the

Bulletin that I've looked at are laced with hefty doses of smugly assumed cultural power, dispensed with the velvet glove of noblesse oblige.

A remarkable case in point is the essay by Georg Swarzenski announcing to the general public that the Emly Shrine had come to Boston. Not published in the MFA *Bulletin* until October 1954, two years after the purchase and his son's letter to Hector O'Connor, Swarzenski's piece is a fascinating cultural document, a precarious tightrope walk rife with contradictions. In the first place, its title, "An Early Anglo-Irish Portable Shrine," is a misnomer of which Swarzenski ought to have been aware. In the 700s, there was no "Anglo" in Irish society, and very little in British. As to provenance, Swarzenski says only that "the object . . . has been for centuries in the Monsel [*sic*] (Lord Emly) family in Limerick County." He provides no details about how the acquisition was made or how much money was spent, revealing only that the museum's purchase (Accession Number 52.1396) came through the "Theodora Wilbour Fund in memory of Charlotte Beebe Wilbour."

Swarzenski is hugely enthusiastic about the shrine, averring that it is one of six surviving complete examples of "evidently analogous works," only one of which, the Lough Erne Shrine, remains in Ireland—in the National Museum. This admission prompts a preemptive justification: "There is a popular claim that such [rare] works, for their national interest involved, should be treasured alone in the representative collections of the native country which are, indeed, and always will be, the particular and unrivaled domain of the arts in this field. However, Anglo-Irish art of this period spread from the beginning over many countries, and the object shows how its national roots had grown to universal human expression and were generally understood and adopted in scattered places of Western and Central Europe." In other words, by its very translatable excellence, this art had been rendered no longer merely "Irish." Swarzenski goes on: "Only a narrow-minded attitude might complain that [the shrine's] purchase, by the Museum of Fine Arts, had deprived the native country of a documentary and sentimental national value."

Swarzenski's argument then takes another specious, and palpably condescending, turn: "On the contrary, the singular subject, accessible now among outstanding works of cosmopolitan rank, will display here the legitimate importance of this realm, and might, especially in Boston, as we hope, contribute to an awakening and deepening of the historic and artistic understanding of this city's Irish population." Implying that such understanding is at present asleep and shallow, Swarzenski appears to be visualizing the great unwashed of South Boston, Charlestown, Brighton, Norwood trooping into the MFA on weekends to be enlightened by exposure to the handiwork of their forebears.

The rest of the essay develops these two incompatible themes. On the one hand, Swarzenski takes pains to refute the originality of early "Irish" art, references to which he always puts in quotation marks. He claims that the famous "Treasures" of manuscript illumination and metalwork that I was to see at the MFA in 1978 mostly derive from continental and Near Eastern models. In one example, he contends that "the figural representations in the *Book of Kells* are copies—the classical mind says caricatures—of a famous continental manuscript." On the other hand, Swarzenski is unable to restrain his enthusiasm for the distinctiveness of the Emly Shrine itself. He asserts that "the richer, more articulate development of the ridge pole . . . is unique for inventiveness and elaboration," and that the technique of cutting the rectangular step pattern into the yew wood first and then beating the silver lines into the surface appears on no other extant reliquaries and is, in fact, "unparalleled in the Western schools of the period."

The shrine appears to have entered Boston with as little fanfare as it left Ireland. There was no significant coverage of its arrival in the local papers. I have been able to find only one reference anywhere—a brief mention in the *Boston Globe*'s weekly column, "Notes of Irish Interest," for October 12, 1954 (buried on page 24), announcing the purchase by the MFA "some years ago" of the "Emly Limerick Shrine." The writer quotes from and paraphrases Swarzenski's "interesting, if somewhat technical, essay on early Irish art," so there may not even have been a press release. I suspect that despite its importance, no one at the museum was looking to draw attention to the acquisition.

The response at the Royal Society of Antiquaries of Ireland (headquartered at 63 Merrion Square, just a few doors from the home of Emly intermediary Hector O'Connor) was something else entirely. In his April 1955 annual address on "The Position of Irish Archaeology," Seán P. Ó Ríordáin, society president and his generation's greatest archaeologist of Ireland, cautioned that "very little advantage has been taken of the powers conferred by the 1930 [National Monuments] Act." He went on, in a section headed "Export of Antiquities," to deplore the loss of the shrine in no uncertain terms:

> Apart from the safeguarding of monuments and the reporting of finds, the 1930 Act gave power to prevent the export of archaeological objects. I wish to mention one sad instance of this

> export, which may be a salutary warning. I know nothing of the details but it was with a sense of shock that it was learned that the Emly Shrine, an important Early Christian reliquary, had left the country. The first public intimation that this had occurred was an article in an American journal. I do not know what were the preliminaries to the export of the shrine but I do know that the Irish public was also unaware of the situation and was therefore given no chance to enter the market for its purchase. One remembers with gratitude the cases in the nineteenth century when outstanding objects were saved by public subscriptions initiated by the Royal Irish Academy or its members.

If, in fact, any sort of storm followed this blistering reaction, the MFA weathered it, and the Boston press did not cover it. In any case, Ó Ríordáin's indictment was not included in the MFA folder on the shrine that was shown to me. Later documents stored there, however, do illustrate a significant increase in respect for the piece over the ensuing years. The Emly Shrine has left the museum only twice since its arrival in 1952. During two years of travel (1977–79) with *Treasures of Early Irish Art,* it was valued for insurance purposes at $300,000. The shrine's second excursion was to an exhibition at the Palazzo Grassi in Venice in 1991, and at this point it was insured for $2.5 million.

The last tantalizing bit of the record is an internal MFA memorandum of September 30, 1994, from a staffer reporting to his colleagues that "a Trina Vargo from the foreign policy division of Senator [Edward] Kennedy's office in Washington DC had called with regard to the interest of an Irish museum in the Emly Shrine. It was unclear whether this was a loan request or a repatriation overture." A follow-up call revealed that an official from the National Museum of Ireland had asked Senator Kennedy to help get the reliquary back. "They further indicated," the memo continues, "that the shrine had been in our collection for 60 years, that it was not displayed prominently, and that they would love to get it, since they had nothing like it." Furthermore, "There was no implicit or explicit implication that the object ought to be in Ireland, or ought not to be here." The memo concludes: "I explained to Ms. Vargo that we did not typically sell objects from our collection to other museums, and we were not interested in parting with the Emly shrine. She will indicate to the National Museum that we were pleased to hear from them, but that we are not interested in pursuing their proposal."

The Emly Shrine has become, for me, something of a cathetic lodestone, one with great drawing power, and the fate of this object has come to echo my own lifelong engagement with Ireland and Irish immigration. I see the shrine as a figure for the interests that have spurred my teaching and scholarship. Within the field of Irish studies, I've sought to establish the existence of a body of literature—that of the Irish in America—that had been variously forgotten, misunderstood, and underappreciated, and to place that body of literature anew within clarifying cultural contexts. When I started out in the late 1960s, the entrenched Anglophile and Anglocentric predispositions in literary studies resisted such an effort. I recall a number of job interviews, some in places now known as bastions of Irish studies, where I was at pains to explain my interest in *Irish,* much less Irish American, culture. More than once, scholars who should have known better responded to my research by making lame jokes, along the lines of "Irish American culture? You mean besides drinking?" Just as a reliquary is, if understood in its context, much more than a container for dead bones, so is a literary tradition much more than antiquarianism or filio-piety. Similarly, I believe that the Emly Shrine was bought quietly and then buried in a back gallery by Boston's Museum of Fine Arts. Yes, the powers at the MFA saw the shrine as valuable, but they could not acknowledge its importance as a work in the Irish tradition. The Swarzenski essay does not so much as admit that there *is* an Irish tradition.

The Emly Shrine was a new treasure at the MFA in the mid-Fifties, during the time I was a Saturday student there. Given the behind-the-scenes nature of the purchase negotiations, I cannot imagine that the shrine was displayed very prominently. I only know that I didn't notice it. But, I can easily verify the contention in the Kennedy memo that the piece has been kept at the margins in more recent years. When I visited the museum in 2001, shortly after discovering its existence, the Emly Shrine was one of six or seven disparate pieces clustered on the bottom shelf of a small case hanging on the wall outside the MFA's main medieval gallery. All were identified only by numbers, and a typed list of the names beside the case explained that these works had come from "Roman Provinces." As the Romans never ventured across the Irish Sea, even this was patently untrue.

I returned five years later to find the shrine in a much better spot but still woefully out of context. Now it rests in the Catalonian Chapel, a small room off the medieval gallery which is dominated by a curvilinear Catalan fresco, described as "among the greatest twelfth-century European paintings in the United States." The shrine is at the bottom center of a four-by-six-foot display case that hangs on a side wall and holds "Precious Objects for Sacred and Secular Use." There are twenty of these, including a "Eucharistic dove" from Limoges, an English marriage casket, a Spanish astrolabe, two Dutch medallions, the escutcheon of a Florentine wool-merchants guild, and very different types of reliquaries from Germany and France. Every piece in this mixed bag is late medieval—the earliest date is 1150; the latest, 1504—except for the Emly Shrine. The shrine is now included in the MFA's general audio tour, where a sonorous, British-accented voice explains that "only nine medieval Irish reliquaries of this early date in this shape are known to survive today," and adds that the name is "for the Emly family of County Limerick who owned it in the nineteenth and twentieth centuries."

The Emly Shrine looks lonely in the Catalan Chapel. Out of time and out of place, it is 300 years older than anything else in the room, and the only Irish artifact anywhere in sight. I think of its place-lore connections with the perilous history of the early church in Ireland, of its shadowy provenance from Henry VIII to the Monsells of Tervoe, of its rarity and stunning aesthetic qualities, which were on public view in its native country only once, in 1853. That this great work of art has survived so much and ended up where it is now seems to me an injustice—one among myriad in the museum trade, to be sure—but sharply poignant nonetheless. Nothing about the Boston setting of this miraculous survivor is commensurate with the Emly Shrine's capacity for wonder. From Huntington Avenue, it's still a long way to Tipperary.

Bringing Peace to One's Fingers

It's easy to recall what it felt like when I was ten or eleven to make art or to stand looking at it. That's because handwork continues to be a haven. It's a straight line from clay whales to the many bookcases and shelves I've built over the years to the ship models I'm now putting together. I had been lucky to discover so young that focused labor can be a wellspring joy, a dependable springboard to reverie and tranquil absorption outside the self. As Frost puts it, "The fact is the sweetest dream that labor knows." Whenever I'm making something by hand, I experience again how time disappears until the body interrupts with eyestrain, backache, hunger, and thirst, and the message is received by the mind with surprise, even amazement: "What? Where am I? Oh, here I am, in the cellar. Working." My favorite expression of this comes from Robert Lowell, a troubled man much in need of art's help for pain, writing just a year before his death at age sixty to his friend and fellow poet Frank Bidart: "It's miraculous, as you told me about yourself, how often writing takes the ache away, takes time away. You start in the morning, and look up to see the windows darkening. I'm sure anything done steadily, obsessively, eyes closed to everything besides the page, the spot of garden . . . makes returning a jolt. The world you've been saved from grasps you roughly."

Early on, I also discovered that the steadying power of immersed engagement carried over to other parts of the day when I wasn't actually working on a piece. Whenever I had a project in hand, it would pop into my head at odd moments. Without warning, I would think about a problem I had just solved—say, how to attach the emperor's platform to the inside wall of my Colosseum—and where I was going from there: how to create the rows of seats for the ordinary Romans. Here was an unexpected blessing. The idea that I was moving something creative toward completion made for a reassuring sense of continuity, whatever frustrations I was dealing with elsewhere in family and school life. This too has continued reliably to happen. When I'm working on something, the calming thought still comes unbidden: "OK. When I get a chance, I will cut—or join, sand, stain, paint—whatever next needs to be done on this project." This reservoir of healthy anticipation is a great incentive to keep something going on my basement workbench, even if it's just a broken soap dish or a lamp that's been shorting out. I see this as a legacy from my father, whose life was filled with continuing tasks that required hand tools and concentrated attention.

In the years after my Saturday classes at the MFA, I continued to make clay models, pencil sketches, and paintings. I took studio art courses until ninth grade, at which point there was no room left in the "college prep" schedule for such frivolities. I had begun experimenting with oils in seventh grade, through the tried (though not true) medium of paint-by-numbers. My father framed one of these, a pedestrian landscape with a farmhouse and cows, and hung it on the wall in our dining room. Even then I could see that there was no contest between the painting and its frame, which was ornately crafted of a lustrous, grainy wood. It was one of several frames that had been left in the back storage room of our Walpole Street house by its previous owners, the Philbrooks. I went on painting sporadically through college and beyond, and at one point I removed my cowscape in order to use the frame for a newly finished picture. I was surprised to find that my father had used as backing for my clumsy, juvenile effort a picture that had probably been in the frame originally—a lovely charcoal sketch of a dreamy-eyed peasant girl, her dark hair gathered under a bonnet. I took this piece to an art historian, who told me that it was from the late nineteenth century, probably European and possibly French. It was no great stretch for me to imagine an artist making this sketch in a studio across the street from John Singer Sargent working on his portrait of the four Boit daughters. I made this discovery a year or so after my father's death, so I never got to ask him where he had found the girl, why he had preserved her behind my lame creation, and why he hadn't told anyone that she was there. Like so much about my father, there's something here that I can't quite get to, a question that's going to stay unanswered.

Bachelard's *Poetics of Space* is invaluable in explaining the attraction of art classifiable as "miniature," a term that covers many of the objects that I've created and those I've appreciated over the years. He sees the concept as a prime stimulus to the imagination: "Values become engulfed in miniature, and miniature causes men to dream," he says, and "the minuscule, a narrow gate, opens up an entire world." Furthermore, this process occurs in the absence of threat: "Miniature is an exercise that has metaphysical freshness; it allows us to be world conscious at slight risk. And how restful this exercise on a dominated world can be!" The passage in which Bachelard cites the medieval creators of tiny, intricate masterpieces—books of hours, illuminated gospels, reliquaries such as the Emly Shrine—is beautifully resonant:

> Unfortunately, being, as I am, a philosopher who plies his trade at home, I haven't the advantage of actually seeing the works of the miniaturists of the Middle Ages, which was the great age of solitary patience. But I can well imagine this patience, which brings peace to one's fingers. Indeed, we have only to imagine it for our souls to be bathed in peace. All small things must evolve slowly, and certainly a long period of leisure, in a quiet room, was needed to miniaturize the world. Also one must love space to describe it as minutely as though there were world molecules, to enclose an entire spectacle in a molecule of drawing.

I can see myself sitting on the big screened porch of our house on Walpole Street on any of a thousand rainy days of my childhood. There's the fresh, clean smell of the rain. The swoosh, swoosh of automobile tires going by out front. The thickening light of late afternoon. I am thoroughly absorbed in the words on a page or the lines on a map, or on the scratch of my pencil or the flow of my brush, or the pressure of my fingers on a lump of clay. I know in my bones that, as far as being alone goes, I've never been happier than I am right here and now.

Homage to Joseph Cornell

When the porch was shut up in winter, I had another place to go. I would step through the dining room door to a dark landing, flip the light switch, and head down cellar to the little jerry-built room where my mother kept stewed tomatoes and my father stored cans of paint. I remember this long-gone alternate refuge for creativity through the soles of my feet every time I hit the cellar stairs to fix a lamp, work on a cabinet, or lash down the half-inch cannons on the deck of Captain Cook's *Endeavor*. Each step down is a step toward recovering that familiar, deep, spontaneous joy. The fact that he took a similar, mundane, daily trip to create his art was one of the things that interested me about the American artist Joseph Cornell when I first saw his work in *Life* magazine in December 1967. It was the end of my first semester in graduate school in American Civilization at the University of Pennsylvania, and our class had already been warned to start looking for dissertation topics. I was so struck by that essay in *Life* that I thought I had found my subject. I had never seen anything even remotely like Cornell's box constructions, and I sat right down and wrote him a letter, declaring that I loved his boxes and inviting myself to visit him on Utopia Parkway (what a great street name!) in Flushing, Queens. At the time, I didn't have the house number, and the letter came back stamped "Insufficient Address."

The *Life* reporter David Bourdon provided a brief aesthetic history. Cornell had made his first surrealist experiments in collage and construction while hanging around the Julien Levy Gallery in Manhattan in the early 1930s, and his first big break was an invitation to participate in the Museum of Modern Art's historic 1936 show, "Fantastic Art, Dada, Surrealism." Cornell had grown up haunting used book and junk stores and the New York Public Library's photo collection. He had made avant-garde films. All coalesced when he experienced a breakthrough revelation about the direction of his creativity: "He passed an antique shop one day and saw a pile of compasses in the window. 'I thought, everything can be used in a lifetime, can't it, and went on walking. I'd scarcely gone two blocks when I came on another shop window full of boxes, all different kinds. . . . Halfway home on the train that night, I thought again of the compasses and the boxes. It occurred to me to put the two together.'"

The *Life* photo-essay contained full-page color pictures of nine Cornell box constructions, and they stopped me in my tracks. As containers, of wood with window-glass fronts, they were quite ordinary. Some were varnished, some plain; some were painted white or blue; all had cracks and scratches and random flecks of paint. Not at all distinguished by their craftsmanship, they looked to have been casually knocked together. (This was indeed the case. A neighbor on Utopia Parkway had made several of the early ones, and later Cornell had taken over what he saw as merely a necessary chore.) But inside the boxes—what treasures! Cornell carried home to Flushing the flotsam and jetsam of his rambles around Manhattan: marbles, clay pipes, straw, twigs, and moss; photographs, newsprint cutouts, and photocopies of dolls and birds and ballerinas, star maps and land maps; metal springs and rings, glass goblets and vials, wooden balls and blocks, wire mesh, dowels, bottle corks, seashells, and canceled postage stamps. In his basement workshop he accomplished an alchemist's conversion, turning random scraps of quotidian junk into arresting and timeless visionary constructions. To look into a Cornell box is to experience a lyricism so piercing and fragile at once that the viewer feels an almost sensible ache. It's like finding yourself in a quiet room still vibrating just after a chime has sounded.

Among the hundreds of Cornell boxes, three groups are my special favorites. There are those featuring the Medici children, aristocratic kids whom Cornell has adopted by way of photocopies of their Renaissance portraits and placed behind latticed crosshairs in boxes that look like esoteric games, what with the array of numbers, blocks, stars, wooden balls. I also appreciate the wit and whimsy of the bird boxes, which feature an exotic menagerie of parrots and cockatoos and stark-staring owls, surrounded by all manner of *disjecta membra,* of which the birds seem scornfully dismissive. And the night-sky boxes are ravishing, with their deep blue backgrounds, action-painted stippling of stars, and archaic illustrations of the mythic figures for which constellations are named—Orion, Andromeda, Cassiopeia. Often Cornell puts the stable universe in dialectic with human transience by including scraps of newspaper ads for French hotels: "Hotel du Cygne," "Hotel de l'Étoile," "Hotel Royal des Etrangers." These boxes hold loneliness distilled to purity.

Though I never met Cornell—he died in 1972 at age sixty-nine—we have had several encounters over the years. I've made a few boxes in homage and have managed to see several Cornell shows in galleries and museums, including his two big retrospectives in 1981 and 2007. I also spent one

Figure 23. Joseph Cornell, *Untitled (Hotel de l'Etoile, Night Skies, Auriga)*, 1954. Box construction, 19 x 13 5/8 x 8 1/8 in. Lindy and Edwin Bergman Joseph Cornell Collection, 1982.1856. The Art Institute of Chicago. Photography © The Art Institute of Chicago.

marvelous day at the Joseph Cornell Study Center in the Smithsonian's National Museum of American Art in Washington, looking at the marked-up books in his personal library and some of the actual storage boxes from his basement—filled with clock hands, springs, piston rings, playing cards, bird cutouts, and much else, including a mason jar full of rhinestones and containers labeled "mouse dirt," which looks like it came out of a vacuum cleaner. There is plenty of food for thought in that amazing archive, and I hope to go back for more. The example of Cornell's body of work is a cornerstone of my engagement with the arts. He's the artist as autodidactic everyman, and that's a role I much admire and sometimes wish I had attempted myself.

Charley Fanning, Harper

We're always looking for evidence, genetic and historical, to help us understand who we are and how we got to the place we now inhabit. Looking back at Joseph Cornell, my MFA class, and clay modeling, it's clear that I've had a consistent interest in the visual arts all along the way. Moreover, I realize now that I never treated the idea of becoming an artist as an option serious enough to be explored with family, friends, or teachers. My thinking here was private, incremental, at least partly unconscious, and never articulated. And yet it was certainly all decided before I entered high school. Why was this? One obvious reason was the absence of in-house precedent for such a life when I was growing up. As far as I knew then, there had been no artists perched anywhere on my family tree of New England Yankees and immigrants from Ireland and Germany. The Yankees had been farmers and tradesmen and small business people. The immigrants had been farmers, tanners, printers, and reluctant soldiers. None had gone to college, and most hadn't finished high school. All had worked for a living without much choice in the matter of how to go about it.

In my immediate family, my father is the strongest candidate for possession of any gene for aesthetics that may have come down to me. He worked miracles with his hands in the realm of nuts-and-bolts maintenance of automobiles, houses, and public school buildings. He had been a ship-construction welder. He had an artisan's reverence for good tools, for keeping them sharp and clean and dry and rust-free. He had kick-started my own childish creativity by showing me how to make clay whales. And there was one other piece of evidence: he had had a camera, a good one, and according to my mother he had enjoyed taking pictures. I never saw him in action, though, because the camera got broken before I could have remembered anything about it. There are a lot of photographs from the early years of my parents' marriage, including the wedding itself and honeymoon trip, pictures of my mother's extended family on Wilson Street, even some of me as a baby, but these trail off before my brother's birth in February 1945, and I reckon from this that the accident happened around that time. As related by my mother—my father never discussed it—the story was one of our family's few wholly didactic anecdotes. It was short and clear with an irrefutable conclusion. Dad had lent the camera to a friend who had taken it to the beach and dropped it. Some grains of sand got stuck into the works and couldn't be gotten out. And that was that.

We still had the camera throughout my childhood. It was in the bathroom closet in its original black leather case, buffed to a sheen by handling. Though useless, it was still beautiful, and I can remember turning it over and over in my hands, marveling through my fingertips at the mystery of heaviness and delicacy joined in a small box the size of two fists. The camera had high-grained leather paneling, shiny steel concentric rings with tiny numbers stuck on their curves, and a lever whose glossy sweep made blurred double images snap to resolution in the middle of a square gray field seen through the viewfinder. The lesson was obvious—don't lend out the most expensive piece of machinery you own—as was the tragic consequence: a means of making lucid images had been lost to invisible, ruinous sand.

As it happens, I have come up with a possible connection—sketchy, but not entirely off the map—between my family and ancestral Fanning talent in the arts. Music, to be specific. As evidence from my end of the line, I have always been interested in music, and I explored the field in directions determined on my own initiative and according to the lights available to me. Thanks to the radio and my mother's singing around the house, I absorbed hundreds of popular songs as a kid. However, I was not encouraged to learn an instrument in school, mostly because I could neither shake the maracas nor even clap my hands with anything approaching regular rhythm. (On the other hand, my brother and sister both played horn in the band in junior high.) Over the years, and with no success at all, I have tried several times to learn to read music and to play—in turn—piano, guitar, banjo, and piano again. The sharps and flats, G-clef and quarter notes remain well beyond me, and it's probably better that way. But my interest has been authentic, and just maybe there's a gene involved, recessive though it be.

I did grow up *listening* to music avidly, and 45-rpm records did in fact open up for me another new world, of comparable importance to my introduction to the visual arts at the MFA. (In his book *Last Night's Fun,* Belfast poet and musician Ciaran Carson reminds us that "record" is from *recordare,* which is Latin for "to get by heart.") In recorded music, then, I was first inspired by the unlikely triumvirate of Elvis Presley, Harry Belafonte, and Ferde Grofé. My first record player was a present from my parents for Christmas of 1956, when I was in ninth grade. It came with three 45s, one of which was Elvis singing "Hound Dog," with "Don't Be Cruel" on the flip side. On up through high school, I used money from my paper route to buy current hit records, from the black pioneers (Chuck Berry, Bo Diddley, Fats Domino, Little Richard) to the white boys who followed them and cashed in (Elvis, Buddy Holly, Eddie Cochran, Jimmy Bowen). I remember paying special attention to the Everly Brothers, especially "Kathy's Clown" and "Wake Up Little Susie," because their high harmonies were just plain thrilling. Also, my friends and I enjoyed making raucous fun of the many teen-death ballads abroad in the land, among them the ur-classic "Teen Angel," the lyrics of which are stuck in my memory: "That fateful night the car was stalled upon the railroad track. I pulled you out, and we were safe, but you went running back." While I did keep up with this pop music, I must confess that I didn't quite get it. This was because, in junior high and high school, the kids I hung out with were way, way behind in the establishment of romantic contact with the opposite sex, and so the themes of rock-and-roll were almost entirely hypothetical.

Ah, but then I heard Harry Belafonte on the radio. His big hit, "The Banana Boat Song" ("Daaay-o, Day-ay-ay-o, Daylight come and I wanna go home") made me a Belafonte fan and collector. The places from Jamaica evoked in the songs were strange and alluring, as were the calypso rhythms that he brought into the American musical mainstream. I got enough of the jokes in the comic numbers—"Zombie Jamboree," "Matilda," "Mama Look a Boo Boo," "Man Smart (Woman Smarter)"—to believe I was getting inside glimpses of another culture. But I responded most to Belafonte's passionate renderings of love for his native island. Here was poetry much more direct and affecting than anything I was getting in junior high English. I still have these songs by heart (*recordare*): "Down the way where the nights are gay / And the sun shines daily on the mountain top" ("Jamaica Farewell") and "This is my island in the sun / Where my people have toiled since time begun" ("Island in the Sun") and "Standing here in the marketplace, / Water come to me eye" (Come Back, Liza"). Reinforcing my interest in Belafonte was the fact that despite my tender years (fourteen) I was allowed to see his 1957 breakthrough movie, *Island in the Sun*, set in the colonial Caribbean. This had been a tough sell to my parents, as the strong suggestion of sun-and-sand steaminess (late Fifties style) had been reinforced by the media controversy over an on-screen interracial kiss between Belafonte and Joan Fontaine. Citing my record collection, I had argued that I was in it for the music. This was partly true, and it worked. Thus, I got some great visual images to go with the music and lyrics.

Before owning a record player I had also been curious about classical music. Unlike the pop songs, this was not a part of our daily family life as radio listeners. The catalyst here was a sixth-grade bus trip to hear the Boston Pops Orchestra. The red-plush foyer, the glittering big hall, the gorgeous sound: all made for another profound awakening. We even got to go backstage because one of my classmates, Teddy Matola, had an uncle in the orchestra. As I recall, he played something very odd—I think the bassoon, or maybe the oboe. After the concert, we were led up the stairs and across the stage, where we saw musicians walking around in their shirtsleeves, and bustling staff members carrying chairs and music stands. Teddy's uncle shepherded us to a corner where Pops conductor Arthur Fiedler was seated at a small table, about to tuck into a cold salmon salad. A formidable figure right out of central casting, with a mane of white hair and a big, drooping moustache, Fiedler was, for most of the Norwood kids, a first brush with celebrity, and it wasn't all that pleasant. The great man was grumpy, and he hurriedly scrawled what was supposed to be his name on each of our programs. He never looked up at us once. I for one had never gotten anyone's autograph before, and it bothered me that when I scrutinized the program in the bus on the way home, I couldn't pick out a single letter—not even the capital "A" or "F." Oh well, I thought, here at least is someone with worse penmanship than mine, and he's doing all right.

But the evening had been important in another way as well, for the Pops had played "On the Trail," the clip-clop, clip-clop movement from *The Grand Canyon Suite* by Ferde Grofé. I was captivated, and when I got my record player, I remembered this piece. By then, the technology included "Extended Play" records. "EPs" were not much more expensive than regular singles—I think they went for a dollar and that 45s were seventy-five cents—but they held more music and also played at 45 rpm, the only speed available on my little square machine. Grofé's suite came on two EP disks in a handsome jacket featuring pictures of the Grand Canyon. I bought it right away, and soon the melodies of its five movements—"Sunrise," "The Painted Desert," "On the Trail," "Sunset," and "Cloudburst"—were running through my head. Next, I picked up an EP version of a work I had heard as background music for Saturday morning children's radio shows—Edvard Grieg's *Peer Gynt Suite,* truncated, but including my favorite sections, "Morning," "Anitra's Dance," and "In the Hall of the Mountain King." As a high school junior in 1959, I used paper-route money to buy a machine that accommodated long-playing records. My first purchases in that format were benchmark LPs in folk and classical music: *The Kingston Trio at the Hungry I* and Van Cliburn playing Tchaikovsky's *Piano Concerto No. 1 in B-flat*

Minor, the piece with which he had famously won a big prize in Moscow. I have since gone merrily on my untutored way as a lover of all sorts of music, paying special attention to the folk scene, which dominated my college years in the early Sixties.

All of which brings me to an Irish Studies conference in Syracuse, New York, in the late 1980s, where I learned of my possible connection to a figure of some note and notoriety in the history of music in Ireland. A featured presenter at that meeting was Janet Harbison, a much respected performer, scholar, and teacher of the Irish harp. As we rose from adjacent chairs to leave a conference session, Janet pointed a finger at my name tag and said, "Now, that's a famous name you have there." "Really," I replied. "How so?" She proceeded to tell me that Charles Fanning had been an Irish harper of the eighteenth century who had in fact taken first prize at the Belfast Festival of 1792, the last formal gathering of traditional wandering harpers in Irish history. I had heard of that milestone event but not of this namesake. Always on the lookout for genetic predisposition, I noted the link with Northern Ireland, from which I knew my great-great-grandfather, Phillip Fanning, had come out to America. I asked Janet where to look for more information, and shortly after the conference I was turning pages in the standard texts, from Edward Bunting's *A Collection of the Ancient Music of Ireland* (1796) to Charlotte Milligan Fox's *Annals of the Irish Harpers* (1911).

The primary source turned out to be the dictated memoir of the blind harper Arthur O'Neill, Fanning's contemporary and chief rival at Belfast and other competitions. O'Neill begins his character sketch as follows:

> Charles Fanning was born in the County of Leitrim in the Province of Connaught. His father, Loughlin Fanning, was a decent farmer and played well on the harp. Charles was principally instructed by Thady Smith, a native of County Roscommon, and a tolerable performer on the harp. Charles Fanning in consequence of his performance on the Harp, became much respected. He never taught any, but merely was an amateur and principally supported himself by the private emoluments arising from his profession.

O'Neill recalls that, as a young man, "I made the best of my way to Charles Fanning's house, where I met father and son, with whom I remained about three weeks very happy, during which time I attended many weddings and haulings home, where the national customs were all supported with the usual conviviality incident to the circumstances and abilities of the parties." All well and good so far, but then comes trouble: "On his first arrival into the County of Tyrone [Fanning] got acquainted with a Mrs Bailie of Terrinaskea in that County, who played on the harp very well. Charles married her kitchenmaid, for which Mrs Bailie was greatly disobliged, as she frequently had him at her table, and had him introduced to genteel Company. She fell out with him and he was not received as usually. Charley and the wife boxed now and then." This last pithy sentence contains a world of adversity, and it's all downhill from there: "He visited Mrs Bailie generally at three months a time in his professional way. His wife was discharged and was generally sneaking after him everywhere. He went from Mrs Bailie's to Derry, and got himself introduced to the Bishop, who seemed to like him well, otherwise he would not keep him. I, Arthur O'Neill, went to Derry where I met Charley, and when I asked him how he was Charley replied that I might 'blow a goose-quill through his cheek,' meaning he was so poor and thin, and this time he had the wife and one or two children to support." After leaving the Bishop's, Charley "rambled about the Nation awhile," then settled again "for a couple of years" on a four-acre plot with house, garden, and four cows, supplied by "a Mr Pratt of Kingscourt in the County Cavan." This place is very near the border of my ancestor Phillip Fanning's home county of Monaghan. When this patron died, his nephew and heir turned Fanning out, and O'Neill relates that "he then rambled as usual."

The Belfast Harpers' Festival of 1792 was a last-ditch effort to preserve and revive traditional Irish harp music. As such, it had been modeled on three earlier events at Granard, County Longford, in 1781 and the two following years. Sponsored by James Dungan, a wealthy Granard native living abroad, these meetings combined harp competitions with gala dress balls for the Longford gentry. At the first event, seven harpers appeared before at least 500 people, and Arthur O'Neill recalls that "they all played their best tunes. Charles Fanning got first premium, ten guineas for 'The Coolin.' I got the second for 'The Green Woods of Truagh' and 'Mrs Crofton,' eight guineas; and Rose Mooney got the third for 'Planxty Burke,' five guineas." (The best known of the very few female itinerant harpers, Mooney had been born about 1740 in County Meath. She was also blind.) Fanning's winning piece, "The Coolin," is *An Chúilfhionn*, which means the fair-headed or curly-haired maiden. One of the most venerable of traditional Irish tunes for harp or voice, it may have been composed as early as 1295.

O'Neill reports further that "the Judges at the first ball were excellent, and there was some deliberation about the first premium between Fanning and me; but in consequence of my endeavoring to appear on this occasion in my very best duds, they decided in favour of Charley, who was careless in his dress, saying, at the same time, that he wanted money more than I did." For the second Granard ball, in March 1782, the audience was even larger, and Fanning again got first prize—reduced to eight guineas—for "The Coolin." In 1783 the patron, James Dungan, came over from Copenhagen, "particularly," says Arthur O'Neill, "to superintend the last and greatest Irish National Ball, respecting harpers, that ever was held in this country." Lord and Lady Longford also attended, and "there were at least 1000 people at the ball." Plainly, this was a significant cultural event. O'Neill graciously records that "Fanning always deservedly got the first, I got the second, and poor Rose Mooney, as usual, got the third."

Some eight years later, in December 1791, a call went out from the civic leaders of Belfast to raise a subscription "to apply in attempting to revive and perpetuate *the ancient music and poetry of Ireland.*" It was proposed "that the harpers should be induced to assemble at Belfast" to compete for prizes. In addition, "a person well versed in the language and antiquities of this nation should attend, with a skilful musician to transcribe and arrange the most beautiful and interesting parts of their knowledge." This was a political as well as an aesthetic and antiquarian venture, for nationalist feeling in Ulster was building fast toward the Rebellion of 1798, and the call for subscriptions included a pointed assertion: "When it is considered how intimately the *spirit* and *character* of a *people* are connected with their *national poetry* and *music,* it is presumed that the Irish patriot and politician will not deem it an object unworthy his patronage and protection." Those attending the ensuing competition included many highly visible nationalist politicians.

The "skilful musician" enlisted to document the gathering was nineteen-year-old Edward Bunting, whose transcriptions from the Belfast Festival (published in the three editions of *The Ancient Music of Ireland* in 1796, 1809, and 1840) did indeed rescue and preserve over 250 tunes of the traditional harp repertoire. Bunting reports that "ten harpers only responded to this call, a sufficient proof of the declining state of the art. . . . The meeting was held in the large room of the Exchange at Belfast, on the 11th, 12th, and 13th of July, 1792." The oldest harper present, and the one most praised by Bunting for his traditional technique, was Denis Hempson from County Derry, aged at least ninety-seven. The youngest was fifteen-year-old William Carr from County Armagh. Rose Mooney was the only woman. Six of the ten were blind, among them Arthur O'Neill, listed as "(blind), from the county of Tyrone, aged 58 years." Bunting registers Charles Fanning as having come "from the county of Cavan" (evidently the site of his most recent rambles) and gives his age as fifty-six.

Edward Bunting brought strong opinions of his own to the Belfast events. For starters, he was no great admirer of the most famous of the eighteenth-century Irish composers for the harp, Turlough O'Carolan (1670–1738), whose baroque tendencies Bunting saw as a decidedly negative influence. In his *Ancient Music of Ireland,* Bunting insists that "the taste for Italian music, introduced by Geminiani and Corelli, seems about this time to have largely infected the works of Irish composers, especially those of Carolan." Bunting believes that Carolan's compositions sacrifice "that inimitable vein of tender expression which winds through the very old music of Ireland" in favor of "movements with wildly luxuriant basses." Certainly, his avowed preference for music in the old style did not incline Bunting to admire the musicianship of Charles Fanning, either, and in reporting the Belfast meeting, Bunting describes Fanning as "the most brilliant performer, but a modernist in style." He goes on to assert that "Fanning was not the best performer, but he succeeded in getting the first prize, by playing 'The Coolin,' with modern variations; a piece of music at that time much in request by young practitioners on the piano forte." Significantly, it was Denis Hempson's much simpler version of "The Coolin," rather than Fanning's elaborate variation, that Bunting collected for his book.

Bunting was much more favorably impressed with two of the other harpers. He remarks on Arthur O'Neill's pedigree, manners, and dress: "He was proud of his descent, and had the *hand* of the O'Neills engraved on his coat buttons, which were of silver, and of half-crown size." He also praises the antiquarian purity of Denis Hempson, "the only one who played the very old, the aboriginal music of the country, and this he did in a style of . . . finished excellence." As Charles Fanning had neither the clothes nor the playing style—nor, for that matter, the lineage or deportment—to suit Bunting, it is not surprising that, despite his having taken first prize, Fanning gets a dismissive, six-line biographical notice in *Ancient Music,* beginning with the wrong home county:

> CHARLES FANNING, the contemporary and rival of O'Neill, was the son of Loughlin Fanning, also a harper, and was born at Foxford, in Mayo, about 1736. His chief haunts were in Ulster, particularly in Cavan, where Mr. Pratt, of Kingscourt, allowed him a free house and farm. He was also patronized by the cele-

Figure 24. A nineteenth-century illustration of the Belfast Harpers' Festival, July 10–13, 1792.

> brated Earl of Bristol, the great Bishop of Derry; but in consequence of having married a person in low life, and of corresponding habits, he never attained to respectability or independence.

Still and all, Fanning did triumph at Belfast. They can't take that away from him. Furthermore, among those agreeing with the judges was none other than Theobald Wolfe Tone, a founder of the United Irishmen and master planner of the 1798 Rebellion. In support of the nationalist dimension of the festival, Tone attended all three days. His journal reveals him as less than whole-heartedly present to the music, but I like his conclusion. On July 11: "Rise with a great headache; go to the harpers at one; poor enough; ten performed; seven execrable, three good, one of them, Fanning, far the best." On the twelfth Tone again got up "with a headache resulting from late house" and "lounge[d] to [the] harpers." On the thirteenth, it was "Rise again with a headache . . . the harpers again, strum, strum and be hanged." I admit to a thrill in hearing my namesake's accomplishment corroborated in the hand of one of the most formidable figures in the history of Irish nationalism—even if he did have a hangover at the time.

Charles Fanning drops permanently from sight after his high-profile victory at Belfast. But who's to say we're not related? After all, Bunting writes, and Charlotte Milligan Fox agrees, that "his chief haunts were in Ulster," and in his frequent rambles between Cavan and Derry, he must have crisscrossed County Monaghan often. This part of Ulster has also had its own distinctive artistic identity. Known as "Oriel," and including central and southern Monaghan, it was very rich in traditional Irish music, song, and literature from the mid-seventeenth through the mid-nineteenth century. Contemporary sources are clear that aristocratic "big house" families in this area remained hospitable to itinerant harpers according to the old custom up through the lifetimes of O'Neill and Fanning. In Monaghan, these families included the Plunketts of Rocksavage House near Iniskeen, for whom Arthur O'Neill played in the 1770s, and the Shirleys of Lough Fea, who hosted Monaghan native Patrick Byrne as their "domestic harper" as late as 1847. (These are the same Shirleys who beat out my family's landlords, the Westenras of Rossmore Castle, in that 1830s contest to build the biggest room.)

To conclude the argument, I reiterate that Arthur O'Neill also says that Charley Fanning had children, and his age—fifty-six in 1792—makes him a possible grandfather, father, or at least some sort of cousin to John Fannin of Monaghan, who was farming six acres at "Urbilkerk" in 1826, and whose son Phillip was my immigrant great-great-grandfather. Such a connection would also explain my grandfather's first name of Charles, which appears nowhere else in his family as far back as I have been able to look. All this is tenuous, but I'm claiming Charley Fanning anyway. He's my ancestor—the artist in the family—unless someone can prove me wrong.

7

A Prelude

Pour l'enfant, amoureux de cartes et d'estampes,
L'univers est égal à son vaste appétit.
Ah! que le monde est grand à la clarté des lampes!
Aux yeux du souvenir que le monde est petit!
—Charles Baudelaire, "Le Voyage"

Fair seed-time had my soul, I am fortunate to be able to say. (William Wordsworth's *The Prelude* supplies all of this chapter's section headings. I'm no Wordsworth, but his extraordinary poem describes a fairly ordinary upbringing—like mine—and that's the point.) In childhood and early adolescence, the compass directing my attention had four cardinal points: the radio, the library, the playground, and school. This compass was familiar, mundane, predictable for an upbringing in American towns or city neighborhoods in the 1950s. Two of its points were solitary pursuits—listening to the radio and looking into books. These, along with the third—playing baseball on playgrounds—were mostly unsupervised by adults. None cost any money. All were tolerated (the radio and baseball) or encouraged (reading and school) by my parents. My own initiative and predilections drove these preoccupations, and I loved all four from quite early on. Looking back now, I am struck by just how well they balanced out and added up to a quietly eventful child's life in which there was always time to breathe, think, imagine, and dream—to wander around in my own mind, day in and day out. How different this was, I'm bound to say again, from the social and cultural engineering of kids and from the pervasive use of television as babysitter that goes on now in so many American families. Along with my parents, whose supportive presence I've discussed in earlier chapters, a host of permission-granters and advocates from outside our home encouraged my pursuits. These people were literally civil servants—librarians, teachers, store owners, business people—and they formed a community of efficacious goodwill within which I and others thrived. For many growing up in my time, the town of Norwood was a pond with ice thick enough to skate on.

Listening, a gentle shock of mild surprise

Mine was the last cohort of American kids for whom listening to the radio was a critical formative activity. I got a healthy dose because we didn't get a television set until Christmas of 1955, when I was thirteen. Practically preconscious, my memories of radio go back to earliest childhood. From as far back as I can recall, listening to the radio was as natural as breathing. I inhaled deeply and all day long until I started school, and thereafter weekend days and every evening. Three kinds of sound were dominant: the music on morning variety shows, the background noise of baseball games, and the urgent tones of the afternoon soap operas.

Whenever I hear the opening bars of his theme song, "Seems like old times, having you around, dear," Arthur Godfrey's adenoidal chuckle comes to mind. Every weekday morning from 10:15 to 11:30, Arthur's complacent, syrupy drawl filled our kitchen. He sounded vaguely sinister to me for a number of reasons. His main sponsor was Chesterfields. (Both my parents smoked, and I already hated the smell of cigarettes.) He shared lots of mysterious inside jokes and harsh laughter with celebrity guests. He often made fun of the ethnic backgrounds of his own cast, who responded complicitly by performing self-mocking numbers. Hale Loki from Hawaii sang of lazy island life (amid lots of jokes about the hula), "Ireland's own" Carmel Quinn cranked out Tin Pan Alley visions of the old sod ("The Same Old Shillelagh," "Galway Bay"), and Julius LaRosa diagnosed love, Italian-style: "When the moon hits your eye like a big pizza pie, that's amore." (It was big news in our house, and elsewhere, when Julius overreached himself by talking back on the air to Arthur, who promptly fired him.)

Along with the heavy-handed ethnic comic relief, however, *Arthur Godfrey Time* introduced me to the great American songbook. Thanks to Archie Bleyer's Orchestra, Jeanette Davis's solo vocals, and the barbershop harmonies of the Mariners' Quartet, I heard as a four- and five-year-old the music of Irving Berlin, George Gershwin, Cole Porter, and all those Broadway shows. Some days I hardly remember my name, but there are hundreds of pop tunes from the 1940s and 1950s the titles of which I still recognize from the first few bars. I also have pretty good recall of the lyrics.

There was also always the ball game—either the Braves (our team of choice, naturally) or the Red Sox (who would do in a pinch). Years before I'd ever seen a professional game, the play-by-play was a part of life just about every afternoon (there were no night games yet) from April through September. The lulling murmur of the crowd indicated that a game was going on somewhere and that, amazingly enough, adults were paying attention. I could hear the cheers and boos and catcalls, the occasional vendor ("Peanuts a dime, three for a quarter!"), the crack of the bat. The announcer's catch phrases were as memorable as the lyrics of the pop songs and show tunes: "Three and two, the big one due." "Top of the order coming up in the bottom of the eighth." "I hear quacking. The ducks are on the pond." "High and deep to left. This one is waaaay back. Going—going—gone! A home run!" I caught the invitation to visualize the game as played that's been missing in the media ever since TV took over: "The runner on first takes a short lead. Torgeson is keeping him close. Spahn looks hard toward first. Here's the stretch and the pitch. Swing and a miss. Strike three. Robinson was thinking fast ball but Warren gave him a slow curve, breaking down and in. A wicked pitch that tied Jackie in knots. He never had a chance."

The endless, slow-moving soaps—where a day's worth of questions, framed by the ubiquitous organ background, could take two weeks to answer—were the most fun to listen to. "The stories," that's what Mum called the cluster of fifteen-minute daytime dramas that followed the midday meal I shared with her in the years before I started school. Baloney and cheese, Campbell's tomato soup, tuna fish on Wonder Bread—eating these still brings back memories of my first exposure to adult "problems." I used to match the faces of people I knew with the voices, and this habit continued through my peak radio years of elementary school and junior high. Good guys looked like Dr. O'Toole, or the grocer next door, Pete Farioli, a man of infinite patience when it came to dispensing penny candy. Loudmouths whose motives were suspect looked like a friend of my parents whose habit it was to burst into our kitchen, turning out his pants pocket so that nickels and dimes scattered over the floor for the kids to pick up. Models for the truly bad guys were in short supply, especially early on, but I made do with our landlord, "Old Wiscalis," and the coal man, Bobby Sinclaire, mostly because his hands were always black. A bit later, these roles fell to Father McDonald, a fire-and-brimstone parish priest at St. Catherine's, and Miss Hedberg, the principal of the Winslow School.

I remember waiting in the kitchen for the hiss of dead air to be broken by the first strains of the organ—a chord struck, then a second, invariably predictive of genre—either up the major scale for the comic or plunging to a minor key for the dramatic. Da-da-da-DAH. And the sound of the voices was enough to determine character. There was the deep bass growl or scratchy high pitch of the bad guys, punctuated by laughter, sharp and mean, as they plotted their dire deeds. The good guys always had pleasant sounding voices, neither too low nor too high. I knew that they would grasp the problem and either make it come out OK or sympathize with what couldn't be changed—the occasional death by auto accident, desertion by a wayward spouse, or penury at the hands of a slick swindler.

Would "Our Gal Sunday," an orphan girl from "the little town of Silver Creek, Colorado," find happiness as the wife of "England's richest, most handsome aristocrat, Lord Henry Brinthrope"? I rooted hard for Sunday, with her plain-spoken practicality, and made fun of her husband and his dozens of snooty relatives. Sitting at the kitchen table, Mum would talk through her nose in a flutey British accent: "Could you pass the oleo, Charles, like a good fellow. Jolly good." This routine never failed to crack me up. And how would "Mary Noble, Backstage Wife" respond to a similar challenge? She was an Iowa farm girl married to Larry Noble, a New York matinee idol whose condescending friends stirred the pot from their supercilious perches in Westchester and Oyster Bay. One Christmas I got my mother a Mary Noble Gardenia Bracelet, studded with simulated seed pearls, "all the rage in jewelry now," according to the announcer. My father had helped with this major purchase, involving twenty-five cents, a box top from Dr. Lyons toothpaste, and two stamped envelopes, one of them addressed to me.

My favorite character in the stories was "Oxydol's Own Ma Perkins," a middle-aging widow who managed a lumberyard in Rushville Center, the generic American small town. "Ma Perkins" was as close to adult real life as I could get. Her son John had been killed in World War II, and she often thought about him. That was real enough. And Ma's two daughters, one also a widow, were far from paragons. Their recurrent ingratitude and thoughtlessness were grist for the mill of Ma's capacious, if slightly whiny, tolerance for all human frailty: "Now, Faye, I don't mean to meddle. All I'm saying is that Carl Michaels is a fine, steady young man, though granted, he's not as flashy as Dr. Andrew White, who seems quite self-assured." Aha. Mum and I knew where that one was going. People all over town brought Ma their problems, and Rushville Center's homespun oracle untangled complexities every evening in front-porch conversations with her old friend Shuffle. Through thick and thin, Ma's only exclamation was "Land-a-Goshen!"—to which Shuffle would answer with a sympathetic cluck. The soothing background noise of chirping crickets lent pastoral authority to their calm, unrattled voices.

I was a sickly child, and my most important illness came when I was seven: rheumatic fever gave me a heart murmur that's been there ever since. It followed and was followed by a barrage of ordinary childhood diseases—chicken pox, mumps, measles (both German and American), colds and flu, bronchitis, tonsillitis—often in multiple visitations, prompting Dr. O'Toole to proclaim, "If it's out there, Charles will catch it and bring it home." Most of the time I would be set up on the couch in the parlor, waiting with a mixture of relief and fear for the doctor to arrive. I wanted to feel better all right, but that often meant a needle was coming, and in those days, needles were long and thick and could really hurt. A large man with a wide face and lots of curly black hair, Dr. O'Toole would come into the room and sit down heavily beside me, plunking his black bag on the floor—noisily, with the sound of rattling needles.

But the bout with rheumatic fever was different. I ended up in the Norwood Hospital, a big, strange, and scary place of bare, white rooms where the lights were always on and strangers dressed in white came and went at all hours. There were plenty of needles there, too, and, more disturbing, looks of concern in my parents' eyes that I'd never seen before. In an ultimately unsuccessful attempt to stave off future problems, Dr. O'Toole also took out my tonsils while I was in the hospital. I was infuriated because the adults had pulled a fast one on me. I hadn't been able to eat or drink before the operation, and afterward, they gave me ice cream and tonic, which made my throat sore.

That illness and, especially, my recuperation, solidified my relationship with the radio. I have a clear memory of arriving home from the hospital. It's early Friday afternoon, and I am just now settled in the bedroom I share with my brother. (Geoffrey has been moved out to my parents' room for the duration of this illness.) About the first thing I think of is the radio. There are two in the house, a big wooden console with a round, cross-hatched speaker in the parlor and a squat, squarish yellow table model in the kitchen. My father is looking down at me, his forehead furrowed with that worried look, so I risk a question that's wildly disruptive of the familiar order of things: "Dad, can I borrow the kitchen radio?"

"I'll ask your mother," he replies, and I know that means yes. "Would you like some tonic?" (In our family, ginger ale cures all ills.) He goes down the stairs directly, and a few minutes later, both parents come into the bedroom. Mum has the ginger ale and three fig newtons. Dad is carrying the radio. He sets it down on the night table and reaches around behind the bed for the outlet. He knows right where it is because he put it there.

On Saturday morning, my first day waking up back in my own bed after the hospital, my mother comes with a wet rag and wipes the layer of kitchen grease from the top surface of the yellow radio. I don't feel so hot. It's not fair that the sun is out, nor that my favorite breakfast of scrambled eggs and toast didn't taste very good. Ah, but I do have the radio right beside me. What time is it anyway? Almost eleven? It's time for *Let's Pretend*! I turn the knob with that sharp click, the feeling of control smooth on my fingertips. Then the crackle of static and small, abrupt explosions of music or voice, as I move the vertical marking line up the row of side-lighted numbers. I get there just in time for the station break: "This is the CBS Radio Network." Then a pause, then a burst of kids' cheering and the first chords of the familiar tune. A chorus of young voices belts it out:

> Come one, come all, the big, the small, we're here with
> *Let's Pretend*.
> You'll laugh, you'll cry, and wonder why, until the very end.
> The joy of storytelling to all we do extend.
> So give a cheer, 'cause look what's here—another *Let's*
> *Pretend*!

This is my favorite show, bar none. It retells all the best known fairytales and some I've never heard before, using child actors who introduce themselves at the end of each episode. I know all their names and am sure, in my mind's eye, of what they look like. Sybil Trent is a blonde girl with short hair and blue eyes. Gwen Davies has long, reddish brown hair and freckles. Michael O'Day, who plays a lot of the heroes, looks like me.

The format is the same even when I'm upstairs in bed, instead of sitting cross-legged on the big, soft chair in the parlor. "Come on, and LET'S PRETEND," the actors and audience shout out in unison. Uncle Bill, the only adult voice on the show, asks, "And now, Sybil, what's the story for today?"

"Beauty and the Beast, Uncle Bill."

"Beauty and the Beast it is. And who'll say how we get to Pretend Land today?"

"It's Gwen Davies' turn," says Sybil.

"Let's go by giant rockets," Gwen calls out. "One for each of you, and the biggest one for Uncle Bill and me. Everybody ready? Three. Two. One. Blast off!" Then the music comes up again, and the story begins: "Once upon a time ..." I close my eyes, and I'm in a kingdom of castles and cottages where an innocent girl, Beauty by name, knowing her family is poor, asks on her birthday for only "one perfect rose." Even that is beyond her father's means, until he remembers that extraordinary flowers surround the mysterious castle in the deep woods whose inhabitants have never been seen. I know going there is a bad idea when the music darkens. Enter the Beast, heralded by a sinister bassoon and tuba theme. He grabs Beauty's father and sweeps him into the castle, just before the middle commercial and the Cream of Wheat Game, which, as always, involves a dumb riddle for which I have no patience.

"What's the cowboy's name for food?" asks Uncle Bill.

"Chow," shouts the audience. (I know they've been prompted.)

"Chow it is, pardners. And you can bet your boots and saddles that the best all-fired breakfast chow on the whole range, right at the head of the herd for flavor, is . . . "

I know where Uncle Bill is going with this, all right, so I close my eyes and tune out the words so as to concentrate on one pressing question: Who is this Beast and what does he look like? All I have to go on are the shouts from Beauty's father as he is being dragged inside the castle: "His eyes! His claws!" But that's all I need. That's all I'll ever need.

After *Let's Pretend* is over, I sleep and wake, fitfully feverish and groggy, all through the afternoon, and, as the bedroom window begins to darken, I realize that for the first time I have the power to venture into the world of nighttime radio. Until now, my outer limit has been "The Lone Ranger," three times a week at 7:30. But here the radio sits, and as the masked rider and Tonto lock away another member of the Cavendish gang with a resounding metal "Clank," I know that even though it's coming on to eight o'clock, I don't have to stop listening. My parents are downstairs—Mum in the kitchen cleaning up, Dad in the cellar, bringing some worn-out appliance back to life. So, I turn the tuning knob slowly—from words to static to music to static to—to what? Something brand new and spellbinding.

A door is opening slowly, creaking and creaking on rusty hinges. Then comes a low, lugubrious voice: "Goooood evening, friends. This is your host, Paul, inviting you through the gory portals of the creaking door, and into THE INNER SANCTUM." Oh, boy, I think. Here comes something. "And now, if your scalpels are sharpened and ready, we'll proceed with the necessary, though a tad unpleasant, work of the evening. Don't worry, though, it's nothing to lose your HEAD over. Eeeeyahhahahahahahhaaaa!"

I bunch up the covers into a hood over my head, and move closer to the speaker until my nose is nearly touching it. I can make out the dim light of the glowing tubes through cracks in the yellow plastic. Then I hear slow, echoing footsteps. Another voice explains that a shadowy figure is walking slowly down a deserted street. It's a man in a long coat with his hat pulled down over his face. Now I see him. He's got Old Wiscalis's flattened, rubbery nose. There's a young woman standing at the bus stop on the corner. The flash of a knife. A scream. My eyes open wide but the radio is gone. There's only blackness. Before I see that the covers are entirely over my head, I am terrified and thoroughly hooked.

In a day or so I became adept at keeping the volume on a thin line where I could make out the voices but my parents couldn't hear that the radio was on. Before I was well enough to return to school, I had discovered that every night had its feast of new people and places, of funny, dramatic, and frightening stories—from coast to coast and backward in time. Once I knew my way around the AM dial—in those days, that's all there was—I was most intrigued by shows that contained what I considered to be glimpses into the world of adults. Chief among these was *Duffy's Tavern.* The show came on well past my bedtime—9:30 p.m. on Thursdays—and often the reception was poor, which added to the allure. Also the sponsor was a beer company. It was a comedy, yes, but with an urban edge and a whiff of the unsavory that set it apart from the domestic trivialities and easy resolution of silly problems in *Burns and Allen, Jack Benny,* or *Fibber McGee and Molly.* Duffy's Tavern was a barroom on Third Avenue in New York City. The show opened with a ringing telephone, followed by "Blatz Beer is on the air. Blatz Beer is everywhere. Welcome to *Duffy's Tavern* starring Archie himself, Ed Gardner." Then came a few bars of "When Irish Eyes Are Smiling," then the ringing phone again, answered this time: "Hello, Duffy's Tavern, where the elite meet to eat. Archie the manager talkin'. Naw, Duffy ain't here."

Speaking in thick Brooklynese, wised-up and blasé, Archie set the show's tone. Nothing phased him, not even finding a corpse in the corner booth: "His last words were 'Bring me the twenty-five-cent blue plate.'" I'd never been inside a bar, never mind out of eastern Massachusetts, but all this sounded real to me. The early Fifties parade of stereotypes seemed both funny and somehow edifying: Eddie the black waiter, play-acting subservience but obviously cynical and funny; Arthur Treacher, a butler on his night off and every inch the British snob; the Mad Russian, a thick-accented flimflam man living by his wits. Even Finnegan the Irish barfly, bibulous, lazy, and sly, didn't bother me. My favorite character was Miss Duffy, the dingbat daughter of the absent owner, indulged by her father in her misguided ambition to become a professional singer. "Blood is thicker than water," she declared, "and no one's thicker than my father and me." Talking about how she spent time in the balcony of the movie theater with her boyfriend, she sounded cute and a little naughty. In the long run, remembering *Duffy's Tavern* helped me to understand Archie's ancestor, Mr. Dooley, in whose saloon on Chicago's South Side my scholarly interest in the history and literature of Irish immigration began.

On the other end of the moral spectrum from Archie and Miss Duffy was another thoroughly distinctive voice. Every so often, as I inched the dial along in search of a new show, I would run into Archbishop Cushing saying the rosary for the city's "shut-ins," as they were un-euphemistically called. His gravelly South Boston-inflected *Hail Marys* cut through static like the drone on a set of bagpipes: "HAIL Mary full of grace, the Lord is with THEE, BLESS-id is the fruit of thy womb, JEE-ZUZ . . ." Cushing prayed three times a day on three different Boston stations, so his ritual intonation was hard to miss. Talk about the Universal Church—his voice was everywhere.

And so it went. Only a list can convey the richness of this world, and I will keep it as short as I can. The Westerns brought cowboys and Indians into my mind. I followed *Hopalong Cassidy, The Cisco Kid,* and, of course, *The Lone Ranger,* but my favorite show in the genre was a little off the beaten track (so to speak). *Straight Arrow* featured a Comanche Indian who saddled up his faithful horse, Fury, and came galloping out of a hidden cave "to take up the cause of law and order throughout the West," as the announcer proclaimed. An orphan who had been raised by whites, Straight Arrow disguised himself in everyday life as cattle rancher, Steve Adams. (I felt in on the secret by recognizing that they shared the same initials.) He turned himself back into an Indian to fight the crooks and claim jumpers who kept showing up around his Broken Bow Ranch. My approval of the show stretched to an investment of paper-route money—I sent away for the "Straight Arrow Rite-A-Lite," a plastic arrowhead that glowed in the dark and contained a ballpoint pen, a compass, and a secret compartment. When it came, I was delighted to find that everything worked—a near miracle for such offers—and for several days I sat happily in the bedroom closet in the dark writing notes to myself.

Silliness reigned on the comedy/variety shows, which were a collage of musical numbers, special guest appearances, and mild domestic satire. In the storylines, all was formulaic, nothing was ever at risk, and so I often found the problems of the protagonists boring. There was little to learn about "real life" adult behavior from the implausible scenes and characters. George Burns was the inevitable straight man to Gracie Allen's head-spinning verbal legerdemain and the predicaments that resulted. Jack Benny was always stingy, a terrible violinist, and about to be thirty-nine years old, and although they squabbled, he and Mary Livingston weren't even married. Red Skelton's alter egos—Junior, Willy Lump-Lump, Clem Kadiddlehopper—were always broadly dumb, and Fibber McGee could be counted on to screw up by opening that closet door, bringing down the wrath of his long-suffering spouse, Molly, along with tennis racquets, bowling balls, and a spare kitchen sink.

I also found most of the action/adventure shows annoyingly implausible. In these, a brace of wealthy and seemingly ineffectual protagonists transformed themselves into disguised vigilantes in order to dispense deus ex machina justice. Newspaper publisher Britt Reid became the Green Hornet —"The Flight of the Bumble Bee" introducing the show was the best thing about it. Playboy Lamont Cranston turned into The Shadow: "Who knows what evil lurks within the hearts of men? The Shadow knows." And of course, bumbling reporter Clark Kent made his telephone-booth transformation every Saturday at 8:00 p.m.: "Look! Up in the sky! It's a bird. It's a plane. It's SUPERMAN!"

Much more to my taste were the hard-boiled radio detectives who came on the scene in the late 1940s on the heels of the wildly popular crime fiction and film noir efforts of Raymond Chandler, Dashiell Hammett, and Mickey Spillane. Here was convincing realism—serious, sour, and above all urban, with tough, cynical voices narrating some very ugly stories. I loved *Twenty-first Precinct* ("Just lines on a map of the city of New York"), *Boston Blackie* ("Enemy to those who make him an enemy, friend to those who have no friends"), *Gang Busters* ("the only national program that brings you authentic police case histories"), and Jack Webb's *Dragnet* ("Ladies and Gentlemen, the story you are about to hear is true. Only the names have been changed to protect the innocent").

As if all this weren't enough, radio also introduced me to my favorite spectator sport. I had never seen a hockey rink, much less a professional hockey game, when I first heard the Boston Bruins on the radio. I had seen and played pond hockey all right, but I sensed that the enclosed, concentrated action of the real game would be something else again. The play-by-play was crisp, clear, and expressive. I could visualize it all: "The puck is in the corner. Flaman digs it out, dodges a check, gets it up to LaBine at the Boston blue line. Leo winds up, crosses center ice, makes a lead pass to Bucyk streaking over the Detroit blue line. Johnny is in alone, he shoots, he SCORES!" There was also here the attraction of the Canadian exotic. Most of the players were from up there, and many had French names and colorful nicknames—Bernie ("Boom-Boom") Geoffrion, Maurice ("The Rocket") Richard and his brother Henri ("The Pocket Rocket"). The storied teams were the Toronto Maple Leafs and the Montreal Canadiens, who won the Stanley Cup five years running in the late 1950s. Also, the National Hockey League had only six teams—the first expansion wasn't until 1967—and it was easy to keep track of virtually all the players and statistics. The road games were on late, often lasting till after midnight, and the winter sounds of swishing skates on ice and the slap of sticks made me feel cozier under the covers.

With the coming of television, the twenty-year Golden Age of Radio was over in short order. By the time I got to high school, my favorite shows were dropping like flies. In January 1959, my high school junior year, four of the soaps with which I was familiar left the air: *This Is Nora Drake, Mary Noble Backstage Wife, The Road of Life,* and (alas!) *Our Gal Sunday.* The true end of the line was Friday, November 25, 1960, when the last six afternoon soaps stopped for good, including *Ma Perkins.* Ma had been on the air since 1933, with the same actress, Virginia Payne, in the title role all the way. At the end of the last show (it was number 7,065), she came out of character to thank everyone involved in the production. Though I was in the middle of my first semester at college and beyond the immediate call of the soaps, I remember listening to this climactic broadcast with my mother. I was home because it was the day after Thanksgiving.

The dazzling cornucopia that was radio back then was a great gift to the developing mind of a child. There was simply no choice—you had to make pictures in your head to explain the sounds coming in through your ears. And where else could you be told exciting stories and also eavesdrop with impunity on the world of adults? The clatter of hoofbeats, echoing footsteps, and creaking doors. The rumble of thunder, a truck starting up, a lion's roar. The crack of a whip, of gunfire, of a ball coming off the bat. From "Bali Hai" and *Oklahoma* to "Bluebirds over the white cliffs of Dover," from Third Avenue to Wistful Vista to the mean streets of Los Angeles, from Ma Perkins's front porch to the castle of the Beast, radio created a steady, recurrent rhythm for my childhood. It provided the cosmic background radiation that proved I was living in an expanding universe.

Figure 25. The Shattuck estate on Walpole Street. Courtesy of the Norwood Historical Society.

And there have read, devouring as I read

When we moved to 145 Walpole Street in the summer of 1951, I was eight years old and between third and fourth grade. The library was also on Walpole Street, so I couldn't get lost on the way, and I made the trip almost every Saturday morning all the year round. It was only a ten-minute walk, downhill most of the way, but often it took me twenty, because there were several provocative sights to see along the way, spots where (in the parlance of my family) I was wont to dawdle and gawk. The first notable place was the brown, shingle-style Tucker house, my mother's favorite on the street, with three floors, many small-paned windows, and a deep veranda curving around the right side. I could see us living there after I became rich. Next door was an austere white Colonial house of determined plainness, on the side of which was a plaque announcing that it had been built in 1806 by Jabez Chickering, the second pastor of the First Congregational Church. I could not see us living there, rich or poor. Further along came a tall, dark gray house with pointy gables thrusting skyward. It was set back from the street and surrounded so closely by pine trees and bushes that only the third-floor attic windows were visible. Here I could see some dastardly crime—most likely murder—being perpetrated, one that I could solve, given the chance.

Best of all, the road I traveled led past the Old Shattuck Estate, an authentic mansion on its own hill with four chimneys, a widow's walk, jutting porches on three sides, and a carriage house bigger than any place we had ever lived in. This was a daydreamer's paradise, not least because I knew that it housed the family's last daughter, Maude Alice Shattuck, a Yankee spinster who was living on there in baronial solitude all through my childhood. "Maude," as we called her, was pronounced "a character" in our house. She reinforced my mother's prevailing view, which ranged from bemused to jaundiced, of Norwood's Yankee "upper crust." ("You've got some crust" was an accusation of pretentious behavior.) A graduate of Smith College, Maude exemplified the high-minded (and haughty) sense of duty ingrained in her caste which could try the patience of relative latecomers to the Boston area like us. For nearly forty years, she served as a trustee of Norwood Hospital, the local Red Cross branch, and the public library. Her letter to the local paper announcing her incumbent candidacy for the last in January 1935 suggests her demeanor: "Editor, *Messenger*: Running for the Library Board is a habit I cannot overcome. I have served several terms. There are doubtless many better qualified than I. Frankly, I enjoy the work. Maude A. Shattuck." As a kid, I was mightily engaged by the thought of this fabulous, mystery heiress rattling around up on her hill. Many of us plotted a trick-or-treat trip up the long drive on Halloween, but no one ever dared to go through with it. The closest we came was one summer Sunday afternoon when three of us ran from tree to tree and got as far as the foundation stones holding up the portico. When a door slammed somewhere inside the house, we ran like hell.

Maude's lawns swept down to the corner of Winter Street, which marked the bottom of the long, gentle incline of my walk down Walpole Street. Just across Winter was a short, steep hill. On the way up, I passed the First Congregational Church, the spiritual fortress of old Yankee South Dedham. Far from the typical white, spare-spired New England Protestant church, this was a dark, forbidding building, low to the ground and brown-shingled, with a squat, square tower. It reminded me of Hawthorne's House of the Seven Gables. This was Maude's church. She went on to sell her mansion and grounds to the "Congos" (as we called them) in 1956, and they promptly tore the place down and put up a new church building. Attached to the church was Pingree Hall, the social center, where, by my mother's wry account, the young Congos took lessons in dancing and deportment: "No, no, Abigail. Use *that* fork." Just past the church was Aaron Guild's rock, the heart of the Yankee town, and on top of the hill was my destination—the Morrill Memorial Library. When I leaned into that last upward incline, my heart lifted. I loved the place.

Norwood's public library was the most beautiful and fascinating building I had ever been inside. An imposing rectangle in the romanesque revival style, it was set well back on a small hill six feet higher than Walpole Street, and reachable by a sweeping concrete semicircular walk with two steps up every five or six feet. The building was made of big gray granite blocks from the state of Maine; most of them were rough-cut with lots of nubbly surface. Eight or ten—spaced across the front, shoulder high—held smooth circles with incised names: Homer, Dante, Shakespeare, Browning, Dickens, Hawthorne, Melville. The roof was made of red tiles, set in closely spaced waves. The windows were many and wonderfully varied in style: tall ones framed by stone columns, small ones with leaded, stained-glass panes, and, on the roof, flattened half circles—"eyebrow dormers," my sister Patti informs me—that looked, in the setting sun, like squinting eyes. There was an inset entry porch that lay under a keystoned romanesque arch on which was spelled out, all in caps, MORRILL MEMORIAL LIBRARY. Above were three arched blind windows with statues in them. The porch floor was made of irregular slate flagstones in muted colors. These I had seen in our next-door neighbor's garden, but never like this—fitted together and lodged in gray concrete.

Straight on through the iron-bolted oak front doors, nearly as large as those at St. Catherine's Church, was a foyer with stone stairs that led up into the main library. The building had so many nooks and crannies, so many rooms, all different and all stuffed with books. There were glowing oak shelves and mahogany paneling; high, mullioned windows, some with stained glass squares; doorways and staircases everywhere. Counting them now, I find that there were five different floor levels. What joy to have the run of such a place! To the left of the main desk was a doorway to the stacks. Here there was a second floor, reached by a circular iron stair and made—magically—out of translucent, thick glass squares. (When I got to Harvard, the glass floors in the stacks of Widener, the largest university library in the world, reassured me by this echo. A library was a library, and I could learn my way around.)

To the right of the main desk, just past a large, ornately carved grandfather clock, was a stairway with narrow, square, mission-style balusters that led up to the second floor Children's Room. Beyond those stairs was the wide doorway to the Main Reading Room. I always looked in there before heading upstairs. The building opened in 1898, and there have been two renovations since my childhood, but the Reading Room is still recognizable. They look less monumental now, but the big, wooden glass-topped tables with matching chairs are still there. Straight ahead across the polished wood floor stands an oak-lined fireplace with marble inlay, in which are carved these words: "This building was erected and presented to the town of Norwood in memory of Sarah Bond Morrill."

George and Louise Morrill, two of the town's leading citizens, had financed the building as a memorial to their daughter, who had died of typhoid fever at age twenty-three in 1896. (George had founded the Morrill Ink Works. He was also Maude Shattuck's grandfather.) Large oil paintings of Sarah and her father hang in the Reading Room to left and right of the doorway. Five-foot-high shelves full of reference books line the walls, and above them on two sides are facing rows of five windows, high and clear, each one topped by a square, stained-glass window. Echoing the windows are semicircular wooden alcoves with scallop-shell crowns, three on each side of the fireplace. I seem to recall that there were statues in these, though now they are empty, and I may be imagining this detail. With or without, the room was a wonder when I first peered into it. To me, this was the heart of the building. It declared that reading was an activity of high seriousness, worth pursuing for its own sake, even by adults.

The first floor was more or less out of reach when I started coming to the library, but the Children's Room soon became my home away from home. Here was a big square space, windows to left and right, and a long counter on the left. On three walls were book shelves only a little bit higher than I was. On the fourth wall, straight ahead, was a small stage complete with a proscenium arch, reachable by a row of three steps. To the right of the stage was the stairway to the library's highest level: the Intermediate Room, a long, low, cozy space tucked under the eaves, with sloping, pine-paneled walls and dormer window seats, from which I could look out the eyelet windows down to the bottom of Walpole Street where it joined Washington Street to become downtown Norwood.

You were supposed to be in junior high to enter the Intermediate Room and take out its books, but I got there much earlier, thanks to my champion, Miss N. Dorothy Shumacher, the children's librarian. A tiny woman with graying strawberry curls, a sharp nose, tortoiseshell glasses, and twinkling eyes, Miss Shumacher had spotted me for special attention when one Saturday in third grade I had taken out the Children's Room limit of three books in the morning and returned them that same afternoon. My attempt to take out three more broke precedent and caused a meeting that involved the town's head librarian—Edna Phillips. (A few years later, I came to know "Miss Phillips" as a friendly woman and the only customer on my paper route who took the *Christian Science Monitor,* but at this point she was a solemn and distant figure.) Even though the transaction messed up the records by registering that I had taken out six books in one day, Miss Shumacher and Miss Phillips threw caution to the winds and let me have the three new ones. Eudora Welty recalled a similar experience with a different result in "A Sweet Devouring," her essay about discovering books. In Jackson, Mississippi, in the 1910s and 1920s, the book limit was two, and it was not to be relaxed for any speed-reading kid. The librarian, who was "the lady in town who wanted to be it," told Eudora, "You know good and well the fixed rule of this library: *Nobody is going to come running back here with any book on the same day they took it out.* Get both those things out of here and don't come back till tomorrow."

Far from wanting to be "it," Norwood's librarians were there to serve and encourage, and the library became the springboard for my earliest public accomplishments. I looked forward eagerly to the Summer Reading Program. The mechanism never varied. You got stickers on a big board for the number of books read. Every year the theme was different: the Circus (clown stickers), Fishing for Knowledge (little goldfish), Mysteries, from Nancy Drew to Sherlock Holmes (magnifying glasses). And there were always prizes at the end—gold-stamped certificates for everyone who finished, pen-and-pencil sets, pads of colored paper, heavy-duty rulers for those who read the most. As a boy who loved to read anyway—witness the six-book day—I always came in at or near the top in this competition. Also, the Children's Room stage was the scene of entertainment successes. While still in elementary school, my friend David Libby and I put on several puppet shows. Based on fairytales but with some original scripting, these were held as part of the Saturday morning Story Hour. In these same fifth- and sixth-grade-years, the stage became the museum setting for my most ambitious clay models.

Ah, the delights of reading. As Welty puts it: "The pleasures of reading itself—who doesn't remember?—were like those of a Christmas cake, a sweet devouring." From the beginning of the adventure, I most prized the new books, which were put out every Friday. I loved being the first to turn the crisp, sharp-edged pages, and I loved the fresh smell of the paper. Picture books came first, of course. Of these, I especially recall two: *Make Way for Ducklings* by Robert McCloskey and Dr. Seuss's *The 500 Hats of Bartholomew Cubbins.* What I loved most about both books was the placement of characters and narration in a specific context that was established by panoramic, bird's-eye views in which my mind could wander at will. McCloskey accomplished this by having Mr. and Mrs. Mallard look down on the Boston Public Garden from the air. Spread out before them—and me—were winding paths, the duck pond, swanboats, bridge, and the island on which they built their nest. (An early reality check came when my brother and I went there during our father's summer vacation a year or two later.) As I said in the Monaghan chapter, Dr. Seuss began with a double litany, in both words and pictures, of the Kingdom of Didd as seen by King Derwin looking down from his palace, and poor Bartholomew Cubbins, looking up from his hut on the edge of a bog—like me peering up Maude Shattuck's driveway or my ancestor Phillip Fanning standing across the lake from Rossmore Castle.

One book—it was my favorite for years—served as a bridge between picture books and "chapter books." This was *The Bears' Famous Invasion of Sicily*, written and illustrated by Dino Buzzati, an Italian writer who had been a journalist in Africa during World War II. Published in Milan in 1945, the book was translated by Frances Lobb and published in the United States in 1947. My wife surprised me by finding a copy recently, and I can see what captivated me about it. In the storyline the noble bears, ruled by the benevolent King Leander, live up in the mountains of Sicily. The ignoble people, ruled by the tyrannical Grand Duke, live down on the plains. Leander's son, the bear cub Tony, is kidnapped by human hunters, and during a famine-ridden winter a few years later, the bears decide to invade the ducal state in search of food and to look for Tony. Perhaps because the war in Europe had ended too recently for fantasy to dominate even a children's book, Buzzati pulls no punches in describing the bloody warfare and its aftermath. Bears are slaughtered in the first, failed attack; people in the second, when the bears triumph. As victors, many bears take on the corrupting habits of the defeated duke's court: they put on clothes, live in luxury, drink heavily, gamble, and fight among themselves. The overly ambitious Saltpetre, a close friend of Leander, attempts to overthrow the king. Under cover of a sea serpent's attack, Saltpetre shoots Leander in the back. In turn, the traitor is beheaded by a loyalist, Dandelion. Mortally wounded, Leander asks his subjects to reject the ways of men and return to the mountains.

There is much else going on here as well. The vocabulary makes no concessions to its young audience, with phrases in Latin, Italian, and French and big words for which the only recourse was an adult dictionary: necromancer, spate, prepossessing, incognito, incredulous, sepulchre. Moreover Buzzati tells the story in alternating prose and verse. Frances Lobb does a fine job translating sophisticated rhymes: "aspirant/tyrant," "sycamore/blackamoor," "tenebrose/knows." Typographically, some of these wouldn't be out of place in a poem by Marianne Moore: "Now begins a hurly bur- / Ly, shrieks and yells and 'Sauve qui peut!'"

The book is mostly text, and there are only one or two full-page color illustrations in each of the twelve chapters. It was these that first pulled me in. All feature wide, sweeping perspective. It was easy to get lost among the crags and castles, town squares and battlefields, and dozens of figures—mostly bears—all over the place. The battle scenes are especially graphic, with fallen bears and men marked by red blots for spilled blood. In one picture there's a cross-cut, dollhouse view of a gambling den where the newly dissolute bears are spread over four floors, playing cards and games, drinking and eating to excess. In another, the treacherous Saltpetre is supervising the erection of a gigantic statue that looks more like him than its supposed subject, Leander, for whom he has promised it. The text of *The Bears' Famous Invasion of Sicily* ends with an image of the ruined monument: "Last year only a few stones remained, crumbling and unrecognizable, piled up in the corner of a garden." In the last picture, a long line of bears snakes its way up the winding road back to their old home in the mountains. At the end of the line, four bears carry the bier on which lies the body of King Leander. These figures and five streaming pennants are in black silhouette. The reminders of World War II and Shelley's "Ozymandias" are clear: "Look on my works, ye Mighty, and despair!"

Shortly after *The Bears* came *Treasure Island*—my first experience of reading a book after I had seen the movie. Here, though, the memory of Robert Newton and Bobby Driscoll soon gave way to the immediacy of N. C. Wyeth's arresting illustrations. These masterful compositions, blocky, elemental, muted in tone but action-packed, pulled me in time and time again, along with Stevenson's own map of the island. Here was Blind Pew, the harbinger of trouble, tapping his way up the path; young Jim Hawkins taking leave of his distraught mother in front of the Admiral Benbow Inn; and the same boy, transformed, facing down the murderous Israel Hands from the crosstrees of the *Hispaniola*. Indeed, it was the Wyeth illustrations on their jackets that led me later on in junior high to the New England historical novels of Kenneth Roberts: *Arundel*, with its revisionist heroic portrait of Benedict Arnold, and *Northwest Passage*, about the exploits of Rogers' Rangers during the French and Indian Wars. These were big books,

Figure 26. The last page of *The Bears' Famous Invasion of Sicily* by Dino Buzzati
Frances Lobb (New York: Pantheon Books, 1947).

and I was proud to be lugging them up and down Walpole Street. Their clear, straightforward narratives never let me down. Even better, most had endpaper maps of the territory, and I was forever flipping back to these to verify and locate the fields of action. The maps made the stories real.

As it happens, one of my oddest historical loops involves N. C. Wyeth. One of my friends in Carbondale, the playwright David Rush, is a Wyeth collector, and not long ago I found in David's copy of the Tercentenary Edition of *The Courtship of Miles Standish,* illustrated by N. C. and published in 1920, this inscription: "A Merry Xmas to you Fred Fanning from Wyeth." This copy had to have belonged to the brother of my great-grandfather, Walking John Fanning. Except for service in the Spanish-American War of 1898, Fred had never left the old home place on Webster Street in Needham, Massachusetts, to which their father had come from Ireland in 1851. The Wyeths were also longtime Needham residents and must have known the Fannings; their houses were less than a mile apart. Hence the gift of the book.

Anyone who's made a living teaching literature looks back—at least they should—with nostalgia at the drive of pure story, Welty's "sweet devouring," with which we all start. I continue to believe that when books become work, especially in service of some agenda or other, then everybody loses—including one's students. As I moved on to junior high and adolescence, I continued mostly to read adventure stories. Not having heard much about "the Classics" per se, I read the sports novels of John R. Tunis, the tales of Edgar Allan Poe, Sherlock Holmes's ingenious unravelings, and the oddly cryptic *Rutabaga Stories* of Carl Sandburg. In seventh grade came my first *directed* reading. I got interested in archaeology and read all I could find about that. Then came astronomy, the Middle Ages, and spelunking (my then-favorite new word and wildest life plan to date). Books were separate from school because reading didn't just happen between Labor Day and the middle of June. Nor was it done for grades. It was year-round, self-justifying, self-sustaining, and something I had discovered on my own.

Though I spent great gobs of time in the summer reading in a rocking chair on our big front porch, perfectly content, I didn't consider myself a loner. I had three or four good friends in the neighborhood, and our house was the gathering place for decisions on what we were going to do on weekend mornings and summer evenings. My parents liked having other kids around, and I remember that in sixth grade my mother taught me, my brother Geoffrey, Dan Callahan, and Richie Ross how to play whist. We played with her every Friday evening that winter, and the next summer the game continued, moving to the front porch or, weather permitting, to a folding card table in the back yard. My father's favorite card game was cribbage, which we also played endlessly on the front porch. He usually trounced me and Geoffrey, and I can hear him counting out gleefully, "Fifteen-two, fifteen-four, and a whole lot more."

As a child in the1940s and 1950s from a somewhat sheltered family with limited funds, the movies and television came too late to be seriously formative, and for this I am grateful. Because reading and the radio were habitual well before I became a moviegoer or a TV viewer, these solitary pursuits were my main portals to experience beyond home and family and into the imaginative life. Norwood had three movie houses: the tiny Guild and the rococo Norwood Theater downtown and the Southern, in South Norwood, the Flats. Double features were the order of the day. After *Treasure Island,* I can recall only a few kids' movies, and none were particularly impressive. In the early 1950s, I was mildly amused by the yearly Abbott and Costello slapstick confection—A and C meet the Invisible Man, Dr. Jekyll and Mr. Hyde, Frankenstein, and so on. After this, I remember most the movies that frightened me: *The Greatest Show on Earth* (1952), with its close-up lions and tigers, the daredevil high-wire acts, and, above all, the noise; *House of Wax* (1953), with Vincent Price's melting face and torture chamber seen with 3-D glasses; and *Them!* (1954), with giant, mutant ants on the attack. I think that my fears—and I did have nightmares after seeing these shows—were a measure of how little live-action entertainment I had seen. I was coming to the movies fresh from the radio and reading.

What I remember most about our own fairly late entry to television viewing at home is the glittering pantheon of early TV comedians. My father didn't laugh much around the house, but he did chuckle hard at Jackie Gleason, Red Skelton, Ernie Kovacs, and Phil Silvers as Sergeant Bilko. The whole family gathered for Groucho Marx hosting *You Bet Your Life,* ostensibly a quiz show but really the vehicle for Groucho's incomparable, spontaneous wit, exercised at the expense of a parade of hapless "contestants": sad sacks in drab and sacky clothes with padded shoulders and flat chests, sheepish farmers in string ties, dazed and smiling DPs with a burning desire to please, like the lady from Yugoslavia whose dowry had been two hogs. All would strain to "say the secret word" so the duck would come down on a swing with a hundred dollars in its bill. Groucho picked them off like sitting ducks, and he didn't always stop this side of cruelty. But the most fun was the wisecracking salesmen who came in roaring to lay their reputations on the line, and left with their tails between their legs. It's interesting to me that most of these great comics would be labeled "ethnic"—Jewish or Irish—today. Perhaps they articulated for my father's generation parts of itself otherwise unavailable for scrutiny in the screwed-down, homogenized Fifties. Several of my radio favorites also crossed over to television, among them Jack Benny, Burns and Allen, Superman, and the Lone Ranger. But by then, I wasn't interested anymore. Seeing them was not believing.

Prolonged in summer till the daylight failed

I was already eleven when Little League finally came to Norwood in the spring of 1954. The notice for upcoming Little League "tryouts" appeared on the front page of the *Messenger* on a Thursday afternoon in late March when there was still snow on the ground. In the three or so weeks before the event, which was scheduled for mid-April, my friends and I talked incessantly about Little League, but always in terms of what our uniforms would look like, how many people would come to the games, and which teams we wanted to be on. Most kids wanted to be on the Red Sox or Yankees. I found myself in something of a bind, because the defection of my favorite team, the Braves, to Milwaukee the previous year was still smarting. I didn't know which team I wanted to join, so I just kept quiet about that.

Playing ball in many forms had been my passion since before I started school. Alone, I bounced a baseball off the concrete front stoop of our house on Winslow Avenue for hours on end. The rhythm of throw, whack, bounce, smack (into my glove) was soothing, yet the action was infinitely various. The tricky, unpredictable hops were as challenging, I thought, as any fielded by my hero, the Braves' infielder Sibby Sisti. Playing catch with my brother in the back yard was the next step up the ladder of competition. Though two years younger, Geoffrey was already showing signs of the natural ability to make his arms and legs move in coordinated ways that would make him a three-sport star by junior high. These games always started slowly, but before long we were hurling the ball, trying to get fast pitches or grounders past each other: "No fair! I wasn't looking." "Yes you were. You just can't catch."

Invariably, we would knock a tomato or two off one of the vines in Dad's garden. These we would throw over the fence to hide the damage. This ruse worked only with the small, green ones, though. Dad always noticed if a near-ripe tomato was suddenly missing, and this was one of the few things we kids did that really annoyed him. He wasn't all that interested in food—maybe because waiting on tables was one of his jobs—but he did love fresh "tums" right out of the garden, washed clean in cold water, cut in half, and salted. Yum. A far worse sin was breaking garage or cellar windows with an errant throw. He reglazed windows so often at work that he hated doing it at home.

Soon after starting first grade, I began getting into pickup games on the Winslow School playground after school with the other kids who lived nearby: the red-head McDonald twins, Dicky and Bobby, emigrés from South Boston with more street-smarts than the rest of us; Stanley Everson, short and tough, with whom I would have my first and only fight in elementary school (he called me "four-eyes"); Johnny Bowler and his little brother Richie, a shy and friendly kid who died of leukemia in third grade. The girls played too: Maggie McCurdy, who lived next door to the school, Linda Soderstrom, Stella Orlando and Jean Connolly. We played way over at the far side near the woods, where we could use the low stone wall between the playground and Maggie's yard as a backstop. Base paths were worn by the traffic of our sneakers, and the bases themselves were ripped squares of box cardboard. A couple of kids had bats, but if they didn't show up, we weren't above using sticks. Our baseballs came from the Five-and-Ten, and after they lost their loosely stitched covers, we wrapped them in fuzzy black tape.

The minimum for a game was three players—pitcher, batter, fielder, with everyone keeping his own score by an elaborate and ever changing set of rules involving distances allowable for a fair ball to either side of the fielder, how to judge swinging for real versus just to stop the ball, whether or not to run to first base and what to do after getting there, and so on. If six kids showed up, then we had a real game, in which those not actually at bat played some of the defensive positions on the honor system, pledged to make every effort to get their own teammates out. This was a recipe for trouble, of course, and it often came: "Anybody could have gotten that one. You didn't try." "Yes I did. It took a bad hop." Or, "You took your foot off the base on purpose." "No, the cardboard moved and I couldn't find it." Or, "Why didn't you throw home?" "I couldn't get the ball out of my glove. Besides, nobody was covering the plate." As no one had catcher's equipment and the position itself was the lowest of priorities, the pitchers never threw very hard. You couldn't strike out. The idea was to serve up the ball so it *could* be hit.

On Saturdays and Sundays in the spring we played real games with eight or nine or ten on a side. In the summer we played every day. In the repeating ritual, two of the best players—everybody knew who they were—would "buck up," throwing out the fingers of one hand for first pick. By third grade I had a reputation as a pretty good infielder, and I was usually chosen somewhere in the middle of the pack. Thanks to my solo practices on the front stoop, grounders were my special province. I loved outsmarting the ball by pure instinct: measuring speed and spin, making the last-second adjustment dictated by a short hop or a stone—and there were stones galore on the playground, which had never seen a rake. Then the satisfying scoop—a thrill in my glove-hand palm that traveled all the way up my arm to the shoulder—followed by the pluck and release of the ball toward first base. God, it was fun. Often we didn't even know who had won or lost when we quit for the day.

All those ball-playing days are one day now. I can feel the spring of possibility in my sneakers as I round the corner and step off the sidewalk onto the grass of the schoolyard. Sunny, cloudy, chilly or hot—it was all the same. We were going to play ball. We got to the field early, when the robins were still hopping around in the dew. We'd be there under the high, blue sky of midday, until the heavy heat and humidity would remind us to run home for dinner. Then we'd be back, playing ball again under the fat, white clouds that rolled in, casting shadows across the field. We would hang on till suppertime, and in the late afternoon of days when it looked like rain, we'd play while the clouds turned gray and threatening. We'd play through the mist that came down, covering our faces and arms like a soothing, damp blanket after the heat of the day. When it really rained, when big splotches turned into a downpour, we would run to the front-porch overhang of the Winslow School to wait it out. Bunching up against the big, green double doors reminded us that the school was ours now. There were no boys' and girls' lines, no bells, no teachers. We couldn't get inside, but who wanted to? We owned the place. We would mill around, hoping to get another half-hour in. When it was clear that wasn't going to happen, we'd run home in the rain. That was OK too. It was exhilarating to arrive at the back door, soaked through and with sneakers squishing, my glasses beaded up and foggy. There was a holiday feel to running upstairs to the bedroom, peeling off all my clothes, toweling dry and changing, then coming downstairs for a supper of hot soup. Here was a fresh, new lease on life—and I hadn't had to take a bath to get it.

The tryouts came around on a cold April Saturday afternoon. I took it as a lucky omen that they were held on my home turf—the playground of the Winslow School. The sky was a mottled gray, but it hadn't rained yet as I walked down Winslow Avenue. I was still filled with simple, anticipatory excitement—until I reached the playground. There I was ambushed by a sudden change in the climate inside my head. From all the way across the field, I could see a lot of kids standing around with baseball gloves and a clump of adults, huddled and talking among themselves. By the time I reached these groups, I was nervous. My stomach turned over, my hands shook, and, despite the chill in the air, my glasses were beginning to fog up.

"Welcome to the Norwood Little League tryouts," a voice boomed out, a voice belonging to a big man in a gray sweatshirt and a Red Sox cap. "Let's get into groups by age. Nine-year-olds over here behind me, ten-year-olds with Mr. Kelly over there, eleven-year-olds farther out, near the woods. We're going to run some drills." He went on to explain that on the basis of ability, we kids would be divided up between major and minor leaguers. Both leagues were going to play a full schedule beginning in late May. Major league teams would have full uniforms. Minor leaguers would get caps and T-shirts. Just like in the big leagues, each minor league team would be connected to a major league team, and there would be chances for players to move up—"or down," he added with a laugh—through the course of the season. After these tryouts, the coaches—and he waved one large hand around to take in the other men—would get together and select the teams. "Everyone picked will get a phone call by next Friday night."

Everyone *picked*? Did that mean not everyone was going to be able to play? This was news to me. My stomach flipped again, then knotted up, as I realized that "trying out" meant that though everyone was going to try, not all would succeed. I walked slowly out to the eleven-year-old group. It was smaller than the others, but I didn't recognize any of the kids. Four of the men ambled slowly along behind us. I didn't know any of them, either. One—he was holding a bat and ball—was the man in the Red Sox cap. "OK, everybody," he shouted out. "Let's line up across the field. We're going to hit three or four ground balls and flies to each of you, and when you get the ball, heave it back in here. Pretend there's a base runner heading for home and you have to nab him." He pointed at the man beside him, who was wearing a glove. The other two men had furrowed brows and carried clipboards with fluttering yellow paper, above which were poised pencils. I swallowed hard. This was a test.

I found myself somewhere in the middle, about ten kids from either end of the line. I looked up and out at a world of indistinct, whitish shapes. My glasses were entirely fogged. I took them off and wiped them on my shirt, then dropped them on the grass, picked them up, and put them back on. I knew every dip and every bump of this field, but it felt different now, and strange. I could feel the woods at my back, too, looming as a threat. What if the ball got by me and was lost in the thick tangle of bushes and small trees? What if I couldn't find it and held up the whole practice? Then we were off. The man hit fly balls and grounders. The kids caught or missed them, and pegged the ball back in. I could see that when a fielder caught the ball easily, the next chance was harder—a higher fly for which he'd have to back up or a sharper grounder with wicked hops. Most did pretty well. After all, we were eleven and had been playing pick-up ball for four or five years. Maybe, I thought, that was why none of the adults said "Attaboy" or "Good throw." Still, the pencils were flying over the clipboards.

Then it was my turn. The first fly ball was on its way out. Little more than a pop-up, really, it came at me in a lazy arc, spinning slowly, slowly, clearing just barely the confusing background of the brick wall and green tile roof of the school. I saw the ball as a black silhouette against the gray sky for only a second, then it came back down, picking up speed. All I had to do was move two steps to my left, but in doing this, I stumbled, took my eye off the ball, and lost it against the brick wall. Bouncing off the top of my glove, the ball hit the ground with a soft plop. In a hurry to get it back in, I didn't throw high enough, and it took three bounces and stopped before reaching the man with the glove. My second fly ball sailed over my head toward the woods. I didn't get a third fly. Instead, a pretty fast grounder came my way. Three feet in front of me, it hit a stone and came up hard, hitting me in the face and knocking off my glasses. I got two more grounders, both soft, and fielded them cleanly. It wasn't much. Just enough to keep my hopes alive.

When the tryouts were over, I started for home by myself in the chill of late afternoon. I turned back at the edge of the darkening field. It looked like a different place. I was shivering. Also, there were tears in my eyes. What was the big deal? I walked slowly, taking much more time than usual to study the houses along the way. Nobody was outside. It had begun to rain, and blank front windows mirrored the gray skies overhead. When I got home, I brushed off my mother's question, "Was it fun?" with a shrug.

"Yeah. I guess so."

"Were any of your friends there?"

"Um, yeah." It was then I realized that some of the kids I'd played ball with for years had in fact been at the tryouts. But I hadn't spoken to them. I hadn't spoken to anybody.

By midweek, I had reconciled myself to being a minor leaguer. That would be OK. I'd have the chance to show my infield skills. The coaches would be so impressed that I would be brought up during the last week of the season to help shore up the "major league" team's defense. We would get into the playoffs, and I would play second base and turn a double play at the right moment, just like Sibby. Everyone would say it was a shame that because I was about to be twelve, this first year of Little League was going to be my only year. I definitely had potential. On Friday, I didn't leave the house after I got home from school, not even to go out in the back yard. I went through the motions of our usual round of activities, but all I thought about was the phone call. We had our Friday supper of fish sticks, frozen french fries, and a can of peas. Knowing the state that I was in, Mum came up with a surprise—Snow's Clam Chowder, mixed with milk and with a big glob of yellow margarine in the middle of the bowl. This was just about my favorite food, but that night it was merely a distraction—one more item to finish up. On Fridays, two of my favorite radio programs were on. But not even *Duffy's Tavern* and *Inner Sanctum*'s creaking door could hold my attention. Instead of settling into the big chair beside the radio, I paced the parlor floor. The phone rang three times: one wrong number, a call for my mother from one of my aunts, and Holman's Catering with a last-minute banquet job for my father for Saturday night.

By bedtime, I had come up with the idea that maybe Saturday morning would count too, at least until 9:30 or so, because the man had said the first practices would start "at 10:00 AM sharp" on school playgrounds all over town. There were so many kids to call, and they'd probably get to the minor leaguers last. I lay awake for a long time, thinking mostly about Little League but also about the humdrumness of the Red Sox (could I ever root for them, even with Ted Williams?) and the unforgivable perfidy of the Braves (how could Spahn and Sibby have deserted us?). Counting something, anything, was our family's tried-and-true remedy for insomnia, so I tried to imagine, one by one, all the hundreds of pop-ups and grounders that had been fielded and booted by the line of kids who had been at the tryouts. Given what was keeping me awake, this was not a particularly smart choice of material. Drifting off to sleep, I had one last disturbing thought. As of the next morning, there would be for the first time two kinds of ball-playing kids in Norwood, where before there had been only one. Some would have caps, worn proudly to school and also during the certain-to-be less-frequent pickup games, and some would not.

Not making Little League was far from the end of organized baseball for me. Later that spring, Paul Fulton, a kid from around the corner on Eliot Street, organized us capless neighborhood kids into "the Demons," a ragtag team that played occasional games on a vacant lot half a block from my house. We called our leader "Uncle Fulty." This was a nod to his entrepreneurial skills, which included negotiating permission to play from the lot's owner, arranging games with similarly constituted teams from other parts of Norwood, and making a deal with a local sporting goods store to get us—at a discount, he insisted—blue baseball caps with big white Ds on them. The

Demons played only three or four games, but they kept us going until school let out, and the town's playgrounds opened up for the summer.

After my failure at Little League, the playground became more valuable. Here was an example of Norwood coming through for me. I marvel now at the simplicity of this system and the great pleasure it afforded so many kids. The town hired counselors, most of them college students on summer vacation, to staff a dozen local playgrounds from the end of June through Labor Day, Monday through Friday, from 9:00 AM to 4:30 PM. Each playground had two counselors, male and female. The clientele was kids of all ages, from preschoolers on up to high school students. For the little kids, activities included pickup sticks, checkers, crafts, puppet shows, doll contests, dodgeball and volleyball, track and field competitions, story hours. For the older kids, it was all about playing baseball (boys) and softball (girls) in the Playground League. Each playground fielded four teams, two "Midget" (up to age ten or so) and two "Intermediate" (the rest of us). Even some Little Leaguers deigned to play. They tended to act as though they were doing us a favor, though, and Little League pitchers were forbidden to risk their arms in playground games, which drove the distancing wedge even further. Still and all, we were in a real league. Scores and statistics were kept by the counselors, who were the umpires as well, and our box scores and standings appeared every week in the *Norwood Messenger.*

In one of these playground games, I had my shining moment at the plate. Norwood's most famous athlete in those years was Richie Hebner, a boy so talented at both hockey and baseball that he could have played either sport professionally. He chose baseball and went on to a creditable, seventeen-year career (with a lifetime batting average of .277) as an infielder with the Pittsburgh Pirates and the Philadelphia Phillies. He was at third base when the Pirates won the World Series against the Baltimore Orioles in 1971. Richie loved to play baseball, anytime, anywhere, including in the Playground League, where he participated (without a scrap of condescension) on his neighborhood's team, Father MacAleer's. Richie was five years younger than I, but I'm still proud to let the record show that one morning in July I hit a triple off his pitching in an Intermediate game between my team, the High School Playground, and Father Mac's.

The playgrounds also sponsored two bus trips every summer, to which I looked forward with great anticipation. One was to Nantasket Beach in Hull, a honky-tonk wonderland with a small amusement park, a mile of ocean beach, and a long boardwalk full of stands selling saltwater taffy, fried clams and french fries, balloons, cards, and trinkets. The other was to a Red Sox doubleheader at Fenway Park, usually on July 4. I started going on these trips at age nine or ten, and each opened up a new world. These were my first experiences of riding on a school bus, of being wedged together and bouncing along with forty other kids, all of us bound for fun. To get to Nantasket, we traveled on two-lane roads through towns I'd never heard of: Holbrook, Rockland, Assinippi, Hingham, Cohasset. To get to Fenway, we negotiated the scary twists and turns of the Jamaica Way, passing Jamaica Pond, the Children's Museum, the back yard of the Mass Eye and Ear Hospital, and mansions old and new, including the home of the legendary James Michael Curley. Formerly Boston's mayor, a congressman, and the governor of Massachusetts, Curley had been the most colorful of old-school politicians, and a man who had been to jail twice for corruption. Was he just another example of wayward Irishness? This wasn't clear to me, because everyone, my parents included, got such a kick out of him. The resounding success in 1956 of Edwin O'Connor's novel *The Last Hurrah* further confused the issue. We couldn't miss Curley's house, because the shutters had shamrock cut-outs, placed, it was said, for the edification of his Yankee neighbors.

At both destinations, I saw more different sorts of people than ever before, colorfully set off against the high, blue summer sky. And both places were unforgettable: on the one hand, the meticulous, focused beauty of Fenway Park, enveloped by the hum of the crowd, punctuated by catcalls and vendors I'd heard on the radio; on the other, the open, rolling expanse of the Atlantic Ocean, with the regular crash of breakers interrupted by screeching seagulls.

The playground system was a great institution, money well spent—and it couldn't have been much—to extremely effective ends. Parents from all over town sent their kids, and the kids wanted to be there. Most of the counselors, though certainly not professionally trained, were serious about the work and did it well. They liked kids and were happy to have the jobs. We were all part of something to which we could fasten placebound, neighborhood allegiance. Summer at the playground was an indispensable part of childhood for me and my friends.

Baseball in the summertime was still possible for the unaffiliated, on into my high school and even college years, by virtue of another town institution—the Twilight League. Any group of kids in their teens or early twenties could sign up to field a team. There was no charge, and the only requirement was that at least six teams wanted to play in a given year. Some were high school and American Legion stars; others, like me, were not. I played for a team with a mildly countercultural name, the Beatniks. There were two games a week, starting at 5:30 or 6:00 PM on fields without lights, so the games usually went no more than six innings. In the summer of 1962, we reached our high point by winning the league title. All of us were in college, and we played against teams of young men many of whom were already in the workforce, or just drifting around, or about to join the armed forces. Having grown up together, we continued to get along fine—another indication that Norwood's social fabric was flexible and encompassing.

A Beatniks box score from the *Messenger* in June 1963 reveals the closeness over time of my group of friends. There were six of us on that team: Dick "Buz" Shea in left field (an undergrad at Boston College, nicknamed for Jim Busby, a Red Sox journeyman outfielder), Dave Drummey in center (a standout high school ball player, community college student, and one of the most naturally funny people I've ever known), Pat Dempsey at third base (another talented high school player and a brilliant math major at B.C.), and at first base, Dan Callahan (then at Georgetown and thinking of going to law school). As usual, I was at second. Our pitcher, Lorin Maloney, a track star at the College of the Holy Cross in Worcester, had gone to Boston College High School. Dan and I had gotten to know him during senior year when the three of us were interested in the same girl, and he had become a friend right away. I notice now that all of us had Irish surnames, but it's another measure of the general lack of ethnic consciousness in those days that we almost never talked about Irishness. It wasn't failure to see the trees for the forest that stifled us either, because our high school and college gang also included three girls from quite different backgrounds: Dianne Daley, the sometime object of our triple affections, who was half Irish and half Polish; Marianne Cooper, whose parents were Jewish, and Madeline Zilfi, the daughter of an Irish mother and a Turkish father. But even these examples of otherness failed to provoke many forays into comparative ethnic studies. Ours was a typical benign ignorance in the late 1950s—before the civil rights movement and Black Pride inspired new curiosity about their roots among other immigrant groups. Before. So much was "before" for us. In high school, we were shaped, for good and ill both, by stasis, and the shock of change, when it came, was just that—a shock.

Whatever imports from the world of death

The communal experience of kids in our town did, however, include one particular day when Norwood stopped being an innocent place. It was

November 5, 1954, six days before my twelfth birthday. That Friday afternoon I looked down at the pile of newspapers that had been left, as usual, at the foot of our driveway for me to deliver and saw a huge banner headline on the front page of the *Boston Globe*:

NORWOOD GIRL, 15
SLAIN IN GARAGE

Followed, in type only slightly smaller, by

STRANGLED BODY DISCOVERED BY NEIGHBOR
Silver Chain Pulled
Tightly Around Neck;
Last Seen at 10 PM

Snapping the twine with my pocketknife, I picked up the top paper and read this lead: "The nude body of a pretty, 15-year-old girl, strangled by a sex murderer, was found this morning on the floor of a garage near her home." My parents would probably have kept the details from me, but as a paper boy, I was getting the story first and unfiltered. Stuffing the papers in my bag, I set off up Walpole Street, stopping every now and then to follow the gripping narrative as it continued on the inside pages.

There were pictures all over the paper: the smiling girl, her distraught parents, their three-decker "tenement," and the murder scene: a two-car garage next door to their house, which was just off Washington Street in South Norwood—the Flats. I was immediately drawn to a *Globe* artist's map of the scene, complete with the relevant buildings. Along with these was a directing arrow to the nearby site of an earlier sensational murder: "13 yr-old Nellie Keras found murdered in cellar of home on Oolah Ave in 1932." Here was another jolt—this kind of thing had happened in Norwood before. A sidebar explained that Nellie had been stabbed to death on Christmas Day 1932 in the third-floor apartment of the building where she lived on the second floor. Her killer was an "immigrant pedler," Ahmed Osman, who had died in the electric chair in January 1934.

On the next afternoon, Saturday, November 6, the *Globe* headline was again a silent shout:

EXTRA
BOY ADMITS
SLAYING GIRL
Neighbor, 15, Reenacts Norwood Crime

ILY GLOBE—FRIDAY, NOVEMBER 5, 1954

Victim, Friend; Left Her Off Near Home

(By Globe Staff Artist Norbert Quinn)

ARTIST SKETCHES NORWOOD NEIGHBORHOOD where teen-age girl was found brutally murdered today.

CHUM

Continued from the First Page

"See You at School"

Slaying Recalls Norwood Girl's

Figure 27. Map of the Annese murder scene, *Boston Globe*, November 5, 1954.

For the next two weeks, my friends and I talked of little else. Because of my special access to the news, I had more details of the murder than most kids, and I was much in demand as an expert witness. Here is what had happened. At about 6:30 on the evening of Thursday, November 4, fifteen-year-old Geraldine ("Gerry") Annese, the youngest of the five children of Mary and Joseph Annese, had gone out on a double date with her best friend, Cynthia Savage, and two sixteen-year-old boys from the nearby town of Walpole. The kids had driven around, stopping at several local haunts—diners, a pizza parlor, a bowling alley. At about 9:45 the group had let Geraldine off at the corner of Washington and Tremont Streets in South Norwood. According to Cynthia, Gerry had said, "I'll see you tomorrow at school" and had gone off up Tremont, swinging her handbag and singing the song "Teach Me Tonight."

She didn't have far to go—no more than thirty yards. The Annese family lived on the second floor of a three-decker at 13 Tremont Street. Gerry had to walk past only the side of a big apartment building that fronted on Washington Street (1201 Washington), a vacant lot, and a two-car garage that was a few feet from the side door of her building. When she came to the garage, she heard a familiar voice calling her name. A boy she knew was standing in front of the garage doors. Somehow he got Gerry to enter the garage, and there he killed her. Death was due to brain hemorrhage and strangulation. The body was found at 7:45 the next morning, Friday, by a young man who came into the garage to get his car for work. The first newspaper reports contained two details that stuck in my mind. Gerry had struggled so fiercely that "one of her fingernails was torn off," and her body was found "unclothed except for her bobby sox."

What was worse, we soon found out that the murderer was not an outsider but a boy from Gerry's neighborhood, also fifteen, who had been brought in for questioning soon after her body was discovered. After eight hours of grilling, he confessed, led the police to the scene, and reenacted the crime. His name was Peter Macarewicz. He lived with his parents, Peter and Adrienne Macarewicz, and two younger siblings, a brother thirteen and a sister twenty-one months. Their apartment was on the second floor of 1201 Washington Street, which meant that Peter could look out his back windows straight across the empty lot to the windows of the Annese apartment. Peter and Gerry had known each other since elementary school (the Balch, just across Washington Street), and both had gone through Norwood Junior High as well. In November 1954, both were attending the Henry O. Peabody School, the vocational annex to Norwood High, and had often walked to and from school together. Peter had wanted Gerry to be his girlfriend and had given her a necklace. She never wore it, and six months before the murder she had rejected him and broken off their walks. Peter was a former Boy Scout and an altar boy at St. Peter's, South Norwood's Polish parish, and the press made much of the fact that he had served Mass on the previous Sunday. On the fatal Thursday evening, one of Gerry's girlfriends had run into Peter in a local variety store and casually mentioned that Gerry was going out with some boys from Walpole. At some point later on, Peter had slipped out of his building through the cellar, crossed the vacant lot to the garage, and waited there in the dark for Gerry to return from her date.

On the following Tuesday, the *Norwood Messenger* went all out, with a tableau of the dramatis personae of the tragedy spread out across the front page above the masthead: pictured were Peter Macarewicz, Gerry's parents, her sister Lena, her girlfriend Cynthia, and her stepbrother Philip DeRose. Then came the man who had discovered the body, followed by a picture of Gerry herself. The accompanying coverage, which I again read as I delivered the papers, had much new and disturbing information. There had been six previous attempted attacks against women in South Norwood since

Labor Day, three of them in the same neighborhood as the murder, and one on the same street. The pressure on the Norwood police had been so great that even though the confessed killer had been captured, the town manager had declared a "state of emergency" in town, and the police chief had issued a "shoot to kill" order "in the matter of sex offenders." Good grief. We kids were much too unsophisticated to recognize all this as the big overreaction that it was. At home, our parents were having whispered conversations which stopped when we came in earshot. Everyone was shaken. The Annese murder was in the papers for months—through Peter's trial, conviction, and incarceration in the state prison at Walpole.

As this spectacular event leached into the general consciousness of the town, my friends and I made efforts to distance ourselves from the circumstances of the crime, in order, I'm sure, to cushion the blow of the murder and make ourselves feel safer. All seven attacks that fall, and the 1932 murder as well, had been in the Flats. The Anneses were Italian; the Macarewitzes were Polish. They lived not in freestanding houses but in three-deckers. Although they were Catholics, they were members not of St. Catherine's parish downtown but of the national parishes in South Norwood that had been founded to serve the new immigrants. Gerry had attended St. George's, with Italians and Lithuanians, and Peter had been an altar boy at St. Peter's, the Polish church. Both teens had been enrolled at the Peabody School, which wasn't quite the same as Norwood High.

On the other hand, the newspaper stories about the murder were full of references to people who were familiar to my family: Norwood's town manager John Kennedy, Police Chief Mark Folan, Sergeant Joseph McNulty, and Patrolman Dick Towne, whose house was on my paper route. Also, because so many mourners were expected, Gerry Annese's funeral was held at our church, St. Catherine's, and the celebrant was Father Carroll, known even to us public-school Catholics as a kind, funny man who was popular with kids. Furthermore, on that first Saturday, the *Globe* had printed a second map on which the whole town was spread out, with markers at places associated with the crime, including the Junior High School (my father's turf) and the center of downtown (my own Friday-night stomping ground). Even my elementary school, the Winslow, was there, along with the public library and our stretch of Walpole Street. The message of this map was proximity. I could see that, as the crow flew, my house was no farther from the Tremont Street murder scene than from St. Catherine's, to which we walked on Sundays. The railroad tracks seemed a flimsy barrier between the quiet streets of my neighborhood and a place

Figure 28. My first-grade school picture, spring, 1949.

where one teenager could brutally kill another. There was no getting around this transforming knowledge. Joined together in this tragedy, Norwood was one town after all, a town where *Dragnet* had suddenly come to life.

Of knowledge, when all knowledge is delight

I hadn't attended kindergarten, but when I got to elementary school, I took to it like Mr. and Mrs. Mallard to the Public Garden. At the end of the first day of first grade, I came running up Winslow Avenue waving a big piece of construction paper on which I had drawn a large, fat, blue rabbit. It was the Wednesday after Labor Day of 1948 and I was five years old. My excitement spilled out in a rush of words. The teacher had read us *Bunny Blue,* a picture book, and then directed us to draw his picture from memory. In the top right corner of my picture was a gold star. Here was praise from the outside world. I was purely delighted. This became one of my mother's favorite stories about me, and "Bunny Blue" was her code phrase for having predicted my success as a student. And, in fact, it was pretty much as simple as that.

Nearly sixty years later and unprompted by research, I can still rattle off the names and recall the faces of my six elementary school teachers. Many people I've asked can do this, and it must be a sign of how strongly the beginning of formal education gets imprinted on us. As the times most often dictated, there were five misses and one, the last, a mister. My first-grade teacher was Miss Cataldo, a short, dark, pretty young woman with short, dark hair. All the boys and most of the girls had crushes on her. It was she who heaped praise on my clay-modeled manger scene at Christmas. Just starting out in the profession, Miss Cataldo resigned and got married a year or two after our class moved on. In second grade, I had Miss Cuff, a tall, thin-faced woman in her fifties with long, gray hair pulled back in a tight bun. I didn't know it then, but hers was a particular sort of West of Ireland look—stoic to grimness, and with piercing blue eyes. But Miss Cuff was really very kind. Deducing that I needed glasses, she moved me to the front row till I got them, and then eased my transition to having four eyes rather than two.

For third grade, I had Miss Kenefick, a short, sometimes grumpy woman with fluffy white hair and kind blue eyes. I knew that she lived with her brother and sister, because they were on my paper route. My fourth-grade teacher, Miss Agnes Marsh, was short and on the heavy side, with reddish brown hair. Probably about forty, she looked jolly and had a hearty laugh, but she turned out to be tough and strict. Plenty of kids, me included, got their first experience of clapping out erasers after school with Miss Marsh. In fifth grade, my teacher was Miss Flora Verderber. Still in her thirties, tall and (as they say) big-boned, she was a definite presence in the school, for she wore visible red lipstick and rouge and had a permanent-waved "hairdo." Also, her dresses were brighter than anyone else's, and they swished around her legs when she walked. She spoke with an impatient, clipped precision. My mother knew her well, because they had grown up together on Wilson Street in Germantown. The Verderbers had come over from Austria.

In sixth grade, I found my first academic mentor, Mr. Francis Lambert, a young teacher with carefully combed brown hair and a moustache, and an outgoing, friendly way about him. Mr. Lambert had many interests and the gift of sharing these enthusiastically with his students. Art was important to him, and he made sure we had time to draw and paint. A fine amateur photographer, he won several prizes in the *Boston Globe* contests. He also loved history and took us on field trips to the Bunker Hill Monument; the USS *Constitution* ("Old Ironsides" at the Charlestown Navy Yard); the original Boston Children's Museum, housed in a mansion on the Jamaica

Way; and the Christian Science Mapparium at the Mary Baker Eddy Library on Massachusetts Avenue, a huge glass globe that you could enter on a catwalk, allowing you to see the world from the inside. He also arranged for us to get do-it-yourself kits to make radios. Because I was a veteran radio listener, this was a tremendously exciting project. I remember a piece of wood, some wires, screws and spools, a few drops of solder. And mirabile dictu, we actually heard voices.

I have never been very good at standardized tests, and those I took in elementary school had me slotted in as an average student. I think this was why I was placed in Mr. Lambert's class, which was a split fifth and sixth grade, rather than in the class of all sixth graders with most of the identifiably "smart" kids. This must have been a teaching challenge for Mr. Lambert, and I seem to have been something of a challenge as well. His summary comment on my report card was, "Slow in complying with requests for better behavior and will sometimes argue unnecessarily with constituted authority." (My mother saved *all* my report cards.) And yet, I could not have had a better experience. Mr. Lambert was a fine teacher, innovative and attuned to his students' potential. On the evidence of my clay models, it was he who engineered my year of Saturday classes at the Boston Museum of Fine Arts. Also, given the manual dexterity involved in my tiny castles and coliseums, he advised that I consider becoming a dentist. This attention came at a good time, as it was also my sixth-grade spring when I got rejected by the Little League. I was lucky to have Mr. Lambert, because he left the following year for a better job in the posh, upper-middle-class town of Wellesley.

I had a number of great teachers in the Norwood schools—I think for two reasons. First, public education was in those years still universally acknowledged as a profession—a calling in the eyes of many—and the community held its teachers in high regard. Status helped to compensate for the relatively low pay, which could in any case be supplemented by summer employment elsewhere. Second, because employment opportunities for women remained severely limited throughout my public-school years—September 1948 through June 1960—many of my female teachers were remarkably intelligent and skilled by any standard of measure. In today's world, some would certainly have opted for careers in medicine, science, the law, business, or university teaching. I found stimulating teachers at every turn.

At the same time, my father provided a humorous, slightly jaundiced perspective about teachers that kept me from idealizing them. As a custodian, he saw their human limitations. There were things around the school that they refused to do or could not do well. A very intelligent man in a low-status position, Dad had to put up with his share of trivial and petty demands, and once in a while he would tell us stories out of school. One teacher broke a high window with a slip of the hooked pole that opened windows from the top. One dropped his morning coffee all over the floor just as the first bell rang, then let the kids in anyway. One was incapable of locking a cabinet but could, and did, lock himself in his classroom. Dad used to say, "School would be a great place, without the teachers," and I appreciated the insider's balance that he gave to my perceptions of the culture of education.

Seventh grade was my toughest year in school. Even though my father worked there and I knew the geography of the Norwood Junior High School intimately from our Sunday morning visits, I faced the usual problems that came with moving out of the protection of the small neighborhood schools from which we all had come. To begin with, for the first time, students were placed in "divisions." We were told that these were random assignments, but everyone knew that "smart" kids and "slow learners" ended up in different classes and that everyone else was somewhere in between. Where did I fit? I hadn't made Little League, but I had been to the Museum of Fine Arts. Because of my many bouts of illness, I had missed a lot of school—on average, thirty days (six full weeks) in each of the first five grades. I began junior high in "7 G," which was definitely not the top of the heap, and started the year with Bs in everything. But by the last quarter I was getting As and A-minuses. This had to be due in part to my improved health: I missed only seven days all that year.

The key figure for me in this transition was Mrs. Brown, a small woman with a tight gray bun of hair and wire-rimmed glasses. As my seventh-grade homeroom teacher, she was my guide into the intricacies of junior high, and I also had her for social studies. She had a reputation for rigid discipline, and no one ever acted up in her classes. She was so tough that no one even knew her first name. We assumed she was a widow, though my father said that he wasn't sure there had ever been a Mr. Brown. But there were indications that she had another side as well. She couldn't quite disguise the fact that she got a kick out of our greenhorn haplessness—dropping pencils, paper, even books, bumping into doors, losing our way, failing to hear the second bell. Her eyes would dance when someone, usually a boy, would raise the wrong hand, the one that was holding up his desk lid, which then would come crashing down.

Another giveaway to her innate kindliness was the fact that Mrs. Brown ran the Norwood Junior High School Stamp Club. It's important to note that the pride and commitment of my teachers in the public schools extended to their willing sponsorship of all manner of activities outside the classroom during free periods and after school. Stamp collecting was a natural hobby for me. Here were little pieces of colored paper with variegated edges, many of them beautiful and issued from faraway places. Stamps weren't expensive either, they could be traded (like baseball cards), and they came with a clear mandate that was dear to my heart—they had to be sorted, organized, and put into a book. The Stamp Club met once every two weeks after school in Mrs. Brown's room. The atmosphere was somewhat more relaxed than during the school day. After all, we were only a dozen or so interested collectors, and we showed up on our own time. We learned how to use stamp hinges (I had been pasting my stamps onto sheets of paper), and to separate stamps from their envelopes over a steaming kettle. We sent for U.S. first-day covers, which came to our houses with "First Day of Issue" emblazoned on lovely envelopes with engraved pictures. With money from our dues of a dime a month, supplemented by her own funds, Mrs. Brown sent for big packets of unsorted world stamps and divvied them up among us, declaring, "You never know what you might find!" I dreamed of finding the world's rarest stamps—the 1847 one-penny red and two-penny blue from the island of Mauritius, mistakenly labeled "Post Office" instead of "Post Paid" and worth half a million dollars each.

Supervised activities such as the Stamp Club encouraged the idea that teachers were people too, but my breakthrough revelation of this fact came on the afternoon of Tuesday, October 4, 1955, when I entered Mrs. Brown's room for a club meeting and heard the familiar sound of a baseball play-by-play broadcast. The source was a table radio, which sat incongruously in the middle of the teacher's desk. Of course, I knew what was going on—this was the seventh game of the '55 World Series between the New York Yankees and the Brooklyn Dodgers. Neither one was my team, but I was partial to the Dodgers because I already hated the Yankees, not least because my father rooted for them so gleefully—just to get our goats. The Yankees were in the middle of their crushing dominance of professional baseball from the late Forties through the early Sixties, and the Dodgers were clearly the underdogs, having never won a World Series in seven attempts. Worse still, five of these losses had been in "Subway Series" against the Yankees. The 1955 series had begun with two Yankee wins at home in the Bronx, but the bleeding was stopped by young Johnny Podres, who won game three at

Ebbets Field on his twenty-third birthday. The Dodgers also won the next two games at home, but the Yankees tied the series at 3–3, setting up the decisive seventh game—at Yankee Stadium.

We hadn't known that Mrs. Brown knew anything about baseball, much less that she was a fierce fan of the Dodgers, but stamps were forgotten that afternoon. She paced the aisles of screwed-down desks and chairs, hanging on every pitch. She let out a big sigh when Brooklyn's Sandy Amoros made the game's biggest play, running down a long fly ball to left by Yogi Berra in the sixth inning and doubling the runner off first. When Elston Howard grounded out to Pee Wee Reese at short to end the game, Mrs. Brown jumped up and down several times, then danced around the classroom, shouting "Johnny Podres! Johnny Podres!" over and over. The Dodgers had won 2–0, and Johnny had come through again, pitching a complete game, scattering eight hits, striking out four. I had never seen such an outpouring of sheer elation from any adult, much less a teacher, much less Mrs. Brown. That night at supper, Dad feigned disappointment in the Yankees loss, but he also shook his head and chuckled.

When I was in eighth grade, my father procured for me a rejected teacher's desk and a library chair from the Junior High. Old and scarred but well made of good wood, they were more than serviceable after Dad patched them up. I could hardly contain my excitement when he and another custodian brought the desk up the stairs and into my bedroom at the front of the house on Walpole Street. Here were seven drawers for all my stuff. Here was a clean expanse of smooth wood on which to spread out and proceed with my various kinds of "work." The first time I sat down there, I felt utterly at home. My head became clear. The cares of the day dropped away. "The game," as Sherlock Holmes often told me in those days, was "afoot." A pleasing, efficacious rhythm came naturally to me. I would pile my books and papers on the floor to my left, then pick up what was needed for one homework assignment and place it all on the empty surface of the desk. Then I was off—turning pages, filling sheets with words and numbers, happily making a mess. And just when the jumble was greatest, there would come the midpoint, the turn. I sensed that a solution was about to emerge, and I could begin the process of subtraction, piece by piece, back to the single sheet that held—the answer. Then, dipping down to the left, I would pick up the next assignment. This has been, ever since, the rhythm of my working life: to move from questioning emptiness to buzzing, inchoate activity to a winnowed fulfillment. It's a process as much visual and tactile as intellectual.

By the time I got to high school in September 1957, I was in pretty good shape to make the most of the experience. My grades had flagged me as intelligent, I was an old hand at the library, and I was a comfortable gladiator in the desk-top arena where "homework" got done. Teachers and fellow students had continued to admire my art work. In ninth grade Ancient History had come my valedictory achievement in clay—the Egyptian Temple of Karnak. With a newly mended easel (again, a junior-high reject), I had begun to paint, and this activity would satisfy my craving for handwork on through college and a bit beyond. I was also entering high school with half a dozen good friends and a wide circle of acquaintances, which made for a level of security I hadn't known since the Winslow School.

My interest in sports continued through junior high and into high school, but I was enough of a realist to know that none of the marquee sports teams, not even baseball, was going to take me on. I went out for cross-country sophomore year, mostly because there were no tryouts. I soon found out why everyone was welcome. Unless you had some talent—and I didn't—running up and down the hills between the high school and New Pond every weekday afternoon was sheer agony. I stuck with it that first fall, running for the junior varsity, but that was that. My best finish was third in a JV race against Walpole. Inspired by watching on TV the Sunday afternoon charges to victory of the amazing Arnold Palmer, I also took up golf. With paper-route money, I bought a cheap set of clubs (the logo was "Johnny Revolta," which made them the butt of many jokes) and a very affordable junior membership at Walpole Country Club (I think it was $75 a year), where I played with my friends Dan, Billy, and Stevie Callahan, whose father was an avid golfer. By senior year, I had improved to sixth (last) man in the match-play roster of the Norwood High golf team, in which position I alternated with Dan Callahan. I didn't win a match, but walking the courses on beautiful spring afternoons was a lot more fun than cross-country, and I continued to play the game for a few more years before losing interest.

Then there was hockey—to me, the most exciting of games. I played with friends on local ponds and listened to the Bruins on the radio, but there was a problem—I couldn't skate. I hadn't started young enough and had never seen the inside of a rink, so my ankles remained weak and wobbly, there was much leaning on my stick, and skating backward was an unattainable skill. I found a solution, though. When I was in my last year of junior high (ninth grade), my Latin teacher, Jack Monbouquette, became Norwood High's varsity hockey coach, and I asked if he could use any help with the office chores. He told me that the team already had a manager, and this turned out to be Frannie Doran, a friendly senior who was happy to take me on as his assistant. I took over the job the following year and held it from then on. This was the beginning of a long and eventful career as a hockey manager, which, oddly and unpredictably enough, would play an important part in my college experience.

In high school, the job involved very little besides collecting pucks, taping sticks, and counting heads on the buses, which took us for practices to rinks all around the Boston area, often at ungodly hours of the morning. Norwood was in the powerhouse Bay State League, and our games were on Friday nights at the Boston Arena, off Massachusetts Avenue in the South End. High school kids from the surrounding towns—Dedham, Walpole, Needham, Natick—would crowd into this aging facility, jamming a concourse that was warm with the smell of hot dogs and popcorn. The cement floors were dark with grime and slick with melted snow. Downstairs, the tiny locker rooms smelled of sweat and piss. It was an exciting place to be, especially during the Christmas vacation games, when everyone was carefree, released from the daily grind, and up for anything.

These were the first hockey games I ever saw, and they were all I expected them to be and more. It's still my opinion that ice hockey is unbeatable as a spectator sport. The combination of grace, guile, and power, the obvious high level of skill necessary to move effectively on skates, the abrupt shifts of speed and momentum, the heart-stopping rush of an attack that involves everyone on the ice, the split-second decision to pass or shoot the lethal, hard-rubber puck—there's nothing like it. I mean high-school hockey or, especially, the college game, where the referees ride herd and the action is unimpeded by grand-standing fights and overall chippiness. Professional hockey used to be more like this—I think because almost all the players were Canadians, and they tended to have egos held in check by reverence for their national game.

I had some very fine teachers in high school. The three who stand out—Ruth Johngren, Jim Dunn, and Betty O'Sullivan—taught, and helped determine, my favorite subjects: French, Math, and English. Miss Johngren was a tall, vivacious woman who brought more energy into the classroom than anyone else I've ever seen. She bounded through the door every day for three years, arms waving, shouting out, "*Bonjours, classe! Comment ça va? Écoutez, Écoutez-moi!*" This was not an act but authentic and formidable joie de vivre. Miss Johngren was able to get us excited about the subjunctive mood, but the real payoff came senior year when we read some literature: Molière, Maupassant, Baudelaire, Rimbaud. With this came an explosive combination of enthusiasm and high seriousness that worked on us well before we understood why such reaction might be warranted. Ruth was a graduate of Radcliffe, brilliant and sophisticated, and we were lucky to have her around. Twenty years later she turned up as a fellow subscriber to a series of film classics at a Brockton movie theater. By then, she had been retired from teaching for ten years, but there was no diminution of energy, intellect, or curiosity. My last memory of her is the great discussions we had in the lobby after showings of *Our Town, Mother Courage, A Threepenny Opera,* and *The Iceman Cometh.*

Mr. James Dunn was an enigma. My homeroom teacher sophomore year, he introduced me to the high school and to the joys of disinterested thinking. Somewhere in his late forties, he had wavy, graying brown hair, perfectly in place, a long face with prominent nose, and wire-rimmed glasses. In those days, all the teachers dressed pretty formally—skirts for the women, jackets and ties for the men—but Mr. Dunn was something special. He was elegant, even dandyish: white pants and seersucker jackets in spring, brown tweeds in fall, and always a sparkling white shirt with a brightly colored tie, figured or striped. He talked to us as though we were adults, in a clipped tone with subtle, understated humor. He was a Norwood native, and my mother told me that he had been quite "literary" as a young man, with a reputation in town for having published a risqué story, "something about pink tights," in a national magazine. She thought it was the *New Yorker,* but I haven't been able to find it there. Maybe he used a pseudonym. Adding to the mystery, he taught math, not English, to which he brought a genius for clarifying analogies.

Twice Mr. Dunn confided in me. In sophomore year I was involved in some mild horseplay during geometry class. He took me out into the hall and said, "Charles, you ought to distance yourself from such trivial behavior. You've got more to engage your mind than this clowning around." One afternoon late in my senior year, he told me that he taught math because he loved literature—so much so that he couldn't bear to discuss it with adolescents. He knew I was thinking about becoming a teacher, and he said I ought to consider taking the same path: "Math, Charles, is a good subject for teaching because it doesn't have anything to do with people. It's predictable and free of emotion, except for the abstract beauty of a geometric figure or proof." I thought seriously about this, because I had liked math since junior high. In eighth grade, I had been so fascinated by learning to do square roots—by hand, of course, as this was well before calculators—that

I had asked my math teacher, Miss Cooney, how to find cube roots. She had stayed after school for two weeks and taught me. In the end, though, I went into teaching by another route.

My English teacher for all three years of high school was Miss Elizabeth O'Sullivan, a bright and lively middle-aged woman from Maine. She never mentioned this, but she came from a large clan of O'Sullivans from County Kerry who had immigrated to the Maine coast in the late nineteenth century. Many were Irish speakers, and they kept the language alive in northern New England well into the twentieth century. Miss O'Sullivan loved literature, especially that which was meant to be spoken aloud—oratory, narrative poems, and plays—and she read to us at every opportunity. Her great love was Shakespeare, and we read more plays than most classes did—not just the then standard sophomore-junior-senior sequence of *The Merchant of Venice, Julius Caesar,* and *Hamlet* but also *Henry IV part I, MacBeth, King Lear, The Taming of the Shrew,* and *The Tempest.* We always acted out the big scenes, and Miss O'Sullivan handed out parts with meaningful looks and a few enigmatic words that got us thinking. "Why am I Brutus today?" "Why is Marianne Cordelia?" "How can Dan be Falstaff?" She never explained.

She wasn't nearly as interested in lyric poetry, and I didn't begin to appreciate that tradition until my freshman year in college. In junior high we had memorized chunks of the Good Gray Classics: "Snowbound," "The Village Blacksmith," "To a Waterfowl," "A Psalm of Life." Also "The Raven" and "Annabel Lee" and some of the *Spoon River Anthology.* A lot of this is still stuck in my head, and there's a special room there for poems distinguished because my mother had also learned them in school. I would come bouncing home from seventh grade and we would trade lines: "'Twas the schooner Hesperus that sailed the wintry sea / And the skipper had taken his little daughter, to bear him company" ("The Wreck of the Hesperus"). And "'Shoot if you must, this old gray head / But spare your country's flag,' she said" ("Barbara Frietchie"). And "This is the forest primeval, the murmuring pines and the hemlocks / Bearded with moss, and in garments green, indistinct in the twilight ("Evangeline").

Another reason for my reluctance to understand poetry as serious business was "The Poet's Corner," a weekly feature in the *Norwood Messenger* to which the Fannings looked forward with relish. Mum and I would read the poems aloud at the supper table, inducing gales of laughter. The authors were all homegrown and worthy descendants of Irish American litterateur Patrick J. Pendergast. All of these folks ignored Ezra Pound's warning to

"Go in fear of abstractions." Our favorite was Katherine Saunders, dubbed by my mother "the poet laureate." A Norwood native and stalwart churchgoing Congo, Katherine had started out as a medical secretary, but in later years she listed her occupation in the street directory as "poet." She published eight chapbooks out of her home on Lincoln Street. Because of its celebration of the old downtown, I am partial to "Hat Happy," which goes like this:

When we were young the hat shop
Was the busiest in town
Hats displayed in windows
Yellows, orange, brown.
Pinks and blues and violets
Lit up every street,
Men adored the pretty things
Wild or prissy neat.

In high school we did read some great poems, but without venturing too far into the vasty deeps of interpretation. In fairness to Miss O'Sullivan, we must have looked to be a fairly naive bunch—even though we were the Honors Class. Maybe *because* we were the Honors Class. We read some Emily Dickinson. "This is my letter to the World / That never wrote to Me—." OK. Wasn't it nice that she wrote us this letter? Yes it was. Full stop. We read some Edward Arlington Robinson. OK. Why is Old Eben Flood so lonely? Well, he drinks too much for one thing, and that causes hallucinations. Full stop. We read some Robert Browning. OK. What's wrong with the Duke of Ferrara? He hasn't treated his wives very well. Full stop. Predictably for New Englanders, we also read Robert Frost. I recently came across a review I wrote of Frost's *Collected Poems* in the May 1959 issue of Norwood High's newspaper, *The Hilltopper.* (The piece had been saved from oblivion by my aunt Rose Riley Fanning, the funny and generous wife of my father's younger brother Phil.) I discussed "Mending Wall," which makes the point "that people must have some reserve and some secrets from others, that we should have an inner sanctum of the mind." (I wonder where that phrase came from.) I declared that "the beauty of Robert Frost's poetry is in its simplicity of thought and execution. He has no need for ten-syllable words or unpronounceable language, for his clear, concise style of free verse [*sic*] flows like pigment from a tube and with it he paints glowing scenes of forests and brooks." Moreover, a Frost poem "flows along effortlessly, the words seeming to carry my mind along as a stick of wood is swept by the current of our river." *Our* river? Wordsworth had his Derwent. I had the Neponset, which curled around Norwood to the south and west, protecting the town.

In the spring of 1960, some of the prizes that went along with finishing up high school came my way. I was one of eleven seniors inducted into Norwood's chapter of the National Honor Society. I was one of fourteen Massachusetts winners of the National Council of Teachers of English Achievement Award. When the yearbook rolled off the presses, my handiwork as Art Co-Editor was visible on every page. In addition to cartoons, drawings, and overall layout, I had slipped in a number of corny puns. The vocational program heading was "They Gave Their Awl!" For our musicians and choral groups, "They Beat the Band." The hockey team "Skated Up a Storm." In baseball "Our Diamondmen Shone Brightly," the tennis team was the "Racquet Raisers," and the golfers were "Birdie Watchers." Talk about innocence.

Twice in the last month of school I made the front page of the *Messenger.* First, I was a cowinner of the high school science fair, and therein lies a tale. In senior year I was having a problem with Physics, where I was headed for a low B. I did not get along with the teacher, Mr. Everett Learnard, in part because he felt that, given my stellar record in everything else, including Advanced Math with Mr. Dunn, I wasn't trying. There was something to this—Physics did bore me—but I also didn't get it. A small, nervous man, Mr. Learnard scurried around in a permanent crouch that accented his receding hairline and furrowed brow. We called him "the Bug." His natural state was sputtering agitation—no one could have gotten more excited about the results of rolling marbles down an inclined plane. His mood was not contagious though, partly because we saw him as a comic figure and partly because our lab was so poorly equipped, consisting of a few cardboard boxes full of inert, dusty stuff reminding me of the scraps of busted machinery that sat in our cellar and garage at home. (My father had grappled to his heart with hoops of steel the old Yankee adage, "Throw nothing away.") In sum, we were experiencing Physics in purest form: nothing in that classroom moved unless someone pushed it.

The stars were not aligned for me along this learning path, and yet my guidance counselor, Mr. Tom White, had gotten the idea that the key to my getting a college scholarship lay in mastery of the hard sciences. There was evidence in favor of this strategy. Sputnik had gone up in October 1957 when we were sophomores, and all America was worried about having fallen behind the Soviet Union in the race for space. Catching up to our

Cold War nemesis was going to require a mighty outlay of exhorting funds to be pitched at school and college science programs. Mr. White persuaded me to put down Physics as a projected major on my applications, and he even parlayed that approach into getting me a private interview with the chair of the Physics Department at Boston College, which he clearly saw as my best shot. My father drove me over to Chestnut Hill on a Saturday morning. After admiring the lab, I ran out of things to say, and the chairman, a tall, ascetic-looking Jesuit, filled up the time by describing in lengthy detail the connection between the Physics major and the college honors program. After this visit, I was sure that Physics wasn't for me, but I kept my own counsel on that one.

I was still no closer to making an A in Mr. Learnard's class, and yet, with the approach of the Science Fair, I began to get an idea. I started thinking not about a project but about what the science fair judges would want to hear. My experience in earlier fairs had led me to deduce that it wasn't so much what you did as how you explained the process. You had to convince the judges that you had used "the Scientific Method." You needed to ask a question or two, then come up with a liberal sprinkling of hypotheses, which you challenged energetically by experiments, which then led to conclusions. Thinking that I ought to play to my strength in math, I came up with a set of experiments involving probabilities in the "flexication" of a geometrical construct called a hexaflexagon. I can't recall where I found these things—Mr. Dunn may have put me on to them—and all I remember is that they resembled the folded-paper objects we had called "cootie catchers" in elementary school. You opened them one way and they were spotless, then brushed them across the sleeve of someone you wanted to annoy (a girl, more often than not) and then opened them again, the other way, to find pictures of bugs. Anyway, I put together a couple of hexaflexagons, then worked out a statistical model that would predict the various combinations when I flipped them around. When I explained the idea in Physics class as a rough equivalent of determining how often bugs would appear in a cootie catcher, I had my friends rolling in the aisles at the reference to our teacher's nickname.

Mr. Learnard was skeptical: "This is a math project, Fanning." (He was the only one of our teachers who called us by our last names.) He did let me into the fair, which was held in the high school gym in early April. My plan must have worked, because "A Theory of Hexaflexagons" was cowinner of first place, along with a sophisticated experiment on "The Relation of Light Paths and Time" by Donald Bamber, the best scientist in our class by far, who was off to MIT in the fall. Mr. Learnard was far from pleased. A couple of weeks later I got an Honorable Mention at the State Science Fair, (Don got a suitably more impressive Second Place), but even that did not help my fourth-quarter Physics grade, which came in at 80 percent. This was my lowest mark since Phys. Ed. in seventh grade, and it was accompanied by a notation that my work habits left something to be desired. Maybe Mr. Learnard had gotten the bug joke.

I remembered my second appearance on the front page upon reading a James T. Farrell story, "The Oratory Contest," written in 1935. The characters are a middle-aged Chicago streetcar driver, George O'Dell, and his sixteen-year-old son, Gerry, who is about to compete in the senior oratorical contest at his South Side high school. A successful student, encouraged by his teachers, Gerry is considering college, though he won't be able to go unless he can get a full-time job and enroll in night school downtown in the Loop. In the event, the boy wins the gold medal. George is moved to tears, and he rushes out to a drugstore to telephone the news to his wife, who is at home with their younger children. When he returns to congratulate his son, he finds only an empty stage. The story ends with George O'Dell's sad epiphany: "He asked himself why Gerry hadn't waited, and he knew the answer to his question." There is no more effective rendering in American writing of the gulf that can develop between working-class parents and their college-bound children.

I felt the shock of recognition here because this was my story too—except for the ending. The Norwood Chamber of Commerce sponsored an annual essay contest for high school juniors and seniors. Under the front-page picture of the three finalists in May 1960, the *Messenger* headline was "Wins Essay Contest Second Year In Row," and the lead was "Charles Fanning, Norwood High School senior, made history Tuesday night when he won first prize in the Chamber of Commerce annual essay contest for the second year in a row." My subject was "The Value of Art in Modern Civilization." (In those days, I was no more afraid of abstractions than Katherine Saunders.) On the night of the competition, held in the Junior High auditorium, my father was not in the audience. He was on duty as custodian, standing at the back of the room. When I emerged from the hall clutching the first-prize check for $25, he was in the foyer leaning on a push broom. I went right over and shook his hand. I was happy to see how proud he was of me, and that was that. Similarly, Dad was also present and also working at our senior class banquet in the high school gym just before graduation in early June. The caterer was Holman's, and when I saw that my father would be serving our table, I was delighted, as were my friends, because we knew we'd be getting extra banana fritters, Holman's signature dessert.

Why wasn't I Gerry O'Dell? First, as I've been saying right along, our socioeconomic status in Norwood seems not to have been an issue for my parents. Our family was comfortably at home in the town. Though the income from my father's two jobs of janitor and waiter was small by any measure, we never considered ourselves poor, and my siblings and I never expected that our choices beyond high school were going to be curtailed. Second, in my memory, the ethos of Norwood High School was essentially egalitarian. As a rule, teachers did not emphasize distinctions between differently "tracked" classes. Athletes were not given special treatment either. They were respected but not by any means venerated. Also, though we were all college-bound and in the top slots of class ranking, my group of friends did not look down on kids who were taking the shop, secretarial, and "general business" courses. Nor were we contemptuous of those who dressed in pink-and-black and spent their weekends drag-racing and drinking beer. Certainly, there were cliques, but I don't recall them as having been vicious or mocking of one another.

All this may sound like a nostalgic fairytale, but I don't believe it is. I've just been looking at our yearbook, with results that back up my memories. There was a rich ethnic mix in our class, though not a racial one. There were very few African or Asian Americans in Norwood at that time. Just about everyone else was represented, though: Yankees, Irish, Germans, Italians, French, Norwegians, Swedes, Finns, Poles, Lithuanians, Syrians, Lebanese, Jews. Also, the numbers reckoning relationships among us are impressive. Of the 284 Norwood High seniors pictured, I find that I could and would have greeted 271 by name. Of these classmates, I count 92 whom I considered as friends and another 38 as close friends. Adding to these the other seven members of our tight-knit gang of eight, the total is 137 identifiable friends. I was not especially outgoing, and I was far from being a charismatic figure in the class, but these numbers don't strike me as surprising. It was simply that kind of school, that kind of town.

Timing was, of course, everything. I find in the yearbook two familiar faces, friends of mine and legitimate school leaders, who had tragic connections to disturbing, divisive times before and beyond the relative calm of the late 1950s. Steve Sacco was an honors student and our student council president. His grandfather was Nicola Sacco, who, along with Bartolomeo Vanzetti, had been accused of murdering two guards during a payroll rob-

Officers of the Class of 1960, Norwood High School

VINCENT LUTKUS, Boys' Treasurer — HELEN ECKHARDT, Girls' A.A. Representative — STEVEN SACCO, President of Student Council — STEPHEN GULLA, Boys' A.A. Representative — JEAN MALACINSKI, Girls' Treasurer — RONALD HARDY, President — INGER HALLSTROM, Foreign Exchange Student — MARY ANN CASHEN, Secretary — BRIAN McTEAGUE, Vice President

Norwood Messenger

The Outstanding Civic Asset Of A Community Is The Integrity Of Its Newspaper

66th Year No. 55 — Norwood, Mass., Tues., June 7, 1960 — SEVEN CENTS

Exercises Set Tonight At 6

Diplomas will be awarded to 298 members of the class of 1960 of Norwood Senior High School at annual commencement exercises scheduled to be held outdoors at 6 o'clock tonight at the H. Bennett Murray Athletic Field.

In case of inclement weather, will be given by Reverend Ray-

Figure 29. Senior class officers on the front page of the *Norwood Messenger,* June 7, 1960.

bery in April 1920 in South Braintree, Massachusetts. Both men were Italian immigrants and known to belong to militant anarchist groups. Those were the days of the "Red Scare," "Palmer Raids" (there had one in Norwood), and a hue and cry for immigration restriction, and the Sacco and Vanzetti trial, convictions, and appeals process became one of the most famous cases in American history. Governor Alvan Fuller appointed a special committee to advise him regarding the last-ditch effort of the defense to overturn the death penalties. Led by Boston Brahmin Abbott Lawrence Lowell, the president of Harvard, this group declared that clemency was not warranted. Despite a widespread international outcry, Sacco and Vanzetti were executed on August 23, 1927. As a little boy in the 1920s, Dante Sacco had been the recipient of his father Nicola's "Letters to Dante," written from prison and published as part of the campaign to exonerate the men. This all happened thirty years before we started high school—not that long a time, but Dante's son Steve, our classmate, never spoke of the burden of painful recollection that his family carried.

Ronnie Hardy was our class president for all three years of high school. The most gifted and mature young man among us, he was fullback on the football team, a talented pianist with a fine bass voice, and a top student. He was also seriously religious in a social-gospel way and spent time volunteering at a mission for the homeless in Boston. With all this, Ronnie was genuine, considerate, self-effacing, and never preachy. We were all sure that he was headed for a life of significant achievement, and the class voted him most popular, most dependable, most talented, and most musical. Ronnie went off to college at Brown and we lost touch, but I knew that he had done civil rights work in the South and had then gone on to an internship in chaplaincy at the University of Massachusetts. As the quagmire of

Vietnam intensified, I heard that Ronnie was active in the antiwar movement in Amherst. Then came the horrible news that in protest against the immorality of America's ongoing folly, he had immolated himself on a quadrangle at the university. Previous to this, though neither had been in our class, I had known two of the half-dozen Norwood boys killed in Vietnam—Jack Concannon, who died in May 1966 at age twenty-two, and Johnny Fitzgerald, who died in April 1968 at age twenty. But it was Ronnie Hardy's death that brought the war home, and with it, full realization that the world in which I had grown up was gone.

8

A Thousand Days at Harvard

"But if our resources have about tripled, the costs of education have tripled, too, so we are no further ahead than before. We haven't really made it easier," Dean Bender says sadly, "for the janitor's boy to come to Harvard."

—"Many Are Culled, Few Are Chosen," *Boston Globe*, May 15, 1960

Applying to Harvard College had been my idea. Though it wasn't the high-flying, ne plus ultra, success-assuring brand name that many perceive it to be these days, Harvard in the late 1950s was certainly a prestigious school, a glittering prize, and I was much impressed by descriptions of the famous faculty, one-on-one tutorial system, and college life in idyllic "houses" along the Charles River. Also, I had done the research about the combination of scholarships, loans, and on-campus jobs through which, the brochures had insisted, anyone accepted at Harvard would be able to attend. On the other hand, Tom White, my high school guidance counselor, advised me to take the full-tuition scholarship to Boston College that I was offered in January of 1960. Because I lived so close, there would be no aid for living on campus, and so I would commute to B.C. with many of my Norwood friends.

I held out for Harvard—the only other school to which I had applied—in part because it seemed to me that I knew more about the place than Mr. White, who was, in fact, a graduate of B.C. and made no bones about his enthusiasm for the place. Also, despite his feelings in the matter, Mr. White had driven me to Cambridge for an interview. I had never been there before, and I loved everything about it: the mellow red brick with white trim everywhere, the colorfully painted towers and cupolas, the meandering little streets off Massachusetts Avenue, the beautiful river that bore my name—an omen perhaps? Here was a venerable, lovely, and serious place. There was no doubt about it. I wanted to be there. I believed, and flatly told Mr. White, that it was worth my while to wait. Naturally, this worried my parents, neither of whom had any previous experience of postsecondary education. Worse still, Boston College had imposed a deadline for acceptance of its scholarship which fell more than a month before the Harvard letters were to go out. Thus, I felt a good deal of pressure.

What happened next is one more measure of how much simpler the times were then. To his everlasting credit, Mr. White called Harvard Admissions about the dilemma I was facing. Miraculously—or so it now seems—the committee agreed to look at my file right away and to tell Mr. White the results. The next day he called me at home after school and asked, "Are you sitting down?" I promptly sat down and heard him say that Harvard had accepted me, with enough combined aid to allow me not only to go but also to live on campus. Because it was so long until the letters would go out, he said, I shouldn't tell anyone except my parents. This I was somehow able to do. In that memorable phone call, Mr. White also informed me that the admissions committee had been impressed by the variety of my activities and accomplishments: the writing awards, my "interest in physics," my art work from clay models to painting, hockey managing, high grades (I was third in the class, behind two girls) and solid (though not by any means spectacular) SAT scores. In short, I was "well-rounded" and seemed to have potential in both the humanities and the sciences. Mr. White also told me that our high school principal had endorsed me as "the strongest all around candidate" from Norwood in his memory. In the mid-Fifties, the school had sent both a football running back and a hockey defenseman to Harvard. Both had made the varsity and played. But no one could recall the last time a non-athlete had gone there.

My official acceptance letter came on May 12, a Thursday. Throughout the process, my parents had had no advice to offer. They never questioned my plans or motives in this unknown territory. I think they felt out of their depth. In fact, silence here for once was efficacious, blessing my ambition and giving me the confidence to make myself up as I went along. It was, though, at this point that my father conveyed the only indication of how important this step was to him. I was, after all, the first Fanning in memory to attend *any* college, and I was bound for Harvard. Dad had never struck me as superstitious, but on May 13, he refused to allow me to mail my letter accepting admission to Harvard because it was Friday. I thought at first that he was joking, but I soon saw that he was absolutely serious. He wouldn't let me out the door. So, the letter stood propped against the lamp on our kitchen table until Saturday morning, when I took it to the mailbox on the corner—"The Box" of our group-generated *dindshenchas*—and dropped it in, slamming home the blue-metal handle with a satisfying clunk.

The next day the *Boston Sunday Globe* carried a front-page story with the headlines, "MANY ARE CULLED, FEW ARE CHOSEN, Harvard Refuses 3600." More than 5,000 young men had applied, and "exactly 1402 youths were admitted," according to reporter Charles Whipple, himself a graduate of the college. Much quoted in the piece was Wilbur J. Bender, who was about to retire from the position of Dean of Admissions and Financial Aid, which he had held since 1952. What caught my eye right away was the follow-up headline on the second page: "Harvard Is Now Less of a Rich Man's College." Bender went on to describe the steps taken in recent years to identify and support promising students from outside the prep-school networks. Indeed, the reporter asserted, "Dean Bender's main concern has probably been to help the poor boy get to Harvard." Hm. Now I was really hooked. I still had my Sunday paper route, and I stood frozen in my tracks in front of the red wagon in which I hauled the bulky Sunday editions from Walpole Street to Westover. To the reporter's question, "Has Harvard done everything possible in this regard?" Bender had replied, "But if our resources have about tripled, the costs of education have tripled, too, so we are no further ahead than before." Then, highlighted in bold print, came the kicker: "'We haven't really made it easier,' Dean Bender says sadly, 'for the janitor's boy to come to Harvard.'" This was quite a moment. The janitor's boy. That was me. And I *was* coming to Harvard. I felt proud, but with a twinge of apprehension about what I'd gotten myself in for. Surely, there were plenty of janitors' boys on their way to Boston College. Should I have been one of them? Well, the *Globe* story caught the attention of almost everyone I knew. We got several phone calls that Sunday afternoon, and Uncle Frank came up from the family house on Walnut Avenue to chew over the notoriety with us.

In recent years, a spate of books has appeared that demystifies and parses the Ivy League admissions process as it operated in the 1950s and 1960s. In *The Chosen: The Hidden History of Admission and Exclusion at Harvard, Yale, and Princeton* (Boston: Houghton Mifflin, 2005), Jerome Karabel reveals that Wilbur J. Bender left his job in a blaze of bad feeling. A pitched battle had been fought during the year before my acceptance over who should get into Harvard College. A "Special Committee on College Admission Policy" had convened in the spring of 1959. On one side, Dean Bender led the traditionalists, staunchly defending the "docket system" and its stated goal of "balance," which favored legacies, graduates of private boarding schools, and other children of the eastern WASP establishment. Bender referred to these prospects as "gentlemen" and "paying customers." The opposition leader was chemistry professor E. Bright Wilson, who advocated a purely meritocratic selection process. Wilson spoke for a phalanx of scientists with serious post-Sputnik concerns about the fate of the United States as a world power. When the debate in the committee turned acrimonious, Bender gave notice that he would resign the deanship effective July 1, 1960. This gesture allowed him to distance himself from the group's final report and also to express his own opinions separately.

The Ford Report (named for the committee chair, historian Franklin Ford) appeared in February 1960, just as the Admissions office was beginning to sift through the dossiers of my class of 1964, the last to be selected under Dean Bender. As approved by Harvard's Faculty of Arts and Sciences in April, the report equivocated on all the major issues, and Bender's anointed successor, Fred Glimp, kept the process pretty much unchanged throughout the 1960s. One section of the Ford Report strikes me as having been especially relevant to my situation. In response to the fact that the percentage of freshmen from the working class had been declining through the 1950s, the report waffled by warning that "it is easily possible to ask a talented boy to jump further, in terms of educational demands and cultural surroundings, than his background will permit." From my perspective, the phrasing here is worth examining. There is the verb "to jump," with its connotations of trivialized overreaching, along with the warning that Harvard's "educational demands and cultural surroundings" may be too much even for "a talented boy" from the wrong side of the tracks. It looks to me now as though denial of permission has been disguised as solicitude.

The issue in the debate on admissions policy was, of course, the process by which the freshman class was selected during Wilbur Bender's reign from 1952 to 1960—and for many years thereafter, it seems. The Admissions Office placed each candidate within three separate classification systems: the "docket system," which was roughly geographical but also contained a number of shaping assumptions; the "typology," which identified a single outstanding characteristic; and a numerical ranking with four metrics and a summary judgment. In the docket system, each applicant was placed in one of twenty-two roughly geographical groups, each with its own "target" number of admissions slots. These groups and numbers were wildly disproportionate. Docket B, for example, spanned eight Rocky Mountain states, and Docket S included all public school applicants from New Jersey, metropolitan New York City, and metropolitan Philadelphia. On the other hand, the East Coast private schools had four dockets to themselves: one for Exeter and Andover alone, one for "select New England private schools," one for other (presumably less select) New England private schools, and one for private schools in the Middle Atlantic states. In addition, the target numbers and percentage of actual admits were significantly larger in these private school dockets than in any others.

The typology consisted of twelve categories meant to describe a candidate's most important characteristic, as determined by the admissions staff. These were fascinating and tricky. For true misfits, there was category O, for "Other." Everyone else had to go in only one of the eleven remaining choices which were also obviously slanted in a number of ways that today look pretty controversial as regards talent, money, and status. (And yet, Karabel finds that "this typology was still in place at least through 1988.") Only two categories registered outstanding intellect: "first-rate scholar in Harvard departmental terms," and those just below that. There was one category for "creativity in music, art, writing." Two were primarily athletic: "All-American—healthy, uncomplicated athletic strengths and style," and "Krunch—prospective varsity athlete." Three looked to be character-driven: "Mr. School—significant extracurricular plus excellent academic record," "Cross-country style—steady man who plugs and plugs and plugs," and "PBH style," which meant congenial to the liberal mind-set of students associated with Phillips Brooks House, the campus center for outreach to the greater Cambridge and Boston communities of less privileged folks. (This one really annoys me, because I did in fact join up at Phillips Brooks House, where I tutored Cambridge junior high kids in math.) Finally, three categories were driven baldly by matters of class: "Lineage—candidate probably couldn't be admitted without the extra plus of being a Harvard son, a faculty son, or a local boy with ties to the university community"; "Boondocker—unsophisticated rural background" (I am not making this up); and "Taconic—culturally depressed background, low income." (This last took its name from a private foundation that supported efforts to attract poor students to Harvard.)

The third system called for a numerical ranking in each of four areas: Academic, Extracurricular, Athletic, and Personal. This was followed by an overall placement ranging from 1 (Clear Admit) to 9 (Clear Reject). In addition to its use by the admissions staff, this last set of judgments was also solicited from high school principals and teachers and from alumni interviewers. Karabel notes tellingly that "Academic" was but one of the four categories, "Extracurricular" and "Athletic" each got their own, as did

"Personal," a hugely subjective term. Thus, there was plenty of built-in bias against overemphasis on intellectual merit. In fact, a version of this numerical scale is still in place. The only difference is that there are only three categories, with "Extracurricular/Athletic" bunched together—I would guess to avoid the heavy-handed focus on athletic prowess alone. Also, there are only five "Overall" ratings, running from "Absolutely superior for admission; truly unusual in the entire applicant pool" to "Not recommended." Having looked at all this, I agree with Karabel's conclusion that "the design of this system was a fateful matter, for systems of classification are also systems of power, favoring some groups while disadvantaging others," and that Harvard's system guaranteed "the set of outcomes that Harvard wished to see." Chief among these, in Karabel's judgment, was the "decisive defeat" of the "ideology of academic meritocracy."

Actually seeing Karabel's presentation of the facts and figures on freshmen admitted to Harvard during Wilbur Bender's reign as dean, I'm amazed that I got in. First of all, while applications were increasing dramatically, places in the freshman class remained steady at 1,400 acceptances for a projected 1,200 who would come. In 1952 a whopping 70 percent of the applicants had been admitted. In 1960, my class of freshmen, that number was under 37 percent. In the same period, the combined median SAT score of admits went from 1181 to 1377. (My score was just about at that median, and my verbal SAT actually decreased between junior and senior year.) Between 1952 and 1960, the median family income of freshmen went up from $4,900 to $5,300, and that of scholarship awardees increased from $4,900 to $7,800. Further, and even more skewed against my candidacy, the percentage of legacies in the freshman class went up from 17 in Bender's first year to 20 in his last, and that of accepted students whose fathers had not attended college went down—from 37 percent in 1952 to 18 percent in 1960. (There seems to have been no record kept for students whose fathers hadn't attended high school, but there couldn't have been many.)

My educated guessing about where I stood in the spring of 1960 within the established categories is also far from reassuring. First, I had to have been in Docket Q, which contained all the public schools in metropolitan Boston—with the exception of the Boston Latin School (the mostly merit-driven magnet school for the city itself), which had its own docket. My docket had relatively few projected admissions slots as compared with the private school big guns. Second, I was an excellent student at Norwood High, but my SATs were not outstanding, so I hardly qualified for either of the two academic dockets. I might have been a borderline "Mr. School," with "significant extracurricular" activities "plus excellent academic record." But, because only one docket placement was possible my money is on "Taconic." That is, "culturally depressed background, low income." My parents hadn't been to college, and my father's two jobs of janitor and waiter were quite poorly paid. Even here, though, my street credentials were suspect. I lived in a town, not a city, and I wasn't part of an ethnic or racial underclass. Somehow, though, I did get in.

There's no mystery about how I paid for Harvard, because I still have just about every record relating to the economy of my four years in Cambridge. (Like my father, I live by the dictum "Throw nothing away.") The record is as sparse and simple as that in my grandfather's checkbooks from the 1920s. I opened my first bank account on July 5, 1960, with a deposit of $30 from my first summer job. The one bank book from Union Savings Bank of Boston, Norwood Branch, took me all the way through college. I closed it out on August 19, 1964, with a last withdrawal of $210, just before heading out west to California for graduate school.

The same pattern held for all four years. Week by week, from late June to early September, I deposited $30 or $40 dollars in the account. After school began, I transferred the total of my summer savings into my checking account at the Cambridge Trust Company in Harvard Square. The numbers are as follows: in 1960, $347; in 1961, $483; in 1962, $352; in 1963, $331. Each year, this money was supplemented by a local scholarship from the Alice H. Plimpton Educational Trust, which supported Norwood High grads with funds from the family that owned Plimpton Press. They gave me $300 in each of my first two years and $500 in each of years three and four. In the cheery letters that accompanied the checks, I also got advice from the trust's executive secretary, Ruth M. Gow, who was a junior high teacher and a friend of my father. In one letter, Miss Gow counseled, "There is just one thing you must watch while you are in debt—and that is don't get married. Just make up your mind to that and you need not worry over any amount you borrow. But the responsibilities of a family is the only factor that may wreck financial plans. So forget your financial worries and make every minute count at this point in your education." This was an easy admonition with which to comply. At the time, I was nineteen and didn't even have a girlfriend.

Harvard had given me a scholarship from the Hall-Mercer Fund that essentially paid my tuition, which was—believe it or not—$1,250 freshman year. By senior year, it had gone up to $1,520. The total for room and board was $1,100, and my resources didn't cover even that much. On the scholarship forms for each of the four years, I put down an estimate of $50 for my family's contribution to my college expenses. The worksheets I've somehow kept reveal the reasons for this. The year before I entered Harvard, my father earned $5,100 a year at his two jobs. Our "annual home expenses" (mortgage, real estate taxes, utilities, routine repairs) totaled $1,500. There were five of us, including my brother in junior high and sister in third grade. The family's main liability was an unpaid mortgage of $5,000 on a house valued at $12,500. Our other assets were an automobile (1951 Plymouth), my father's Straight Life insurance policy (paying $4,000 upon his death), and $100 in the bank. True to the promise of Harvard's brochures, I was able to make up the difference on my term bills with in-house loans and jobs. In the four undergraduate years, I borrowed $400, $400, $600, and $700 from the university. My jobs at Harvard included washing dishes and slinging mashed potatoes behind steam tables, cleaning rooms as a member of the dorm crew, and working in press-box food service at football games. I was paid $1.25 per hour for a ten-hour week, for a total of about $375 for the academic year.

With senior year as a template, here's how I lived. As tuition was covered by my scholarship, I had to come up with $1,100 for room and board plus whatever else it took to be a college student in Cambridge and Boston between 1960 and 1964. My assets for 1963-64 were as follows: summer savings from my job as a meter reader for the electric company ($331), Plimpton grant ($500), Harvard loan ($700), Harvard jobs ($375). The total was $1,906. After paying room and board, I had $806 for everything else from mid-September to graduation on June 11: buying course books, clothes, and food and drink beyond the three meals in the dorm; getting laundry done, riding the MTA; attending movies, concerts, Red Sox games. For each of those thirty-nine weeks, I had roughly $20 to spend. What was it like to live on this budget? I am here to report that, as in my time growing up in Norwood and in large part because of that experience, I never felt deprived in any significant way. What I felt was lucky to have gotten a priceless opportunity. I now had access to *three* new, overlapping worlds: a city, a university, and—unexpected, but no less important—the complex administrative organization of Harvard athletics.

Composition of Place: Cambridge, September 1960

My first and most immediate new world was Cambridge. I doubt that any Harvard freshman in 1960 was less traveled. My whole life had been spent within a thirty-mile radius of Norwood. I had been to Boston a fair number of times: on the train with my father during his summer vacation week, with Mr. Lambert on our sixth-grade field trips, to Fenway Park and Nantasket Beach on the playground bus, weekly during my year of classes at the Museum of Fine Arts, and to the Boston Arena with the Norwood High hockey team. I had also gone ice-skating at Rocky Woods in Medfield, a state park with a tiny lodge and two skating ponds. The farthest afield I had been was a single trip to Cape Cod. I was invited to spend a week in Pocasset with Dan Callahan and his family, somewhere around fifth or sixth grade. In our high school junior year, my friends started to get their drivers' licenses, and from then on we cruised the back roads of the towns around Norwood. Route 109 in still-rural Westwood was a favorite drive, from the gloomy, pine-shaded Westwood Lodge, a "rest home" (which, we heard, housed the likes of Judy Garland on occasion), to the Bubbling Brook, a cottage with a small stream and a goat behind it, where we got orange freezes and coffee frappes. On occasion, we ventured as far as North Attleboro—almost to Rhode Island. We did pop over the line once or twice but never stayed long. Mostly, we rode up and down Route 1 between the Howard Johnson's restaurants in Dedham and Walpole, stopping briefly at each, before settling at Art Johnson's food stand (no relation to Howard), Norwood High's preferred hangout and the dispenser of great fried clams.

We had graduated from high school on a clear, cool evening, June 7, 1960, at 6:00 PM, with risers and folding chairs set out on the grass in front of the high school. We processed to the strains of "Pomp and Circumstances." The seniors sang "The Halls of Ivy" and "Moments to Remember." Our president, Ronnie Hardy, presented the class gift to the school. The main speaker, "prominent Boston attorney" Henry M. Leen, holder of "three degrees from Boston College" (he looked pretty well off—had I made the wrong choice?), told us to "cling to your faith, your ideals, and the moral truths impressed upon you in the home, the churches, and the classrooms." Furthermore, "Give of yourselves. And above all, cherish and preserve the moral and spiritual values that have made America great." We received medals and prizes from Superintendent Lincoln D. Lynch, and diplomas from Principal Charles A. Hayden. We sang the school song ("There's a school on the hill called Norwood, and her sons and daughters too") and "The Star Spangled Banner." We recessed. And we were launched. Everything went as it had always gone. There was not, as far as I can recall, a single shred of irony in the event from start to finish.

One indication of the new experience that lay just ahead for me on the other side of summer occurred on a Friday evening in June, when we piled into the Callahans' car and drove straight into the city to the Boston Arts Festival at the Public Garden. Japanese lanterns strung along the walkways reflected in shimmering waves off the surface of the lagoon, around which the swan boats glided in a rare nighttime outing. Scattered tents, open to the breeze, held paintings, sculptures, prints, architectural models. The papers had been full of complaints that there was too much nonrepresentational art in the show. I hadn't seen much of this before, and my eyes were opened—my ears too, as the sounds of the New York City Opera Company singing *The Taming of the Shrew* filled the air. The place was magical. And I was about to go to college right next door in Cambridge.

My friends and I got our first day-long jobs that summer, and at the same place: six of us found ourselves "working for Abe," Abraham Shagoury, a successful Norwood contractor, putting in lawns around the just completed houses that lined brand-new streets named for his daughters. Dark and muscular, invariably dressed in a spotless white T-shirt, Abe was a man of few words, all of them deep-voiced, gruff, and salted with profanity. He had a few cryptic epigrams, of which I only remember one: "A dollar a day. Tomorrow, two days, two dollars." Abe had a gift for the element of surprise when arriving at the job site. He would cruise up to within a foot of our straining rumps in his nearly silent late model Chevrolet, and scare the living daylights out of the whole crew with a tap on his horn. It was fairly hard work when the sun was out, which was most of the time. We spread out the piles of loam, then raked out the rocks, scattered grass seed, and watered it in. Our foreman was Pat O'Donnell, a small, wiry, tightly strung Irishman who worked tirelessly all the livelong day, which went from 8:00 AM to 4:30 PM, with two fifteen-minute breaks and a half-hour for lunch. Every day Pat finished his lunch in ten minutes, tops, and he expected us to be close behind. He looked on us "college boys" with undisguised bemusement that shaded on occasion toward contempt, but he was a pretty good egg overall.

A much recounted highlight of the summer was the time Pat asked me to get "a bag of seed" from the bed of the truck. I thought he had said "a bag of C," short for cement, and so I toted a fifty-pound bag to the side of the front yard we were working on. Pat was speechless with incredulity, but he recovered quickly enough to ask, "What the hell am I supposed to do with this, Charlie? Make a cement lawn and paint it green?" We all started at the Massachusetts minimum wage of $1.25 an hour, which was boosted by a dime after two weeks for the workers who caught on the fastest. This was a step I never made, but really it made no difference. The job provided endless fodder for evening discussions while we drank beer in somebody's car. The shared suffering brought us closer together.

We spent many evenings all summer long at the Blue Hills Drive In over on Route 138 in Canton, where the price was definitely right at "$1.10 per carload." There I saw such classics of the jejune as the teen-flick *Because They're Young* (starring Dick Clark and Tuesday Weld), the cautionary tale *I Passed for White,* and the movie version of James T. Farrell's *Studs Lonigan* (with a very young Jack Nicholson as Studs's adversary, Weary Reilly). The most fun was the drive-in reprise of Alfred Hitchcock's classic *Psycho.* We'd all seen it in the theater earlier in the summer, but revisiting the Bates Motel outside in the dark was not to be missed. At the Blue Hills I also saw Sean Connery's first star turn in Walt Disney's *Darby O'Gill and the Little People,* a piece of classic green-tinted schlock replete with bibulous, gullible peasants and clever fairy folk, a leprechaun king, and the banshee's wail. Still, I knew and cared far too little about my own or anyone else's ethnicity to be offended by the cartoonish stereotyping in Walt's rendering of Ireland and the Irish.

At Christmas vacation time during my Harvard years, some of my friends and acquaintances talked about going skiing at Stowe, Mad River Glen, even Switzerland. I, on the other hand, would be looking for a New Year's Eve date to take with my friends to the Hi Hat in Allston, a "Bar/Lounge" at Harvard Street and Commonwealth Avenue that we had picked out for its quintessential sleaziness. The greats of jazz had played there in the Forties, but we knew nothing of that. Now, there was a ragged trio of old timers pumping out the standards to a clientele of bedraggled hard-luck types, many of them alone on December 31. At midnight, there were some tears from the locals, a free plastic glass of cheap champagne, and "Auld Lang Syne." We were young and dumb, of course, and found the spectacle entertaining, though not, I think, in a mean way. At least, we never laughed at people openly. We also spent the occasional vacation evening in the "Combat Zone," the network of bars, strip joints, and peep shows that littered Tremont Street and environs between Boston Common and Chinatown. Here our favorite performer was Roger Pace, a hopped-up oddball who billed himself as "the White James Brown" and came with his own "Cape Man," a grizzled character who shuffled on stage to wrap the exhausted star in a red cape at the end of his grueling version of "Please, Please, Don't Go." (Roger had borrowed this bit of showmanship from the black James Brown.) We were a long way from Gstaad, but I couldn't ski anyway.

Figure 30. Harvard Square looking north, April 1964. Lenscraft Photos Collection, Cambridge Historical Commission. Courtesy of the Cambridge Historical Commission.

My first trip to Cambridge had been for my Harvard interview the previous fall; my second, for the state Science Fair at MIT in the spring. During the summer my friends and I had circled Harvard Square tentatively two or three times, getting the lay of the land but without getting out of the car. Thus, it was quite a big deal when I drove to Cambridge with my parents on a Sunday afternoon in mid-September of 1960 to move in. The trip would become second nature: from Norwood via Washington Street through Dedham (my grandfather Fanning's hometown) to the twisty, tree-lined Jamaica Way, past Jamaica Pond and James Michael Curley's mansion, then left at Longwood Towers, through the back streets of Boston University, over the bridge onto Memorial Drive, then left along my river, the Charles, past the boathouses, and right onto Boylston Street and up to the center of the Square. It took only thirty minutes, door to door, to reach my brave new world.

Directed by a cardboard sign, Dad drove the old gray Plymouth straight on through the gates into Harvard Yard. I picked up my first ever room and mailbox keys, and we proceeded left, pulling up in front of Stoughton Hall—my freshman dorm. It was a red brick building—what else?—small but freighted with history. The original structure had been paid for in 1700 by Lieutenant Governor William Stoughton, who had presided over the Salem witch trials. Damaged during the Revolutionary War, it was torn down in 1780 and replaced in 1805 by a new building, designed by Charles Bulfinch. I set up shop in Stoughton 4 on the ground floor of the south entry, in a room with two big windows overlooking the College Pump, an ancient contraption emblazoned with the motto "Your wooden arm you hold outstretched to shake with passers-by." I opened the door to walls of blond wood and exposed brick, and an expanse of linoleum-covered floor on which stood two beds, desks, bureaus, and bookcases. I had a name and hometown for my roommate—Ed Boedeker and St. Louis, Missouri. His clothes, typewriter, and dictionary were there, but he wasn't, so my family and I had the place to ourselves to unpack. This took half an hour. I then walked them out to the car, hugged my mother and shook my father's hand, and in a flash I was waving them off and stepping back inside the open door. I felt a predictable mix of loneliness, apprehension at the challenges ahead, and a welling-up of pure excitement at the newness and unpredictability of what was about to happen. I had made it. I was a student at Harvard.

Our entry was full of interesting kids. Four of us stayed together to share rooms as upperclassmen at Winthrop House: my roommate Ed, who persisted as an English major even after deciding to go pre-med, and who was the son of a prominent St. Louis attorney; Jere Johnston, one of the nicest people I've ever known, the son of a career naval officer from Rowley, near Newburyport, Massachusetts; and Larry Gillis, an Andover grad whose father was the police chief in the shady city of Revere, just north of Boston. Others I remember from that first dorm include Jerry Lander and Art Hessel, two more St. Louisans, one serious, the other funny, headed for medicine and the law; Rich Hazeltine from New Jersey, a legitimate math and physics star and the son of the inventor of an indispensable radio transistor; Steve Carnovsky, a witty Manhattanite whose father was the noted Shakespearian actor Morris Carnovsky; Norm Leavitt and Dave Seidman, old friends from Bronx High School of Science; and Stan Abrams from Providence, a good-natured scratch golfer with a perpetual tan. It looks as though we were overloaded with Easterners, but it was still a good start on a wide and diverse acquaintance that would expand in the following years.

So, Cambridge. In the fall of 1960, Harvard Square was a real city neighborhood, a dynamic, shifting combination of urban grit and Ivy League panache, of the seedy and the tweedy. I loved it all. This heady mix is long gone, for the old townie places were relentlessly driven out by high rents, slick entrepreneurs, and upscale national chains, rootless and ruthless. But when I arrived, there were varied, engaging, indigenous spots around every cobbled corner. The most salient marvel was the Harvard Cooperative Society—the Coop—where I got a plastic card with my name on it, assuring me an end-of-year rebate on all purchases made there. Well before the age of the credit card, this was quite a big deal, as was the 10 percent discount to Coop members who paid cash. A virtual general store, the Coop sold books, clothes, Harvard-labeled paraphernalia, paper and pens, typewriters, furniture, lamps. You name it. Across from the Coop, dead center in the Square, stood Out of Town News, a low, iron-roofed kiosk that carried magazines and newspapers from all over the world. And right underneath it was the Harvard Square Station of the MTA. On the way downstairs, a big sign announced "Eight minutes to Park Street." Boston and the wider world were accessible as never before. I could go there on a whim.

The Square had two theaters, the University for first-run movies (on a single screen), and the creaky, comfortable old Brattle Theater for "art films." Ingmar Bergman's *The Seventh Seal* was showing the week I started school. There were also a Woolworth's, two pharmacies, two ice cream parlors (Bailey's and Brigham's), and Varsity Liquors, which almost never checked IDs. (The drinking age was twenty-one, which a good chunk of the clientele had not yet achieved.) Crucial to the life of the place were the four all-night cafeterias—Hayes-Bickford, the Waldorf, Albiani's, and Hazen's—each with its loyal cadre of nighthawks. There were several well-worn bars where town and gown mingled, stool by stool, mostly without incident. The Wursthaus served decent German food and cheap draft beer. Whitney's was a hole-in-the-wall where the equipment men from Harvard athletics hung out after work. Jim Cronin's, down on Mt. Auburn Street, past the MTA carbarns, was a big place criss-crossed with chummy wooden booths, serving cheap food and draft beers for a quarter. (The poet John Ashbery, an undergrad in the 1940s, recalls "late night beers at Cronin's, Cambridge's answer to *La Coupole*.") There were several places to get your hair cut, from the vast Harvard Barber Shop on Mass Ave—"Nine Chairs, No Waiting"—to the small shop tucked in the basement underneath Elsie's ("Home of the Roast Beef Special"), which had been frequented, it was said, by the Kennedy boys.

I realize now that I was comfortable right away in Harvard Square because it was so much like downtown Norwood—though with an urban edge. The streets were filled with stores and spas run by people whose names were on the signs out front: Libby's Market, Kahaly Brothers

Grocery, Frank Cardullo's International Foods, Tommy's Arcade Lunch, Bob Slate Stationer, Dickson Brothers Hardware, Olsen's Cards and Gifts, James F. Brine's Sporting Goods, Shea's Dry Cleaners and Launderers ("15 cents per pound, everything folded"), Felix's Newsstand (which also repaired shoes and blocked hats), Briggs and Briggs Music. Entering Leavitt and Pierce Tobacconists was like stepping into the nineteenth century Ivy League: old team photographs and oars hanging on the walls, oak cabinets, a vast array of pipes and chess sets, the heady smell of tobacco everywhere. Also there for private-schoolers and preppie wannabees were the Tennis and Squash Shop and the two "exclusive" clothing stores, J. Press and J. August. These were not, of course, part of my scene, but I did pick up the uniform—we still had to wear jackets and ties to every meal—of chino pants, blue Oxford button-down shirts, and striped ties. I went into J. August once, looking for a tie, but the prices drove me right back to Murray's Outlet in Norwood, where chinos could be had for $2.59 and "Men's Sport Coats" for under twenty bucks.

The wondrous cornucopia of bookstores spilling out all around the Square established for me a lifelong enthusiasm. There were so many that I can't remember them all. At least four—the Coop, Barnes and Noble, Phillips, and the Harvard Bookstore—carried course books and general-interest books-in-print. The cosmopolitan Schoenhof's, where the clerks spoke several languages, was the place for foreign books from everywhere. For my French courses, I bought there—for $2.50 each—the marvelous Classiques Garnier editions of Flaubert, Baudelaire, and Stendhal. These were not simply paperbacks, but real books, bound beautifully to last on heavy paper in copious signatures laced together with white thread, and covered in stiff papers of a dazzling, high-gloss yellow.

My first experience of used and antiquarian (a new word) bookstores was in Cambridge as well. On the side streets off Mass Ave, transient, dusty stores came and went, full of castaway book-club hard covers and ratty paperbacks, poorly organized and crammed into sagging pine shelves. There were also spic-and-span shops that looked as established as Harvard itself, with books beautiful and rare, ranged meticulously on dark wood shelves and in locked, glass-front cases: first editions, signed editions, incunabula (another new word). Two that come to mind are the Pangloss Bookshop and Mandrake Books, each a small museum, curated by a gruff, gray-haired proprietor who suffered no fools but would deign to answer intelligent questions, though with little grace. Because learning to read lyric poetry in my freshman literature course had been a revelation, my favorite of these was the Grolier Poetry Book Shop. Up a short, steep staircase on Plympton Street the tiny, cluttered Grolier was a legendary kingdom of verse, where one could rub elbows with the poets themselves. I didn't know who they were, but I knew they were poets, all right, flopped on the lumpy old couch and armchair or turning over the piles of books on the big central table. The ruler of the place was Gordon Cairnie, a tall, stooped old man, austere and preoccupied, who had founded the store in 1927. He seemed much more interested in his cat than in barging, clumsy students, but the door stood open, and the Grolier was an affordable gold mine, as new paperback poetry collections sold for a dollar or two.

Grafted onto the flat end of the wedge-shaped Lampoon building was the Starr Bookstore, where the wares ran the gamut from old Penguin paperbacks to borderline rare books. There I made my first roughly antiquarian purchase—a set of J. M. Dent and Company's *Temple Shakespeare*, published in London at the turn of the twentieth century. This was a forty-volume edition in pocket format of all the plays and poems. Each book was three by four inches, which appealed to my love of miniatures. I thought long and hard about what was a major economic decision—I think the set cost $25—but I've had these books ever since, and they remain fresh to the eye and hand. Their covers are thin but substantial board of a deep maroon, embossed with the Dent coat of arms. The paper is thick and watermarked with rows of fine lines. The still perfectly legible text is in two colors, crisp black with bright red highlights, and each volume features a frontispiece illustration protected by a sheet of onion skin on which is printed a poem about Shakespeare by another writer. And there's a thin linen bookmark set into the sturdily sewn binding. A useful preface, glossary, and set of notes completes each book. These small gems testify to Dent as a pioneer in providing well-made books for people without much money.

Cambridge also gave permanent shape to my taste in music. Here there was a flurry of early signals followed by one confirming event. My interest in folk music had begun in high school with exposure to the commercially successful recordings of Harry Belafonte and the Kingston Trio. I had followed up by tuning in to the heavy folk representation on Harvard's student radio station, WHRB, which ran several weekly folk music "hours" and a famous "Folk Music Orgy" twice a year during exam period. Then there was Peter Warshall, one of my entry-mates in Stoughton, a savvy Brooklyn native and graduate of Stuyvesant High who actually *knew* many of the Greenwich Village lefty singers and songwriters, including Ramblin' Jack Elliott, Fred Neil, Pete Seeger, and the Weavers. He even mentioned

Woody Guthrie. (I think his parents were a part of that scene.) It was Peter who pointed me down the street and around the corner to the Club 47, that early, iconic site of the Folk Revival. The place was at 47 Mt. Auburn Street, next door to Kahaly's Grocery, which looked and smelled enough like Farioli's in Norwood to make me feel at home there. The Kahaly brothers even smoked cigars, as had old Mr. Farioli. Anyway, it was three steps down off street level to get into the club, and the wooden stage, painted black to disguise its makeshift nature, was shoved right up against the big plate-glass windows. Anyone walking by could see the backside of the Cambridge folk revival just getting off the ground.

There I saw and heard, from both inside and out, a host of great and lively musicians: fellow Harvard students Tom Rush and Ted Alevizos; Jim Kweskin and his Jug Band, with Fritz Richmond on the washtub base and Geoff Muldaur and Maria D'Amato on vocals; the blues duo of Sonny Terry and Brownie McGhee, who played and sang harmoniously together but never spoke offstage because, it was said, they detested each other; and the Cambridge folk scene's major domo, Eric Von Schmidt, famously referenced by Dylan on his first album (*Bob Dylan,* 1962) as having introduced Bob to "the green pastures of Harvard University." I picked up on Dylan right away as well—along with everyone else—and his album releases were big events throughout my college years and beyond. Most memorable to me, though, was Joan Baez, nineteen years old in the fall of 1960, tall and thin with long black hair, laughing brown eyes, and that amazingly pure and piercing voice. She was virtually my age, for crying out loud, and yet what a presence! My initial record purchase in Cambridge—at the capacious, stuffed Briggs and Briggs, which, like Irving's Record Shop in Norwood, had a listening booth—was Joan's first solo album, from Vanguard, which came out in November. I listened over and over to those Child ballads and Appalachian folk tunes, and they are with me still: "Mary Hamilton," "Silver Dagger," "East Virginia," "All My Trials." And there she was, in person, on any old Sunday evening, just a five-minute walk from my freshman dorm.

The musical capstone event of freshman year for me was a spring concert by Pete Seeger. I had mentioned to Peter Warshall that I loved Seeger's banjo riffs with the Weavers, and I wondered if more of that kind of thing was out there. He recommended a little-known album, *The Goofing-Off Suite,* a ten-inch 33 ⅓ record that Pete had made for Moses Asch at Folkways in 1955. Sure enough, Briggs and Briggs had it. Mostly instrumental—banjo, mandolin, chalil, and guitar—with a few lyrics and a lot of humming and whistling, this became my favorite record. Emblematic of Pete's unpretentious, high-energy, eclectic, and thoroughly democratic musical faith, the *Suite* rang a whole carillon of bells for me. Songs of the Depression ("Time's a Getting Hard," "Barrel of Money Blues") reminded me of my father. Irving Berlin's "Blue Skies" was a song my mother had sung along with on the radio. "The Girl I Left Behind Me" was an Irish folktune. I knew the familiar classical melodies that Pete had arranged for banjo: Bach's "Jesu, Joy of Man's Desiring," a theme from Beethoven's *Seventh Symphony*, the "Ode to Joy" from his *Ninth*. There was even a piece—"Anitra's Dance"—from my old standby, Grieg's *Peer Gynt*.

In early April of 1961, Harvard's Student Council invited Pete Seeger to Sanders Theater, the lovely wooden performance space at one end of Memorial Hall. The context for the invitation was the conclusion of Pete's trial for contempt of Congress for refusing to answer questions in 1957 before the House Un-American Activities Committee. The long-delayed trial had taken place in March 1961. Pete was found guilty and, on April 4, sentenced to a year in jail. The trial had made him a visible and much admired figure among American liberals who had deplored the actions of the HUAC in the Fifties. Also, he was a member of the Harvard Class of 1940—hence the invitation. But then came trouble. Harvard President Nathan Pusey refused to allow the concert to go forward, declaring, through Dean of the College Robert Watson, that "lawyers advise against the University getting involved in cases still pending in court." (Pete's conviction was under appeal. In fact, it was overturned a year later.) This caused a furor about free speech that spread so fast and far that Pusey relented two days later. In a lame attempt to save face, the president said that the concert could go on because the Student Council had assured him that it would be "a purely musical event."

When it came, the concert on May 18, 1961, was thrilling. Pete strode onto the stage with his banjo to a five-minute standing ovation. Proclaiming that "You are my jury!" he sang a song about voting rights in Tennessee, and one about a girl killed in the Polish resistance in World War II. He sang the Weavers' favorites, "The Union Maid" and "Banks of Marble" ("I have seen the weary miner scrubbing coal dust from his back. / I have heard his children crying, 'got no coal to heat our shack'"). He sang three songs that the HUAC had criticized specifically: "Midnight Special," "The Hammer Song," and "Wasn't That a Time," introducing them by declaring that "I'll stand or fall by these songs. And I've got a right to sing them for every kind of group." The evening ended with three thunderous encores. In an interview in the *Harvard Crimson* after the concert, Pete laughed at President Pusey's rationale: "It's hard to sing American folk songs without touching on politics. In the broadest sense, all folk songs are political. You know," he continued, "even love songs can be propaganda. Take a song like 'Careless Love,' which is about unrequited love. That's propaganda for unrequition." After all this, I was committed to folk music for the long haul.

Still, the Sixties were not yet "The Sixties." Though the folk revival was in place, the Beatles and the Rolling Stones were just getting started over in England. Signs of the coming cultural upheavals were minimal when I started at Harvard. Timothy Leary and Richard Alpert had appointments in the Psychology Department, but their experiments with mescaline, psilocybin, and LSD were still at the rumor stage my freshman year. (Leary and Alpert would be fired in spring 1963 for unauthorized involvement of students as subjects.) By senior year, only one of my friends had even talked about smoking pot. Similarly, campus rioting was still relegated to a rite of spring. In April of freshman year, the issue that brought undergrads into the Square two nights running was the abrupt switch of the language on Harvard diplomas from Latin to English. Adding fuel to that fire was the announcement that Radcliffe diplomas would remain in Latin for the time being. Students threw eggs, police threw a few tear-gas canisters, four undergrads were arrested, and the crowd marched to the president's house chanting, "Latin, Si! Pusey, No!" A "gang of forty" from Kirkland House threatened to retaliate by wearing Madras jackets to commencement. ("Hold on a minute," I thought. "I have a Madras jacket.")

The Life of the Mind

In midsummer before freshman year, I had a healthy omen of intellectual things to come in the form of a letter informing me that I'd been accepted into a "Freshman Seminar." Then a recent innovation meant to break down the barrier between senior faculty and undergraduates, these very small classes, the brochure had warned, were extremely competitive. You had to apply in the summer with an essay targeted toward a particular course, and I was accepted into Professor Kenneth Schuyler Lynn's American literature seminar on Hawthorne and Melville. Lynn's was a fairly famous name. A full professor, he taught the spring term of English 70, the American literature survey, and had published several books on nineteenth-century literature. He also could have posed for pictures of the model Harvard professor.

A handsome man in his early forties, with wavy blondish hair and blue eyes, Lynn wore tweed jackets with elbow patches, crisp white shirts, tastefully muted ties, and creased trousers. (They all dressed like this, except for the European intellectuals, who tended toward a distracted, mild dishevelment.) Lynn even smoked a pipe.

At the first seminar meeting, I was further heartened to discover that there were only four of us. Seated at a small round table in Lynn's office, we were a cross section of Harvard freshmen in the fall of 1960. I was the one working-class kid from an ordinary public high school. Franz Jevne was the product of upscale public schooling in the affluent Minneapolis suburb of Edina. He and I became friends—at first because we were the least articulate seminar members. He was also a hockey player, which further connected us. David Rounds was a Connecticut preppie from Hotchkiss School, very smart, well-prepared, and enthusiastic about literature. He went on to graduate *summa cum laude*. Gail Thain, a Radcliffe student, was from Evanston Township High in the upper-middle-class bastion of Evanston, Illinois, just north of Chicago. Now Radcliffe in those days was still a distinct entity, with its own fiercely competitive admissions process. Because there were 1,200 of us in the freshman class but only 250 Cliffies, many Harvard students were convinced—for the most part rightly—that they were a lot smarter than we, their male counterparts. Gail was indeed brilliant. She went on to become Bennington College's youngest president at age thirty. Still and all, after a slow start I held my own in discussions, and Lynn wrote that I'd done the best of the four of us on the final essay. In retrospect, this was probably because the seminars were ungraded. We simply got "credit" at the end, and it's likely that David and Gail, who were much less naive than I was about college, had put less energy into the assignment.

My other courses that first fall were pretty ordinary. The freshman writing course was General Education Ahf. I've long forgotten what those letters stood for, but—I admit this is looking a little scary—I still have my essays. My first effort got a grade of C with the comment, "Your paper is well written, but ill-conceived." This became the pattern all through a string of Cs in the fall semester—almost every paper was "well written," but the problem was content: my choice of subjects was unfortunate; I didn't develop themes well; the result was often superficial. This was predictable. Though I wrote competently, I didn't have a lot to say—in part because I hadn't had much experience in the world, and also because my high school teachers had not demanded much in the way of specifics. Expounding on "The Value of Art in Modern Civilization" was fine for the Norwood

Chamber of Commerce, but it wasn't going to get me far at Harvard. I did work my way from Cs to Bs and ended up with a straight B for the course, which was about as much as I could have expected.

Math 1A, the introduction to calculus, provided the swan song for my projection into a career in physics, about which I had never been enthusiastic. The course was taught entirely in small sections, and mine was led by Mr. Parikh, an Indian grad student whose accent made it harder to grasp the already slippery fundamentals of differentiation and the analytic geometry of the straight line. Though I haunted his office hours, where I still understood only every third sentence, I managed only a C-plus at the end of the day. And that was the ball game for the hard sciences. I had already anticipated this outcome by also taking Natural Sciences 3, a historical gallop through astronomy, chemistry, and physics from Heraclitus to Einstein. The course did count as a general education science requirement, even though—and this was crucial—there was no lab. Everyone in there was oriented toward the humanities or social sciences, and we all saw the course as a life preserver. From that skeptical perch, we viewed the professors, perhaps unfairly, as both crushing bores and figures of fun. Noted historian of science I. Bernard Cohen was, in fact, something of a blowhard. Portly, mustached, given to three-piece suits and bowties, he had a complacent strutting demeanor and a rounded, mellifluous, soporific voice. His much younger acolyte, Owen Gingerich, provided most of the humor. A mousy, tentative man, he could be counted on to screw up the hands-on stuff during lecture. The standing joke was that every experiment illustrated Heisenberg's uncertainty principle. No matter. I did very little work, came out with an A-minus, and said goodbye to science.

During the summer before college, I had come upon a newly published book that reinforced my high school view of poetry as in large part a waste of time. *The Powers of Poetry* by Gilbert Highet contained "appreciations" of poets, biographically based, breezy, and shallow, along with unexciting essays on melody, rhythm, and "Obscurity in Poetry." In the climactic piece "What Use Is Poetry?" Highet comes up with four flat justifications: it's musical, it can be "better than prose for telling a story," it's mnemonic, and it's an "aid to life." Ho-hum, I thought. Even at seventeen, I recognized Highet's essays as vacuous fulminations, despite the Oxford University Press imprimatur of his book. But then came a revolutionary turn in my thinking. I enrolled in Humanities 6, an introduction to literature that came highly recommended to prospective English majors. Professors Reuben Brower and Richard Poirier ran this course—strictly by the tenets of the "New Criticism," which dictated that a work of literature ought first to be examined as a self-contained art object. There was no claim that this was the only viable way to approach a piece of writing, but it was clearly the place to begin. I can see now that this technique appealed to me for two reasons. First, as I was coming from a background less sophisticated than some other students were, examining literature on its own, devoid of contexts that weren't yet available to me, created a more level playing field. Second, exegesis appealed to my love of maps and miniatures. In close reading, a poem or paragraph became a focused field of thought and feeling. And so, using the tools of new criticism turned me into a lover of poetry. In spite of Mr. Dunn's warning, I started to think about a career that involved the heart, not the head. Maybe I'd become an English teacher.

The Hum 6 lectures were beautifully wrought. Poems opened up like blooming flowers: Yeats's Byzantium poems and "Lapis Lazuli," Keats's Odes, the wonders of the sonnet form as practiced by Shakespeare, Wordsworth, Hopkins, Ransom. Both Brower and Poirier were working on books about Robert Frost, and his poems figured heavily in the course as well. There was drama, too. Immersed in the knotty language puzzles of *Troilus and Cressida,* we had the bonus experience of getting to see a production at the new Loeb Drama Center. (I remember the arresting performance of Harvard senior Mark Mirsky as the villainous Thersites.) And there was fiction, for I read Joyce's *Dubliners* in Hum 6 and began a lifetime of marveling at the spectacularly precocious achievement of an Irish writer in his early twenties. The approach of close reading was further reinforced in my French literature courses, where lectures were followed by small sections in which *explication de texte* was the order of the day.

To try out the English major, I signed up for an upper-level course, English 141, the Eighteenth-Century Novel, for the spring term of freshman year. This turned out to be a hugely challenging affair, for the reading list was chockablock with the biggest novels going: *Pamela; or, Virtue Rewarded* (abridged to a mere 600 pages), *Clarissa Harlow, Tom Jones, Humphrey Clinker, Tristram Shandy.* The titles alone still strike fear into my heart. I have returned to only one of them—*Tristram Shandy*—for its humor, encyclopedic quirkiness, and the Irish roots of its author, Laurence Sterne. I lost my first spring break to feverish ingestion of these doorstop books, but there was a silver lining. The lecturer was Professor John Bullitt, every bit as pompous as I. B. Cohen, though a very different type—a slim, tailored WASP with the look of a U.S. Marine, right down to the ramrod posture and closely cropped head. His lectures were heavy on biography and light on intellectual content. But one of the section leaders became my mentor and friend—thanks to the tutorial system and my sophomore-year placement in Winthrop House, where he lived and worked as a graduate student. This was David Littlejohn, a native Californian who was bright, witty, genuinely funny, and really interested in students. David took me under his wing and made my sophomore and junior years as an English major worthwhile. In sophomore group tutorial the highlight was reading Yeats's poetry straight through. What a joy and study this was. Junior year, David agreed to take me on in an independent tutorial. As a program requirement, I needed to learn some Middle English, and so we worked our way through Chaucer. I've never worked harder nor enjoyed it more.

All the while, David was finishing up his dissertation on Samuel Johnson and successfully wooing the Winthrop House senior tutor's secretary, Sheila Stannard, a tall and striking Englishwoman who was also irreverently quick-witted and a lot of fun. In December of sophomore year, everyone took notice when she played Alithea Pinchwife in the Winthrop House production of William Wycherley's 1673 sexual farce *The Country Wife*. David married Sheila and took her back to California in the summer of 1963, when he took an assistant professorship in English at Berkeley. We kept in touch, and, as he put it, he "sold" me to his new department as a grad assistant on fellowship for the fall of 1964. And that's how I ended up out there in the wild west during the semester of the Free Speech Movement, when the academic world turned upside down. But that's another story.

These small-group experiences were the heart of undergraduate intellectual life. Most of us never got to know the famous professors whose lectures we attended. In my interest areas of history and literature, these included Oscar Handlin, Arthur Schlesinger Jr., Frank Friedel, H. Stuart Hughes, Jared Whiting, Douglas Bush, Harry Levin, and Perry Miller. They were names to me, and not much more. Some were good lecturers, some not. Douglas Bush was the erudite master of two literary centuries, the seventeenth and nineteenth, but he was also a world-class droner with minimal affect. The joke about Bush was that if he finished up with Milton's *Paradise Lost* in the middle of a class, he would simply turn the page and begin talking in the same monotone about *Paradise Regained*. Though Oscar Handlin practically invented American immigration history—using the Irish, as it happens—he could be counted on to put half his class into a doze by 10:20 of a Tuesday morning.

On the other hand, the best lecturers projected a combination of brilliance and passion about their subjects and contempt for the frivolity of undergraduates. Harry Levin would look down his nose at us from the heights of the podium in Lowell Lecture Hall and suggest a dozen sources for the proper study of *King Lear*, "though of course, I realize you're much too busy to consult these." The champion on this theme was the great scholar of colonial America, Perry Miller, who thundered at us from his lectern in the fall term of the American literature survey like Melville's Father Mapple from the pulpit or, a better fit, Captain Ahab on his quarter-deck. As scrupulous and tortured as his hero, Jonathan Edwards, Miller exemplified the intellectual life as fierce, uncompromising commitment. The big news among English majors my senior year was the promise that Miller was going to teach the second half of the survey in the spring of 1964. At last, we were going to find out what he thought of "the moderns," and the prospect was not bright for Hemingway and Fitzgerald. Sadly, we were denied those lectures, as Miller was found dead in his apartment at the top of Quincy House in December 1963, having wrestled his personal demons to a draw.

One other lecture course stood out—Fine Arts 13, the two-semester survey of art history, which I took as a senior. Right from the start, I loved everything about the experience. Going down into the bowels of the Fogg Museum for the lectures was a happy release from the cares of senior year and the outside world. When the lights dimmed and the first slides went up, we were off to the races. It was a gallop, of course, from archaic China to abstract expressionism, with the semester break splitting the Renaissance in two. But the intellect and passion of both lecturers—Benjamin Rowland in the fall, Seymour Slive in the spring—were evident throughout, despite the elementary level (for them) of the discourse. The two professors seemed matched to their specialties. Small, thin, ascetic looking, Rowland was an expert on ancient India and the Middle East. Slive was as substantial and fleshy as a Dutch burgher, befitting his focus on the Northern Baroque. (It's probably a good thing that I hadn't taken this course as a freshman, for I might then have majored in Art History, thus virtually ensuring that I'd never get a job.)

In the fall of 1963, therefore, I began to make thoroughly enjoyable regular visits to three museums: the Boston Museum of Fine Arts, Harvard's Fogg, and the Isabella Stewart Gardner Museum. I had been back to the MFA only a few times since my seventh-grade art classes, but now I found myself once again in those dusty "Oriental" galleries, gazing at the *Nine Dragon Scroll* and *The Burning of the Sanjo Palace*. It was a homecoming of sorts, and the familiar surroundings encouraged the idea that, yes, I had arrived somewhere, that a circle had been closed. When he got to the early Middle Ages, Professor Rowland paused to note the "breathtaking complexity" of Celtic art. Examples included the Sutton Hoo Ship Burial, the Battersea Shield, and the books of Durrow and Kells. I don't think he mentioned the Emly Shrine.

Professor Slive had just arrived at Harvard. He began the spring semester con brio in the High Renaissance, then moved happily into the Northern European sixteenth century (Bosch, Bruegel), and, from there, into the harbor of his great love, seventeenth-century Dutch painting. Like Perry Miller, he took every opportunity to point out the youthful accomplishments of the artists on the syllabus, at the expense of his audience of callow undergrads. With a slide behind him of the beautiful pencil sketch of a Greek statue that Picasso had drawn at age five, Slive hurled a question at us: "And what have *you* done?"

The MFA was world renowned for its Asian holdings, and thus it was Slive's assignments that introduced us to the riches of the Fogg and the Gardner. The Fogg Art Museum on Quincy Street is a jewel in Harvard's crown. Designed by the crimson-tinted firm of Coolidge, Shepley, Bulfinch and Abbott, it features an elegant three-story interior court of travertine marble modeled on Italian originals. To the right of the entry is Warburg Hall, two stories high and capped with a French sixteenth-century carved oak ceiling from Dijon. My favorite place in the Fogg was the narrow gallery running along Warburg on the second level, a place for small gems of the collection and a clear view of the comings and goings in the hall below. My favorite piece in the museum was a tiny drawing by Rembrandt, *Winter Landscape* (c. 1648–50), which I loved for the miraculous economy of its making. Blank paper and a delicate wash evoke snow, sky, and a road. A few strokes bring out a fence, a bare bush, and a house or barn in merest outline that somehow achieves solidity. It must have taken him ten minutes to do. Less is more when you have the steadiest hand and the largest imagination on the planet.

"Mrs. Jack" Gardner's faux Venetian palazzo, perched on the edge of the weedy Fenway, was the outstanding discovery of my senior year. What a spot. Slive sent us over there every couple of weeks, first to gaze upon Botticelli's *Madonna of the Eucharist*, a Raphael *Pietà*, and Titian's *Rape of Europa* (which he called "probably the most important painting in Boston"), and then to see "a few smallish Rembrandts" and, "not to be missed, his only seascape, *The Storm on the Sea of Galilee*." With a catch in his breath, Slive also directed us to "the one Vermeer in Boston," *The Concert*, a stun-

Figure 31. Rembrandt Harmensz van Rijn, *Landscape with a Farmstead ("Winter Landscape")*, c. 1648–50. Brown ink, pale brown wash, and incidental marks in black chalk on cream antique laid paper, prepared with light rose-brown wash, mounted overall, framing line in brown ink; actual: 2 5/8 x 6 5/16 in. Harvard Art Museum, Fogg Art Museum, Bequest of Charles A. Loeser, 1932.368. Photo: Allan Macintyre © President and Fellows of Harvard College.

ning, still portrait of three performers: a woman seated at a pianoforte, a man with his back to us holding a stringed instrument, and a female singer, standing with one hand in the air, poised between notes. Slive pointed out that the painting hanging on the wall behind the singer is Dirck van Baburen's *The Procuress*, which had been owned by Vermeer "and is now, in a twist of fate that benefits us, hanging in the MFA, just across the road from the Gardner!" And what, Slive wondered, could Vermeer have meant by inserting this reference to illicit sex into a picture otherwise so decorous? Here was "food for thought—a mystery within a masterpiece." (In a terrible calamity, Rembrandt's *Storm* and the Vermeer were stolen in the great art theft from the Gardner on March 18, 1990. Two decades later, they've not yet been recovered.)

Once I had found the Gardner Museum, I came to love the Sunday afternoon concerts there. These provided respite from both post-college planning and the national upheavals that gathered steam through the fall of 1963 and on into 1964. I used to sit in one of the third-floor nooks overlooking the courtyard, ablaze with bright flowers even in the dead of winter, and let the music wash over me. As Thomas Kinsella says, "At such a time I wouldn't thank / the devil himself to knock at my door." Getting to and enjoying that place can stand for the lasting gift that was my academic experience of Harvard College. Lectures, seminars, tutorials, conversations—all reinforced a conviction that was all the more powerful because never stated outright: the life of the mind was worth living. I came to believe that by accretion and arrangement of small bits of information, valuable patterns and insights could emerge. As Frost has it, "What was that whiteness? / Truth? A pebble of quartz? For once, then, something."

The Irish-Yankee Confrontation

Harvard's great scholar of Irish history and literature was John V. Kelleher from Lawrence, Massachusetts, who came to hold the first endowed chair in Irish Studies in the United States. That position was established by Henry Lee Shattuck, a Boston Yankee of great intellect, curiosity, and drive, who left his mark on Harvard, the Museum of Fine Arts, and several other New England institutions. As an undergraduate, I didn't know John Kelleher at all, though he became a mentor and friend later on. In the early 1970s I came upon John's essay, "A Long way from Tipperary," which had appeared in *The Reporter* for May 12, 1960—coincidentally, the same day I got my Harvard acceptance letter. In this piece, which, like everything he wrote, accomplishes much more than its purported aim—here he was reviewing George Potter's history of Irish America, *To the Golden Door*—John sums up the vexed origins of the tension between nineteenth-century Irish immigrants and their WASP welcomers in a flash of conciseness and clarity.

> The Irish-Yankee confrontation is the richest still-unrealized tragi-comedy in American history. On the one side, the Irish, fleeing from a homeland where they had been racked, robbed, and demoralized by an imposed aristocracy of Protestant, Puritan, Anglo-Saxon derivation. On the other, a Protestant, Puritan, Anglo-Saxon people who had, when the Irish arrived, just about completed a city and a society made in their own best image. More thoroughly than ever before in history the sins of the fathers were visited on the second cousins once-removed. The mutual despair and hatred re-echoed from the welkin. No wonder that assimilation is not yet quite complete in and around Boston. Nor that the drama remains to be written. The dramatist would have to re-imagine the tale with entire sympathy for both sides and full understanding of the two histories and unfailing consciousness of the irony.

I arrived at Harvard with little sense of how those long-established animosities had played out there and elsewhere in Boston and New England.

By the time I was growing up in Norwood, the town had been predominantly Irish and Catholic for so long that I had no consciousness of discrimination and prejudice along those lines. As I have said, we were unthreatened by the Yankees and tended to see them as figures of fun—Joe Gould, Maud Shattuck, Katherine Saunders. To be sure, I knew a few stories—Catholic children snared by the New England Home for Little Wanderers, the sign in a downtown store window warning that "No Irish Need Apply." But I had no idea till much later of the litany of Boston Irish and Catholic grievances against the Protestant establishment: the burning of the Ursuline Convent in Charlestown by a nativist mob in 1834, the poisonous public letters on Irish immigration by Edward Everett Hale (my grandfather Balduf's namesake) and others during the Famine, the "Nunnery Committee" that investigated convents for suspected immoral activity in the Know-Nothing 1850s, the mandated recital of Protestant prayers in the public schools, the exclusion of priests from the bedsides of their parishioners at Boston City Hospital, the prohibition against Catholics in the Yankee "white shoe" law firms (Hale and Dorr, Ropes and Gray) into the 1930s. Nor had I heard of the notorious 1950 debate about the "Dover Amendment," in which local governing bodies in the neighboring town of Dover tried to keep the Dominican religious order from setting up a seminary at the estate they had purchased there.

Norwood's Irish Catholics had faced no such problems for a long time. My parish church, St. Catherine of Siena, had been an early (1908) ambitious project by the architectural firm of Maginnis, Walsh and Sullivan, which went on to design several monumental Gothic Revival buildings at Emmanuel College, St. John's Seminary, and Boston College. An extensive assemblage of church, school, rectory, and convent, St. Catherine's made a statement: we had arrived. But growing up in the 1950s, none of us knew where we had come from, and our parents weren't likely to tell us much about what the journey had been like. It had, in fact, been pretty smooth, as these things went. Of course, Dover was a Yankee fortress, and so was Dedham, founded in 1636. However, Norwood's secession from Dedham in 1872 had been a crucial safety valve, alleviating the pressures created by the great immigrant influx of the later nineteenth century.

My parents' Irish and German forebears had been in at the creation of the new town, and that had made all the difference. No one I knew had experienced anything like the shock of unearned animosity at Boston Girls' Latin School in the 1910s, recalled by poet Louise Bogan: "It was borne in upon me, all during my adolescence, that I was a 'Mick,' no matter what my other faults or virtues might be. It took me a long time to take this fact easily, and to understand the situation which gave rise to the minor persecutions I endured at the hands of supposedly educated and humane people." (Bogan made sure that the jacket copy for her first volume of poetry, *Body of This Death* in 1923, announced that "Louise Bogan was born at Livermore Falls, Maine, in 1897, of Irish-American parents. Her father's people came from Londonderry, and her mother's from Dublin.")

As I headed off to Cambridge, I was told no stories of injustices perpetrated against the Irish, nor was I warned by Catholic voices to "keep the faith." In 1960, as a matter of fact, the spread of communism was perceived as much more of a threat than Protestantism to Catholics or vice versa. The John Birch Society had recently been founded in the Boston suburb of Belmont, and I had friends whose parents and older siblings were joining up. So, I heard a few references to the "little red schoolhouse on the Charles," but even these were mostly tongue-in-cheek.

There had been evidence of Irish-Yankee confrontation specifically at Harvard, too, but I hadn't heard any of those stories either. Though I missed them by only four years, I had not known about the army of 400 maids, known universally as "biddies," presumably because so many were of Irish background, who had cleaned the rooms *and* made the beds of Harvard undergraduates five days a week until 1956, when they were replaced by "dorm crews" of student workers. The last pay rate for the maids had been eighty-five cents an hour, whereas the first students to take the job, though they neither made beds nor dusted, earned $1.15. In 1930, Harvard had gotten some terrible press when, on the same day it received a $5 million unrestricted gift, the university fired twenty maids rather than raise their pay by two cents an hour. Nor had I heard the compelling anecdote in Cambridge native Julian Moynahan's novel, *Where the Land and Water Meet* (1979), in which the narrator recalls "the heyday of the Gold Coast residence halls which lined the little streets running down from Massachusetts Avenue to Mount Auburn Street. There on freezing winter afternoons the gilded youth heated pennies red hot at comfortable fires and showered them down into Bow and Plympton streets, where ragged urchins from Saint Paul's parish—and mixed with them more than a couple of adults down on their luck—fought each other in the snow for the privilege of blistered fingers."

Certainly, the ruling presence of Yankees at Harvard was undeniable. The tone was set by the cadre of administrators with whom we first came in contact as undergraduates. The Dean of the Faculty of Arts and Sciences was McGeorge Bundy, a Boston Brahmin by way of the Groton School and Yale. The Dean of Harvard College was John Usher Monro of Phillips Academy Andover and Harvard '35. Dean of Students and chief disciplinarian was Robert B. Watson, of St. Mark's School and Harvard '37. Most immediately, the long, Hapsburgian face that looked out grimly from the first page of our *Freshman Register* belonged to Dean of Freshmen Francis Skiddy von Stade Jr. of St. Paul's School and Harvard '38, who as a freshman had brought his own polo ponies to Cambridge.

In my first year at Harvard, I had defining encounters regarding both Catholicism and Irishness—one positive, one negative. Just after high school graduation I had turned up at Mass at St. Catherine's on a Sunday morning in June. There I ran into my Thursday-school nun from eighth grade, a smart, funny, and kind woman whose tutelage had been much the best thing about the entire Confraternity of Christian Doctrine experience. She knew me right away, said "Good morning, Charles" with a big smile, and shook my hand in warm congratulations for my acceptance at Harvard. Not a word was said about avoiding the Commies and keeping the faith in heathen Cambridge. I think it was largely on the basis of that pleasant farewell that I showed up for the opening reception for Harvard Catholics in the fall. In 1959, Harvard had given an honorary degree to Cardinal Richard Cushing. That gesture, along with the increasing number of Catholic undergraduates, had resulted in the opening of Harvard's first Catholic Student Center in 1960. Identified as a Catholic on my profile for selection of freshman roommates, I had received an invitation to the reception at the Center, which was housed at Harvard Square's venerable Catholic church, St. Paul's, at the intersection of Bow and Arrow Streets. There I was greeted by the booming voice of Harvard's first official Catholic chaplain, Father Joseph Collins, a big, friendly man in his forties. When I told him I was from Norwood, his eyes lit up: "Norwood! *I'm* from Norwood, too! Who are your parents?" I said my father was Chick Fanning, and he nodded in recognition: "Oh, yeah. I know the Fannings all right." But when I said that my mother was the former Pat Balduf, Father Collins exploded with glee: "Pat Balduf! We went to high school together. Class of '31. Why, Charlie, I used to dance with your mother!"

Over the next four years, Father Collins came to represent for me the best of Boston-area Catholicism. Born in Norwood to Irish immigrant parents in 1914, Joe Collins was one of six kids. He played baseball at Norwood High and at the College of the Holy Cross in Worcester, where he decided to become a priest. He studied at St. John's Seminary in Brighton, was ordained in 1940, then joined the army as a chaplain and served through the Battle of the Bulge in 1945. Returning to Boston after the war, he was assigned to St. Paul's, where he helped start the famous archdiocesan choir school which is still going strong. As Harvard's chaplain, he became good friends with a number of Catholic faculty, among them Robert Kiely, who became Master of Adams House, across the street from St. Paul's, and William Alfred, professor of Old English and a playwright as well. When Faye Dunaway was starring in Alfred's play about the Brooklyn Irish, *Hogan's Goat,* she met Father Collins, and he later instructed her in Catholicism and officiated when she came into the Church.

With this secure grounding all the way back to Norwood, being Catholic at Harvard raised no disturbing issues or anxieties for me. On the other hand, my faint and unreflective sense of Irishness did get a jolt when I attended my first St. Patrick's Day parade in South Boston in the spring of freshman year. I'd heard of it, growing up, but no one I knew in Norwood had made the trek to South Boston to attend the parade. March 17 meant very little to us. To acknowledge the birth in Ireland of her mother, Johanna McAuliffe, my mother did insist that we wear something green on that day, especially after we moved to Walpole Street, where our next-door neighbor—a Baptist from Alabama—always put on an orange sweater to mark the occasion.

From Harvard, "Southie" was only a subway ride away, without even a change of train. So, on March 17, 1961, with a couple of friends from Stoughton Hall, I made my first ethnic pilgrimage. The *Boston Globe*'s lead for its parade story that day underlined a contrast of which I was slowly becoming aware: "As Harvard boasts of THE game, today Boston's Irish boast of THE day." The seventeenth was a typical March day. The temperature was in the twenties with snow flurries and a cutting wind when we came up out of the Andrew Square T station. Southie was emphatically down-at-heel in those days, and the scene was really pretty dismal. Dorchester Street was lined with seedy bars, package stores, little groceries, and three-decker apartment houses. Dirty gray snow lay heaped on every corner. The crowd was large and enthusiastic but territorial, and a bit frightening. Families had staked out spots on the muddy sidewalks with lawn chairs, and seemed in no mood to let strangers block their view, not even in transit. Teenagers in gangs of five or six stalked up and down, looking for trouble. Fights broke out here and there and the police let them run their course. I'd never witnessed public drinking before, so I was surprised to see many people carrying open cans and bottles, some obviously my age of eighteen or younger. Some of the drunks were also drunker—by a quantum leap—than I'd ever seen anyone be. I remember one unshaven old guy stumbling around, carrying a dusty, framed portrait of a man with a bushy mustache in a bowler hat. To anyone within earshot, he explained, not very coherently, that this was a picture of his father's cousin, Patrick Collins, who had been "a great lawyer, and not just a lawyer, but a graduate of Harvard Law School, and then the first Irish mayor of Boston and a Congressman, too." (He was mostly right. A native of Ireland, Collins had graduated from Harvard Law School and been a U.S. congressman in the 1880s. He hadn't been the first Irish mayor—that was Hugh O'Brien in 1884—but he had been mayor from 1902 till his death in 1905.)

I got myself dug into the side of a snow pile on East Broadway to watch the parade go by. There must have been two dozen high school bands and drum-and-bugle corps, each announced by a colorful, silky banner: St. Columbkille's Brighton, St. Peter's Dorchester, St. Ann's Neponset, Sacred Heart Roslindale, and on and on. Of course, the Southie parishes got the biggest cheers: St. Augustine's, St. Brigid's, Gate of Heaven. There were baton-twirling majorettes in cowboy boots, national guard units, Boston policemen on horses, firemen on foot, dogs wearing green caubeen hats, people dressed as leprechauns. The green-themed floats sponsored by local businesses were makeshift, ragged, stereotypical: St. Patrick driving out the snakes, Molly Malone wheeling her wheelbarrow, the pot o' gold at the end of Finian's rainbow, painted cardboard round towers and ruined castles. There were politicians galore walking behind black, shiny cars with their names on the side emblazoned on paper signs: Mayor John Collins (Patrick's descendant, perhaps?), Governor John Volpe, United States Senator Ben Smith (the Harvard roommate of newly elected President Kennedy, appointed to keep the seat warm for JFK's brother Ted, who wasn't yet thirty). The least comfortable pol was Brahmin Senator Leverett Saltonstall, who waved tentatively from the back seat of his car while smiling weakly and projecting the desire to be anywhere else but here. I was surprised to discover that watching this shabby spectacle with my new Harvard friends made me uncomfortable, even embarrassed. Though we were served beer easily in the taverns, our ages unchallenged, this new experience wasn't nearly enough to save the day.

In early October of freshman year, two things had happened within days of each other that, taken together, constituted the beginning of a dialectic in my own head on matters of social status and stereotyping, of the Irish versus the Yankees—of cabbages and kings—which would continue throughout my undergraduate years at Harvard. At the time, though, I had no idea that the two events were connected at all. One Saturday morning, my roommate and I woke up to find that two small envelopes had been slipped under our dorm-room door in the early hours. Both were addressed to Ed, and they were invitations to get-acquainted meetings of two "Final Clubs." Before coming to Harvard, I hadn't known that these organizations existed, but I had heard since that there were twenty or so scattered around the back streets of Cambridge. Each had its own building, each was open to members only for lunch and camaraderie, and all had spots on a rigid social ladder, dictated by family, geography, and secondary school. At the bottom were parvenu clubs, some rowdy enough to be nearly fraternities, and open (good Lord!) even to midwesterners and the occasional graduate of a public high school. At the top were havens from hoi polloi available only to pedigreed offspring from the dizzying heights of the eastern WASP establishment and private-school network. As I recall, the A.D. and the Porcellian contained the richest and thickest cream of that crop.

Fair enough. I knew I couldn't afford the dues or extra meal charges for *any* club. Nor did I know any upper classmen who might have thought of asking me along. (I didn't know any upper classmen, period.) And yet, with stunning naiveté, I had managed to think that one of those envelopes might have my name on it. This idea must have been a carryover from my high school accomplishments and local fame in Norwood the previous spring. I wasn't crushed by the exclusion, just disappointed. It was a glancing blow, a brief chill delivered by the cold wind of privilege from which my sheltered town life in Norwood had protected me for so long. My reaction was irrational but nonetheless real. For the first time, I saw myself as Dean Bender's "janitor's boy."

Final Club members were easy to spot, or so I thought. They were the descendants of the daughters of Edward Darley Boit—poised and snooty preppies in tweeds and khakis and rep ties who had come from schools I'd never heard of: St. Mark's, St. Paul's, Groton, Choate, Middlesex, Andover, Exeter. Everyone was familiar with their generic identification as "St. Grottlesex" boys. For many of them, appearing to work hard at anything except skiing and getting drunk at debutante balls was decidedly déclassé. They scorned "grade-grubbing" and embraced the "gentleman's C" (a term I heard for the first time that fall), while passing blithely through Harvard on their way to State Street or Wall Street. This was, of course, a stereotype, and one that I was soon to begin revising. And yet, like all such, it had a kernel of truth, and it occurs to me now that perhaps ours was the last college generation in which significant numbers of young men were able to carry off this role without compunction.

The most visible example of the type these days has to be former President George W. Bush, a graduate of Phillips Academy in Andover and the Yale class of 1968, born in New Haven, the son and grandson of hugely prestigious Yalies. A legacy if there ever was one, Bush entered Yale never having appeared on an honor roll, having earned mediocre test scores and participated in no noteworthy extracurricular activities. I was reminded of his St. Grottlesex-ness when, just four months into his disputed presidency, Yale gave Bush an honorary degree in May 2001, which also marked the university's 300th commencement. I was delighted to see that Yale's unseemly haste ("Thrift, thrift, Horatio!") was rewarded with an address worthy of the occasion. The *New York Times* reported that the president's speech was "a lighthearted, gamely self-effacing and oddly defiant rendering of his college days, which he likened to a college daze." Bush recalled visits to the Sterling Library with classmate Dick Brodhead, subsequently Yale's dean: "We had a mutual understanding—Dick wouldn't read aloud, and I wouldn't snore." He referred, as the *Times* put it, "to activities that sometimes blotted out memory." ("If you're like me," said he, "you won't remember everything you did here. That can be a good thing.") The odd defiance came in when Bush both admitted to a lackluster academic record and allowed as how it hadn't made any difference to his career: "To those of you who received honors, awards, and distinctions, I say, well done. And to the C students, I say, you, too, can be president of the United States." Ah yes. Reading this, I felt a wave of nostalgia for the legacy boys of yore. Here again, untarnished by the passage of forty years, was the combination of shameless insouciance, entitlement, and anti-intellectualism that I had first observed in the fall of 1960 in Cambridge. Of course, this was four months before the imposed, unearned, and temporary gravitas that fell on President Bush's narrow shoulders on the next September 11.

Harvard Hockey

The antidote to the minor pangs of rejection by Harvard's clubs came unexpectedly. A few days after my letters of invitation failed to arrive, I answered a knock at the door in the early evening to find two young men of medium height, both dressed in blue button-down shirts, ties, jackets, and dark slacks. The more slightly built of the two introduced himself as Jim Lombard and his friend as Benny Baker. They were, Jim said, the managers in charge of Harvard hockey for the upcoming season. I remembered then that I had responded to a notice in the *Crimson* a couple of weeks earlier announcing that anyone interested in hockey managing should send a note to the Department of Athletics. Because I loved the game and had enjoyed my experience as hockey manager in high school, I had been excited to discover that a system was in place at Harvard.

In fact, the job was a real challenge, requiring organizational skills and the shouldering of significant responsibilities. Freshmen candidates—there were about ten of us—ran after towels, water, pucks, and newly sharpened skates while learning the system and the personnel involved: coaches, equipment men, trainers, players, and other managers. As sophomores, the surviving candidates competed for the positions (held junior year) of varsity, junior varsity, and freshman team manager. In senior year, the varsity manager moved up to become the undergraduate manager, in charge of the whole operation—some twenty managers in all. The three team managers arranged training meals and the practice schedules at home for their teams as well as planning everything to do with away games—transportation, hotels, meals, practices. They served as liaison between the coaches and their teams and the Athletic Department, and they hired and paid the game referees. They even gave tours of the college to prospective players. The varsity manager also dealt with the press (verifying facts, setting up interviews, or barring the door) and the ticket offices (arranging for complimentary and reserved tickets to be left for pickup at both home and away games). The undergraduate manager even did some of the scheduling, especially for the freshman and JV teams.

I enjoyed the freshman competition a lot. While learning my way around Dillon Field House and Watson Rink, I made some friends among freshman players and managers and saw a lot of hockey games. At the end, I was eager to continue in the program. As part of the sophomore competition, each candidate had to plan and go along on at least one varsity trip. I drew the first of these—a midafternoon game against Bowdoin College in Brunswick, Maine, on Saturday, December 2, 1961. We weren't staying overnight, so all I had to do was hire the bus, find a restaurant to serve us a pre-game lunch at about eleven in the morning on the day of the game, and arrange for boxed meals from the Bowdoin dining service to eat on the way back to Cambridge that night. By telephone, I had set up the lunch with a Red Coach Grille off the Maine Turnpike, but when our bus pulled into the parking lot, I looked up from my clipboard (ubiquitous tool of the manager's trade) and saw to my great dismay that the restaurant had burned down. Swallowing hard, I rose from my seat behind the bus driver, turned toward the upturned faces of the varsity team, coach, and trainer, and said: "Well, sometimes things just happen." Everyone laughed, and even the coach smiled. Luckily, there was a working phone booth under the blackened restaurant sign, and when I called the Red Coach number I'd used to set up the meal, an employee explained that, yes, that restaurant had been destroyed by fire a few days earlier, but that another place, which lay just two exits farther north along the Pike, could accommodate us. All went smoothly from there, and it soon emerged that my cool response under pressure had set me apart from the hitherto anonymous group of sophomore managers. The story made it all the way to the higher-ups in the office of the Department of Athletics.

The last and hardest test in the competition was arranging an overnight trip for the varsity team. Mine was a game against Cornell at Ithaca, New York, in early February of 1962. For me, the challenge involved two first experiences that I doubt were new for anyone else on the trip: I had never been on an airplane or stayed in a hotel. The plane ride turned out to be eventful. It was a typical winter's morning in Boston with snow falling lightly but steadily as our bus pulled onto the tarmac and stopped beside a small—a very small—twin-propeller aircraft. I climbed the rickety stairway, ducked my head into the cabin, and made my way up the narrow aisle. The incline was disturbingly steep, and there were only two seats per row on each side. We were sharing the flight with the wrestling team, and our combined group of forty filled the plane. As soon as we were settled, I saw two men carrying what looked like fire extinguishers walk up to the wings and begin to spray something on them. In response to my worried look, my seat-mate, the undergraduate manager Benny Baker, explained that they were deicing the wings before takeoff. This did not sound good, but I held my tongue and tightened my seat belt. The twin engines revving up made by far the loudest noise I'd ever heard, and as we rose into the gathering whiteness, the plane bucked a few times. I must have turned green, because Benny patted my knee with a laugh: "Hang on, Charlie. We're doing OK. Nothing to worry about."

I had to confess that this was my first airplane ride, and *that* word was definitely out by the time we landed in Ithaca two hours later. Back on solid ground—what a relief —I checked off the players on my clipboard as they went from the plane to the waiting bus, and most had something to say, on the order of "It was touch and go there for a while, wasn't it?" or, "I hear the weather going back is going to be really bad," or, "Did you leave anything on the plane, Charlie, like maybe your breakfast?" We stayed without incident at the on-campus hotel run by Cornell's hotel management program, where the staff were tripping over one another to treat us well. And why not? we mused. They were getting graded, weren't they? Harvard lost 2 to 1, thanks mostly to the play of Cornell's All-American goalie, Laing Kennedy, but from the managerial perspective, everything went just fine.

We flew back to Boston after the game, climbing into a blessedly clear sky above Ithaca around midnight. Having counted everyone else, I was the last person onto the plane, and I found myself sitting in the back row beside the varsity coach, Ralph "Cooney" Weiland. I was nervous, because he had looked to be aloof and crusty, almost forbidding, in the few contacts we'd had. His status as a bona fide legend in the professional hockey world that I had followed avidly since childhood made him an even more formidable figure. Born in 1904 in a tiny town, Seaforth, Ontario, a few miles inland from Lake Huron, Cooney had been a brilliant center-ice man who had come up through junior hockey and arrived in the National Hockey League as a member of the Boston Bruins in the 1928–29 season. That year the Bruins won their first league championship, the Stanley Cup. In his second Bruins season, Cooney scored forty-three goals and thirty assists in forty-four games, obliterating the previous NHL points record of fifty-one. He ended his playing career as captain of the 1938–39 team, which won Boston's second Stanley Cup. He then took over as Bruins head coach, and led the team to its third championship in 1941. After moving on to coach in the American Hockey League, he came to Harvard in 1950. Cooney was fifty-six and had held the Harvard job for ten years when I met him. In January 1960, four of his players, including the famous Cleary brothers, Billy and Bobby, had been on the U.S. Olympic hockey team that won the gold medal in the winter games at Squaw Valley, Idaho. Now, here we were in February of 1962, hurtling through the dark, cut off from the rest of the plane by the low lights and throbbing engines. Eyes glittering behind big, black-framed glasses, Cooney began to ask me about myself. He must have been sizing me up for the managerial competition, but I remember being struck by the fact that this hockey giant was really listening as I spoke about Norwood, my father's jobs, my brother's high school hockey career, and my own love of the game as played on the local ponds.

Although opinions were solicited widely, only three people actually voted for managers: Coach Weiland, undergraduate manager Benny Baker, and the varsity team captain. In 1962 this was Dave Grannis, a cheerful bear of a man from Minnesota with a short crew cut and arms like a lumberjack. After I won, Jim Lombard (who was still in Cambridge, working in the Harvard administration while deciding what to do next) gave me a sealed and notarized letter that read: "Today, August 10, 1961, I have stated my belief that Charles Fanning will win the Harvard Sophomore Hockey Managerial Competition in the Hockey season 1961–62." This was quite a prediction, because I am pretty sure that all my predecessors in the job were WASPs from private schools. Jim and Benny were both graduates of Milton Academy. My three closest competitors for manager (and their prep schools) were Todd Gray Moxey (the Haverford School), Buckner Ashby Wallingford II (St. Mark's), and Prescott Bigelow Crocker (Milton Academy). The fact that we came from such different backgrounds was never an issue, however. We all loved hockey and got along well. And, thanks to Benny Baker and his varsity manager, Neal Ryland, the competition was always low-keyed and unthreatening in tone, with clear challenges unambiguously set and, I believe, fairly judged.

Over the course of my two years as varsity and undergraduate manager, Cooney Weiland and I became friends. We had both grown up far removed from the eastern establishment elite that still controlled the world of Harvard athletics. (Cooney had a double dose, for he also coached the golf team, whose home course was "*The* Country Club" in Brookline, which, like *The* Game between Harvard and Yale, required no additional qualifier.) I'm sure that he saw me as a kindred spirit, another outsider in the cold-roast Yankee world of Harvard hockey. Besides, I was smart, efficient, and even quieter than he was. We both saw the incongruity and potential for humor in rubbing shoulders with Harvard hockey's parents, alumni, and supporters—those thin, stiff, ascetic-looking bankers and brokers, with their beefy, florid ne'er-do-well relations in tow—folks with brass-plated New England and New York names: Lodges, Whitneys, Taylors, Hutchinsons, Sargents, Putnams. Indeed, I sometimes put tickets into the bony palm of the apotheosis of that prickly tribe—Leverett Saltonstall, Harvard '14, formerly the governor and in the early Sixties the senior senator from Massachusetts. (In Norwood, the defection to the Republican Party of a prominent Irish American citizen-about-town had been marked by his ever after being known as "Saltonstall Murphy.") And now, here was the man himself, looking only a little more relaxed than he had at the St. Patrick's Day parade, seated as though carved in granite right behind the timekeeper's booth at home games, rooting (albeit silently) for one of his relatives—

a grandson, I think, or a godson. As manager, I had access to pretty good seats too, and one night my father found himself seated beside Saltonstall. Dad stuck out his hand, and said, with a twinkle in his eye, "Evening, Governor." Memories were made of this.

Cooney and I talked often after practices and during trips. He told me about being a kid in Seaforth—how, like me, he had played hockey on the ponds, every day from the first winter freeze to the thaw that often didn't come until April. He had graduated to outdoor rinks in his early teens and then been invited to join his hometown Junior-A team at fifteen. He told me about deciding to move ninety miles north to Owen Sound, Ontario, in 1923, after high school, ostensibly to train as a pharmacist, but really to play for the Owen Sound Greys, a much better Junior-A team. When I asked him if this had been a hard decision, he said that it had been lonely "up there" at first but that he came to recognize Seaforth as a small place with few opportunities. His eyes narrowing, Cooney then said, "Remember this, Charlie. The game fish always swims upstream." Then he repeated the phrase, thereby lifting it from cliché to valuable advice: "The game fish always swims upstream." The following year, 1924, the Greys won the all-Canada Junior-A championship. Cooney said that he'd never had a bigger thrill in hockey than hoisting the Memorial Cup. He did not tell me that he scored an amazing sixty-eight goals in twenty-five games that season. Nor did he ever talk about his accomplishments as player and coach during those championship seasons in the National Hockey League. I did ask him once how he had scored so many goals. Cooney was so small—five feet seven inches and 150 pounds—that I was curious about how he had done it. He replied, "Patience is the key, Charlie. You have to be patient. You slip around the defenseman with a couple of dekes [feints], then come in on the goal at an angle. Then you change speed—go faster or slower—and cut across the mouth of the goal. Then wait—wait—wait until the goaltender commits himself, and just as he starts to split, you gently slip the puck between his pads or flip it over his shoulder."

On occasion, I was able to serve as a conduit between Cooney and the team. As I saw it, there were two kinds of players capable of creating trouble for the coach, other players, and themselves: sensitive brooders and buoyant free spirits. There were only a few of each, and they didn't get along with one another, either. I had some clues about the brooders, who tended to be working-class kids like me but with bigger chips on their shoulders about the disparity between their previous experience and Harvard. But I was wholly at sea with the entitled kids who sneaked off to ski in New

Hampshire, thus risking injury, simply because they didn't want to lose an entire snow season. In all such matters, I relayed Cooney's worries to our varsity captain, Gene Kinasewich, a level-headed, thoughtful young man and a prodigiously gifted athlete, who became a good friend.

Gene's story was amazing. He was the second youngest of the thirteen children of Ukrainian immigrants to the Canadian province of Alberta. His parents both died when Gene was ten, leaving their close-knit offspring to fend for themselves. Like his Harvard coach, Gene was recognized in his early teens as a great hockey talent, surely headed for the NHL, and as a high school sophomore he joined the Edmonton Oil Kings, a crack Junior-A team affiliated with the Detroit Red Wings. There he was found by my manager-friend Jim Lombard, whose passion for Harvard hockey extended to informal, self-financed recruiting of prospects. At Jim's urging, Gene applied for and received a grant for an extra high school year at Deerfield Academy, from which he was accepted into Harvard's class of 1964 with a scholarship based on grades and need. He came for the education, believing that he'd probably be declared ineligible to play hockey because he had accepted $1,122 in expense money over two years from the Oil Kings.

At Harvard, Gene endured a roller coaster of contradictory decisions with maturity far beyond his years. He was shut out from freshman hockey, but allowed to play in his sophomore year by the Ivy League's eligibility committee. Thanks in part to Gene, who led the team in scoring with twenty goals and twenty assists, the 1961–62 team achieved a record of twenty-two wins and only five losses. Harvard won the Ivy League title and finished third in the Eastern College Athletic Conference (ECAC) championship. The team also won the locally prestigious Bean Pot Tournament, in which four schools (Boston University, Boston College, Northeastern, and Harvard) competed at the Boston Garden, home of the Bruins, on the first two Mondays in February.

On September 16, 1962, as everyone concerned was beginning to think about the new hockey season, a bombshell hit. The ECAC eligibility committee ruled again that Gene Kinasewich was ineligible to play, declaring that his acceptance of the Oil King money had made him a professional. Harvard appealed, and Gene went down to New York on December 12 to plead his case. He spoke to the committee on his own for over an hour. The *Globe* reported that "he discussed the entire amateur hockey picture in Canada as it affected young boys." Against all odds, the ECAC reversed itself, explaining that "personal financial hardship" had been a sufficient mitigating factor when Gene was playing Junior-A hockey. That evening, he took the ice at Watson Rink to a thundering ovation. Harvard beat Northeastern 8 to 1, Gene got two assists, and the 1962–63 team was off and running toward a most extraordinary year.

What a season to be varsity manager! For the third year in a row, Harvard won the Ivy League, beating Yale twice along the way, and we also won the Boston Arena Christmas Tournament, with a 3–2 overtime victory over Colorado College. The only regular season blemish was losing to Boston College in the Beanpot finals, but this loss was redressed nine days later when we beat B.C. in a home game at Watson. In those days, Harvard often dominated the Ivy League in hockey, and while it was always nice to beat Yale, our biggest rival in the early Sixties was Boston College, because they were both local and always very good. My feelings here were heightened by the facts that B.C. had been my only other prospective college choice and that so many of my Norwood friends had gone there. I was aware that some on both sides of the Charles River saw the rivalry in class and religious terms—upper-crust New England WASPs versus Boston Irish Catholics. Indeed, one of my fellow managers was wont to ridicule B.C.'s so-called subway alumni, the non-college-educated local supporters of the Eagles, by mimicking them in a thick Boston accent: "Hah-vahd's got more money than Gawd." (This was well before the transformation of Boston College from a commuter school for first-generation college students to a pricey national university with serious upper-middle-class cachet.) I tended to ignore this line of attack. He may not have known anything at all about my story, I reasoned, and as I heard nothing like this from anyone else, I didn't let it bother me.

Harvard's Faculty Committee on Athletics had decreed that the hockey team could not participate in the NCAA tournament, citing the recruiting practices and commercialism of schools in the Western League. Thus, the ECAC tournament would end our season. We beat Colgate in the first round on Tuesday, March 5 and Clarkson in the semifinals on Friday. Here I have a telling memory of our goaltender, Godfrey Wood. A Brookline native and Milton Academy graduate whose father had been a famous amateur tennis player out of the Longwood Cricket Club, Woody was tall, slim, blond-haired and blue-eyed. He looked like Jay Gatsby without the parvenu sheen. In the three years of our contact, I saw not a single indicator of his having been to the manor born. As well, he was a great goalie, not least because of his unflappable temperament. Ours had been the first game on that Friday evening, and Woody went home early to get some rest, rather than waiting to see who our opponent in the finals was going to be. He left the rink forgetting to take along a sleeping pill that the team doctor had wanted to give him. It was my job to take the pill back to Woody's dorm room, and, instead of leaving immediately, I stayed on to watch Boston College defeat St. Lawrence. I saw my doing so for what it was—a small but palpable pettiness—but I just had to know which team we'd be playing in the finals. It was close to one in the morning when I got back to Cambridge and knocked on Woody's door. This was the most important night of his hockey-playing life, and I would certainly have understood had he been annoyed at my tardiness. Yet all he said was that he really appreciated my bringing the pill, and that he'd been sitting up studying for a midterm exam.

This was one of many hockey experiences that substantially undercut the charge of WASP elitism provoked by my club rejections and brought me to a more balanced understanding of what, for lack of a less hifalutin term, I'll call the New England Yankee mind. When Jim Lombard and I had lunch at the Wursthaus, Jim would always take the bill and divide it up meticulously, including a fair adjudication of the tip—to the penny. I believe that he simply couldn't help himself. Even treating me to the tune of three or four dollars would have been too grand a gesture. Because possibly construable as noblesse oblige, such perceived condescension was a cardinal sin and out of the question. The same internalized prohibition governed the way that rich and powerful Boston and New York WASPs would accept without question my dispensation of tickets to big games. They may, at times, have gone around me to the HAA ticket manager, but I know it didn't happen often, and if it happened, I never knew about it. The moguls and pashas of the Brahmin establishment pulled no obvious rank on me. What I saw was genuine consideration for the feelings of others, along with a determination not to claim the perquisites of special status. Hence, as well, the threadbare tweeds and legendary cheapness of the Bostonians, as in the serving at dinner parties of canned tomato soup and barely identifiable cuts of meat.

In any case, through my four-year association with Harvard hockey, I got to know enough real Yankees to discover that, as Louis MacNeice says of the world, the truth about them was "crazier and more of it than we think, / Incorrigibly plural." Hockey demystified WASPs for me in much the same way that going to Harvard College itself had demystified Harvard. In both cases, familiarity inoculated me against an ailment that is still detectable—and not only in New England: exaggerated regard for the people and the school and an unwelcome, accompanying feeling of inferiority. When I tell people I went to Harvard, some still respond, with a resentful edge of tone, "Oh, you went to *Harvard*." Because I know the ordinary realities behind the increasingly overblown reputation of the place, I've been spared all that awe and animosity. "Yes, it was a good school," I reply, "but there are a lot of good schools, and I'd have enjoyed myself at any of them."

The climactic ECAC championship showdown against Boston College on Saturday, March 9, 1963, closed another circle for me, for it was held at the Boston Arena, where I'd first seen a supervised hockey game in a rink. That evening, the rickety old place was jammed to capacity with 5,900 people, and the game was a classic. B.C. scored twice in the first period. Harvard's first line of Jorgensen, Fryer, and Kinasewich—the press called them our "JFK line"—kicked into action in the second period, with Gene scoring at 15:54 to tie the game at 2–2. Harvard outshot the Eagles 18–4 in the third period, but scored only once—Gene's second goal, at 8:43. Three minutes later, B.C.'s Jack Leetch tied the score again, and that's how the regulation game ended. It all came down to the hair-raising prospect of the sudden-death overtime, which began disastrously with Harvard getting a dumb penalty for having too many men on the ice. Shorthanded for two minutes, we managed to keep the Eagles from scoring, thanks mostly to the heroic play of Woody in goal and All-American Davey Johnston on defense.

The dénouement was impossibly romantic. Taking a pass from Davey at center ice, Gene flew down the right boards, left two B.C. defenders spinning in their tracks, then cut sharply across the mouth of the goal. He held the puck till the goalie started his slide, then flicked it smartly between his pads. Gene's move was a carbon copy of his coach's preferred scoring technique, a veritable homage to Cooney. Wahoo! The clock stopped at 4:49. The Arena erupted in cheers. Harvard had won. When the red light when on for Gene's third goal, I smashed my clipboard so hard against the rink boards that it broke into two pieces.

For the second regular-season game against Boston College, I had made an exhorting poster for our locker-room wall. When we won, I decided to make another, then another, as the team piled up victory after victory toward the Ivy championship and the ECAC tournament. Like Bartholomew Cubbins's hats, each was more ornate than the last. After the final victory, the ninth in a row and Cooney's 200th win as Harvard coach, I got a mention in the *Globe*: "Charlie Fanning, manager of Harvard's hockey team, has been painting signs and hanging them in the locker room for each of Harvard's last seven games. The one he made for the ECAC championship game read, 'It's Eagle Day Again. Let's win No. 200.'" Hours after the great game, some of us ended up at the Hayes-Bickford in Harvard Square, eating breakfast at 3:00 AM. We plastered my final poster on the wall beside our table with tape provided by the cashier. A shining moment, that one.

I walked back to Winthrop House with that year's undergraduate manager, Neal Ryland, a scion of the Old South from Richmond, Virginia, who had come to love hockey in prep school. As we were passing an unmarked, nondescript building, he paused and seemed to be thinking hard. Then he invited me in—this was his club—for a celebratory drink. "OK," I said. I knew he was breaking precedent, because only club members were supposed to be allowed into one another's lairs, but I made no other comment. We went down behind the front stairs and Neal unlocked a basement-level door. I found myself in a small, dark, musty room with a bar across one wall. Rummaging in an old fridge, he came up with two beers. We clinked the cans together and drank. Neal certainly knew that I wasn't a member anywhere—I hadn't even been asked into the Hasty Pudding Institute—so, in his eyes, this was quite a gesture. To me, however, the whole ritual now seemed kind of silly. I was beyond all that fiddle.

Harvard hockey gave me much else as well. The experience of managing brought me an appreciable expansion of skills and self-confidence. Never much of a talker, as undergraduate manager, I ran meetings of my staff and represented hockey on the Undergraduate Managers' Council. From this group, I was elected managers' delegate to Harvard's Undergraduate Athletic Council, which met monthly with the Faculty Committee on Athletics to determine policy and rule on issues. All told, the job in my junior and senior years took up at least forty hours a week between October and March. I traveled by bus and airplane to all the Ivy League schools and to many other colleges throughout New England and upstate New York. By the end of the 1963–64 season, I had won two "major H" varsity letters, and I knew a whole lot about how Harvard athletics operated from top to bottom, from the office of Athletic Director Dolph Samborski, Harvard '25, to the equipment rooms at Dillon Field House. But the people I got to know were the best thing about the job.

It turned out that many of the men and women on the support staff for Harvard athletics were Irish Americans from Boston-area ethnic enclaves: North Cambridge, Cambridgeport, Somerville, Allston, Brighton. It's safe to say that these folks recognized where I, a working-class Irish Catholic from Norwood, was coming from. I especially remember three. The head of the equipment room at Dillon Field House was Jimmy Cunniff, whose parents had come over from Ireland to Cambridge to escape the Irish Civil War

Figure 32. Captain Tim Taylor and Coach Ralph "Cooney" Weiland in the locker room following the ECAC Championship win over Boston College, March 9, 1963.

in the early 1920s. Their neighborhood, between Harvard and Central Squares, was known as Kerry Corner. A bachelor, Jimmy lived with his three sisters in the house on Banks Street where he had been born. He had started to hang and help out around the Harvard athletic fields in his early teens, and he was hired by the HAA at age seventeen in 1943.

Long before he became a boss at Dillon in 1962, Jimmy's reputation was established as a person to whom the old adjectives still applied. He was humble and generous and wholly dedicated to Harvard's athletes. A big and very strong man, he was extremely quiet—slow to speak, slower to anger, easily overlooked in a crowd—but he understood how some kids were struggling to make it in college, and his unobtrusive good deeds were legion. He lent money, meals, even his car to students in need, and he paid his own airfare to far-flung tournaments in order to free up a seat for one more second-string player. Everyone had a Jimmy story, me included. When I told him that my brother wanted to be a goaltender for Norwood High, Jimmy invited Geoffrey over on a Saturday afternoon to skate around at Watson Rink and then sent him home with an old but serviceable set of goalie pads, the first he'd ever owned. Jimmy died young—at forty-six, in January 1972—from a cancer that hadn't been diagnosed in time, and his funeral at St. Paul's was packed with over 400 people.

I also got to know John Patrick "Jack" Fadden, Harvard's head trainer. A legend in his own right, Jack came to Harvard as assistant football trainer in 1920 and stayed for over sixty years. The son of Irish immigrants, he had been born in West Roxbury in 1899. Jack also worked for the Boston Red Sox, serving as their head trainer from 1950 to 1965. He became one of Ted Williams's few close friends in the Sox organization—in part because Ted valued his frankness and humor as much as his skill as a trainer. Most visible during football season, Jack was also available for consultation to Harvard's winter sports teams until he left for spring training in February, and he solved many fitness problems for hockey players. In 1966, Harvard started giving the John P Fadden Award to the senior athlete who has overcome the greatest physical hardship to contribute to an intercollegiate team. I have one special post-college memory of Jack, who died at age ninety-one in 1990. During my backpacking solo trip to Ireland in 1973, nine years after I had last seen him at Harvard, Jack recognized me on a bus way up in Mayo, his family's home county. He hailed me warmly, treated me to a big meal at a pub in Ballina, and insisted that I take a $20 bill, "to help keep body and soul together."

At the Department of Athletics, 60 Boylston Street (now JFK Street), the managers' secretary was Marion Kenealy, the granddaughter of Irish immigrants to Boston. Almost from the day of my first appearance in her office on the third floor, I was the apple of her eye. Marion was in her late fifties, small, with curly white hair, lively blue eyes, a sharp tongue, and a soft heart. She was the calm center of the storms that brewed in late October when fall and winter sports overlapped and the imperious football managers made their demands for precedence over everything else athletic as *The* game approached. None of these cut any extra mustard with Marion. Yet when things got busy in the middle of our season, Marion offered to type course papers for me on her lunch hour and after work, and when I accepted (which was often), she never let me pay. Several times she had me over to dinner at her Commonwealth Avenue apartment in Brighton, a third-floor walk-up where she lived alone. She spoke often about her mother, Mary Kenealy, who had raised Marion and her sister Kathryn on her own in a Jamaica Plain apartment. Marion was tough, competent, funny, and incapable of self-pity. When she retired, old managers came in from all over the country to honor her with a dinner.

In the late fall of senior year, I got a little too busy for my own good. Running the hockey program was one thing, but trying to figure out what to do after graduation was starting to get on my nerves. I knew I wanted to teach—but in high school or in college? What about grad schools—could I stay at Harvard? Should I give Boston College another chance? What about following David Littlejohn out to Berkeley? Didn't the University of Toronto Institute for Medieval Studies sound interesting? And here came a new round of applications for admission, fellowships, and teaching assistantships. How could I get everything resolved and finished? I found myself losing sleep. So, to see if I could bring back a measure of peace to my fingers—and inspired by Fine Arts 13—I set up the old easel in my bedroom at the top of Winthrop House, overlooking the river, and began to paint again for the first time since high school.

I managed to finish two landscapes with oils as Christmas presents for Marion and Cooney Weiland. Marion's picture was a bright spring scene with green fields, splashes of flowers, and a red barn. She hung it between the two front windows of her apartment and told me that it cheered her up on rainy days. The picture I painted for Cooney was a snow scene. There was a small village tucked under a range of hills and a frozen pond in the foreground. He called me up a couple of days before Christmas to say that he and Gert both thought it was a wonderful gift.

Cooney coached for a few more years. I saw him occasionally at hockey games and gatherings, and he always greeted me with a warm handshake and a complicit nod. We last met in the early 1970s. My girlfriend at the time, Fran Purcell, now my wife, was then living in Wayland up the street from the Weilands' house, and we dropped in on the spur of the moment one Saturday morning in June. Cooney and Gert welcomed us, and we got to meet Cooney's brother, who was visiting from Seaforth. In 1990, five years after Cooney's death, Gert wrote me, enclosing a photograph she had just found of her husband standing in front of my painting. "While it isn't too good of Cooney," she said, "I think it is pretty good of my favorite work of art." She went on, "We were so happy with it and so proud of it and I decorated our living room around it really. . . . So you see all the loving labor you put into it has been appreciated and enjoyed all these years and I thank you again and again."

The Poet and the Politician

Two famously archetypal figures framed my college experience. Early in the fall of 1960, my Norwood friend Marianne Cooper invited me over to Tufts, where she was a freshman at Jackson, the women's affiliate, to attend a poetry reading by Robert Frost. She told me that there was also going to be a reception after the reading, and, remembering my high school interest in Frost, she said that if I brought along a book, he'd probably sign it. I had never been to a poetry reading—Katherine Saunders hadn't given any—and I ran right out to the Grolier and bought a hard back copy of Frost's *Collected Poems* for $6.00. Though getting to Medford from Cambridge was a public transportation challenge, I made it in plenty of time. "The great act," as Robert Lowell called it in his poem about Frost, was in full bloom that evening: the white thatch of hair, the shuffling gait and disheveled suit, and, above all, a wry, raspy voice that seemed to embody New England. I heard some of my favorite poems and some I hadn't known about at all. One of the latter, "Provide, Provide," carried the force of revelation. This was no kindly old sage in the Good Gray tradition but a teller of hard truths. The poem ends, "Better to go down dignified / With boughten friendship at your side / Than none at all. Provide, provide!" And then, with a dry, mordant chuckle, Frost added, "or, as I like to say, someone else will provide for you." The gathering after the reading was small, and I was able to walk right up to the little table where the poet was sitting in wary state. Knowing nothing of signing protocol, I put my book right in front of him—still closed. He looked down at the book, then up at me. Smiling slightly, he opened it to his frontispiece photograph and wrote, "Robert Frost 1960."

The Kennedy-Nixon election dominated that same fall semester of freshman year. My parents were certainly for JFK. My father recalled having shaken his hand backstage when Kennedy had given a speech at the Norwood Junior High School two years earlier during his 1958 campaign for the U.S. Senate. My mother commented often on his good looks, charm, and way with words. Because I was at Harvard, Kennedy's victory in November seemed especially meaningful, and I felt still closer to the action as the rumors began to fly about the possible migration of advisers from Cambridge to Washington: Arts and Sciences Dean McGeorge Bundy, Archibald Cox from the Law School, economist John Kenneth Galbraith, historians Edwin O. Reischauer and Arthur Schlesinger Jr. In early January we heard that the president-elect would be attending a meeting of the Harvard Board of Overseers, of which he was a member. On the day, the Yard was closed to the public but jammed with students. I had only to step outside my dorm to join the buzzing crowd around University Hall, just across the lawn. Kennedy arrived at about ten o'clock. Seizing the moment with characteristic élan, he sprang up the stairs, turned toward us, waved, and said, "I have come to speak to President Pusey about your grades. I shall represent your interests." Everyone laughed and cheered heartily. Camelot was upon us.

Two weeks later came Inauguration Day, January 20, 1961, with its extraordinary meeting between Kennedy and Frost at the ceremony in front of the U.S. Capitol. On a somewhat different scale, it was a big day for me too. At 9:15 AM, I took my first final examination as a Harvard student. Overnight there had been a huge snowstorm, and I waded through knee-deep drifts to get to the exam site, Lowell Lecture Hall. The course was Hum 6, and one of the questions—an obvious homage from Brower and Poirier—asked for an exegesis of Frost's poem "The Onset." When the exam was over, I made my way back to Stoughton Hall, where someone had set up a tiny black-and-white TV. I got there in time to see the eighty-six-year-old poet confused by the sun-dazzled snow that had fallen in Washington as well. Unable to read the text of the brand-new piece in heroic couplets that he'd written for the new president, Frost recited from memory "The Gift Outright," a deceptively nuanced poem of 1935, in which the speaker generalizes with reserved hopefulness about the American land, "vaguely realizing westward, / But still unstoried, artless, unenhanced." He ended with a flourish, by changing the poem's final line: "Such as she *would* become, *has* become, and I—and for this occasion let me change that to—what she *will* become." All this came as a bonus along with Kennedy's inaugural address, with its rhetorical flair and ringing call for public service: "Ask not what your country can do for you. . . ." When we graduated four years later, 16 percent of the class of 1964 joined the Peace Corps. Only engineering, research, and technical jobs claimed more of us.

There was plenty of news during the thousand-day presidency that followed, and everyone I knew at Harvard took special note of the dramatic ups and downs of Kennedy's journey. We admired the hubris and deplored the failure of the invasion of Cuba in April 1961. Establishing the Peace Corps created a new and exciting option for immediate post college life. The challenge to put a man on the moon and the defiant *"Ich bin ein Berliner"* speech stirred our imaginations. As the fate of the world hung on the outcome of the Cuban missile crisis in October 1962, we in Cambridge felt a special tie to JFK. When Khrushchev backed down, most everyone felt that this stunning victory had canceled out the Bay of Pigs disaster.

In June of 1963, my interest in Ireland got a significant boost when President Kennedy made an official visit to the old sod. His trip took on the aura of a triumphal return, with huge crowds at every stop. When JFK visited his great-grandfather's home county of Wexford, I remember wondering why I didn't know anything about where my own Irish forebears had come from. That question shaped my career as a scholar of Irish-American life.

Meanwhile, as a newly declared English major at Harvard, I had followed up Hum 6 in the best possible way by enrolling in the fall term of sophomore year for "Shakespeare's Sonnets," a course taught by Theodore Morrison. A novelist, translator of Chaucer, and poet, he had also been founding director of the Breadloaf summer writing school and had held that post for over twenty years. Professor Morrison was a fine, gently encouraging teacher. I was pleased to be using my *Temple Shakespeare* volume of the *Sonnets* as we progressed in a leisurely way from 1 ("From fairest creatures we desire increase") to 154 ("The little Love-God lying once a sleepe"). Once we got going, there was plenty of cross-referencing among the poems and some to wider literature, but primarily Morrison showed us how to be concerned with each sonnet as a separate technical construct built for discoverable thematic ends. I loved it. I began to speak more often in class than previously, and sometimes I stayed after to talk.

One day, Morrison asked me over to his house on Walker Street to borrow a new book about the sonnets that wasn't in the library yet. This was the first time I'd been inside a faculty member's home, and despite getting soaked through in a sudden rainstorm, I wasn't disappointed. The house was a Cambridge classic—old, white-clapboarded, with big windows and black shutters. The book-lined study had a floor of wide pine boards, burnished to gold. There was a fireplace with burning logs, and the flames were reflected in the tiny panes of a set of French doors, against which the rain was pelting. We talked briefly about the book—it was J. B. Leishman's

Themes and Variations in Shakespeare's Sonnets—and I was on my way. I had borrowed a book, but I'd also found a model of the kind of place in which I could see myself doing a life's work in literature.

In class, Morrison referred often to Robert Frost—yet another connection—as both a latter-day master of the sonnet form and a dear friend. I did not know until the Frost biographies began to come out years later that Morrison's wife, Kay, had practically saved the poet's life after the death of his wife, Elinor, in 1938. Kay Morrison had taken over as Frost's secretary, organizer, and closest confidante, a post that she still held when I met her husband. She and Frost, it seemed, may also have been lovers briefly, but the friendship among the three survived and deepened thereafter. Two of Frost's finest love poems, both sonnets, had been dedicated to Kay: "The Silken Tent" and "Never Again Would Birds' Song Be the Same."

Robert Frost's final book, *In the Clearing,* was published on March 26, 1962, his eighty-eighth birthday. Though uneven—some of the poems are pretty light—the collection was a smash hit, and it was worth having, I thought and still think, for a couple of gems. My favorite is "Away," one last picture of a man striking out into the woods alone. The poem ends in characteristically whimsical but authoritative affirmation: "And I may return / If dissatisfied / With what I learn / From having died." In December 1962, Frost had prostate surgery, followed by a pulmonary embolism. Death came on January 29 of the new year. Two days later there was a private memorial service at Appleton Chapel at the back end of Memorial Church in Harvard Yard.

I saw President Kennedy one more time. On a beautiful, sunny Saturday, October 19, 1963, he attended the Harvard-Columbia football game at Harvard Stadium with his aides Larry O'Brien and Dave Powers. He stayed through the half-time show—both bands made brief, comic references to his presence—then left quietly. Because of my connection with the Athletic Department, I had a job in the press box at football games that consisted of running errands and fetching refreshments for the sports writers. There may have been Secret Service men up on top of the Stadium that day, but I certainly didn't see any. When word spread that the president was leaving, I walked out the side door of the press box and looked over the back wall. Down at the bottom were three idling limousines, and sure enough, a group of men emerged. I had a clear view of John Kennedy. As I watched, he shaded his eyes and waved, then ducked into one of the cars and was driven away.

A month and three days later, on Friday afternoon, November 22, I found myself on an el train pulling into the old, familiar Forest Hills Station, on my way home to Norwood. This was an unexpected trip, as Thanksgiving was the following week, and I'd been planning to stay in Cambridge until then. Now, the train screeched, then shuddered to a stop, and as my right foot hit the platform, I thought of the morning only a year before when, on this very spot, I had run smack into Jack's youngest brother Teddy, shaking hands during the Senate race for which he had barely been eligible, having just turned thirty. The holder of undistinguished Harvard College and University of Virginia law degrees, the former tainted by a cheating allegation, Ted had had little more going for him than his name. But that, especially on the heels of the resolved Cuban missile crisis, had been plenty. The refrain, ineffective though true, of his opponent in the primary had been, "If your name were Edward Moore [Ted's middle name was Moore], you couldn't have been nominated for dog-catcher of Suffolk County." That earlier November morning, Ted had been apple-cheeked, fresh-faced, clueless. I knew that both he and his brother had been undergraduates in Winthrop House, and as we shook hands, I told him that I was there now, in suite H-41, and that the place still housed a lot of athletes. He told me what entries and rooms he had lived in, and we agreed that it was a superior dorm. I thought that he looked a little wistful talking about his college years. So many responsibilities and troubles lay ahead, some of them unimaginable. I wished him luck, then went downstairs to catch the bus for Norwood.

But today there were no handshakes. At every el stop, working people and school kids, let out early on the heels of catastrophe, had stumbled onto the train, stunned and shocked at the bold headlines on the EXTRA editions clutched in their hands. At every stop, men and women, black and white, got on with tears in their eyes. Many held rosary beads and cried openly, especially at the old South End and Roxbury stops named for colonial bluebloods—Dover, Northampton, Dudley, Egleston Square—long since transmuted from fashionable Yankee addresses to sanctuaries for the Famine Irish, and now on their way to becoming havens of urban opportunity for African Americans migrating up from the South since World War II. On every face was the one question: how could this have happened to him?

Between Dover and Northampton, the train, as always, had slashed across the face of the Cathedral of the Holy Cross, the symbolic heart of Boston Catholicism since its completion in 1875. In a marker of past anti-Catholic feeling, the arch framing the nave entrance had included bricks retrieved from the Ursuline Convent in Charlestown, destroyed by a nativist mob in 1834. I had heard that the placement of the el was no mistake, but

Figure 33. Holy Cross Cathedral and the elevated tracks, June 1920. Photograph by Leon Abdalian. Courtesy of the Boston Public Library, Print Department.

a clear message from the city's Yankee establishment about who exactly was in charge of America's Athens. In 1902, city planners had run the el tracks right down Washington Street in front of the beautiful church, thereby cutting the exterior perspective in half and creating a permanent source of noise and dirt. Beside me on that Friday afternoon, I heard a man say softly to his neighbor that of course Jack's funeral was going to be there.

Thirty minutes earlier, I had walked back up from Winthrop House and the river with a hastily packed bag, passing people gathered in small groups around transistor radios. As I entered the MTA shelter at Harvard Square to ride the clanking wooden escalator down into the dark, the bells of Memorial Church began to toll. Thirty minutes before that, I had been standing in line in the high-ceilinged, marble lobby of the Cambridge Trust Company, waiting to withdraw $20 from my savings account for the weekend. I had been twenty-one years old for eleven days, and the world was my oyster. The big Roman-numeraled clock on the wall read 12:50—within an hour of the rifle shots a thousand miles away—as my friend Curt von Kann came through the front door, spotted me, and hurried over. "President Kennedy's been shot in Dallas," he said. "They think he's dead."

New Pond

The memory of one winter day's discovery at George Willett's—and my mother's—"New Pond" in Norwood remains the most vivid of my childhood. It's nearly dark there at 4:30 on a crisp, cold, early January afternoon during Christmas vacation from sixth grade. I'm far from being a good skater, which adds a touch of danger to what I'm about to do, for I know that every year people drown by falling through the ice on one or another of the dozens of ponds that dot the bumpy crust of eastern Massachusetts. Already this winter two boys have drowned in our area, one in this very pond. But three weeks of temperatures in the teens and single numbers have allayed most parents' fears. The ice looks thick and safe.

As I sit on a log lacing up my skates, I can see three small fires reflecting off the ice. One is at the edge of the narrow, snow-crusted beach just ahead. I can hear the crackle of the burning pine brush and smell bubbling resin, and I'm just in range of the shimmering heat. Another fire is some hundred yards down the curving shoreline to my left, on the edge of a thick pine wood that I recall as being hard to reach on foot in the summer. The third fire is the most intriguing. It's on the tiny island in the middle of the pond, a place I've never been in summer because I can't swim yet. But I remember having seen high school kids on dates sunbathing there when we were picnicking on shore. There are several small evergreen trees, rocks and bushes, a swatch of sand. To me, it's an exotic place—a hitherto unreachable site of ritual boy/girl activities well beyond my ken and a favored location for my cozy daydreams of escape and self-sufficiency. (Last summer I read *Robinson Crusoe.*)

Now I can make out shadowy figures in the light that flickers off the rocks and ice. And suddenly I see that I can get there on my own two skating feet. I've been dropped off with friends, but they're all hockey players and are already on the ice, getting into pickup games. I'm in no hurry to join them, given my meager skating skills, so I'm alone as I stand, walk unsteadily down the beach and step out onto the ice. The moon is up and nearly full, so the hockey games will last at least another hour. I skate out toward the island, first slowly, then picking up speed, and my heart beats faster and faster. But as I get nearer, something curious occurs. This centering place of my summer dreams starts to turn ordinary. Even the spectral moonlight can't keep this from happening. The flickering light of their fire brings out the faces of teenagers rapt in their own dance of awakening, but these are kids I know, the older sisters and brothers of my friends and classmates. They're laughing, singing scraps of a song I've heard on the radio—Hank Williams's "Poor Old Kalija." They warm their hands and toast what look like hot dogs, and just now the sharp pork smell comes across to me—a link with summer, but even so, one that further demystifies the island.

Abruptly, I decide not to glide into the little cove. I'm shy of these older kids and, more important, leery of ruining my imagination's Lake Isle. Nor will I explore the island's other side, for I'm reluctant to witness the still lyric woodsiness dissolve into the merely mundane. Instead, I lean and swerve left and continue on past the middle of the pond. I can't see the ice all the way to the other bank, and so I do not know whether the solid surface will extend or thin to danger or even end in open water. Just as this chilling prospect hits, I clear the island's sheltering lee, and a strong gust of wind at my back pushes me on so strongly that to stop I would have to drop to my knees and skid.

I've never gone this far out before. But fear gives way before my awed apprehension of the expanse of black, black ice, the crack and boom of its settling as the temperature drops, the pure, clear air, the moon a dazzling white, its craters outlined as on a map. Orion, the mighty hunter, with his four-square marking stars, my talismanic constellation since the astronomy part of last summer's reading binge, heaves up toward midsky, jauntily tilted off center yet a massive and serious presence, a whole other galaxy hanging from his belt.

I push farther and farther out. The sounds of hockey games and songs and shouting recede. The three fires flicker and blur. Alone on that sweeping stretch of ice, I feel something for the first time—a sense of release into

Figure 34. San Francisco, September 1964. Photograph by Gerry Pearson.

possibility. I cannot then say these words, but at that moment I begin to realize that we are all more than and different from the sum of our familial, social, and economic parts. Here is where it dawns on me that there is an adventure opening up over my head and under my feet. I feel my skate blades respond to the pressure of will. I am cutting a gradual, slow arc. It's a signature: risky, uncharted, my own.

Acknowledgments

My thanks to the William R. Perkins Library at Duke University for permission to quote from the Letters of Private Fisher A. Cleaveland of Company I, 35th Massachusetts Volunteer Infantry, and to Mark Farrell for his permission to quote from his great-grandfather's diary, the *Civil War Diary of Sergeant Henry W. Tisdale, Co. I, 35th Massachusetts Volunteer Infantry 1862–1865*. Thanks also to the following institutions for their permission to publish photographs: the Art Institute of Chicago; the Museum of Fine Arts, Boston; the Boston Public Library Print Department; the Estate of Dino Buzzati, author of *The Bears' Famous Invasion of Sicily*; the Cambridge (Massachusetts) Historical Commission; the Fogg Art Museum at Harvard University; the Library of Congress Prints and Photographs Division; the Norwood Historical Society; and Bryant F. Tolles, author of *Norwood: The Centennial History of a Massachusetts Town*. Detailed citations for these accompany the captions of the pictures. All photographs without citation have been provided by members of our family, to whom great thanks are due for having preserved these pictures.

Three colleagues at Southern Illinois University Carbondale have been instrumental in this project. My thanks go to Richard "Pete" Peterson for his early exhortation and connection to the world of creative nonfiction, and for the example of his own autobiographical writing; to Beth Lordan for her steadfast encouragement of my non-academic writing over many years and for her helpful reading of this manuscript; and to Ed O'Day for his clarifying perspectives on Irish American studies and his guidance in the wilderness of genealogical research.

Thanks also to Jim Rogers, editor of *New Hibernia Review* and my good friend, for encouraging my work with the example of his own, and for publishing part of chapter 6 as the essay "Lodestone: Following the Emly Shrine" (*New Hibernia Review* 13 [1]: 9–19). I am also grateful to the editors of *Creative Non-Fiction* for publishing the essay that contained the kernel of this book, "I Haven't Been That Far, But I've Been to Norwood" (*Creative Non-Fiction* 14 [2000]: 56–70).

My first cousins Francis Fanning and Margaret Fanning have been the most diligent historians that any family could wish for. Ellen MacDonald has been similarly astute in discovering the details of our shared German ancestry. I thank them for their generosity.

I owe my acquaintance with Patrick J. Pendergast's poems and Frank L. Sweetser's demographic study, *The Social Ecology of Metropolitan Boston: 1950* (Boston: Massachusetts Department of Mental Health, 1961), to Jim Callahan. And thanks go also to my best and oldest Norwood friends, Dan Callahan, Steve Callahan, and Lorin Maloney, for their encouragement of this work and the contribution of their own memories of our shared childhood and adolescence.

My brother Geoffrey has provided a valuable perspective and many crucial memories I would certainly have missed. My sister Patti has been greatly encouraging of this project and tireless in her gathering and passing on of countless gems of her own impeccable research into family, Norwood, and Massachusetts history. My great thanks to both.

I am grateful every day for the love and support of my wife Fran and our son and daughter, Stephen and Ellen. This book is for them.

www.ingramcontent.com/pod-product-compliance
Lightning Source LLC
Chambersburg PA
CBHW030638270326
41929CB00007B/117

* 9 7 8 1 5 5 8 4 9 8 1 0 5 *